DISTANCE EDUCATION IN CANADA

Distance Education in Canada

Edited by Ian Mugridge
and David Kaufman

CROOM HELM
London • Sydney • Dover, New Hampshire

© 1986 David Kaufman and Ian Mugridge
Croom Helm Ltd, Provident House, Burrell Row,
Beckenham, Kent BR3 1AT

Croom Helm Australia Pty Ltd, Suite 4, 6th Floor,
64-76 Kippax Street, Surry Hills, NSW 2010, Australia

British Library Cataloguing in Publication Data

Distance education in Canada.
   1. Distance education – Canada
   I. Mugridge, Ian II. Kaufman, David
   371.3   LC5808.C2

   ISBN 0-7099-4619-8

Croom Helm, 51 Washington Street, Dover,
New Hampshire 03820, USA

Library of Congress Cataloging-in-Publication Data

Distance education in Canada.

   Includes index.
   1. Distance education–Canada. 2. Distance education
–Canada–curricula. I. Mugridge, Ian. II. Kaufman,
David.
LC5808.C2D57   1986   378'.03   86-8828
ISBN 0-7099-4619-8

Printed and bound in Great Britain
by Billing & Sons Limited, Worcester.

Contents

Section 5: USE OF TECHNOLOGY

Preface

John S. Daniel

During a television broadcast just before his government was elected Prime Minister Brian Mulroney identified 'opportunity' and 'civility' as Canada's most distinctive qualities. Such a country should provide fertile ground for the nurture of distance education - which combines the aim of expanding the possibilities for learning with special concern for the individual student. This book documents, in a fascinating manner, the development of distance education in Canada since its beginnings last century and particularly in the last twenty years. Even if the image that emerges is of an exciting laboratory of experiments rather than a showroom of finished products it is clear that distance education has already made Canada more Canadian. Opportunities for individual Canadians to achieve their potential through study gave increased and new standards of civility have been set in the treatment of students.

The growth of distance education in recent years has been typically Canadian in other ways. A vibrant new sector has developed despite a virtual absence both of government policy and of a tradition of correspondence education - except at the secondary school level. In the opening chapter Peter Rothe writes of the 'national potpourri' of providers of distance education. He notes that since few of these providers could buttress their offerings with previously established institutional authority their courses and programmes have had to succeed or fail on their own merits. This is as it should be. The fragility of the institutions and of their governmental support makes the field exciting.

John Ellis, who reviews government policies - or rather their absence- is surely right to urge that the policy vacuum remain unfilled. It is undeniable that distance educators have been even more frustrated than their conventional collegues by the balkanisation of jurisdiction over education in Canada. When the responsibility for the education of only 25 million people is divided between ten provinces and two territories, each of which already has an extensive infrastucture for face-to-face teaching in place, few distance educators can hope to achieve the mass enrolments and consequent economies of scale that are such a politically attractive feature of the enterprise in other lands. But such is life in the Canadian mosaic. Since the partriation of the constitution in 1982, the provincial jurisdiction over all forms of education and the federal control of broadcasting must be taken as given. 'Statutory permissiveness' is more likely to encourage institutions to remain responsive than a multiplicity of policies each applying to small provincial populations.

The contributions to this book examine from various perspectives both the warp and the weft of the complex fabric that distance education has woven in Canada. In so doing they tell us much about the development of Canadian society itself.

Running through the whole text is an unfeigned tone of concern for the individual citizen that would sound remarkable in most parts of the world. The Canadian values of opportunity and civility are manifest in a series of assumptions: that people wish to learn throughout their lives; that they deserve flexible systems for this purpose; that government must promote such systems; that people need assistance in adapting to new learning strategies; that independent study must not be solitary confinement; that institutional success is measured by repsonse to learners' needs; that jobs in distance education must be as fulfilling as those of conventional educators.

This generosity of spirit in matters educational may indeed be a particularly Canadian virtue - but it is also a product of the environment in which distance education began the phase of growth that occupies much of the book. By the late sixties the greatest worldwide boom in history had already lasted twenty years and come to seem like the economic norm. Technology was transforming communications in other fields but had hardly touched education. The dictum that 'the medium is the message' had been pronounced in Canadian Academe and some felt that its application should begin at home.

Most countries that expanded distance education then did so in order to increase access to education. Technological innovation was simply a means to achieve this primary objective, though it did help governments to package the projects in a politically attractive manner.

In Canada it was the other way around. Those who initiated the Télé-université, the 'second' Athabasca University, the Open Learning Institute and the Knowledge Network were motivated first and foremost by a desire to create 'innovative learning systems'. Increasing access to education was a distinctly secondary concern for these institutions at their moments of inception. I am glad that this book does not support a revisionist version that would have it otherwise. Jocelyn Calvert, in her chapter on research, implicitly confirms the unworldly atmosphere in which these events took place by mentioning that she found only one Canadian article on the economics of distance education!

It was not long, of course, before the projects had to become less innovative and more useful. You cannot change your mode of operation to suit every passing instructional or technological whim once you have begun to serve large numbers of students. This process of maturation comforted provincial ministries of education. They began to see outputs whose cost-effectiveness they could analyze. But it was a disappointment to the professionals of technological innovation, many of them in the ambit of the federal government. This group had hoped that distance education, would provide an ongoing application of the interactive satellite technology and videotex systems that were being developed with public funds. The innovators, along with some working in the institutions themselves, failed to realize that distance education students are not suitable guinea pigs for new inventions. To be useful in distance education technologies must be thoroughly domesticated - in the literal sense of being taken for granted in most households - and well established. At present the audiocassette, as James Leslie describes, is just at the right stage of development to be an important technology for learning at home.

Too often, unfortunately, their sensible avoidance of brand-new technologies for communicating with students has prevented institutions from receiving proper credit for using advanced technologies in their internal operations. John Bottomley does a service in documenting Canadian distance education's role as a world pioneer in the use of state-of-the-art technology for processing and printing text. The difference between integrated text-processing and photocomposition systems and older methods is a kind, not of degree, and in that sense they are revolutionary. As an example *Learning at a Distance*, the advance publication of the 1982 Vancouver World Conference of the International Council for Distance Education, which is the most widely quoted source in this book, simply could not have been produced without such technology.

The reader will note, perhaps with a tinge of regret, that radical curriculum innovation is no longer high on the agenda of Canada's distance educators. But for the student this is surely a healthy development. Combining distance education with curriculum reform makes sense in less-developed countries that inherited colonial educational systems whose main purpose was to train people for white collars. In Canada, however, one can assume that the conventional secondary and postsecondary curriculum has evolved in response to Canadian needs. Most distance education students want to be rewarded for their efforts in hard academic currency. The corollary development, as noted in the chapters on Athabasca University and the Télé-université, is that those working withing the institutions have gradually pushed them towards organisational structures and job categories more closely resembling those of conventional universities. No doubt this has promoted greater institutional stability although at some sacrifice in responsivenes to student needs. The variety of approaches to course design and development that are found across the country clearly indicates, however, that there is no single best way of organising the enterprise.

Much greater agreement is to be found on the functions of student support services. This area has attracted the attention of some good minds in several countries in the last decade. The analysis given by Ethelyn McInnis-Rankin and Jane Brindley is evidence of the substantial progress that has been made in understanding what services are needed and how they can be provided. Only ten years ago most papers on this subject fell into the 'here's-how-we-do-it-at ...' category. The debate has now become much more sophisticated and Canada can be proud of its contribution to this process.

While much of the book concerns the record of individual institutions or examines long-standing generic issues in distance education it is good to see, in the chapter on consortia, some discussion of an important new trend. The recent increase in interinstitutional co-operation has indeed been startling. In some cases, like the rapprochement of the Open Learning Institute and the Knowledge Network, powerful marriage brokers may have provided a push towards the altar. But in Ontario the universitites have produced a joint calendar of distance education offerings on their own initiative. Norman McKinnon writes of the increasingly systematic co-operation between the government correspondence schools in the various provinces.

Inevitably for a book published in the mid-1980s, the experience of the universities, and particularly of the specialised distance education univer-sities, receives disproportionate attention. However, these people have an exciting story to tell and it is an important chapter in the development of education in Canada. No doubt by the turn of the century the emphasis will be different - interinstitutional co-operation will probably have gone much further and the line between private and public sectors will be more blurred. Some of today's newer technologies will have become sufficiently domesticated to be incorporated into distance education systems.

But some things probably will not change. Dan Coldeway concludes from studying learners that their motivation and behaviour as students have more influence on their success than any personal or demographic factors. No doubt this will still be true in the year 2000. Though here again Canadians and distance education seem well suited to each other. International comparisons show Canadians to be an unusually motivated lot where their education and health are concerned. Among the world's peoples, Canadians rank only 21st in alcohol consumption and second-from-the-last in cigarette smoking. Such behaviour makes them well qualified in the self-discipline distance education will likely always require. Let us hope that they pause occasionally in their studies to remember those energetic people who built Canada's contemporary distance education networks and provided them with the opportunity to study in the convenience of their own homes.

Acknowledgements

First, we wish to thank our contributors whose willingness to write for this volume we gratefully acknowledge. We appreciate their patience in the face of long silences punctuated by requests for material. In editing the essays, we have attempted to impose uniformity of format without interfering with the style or content of individual contributions. We are grateful for these contributions and trust that their authors will regard the finished product as an appropriate setting for their efforts. In particular, we would like to mention John Daniel, the author of the preface, who, in spite of his heavy workload, willingly reviewed the other contributions and wrote his own in a very short time.

Like our contributors, our publisher David Croom has shown extraordinary patience; and we especially appreciate his initial willingness to accept our proposal and his graciousness in dealing with our requests for more space and time before we could bring it to fruition. Ronald Jeffels, Principal of the Open Learning Institute, provided funds for the editing and production of the manuscript; and we gratefully acknowledge this generous and essential contribution. Jeanne Meisen of the British Columbia Institute of Technology arranged for the use of a laser printer for drafts and final copy of the manuscript. Les Ferch provided immensely valuable service in untangling the intricacies of computer hardware and software. Terence J. Ollerhead edited the manuscript and Michelle Philippe undertook to co-ordinate its production through the many revisions. This is a simple statement of fact; but it by no means describes their contribution. They have not only done what they agreed to do: they have far exceeded it. The manuscript would not have been produced as well or as quickly without their help. We are enormously grateful.

David Kaufman   Vancouver, British Columbia
Ian Mugridge   January 1986

Section 1: OVERVIEW

Introduction

David Kaufman and Ian Mugridge

The essays in this book do not attempt to give a comprehensive account of Canadian activities in distance education. Authors have been asked to present a conceptual overview of their area and to discuss the major issues. They have also been instructed to give examples or case studies rather than to attempt a complete national survey. This has resulted in a book which emphasises rationale, theory, models, and issues in Canadian distance education. Many examples are given throughout, and readers who wish to obtain a complete picture are advised to read the whole volume.

Our approach has also resulted in some notable omissions. No attempt has been made to deal with distance education in the Canadian North, for example, although the work of Inter-Universities North is discussed. The growing number and extent of programmes in technical and vocational subjects has not been dealt with comprehensively, or the increasing involvement of Canadian distance educators with their counterparts overseas, both as advisers and in co-operative projects.

These examples are obvious ones; and readers - and reviewers! - will doubtless think of other areas the coverage of which could have enhanced the value of this collection. Instead, we have tried to encourage our colleagues, most of whom are or have been closely associated with distance education in Canada, to present a picture of its development, of the situation in the mid-1980s, and of its potential.

Peter Rothe traces the roots of distance education in Canada, using the concept of institutionalisation. His paper illustrates the surprising range and diversity of activities that occurred during the past century before the recent 'discovery' of 'distance' education and the change in its name from 'correspondence' education.

In his essay on government policy, John Ellis makes the point that basically there is none. The federal government has no direct constitutional role in education and distance education has thus been developed across the country by provincial governments and often by individual institutions simply doing what circumstances dictated. Distance education in Canada, is consequently, extraordinarily diversified: private and public institutions and agencies co-exist; institutions devoted entirely to distance education work, sometimes within the same jurisdiction, with others which offer both face-to-face and distance instruction; public communication networks serve both types of institution; and so on.

The euphemism for this situation would probably be 'diversified'; but it could also be - and has been - characterised as 'chaos'. But, if this is an accurate description, it is nonetheless chaos out of which a good deal of commonalty seems to be emerging. Frequent references to collaboration, to

1

co-operation, and to consortia occur throughout this book. While we do not accept the conclusion of Abram Konrad's essay on consortia - that they are necessary partly because distance education institutions probably cannot achieve their objectives alone - this and several other essays make clear that the movement towards interinstitutional co-operation is growing rapidly and will probably continue to do so. Discussions about distance education consortia at the British Open University conference in 1979 on the education of adults at a distance concluded that, while it was a good idea which few would dispute, an equally small number would implement it. Increasingly, this is not the case.

The co-operative arrangements discussed in this book give ample evidence of this. Norman McKinnon's essay, for example, deals with the remarkable amount of collaboration which exists among the provincial correspondence branches. It is no accident that the development of a major body of material for the teaching of English as a second language is emerging from this group. Robert Sweet also lists some of the co-operative activities at the university level - the Atlantic provinces consortium, the Western Canadian Committee on University Distance Education, the Open University Consortium of British Columbia, for example. On the international level, both Athabasca University in Alberta and the Open Learning Institute in British Columbia, two institutions which have maintained a co-operative relationship since the establishment of the latter in 1978, have joined the International University Consortium and are actively pursuing collaboration with institutions outside Canada.

The effect of these developments is that for whatever reason - and economic necessity has played a part in the process - distance education is increasingly becoming a co-operative activity. The traditional and frequently wasteful tendency of academics to believe that no other institution or individual can develop a programme or course as well as they can - the emphasis on what the Australians call the 'NIH factor' for Not Invented Here - is being eroded to such an extent that it seems possible, although not yet likely, that Canadian distance education agencies will not merely become increasingly collaborative but will also set a compelling example to such agencies around the world.

The sharing of experience, expertise and courseware should not, however, reduce the importance of one other aspect of the Canadian experience in distance education. It is most clearly stated by Barry Brown and Danielle Fortosky when they say that there is no single formula, no single recipe for the development of any aspect of distance education in Canada, that development should be and has been governed by the regional context, by the local or individual needs of each section of the country. All or almost all of the essays in this volume bear this out in their different ways.

Distance educators must learn to adapt or to create according to their region's physical and demographic requirements, its technical and other resources, and its cultural imperatives. A system which would be effective and useful in one part of Canada is likely to be inapplicable elsewhere. This is illustrated by the diversity of approaches among Canadian provinces and institutions; and it is likely that this diversity will remain, despite the growth of collaborative activities and the increasingly varied use of technology. A diversity of approaches is being used in institutional programme and course development. However, several commonalities are apparent. Some of these are: (1) the use of co-operative and collaborative practices, as discussed above; (2) the application of systematic course design, employing several people with complementary skills; (3) the move towards use of electronic media to complement the use of print; (4) the use of computer technology in student services, course development, production and instruction; and (5) the variability in learner backgrounds and skills but similarity in type of student served, i.e. the adult part-time lifelong learner.

The growing use of technology is the final major theme which emerges from this collection. Increasingly, the requirements of old technologies and the development of new ones are influencing the development of both distance education and conventional forms of education. The traditional means of communication for distance education - print, the telephone, the mails - are changing and perhaps losing their dominance. Most distance programmes still rely heavily on printed material; but the resources available are widening its potential. The telephone is also no longer the simple two-way means of communication it has been, even though such communication will continue to be used heavily. The mails are perhaps losing importance largely because they can be unreliable: Margaret Norquay comments-perhaps rather wistfully - that, in the 1930s, it was possible for questions about 'Farm Forum' to reach the broadcast centre from the Prairies within a week!

Despite Charles Shobe's well-founded warning, there is always a tendency to do the same old things in the same old ways; but the overwhelming evidence of these essays is that the tried methods are frequently being used in imaginative and effective ways. Barry Brown and Danielle Fortosky make the point that strategies need be limited only by the imagination and resources available. While resources are frequently more limited than in the past, our imaginations are perhaps being applied in significant new ways.

Two contributors make this point very clearly. Glen Farrell in his essay on future directions and Ross Paul in his on Athabasca University both state that the future depends on substantial use of new combinations of media. This will probably mean a movement away from 'pure' distance education (or 'correspondence study') as it has often been understood in the past, towards what Farrell calls 'open learning' systems. The obsession with gadgetry which many have thought a danger in recent years now seems to be diminishing. Distance educators in Canada are applying themselves and their resources to the development of ways in which they can reach most effectively the maximum number of students. The research agenda sketched by Jocelyn Calvert will, if implemented (and research may be one of the areas which has suffered significantly during the restraint which has hit most provincial systems in the last few years), undoubtedly further this process.

Distance education in Canada in the mid-1980s appears to be expanding and healthy, responding to the needs of students, many of whom have only recently been able to gain access to educational or training opportunities. Increasingly, the lines which hitherto existed between distance and face-to-face education are being blurred or eliminated as distance education gains more and more widespread acceptance among educators in general, and as the techniques applied to both become more and more consistent with each other.

An Historical Perspective

J. Peter Rothe

Canada's distance education landscape is dotted with many organisations, departments and agencies providing a variety of services according to regional demands. Any institutional uniformity of distance education can be gleaned through their historical developments and a subsequent historical analysis. The extent to which Canada's distance education reflects institutional characteristics in an historical sense will be the goal of this analysis.

In common usage, institutions are often interpreted as organisations such as hospitals, universities, or asylums that contain people. In the same vein, they may also be perceived as large societal entities which hover over the life of the individual like the government, the economy or the educational system. In an analytic sense, however, institutions are defined as patterns of recurring acts structured in a manner conditioning the behaviour of members within the organisations. (Robins 1976) They share particular values or sets of values and they project value(s) in the social system in terms of attitudes and acts.

Yet, historical descriptions of Canadian distance education reflecting the concept of institutionalisation and its development have not been prominent in the literature. Eisenstadt (1966) acknowledged the importance of institutionalisation by writing 'of the necessity to develop an institutional structure which is capable of continuously "absorbing" the various social changes which are inherent in the process of modernisation'. (1966:vi) Further, Riggs (1964) and La Polambara (1968) say that institutionalisation is a primary prerequisite for stability. As Pennock wrote, 'the process of institutionalisation is as surely part of development as are specialisation of function and differentiation of structure. It is when certain forms and procedures become the accepted ways of doing things that they become effective instruments of stability and legitimation'. (Robins 1976)

Pennock's statement when related to distance education raises several questions: To what extent were Canadian distance education organisations established to become institutionalised and thereby attain regional stability and legitimation? 'Can one safely say that the conglomeration of regional distance education organisations reflect a Canadian distance education institution?'

To address these questions an analytic framework originally developed by Huntington (1965) and Robins (1976) will be used to appraise the history of Canadian distance education.

ANALYTIC FRAMEWORK

Four basic criteria are relevant to the study of institutionalisation: complexity, autonomy, coherence and adaptiveness. Although the criteria are interdependent and overlap, for clarity they are described as individual units of analysis.

Complexity

Complexity relates to the rational, logical integration of units in an organisation. Work associated with each organisational function can be divided into specialised tasks which can then be organised into distinctive subunits or departments. Activities necessary for the accomplishment of overall objectives are first determined. Interdependent tasks are distributed to appropriate specialists, assigned to departments and co-ordinated by formally appointed superiors. Organisations which have a variety of specialised units are better able to meet demands creating technical and economic advantages.

Autonomy

Autonomy includes such features as making important decisions, generating one's own resources, defining goals, establishing mandates and philosophies and developing a model of operation.

Autonomy provides the organisation with legitimation of its activities and assurance of its right and responsibility to carry out certain programmes. Legitimation permits the organisation to operate in a certain sphere and to claim support for its particular activities. Finances provide the organisation with the capacity to mount its programmes, recruit and retain personnel, purchase hardware, and acquire other elements necessary to exercise its legitimate authority.

Coherence

Coherence involves an organisation's right to integrate goals and means, negotiate internal and external conflicts, ensure appropriate rules of conduct, and attract individuals with similar ideas, ideals and philosophies. More precisely, coherence includes the provision of guidelines, rules and regulations, and operating procedures which routinise organisational problems and allow for workable solutions. Also, coherence reflects the organisation's arrangements with other organisations particularly with respect to scope of activity and pursuit of resources.

Adaptation

Adaptation features the extent to which an organisation can innovate or structure its mode of operation or goals in accordance with changing times and client needs, while retaining a complex, autonomous, coherent structure.

These criteria provide a filter for analysing 'relevant' Canadian distance education developments occurring from the 1960s to the 1980s. The organisations described in this chapter provide 'benchmark' or 'milestone' progress. For the sake of brevity a selected cut-and-paste reproduction of

Canada's distance education past is presented. To do otherwise goes beyond the limits of a single chapter. But, before precise distance education developments are analysed, a historical glimpse of relevant events before 1967 is provided to establish a broader context for the institutionalisation of Canadian distance education.

EARLY FORERUNNERS OF DISTANCE EDUCATION

It can be argued that, in the 1970s, the British Open University influenced the Canadian distance education scene. However, earlier events are noteworthy. For example, in 1889 Queen's University began credit correspondence courses in the Faculty of Arts and Science. In 1907, the University of Saskatchewan provided off-campus learning opportunities such as 'Better Farming' demonstration trains, the 'Homemaker' short courses and 'Canadian Youth Vocational Training Workshops'.

The first prominent Canadian mediated adult open learning system, the Antigonish Movement, was initiated in 1935. It was a joint venture of the Canadian Broadcasting Corporation, the Canadian Federation of Agriculture and the Canadian Association for Adult Education. (Conger 1974) This programme was St Francis Xavier University's Dr Coby's six principles:

1. individuals can develop their capacities through social organisation;
2. social reform must come through education of the citizens for constructive social action;
3. economics is the first principle of education;
4. group action is essential for success;
5. effective social reform involves fundamental changes in social and economic conditions; and
6. everyone deserves a full and abundant life. (Conger 1974:9-10)

As part of its contribution, St Francis Xavier University's Extension Department organised people into small community groups and supplied them with study materials.

The movement's programme, entitled 'Farm Radio Forum', included educational broadcasts, study clubs, regional organisers and printed materials. It was based on forums or discussion-listening groups. The national offices distributed broadcasts and written materials designed to stimulate thought and understanding among rural listeners. The 'Farm Radio Forum' was intended to widen people's horizons and help improve farmers' conditions during the depression.

The two-way communications process included broadcasts and written study materials from the national office. The forums replied with reports describing the local discussion of these.

The 'Farm Radio Forum's impact on rural Canadian society in fashioning an activist approach on the part of the farmers to socio-economic problems became the basis for the establishment of the National Film Board of Canada in 1939. Like the 'Farm Radio Forum', the National Film Board was based on the philosophy that education should be active and attached to the economic processes and current happenings of the world. Two noteworthy developments of the National Film Board were its 1967 involvement with Memorial University Extension Service's Challenge For Change Programme and its 1968 participation in TEVEC, a social awareness programme for rural Quebec.

On the west coast, the University of British Columbia's Centre for Continuing Education was charged to manage the university's credit correspondence programme. From 1950 to 1973, this division offered a programme of up to 18 courses developed and tutored by the Faculty of Arts. In 1966, the University of Regina became active in traditional off-campus credit delivery. An instructor travelled by car to a classroom in a distance centre. Later the university became actively involved in NORTEP (Northern Teacher Education Programme) centred at La Ronge. This programme emphasised social work, mathematics education and psychology.

Such examples provided a context for the phase of rapid distance education expansion up to the 1980s. The most relevant developments of the 1960s, 1970s and 1980s are herein described and analysed.

Memorial University

In 1967, Memorial University's Extension Service organised and maintained a learning process entitled FOGO, a programme named after Fogo Island and based on community use of videotaping local experiences. Over a short time, it became a valuable tool for rural and semi-rural community development in Newfoundland. According to the Director, 'we were able to use the expertise of locals to speak to their peers. In rural communities films began to be used as a link to provide access to information from one group to another.' (Gwyn 1972:9)

Each one of the Extension Department's nine field representatives was given a camera, tapedeck and monitor. They were to practice the Extension Service's autonomous philosophy: 'Extension is not an advocate of any particular point of view; our philosophy is to lay the groundwork so that people can make their own decisions. At the same time, we work to create self-awareness, and to accelerate the learning process. This is why we use film and VTR - and in all of it the key is the fieldworker.' (Gwyn 1972:9)

Rather than provide field representatives with formal guidelines, representatives were allowed to use the films as they saw fit. Some used them better than others; others not at all.

FOGO was originally devised to provide institutional adaptiveness by implementing a delivery system relevant to the rural scene. However, coherence difficulties resulted. To illustrate, complaints arose about poor communication procedures between co-op members and Memorial University's Board of Directors, about the difficulties of dealing with external government planners and about the lack of opportunities for young people to participate in meaningful study. The following question raised by a programme participant clearly illustrates the lack of complexity yet required of an institution evident at Memorial University in 1967: 'Why is it all we hear about is becoming a teacher or a nurse when what FOGO is going to need are food technologists who know about processing fish; and engineers who know about refrigerating plants.' (Gwyn 1972:6)

In 1969, Memorial University's Extension Service expanded its course offerings because ninety-nine per cent of its courses addressed teachers as the major group of students. Each off-campus centre (ranging from 10-21, depending on demand) with at least fifteen students registered had a part-time local co-ordinator. They acted as registrars, collectors of fees, comptrollers, librarians, bookstore managers and liaisons between instructors and students. This structure was insufficient to meet local demands because off-campus courses could only be taught at centres where at least fifteen students registered. The Extension Service lacked the complexity to meet the needs of smaller communities where less than fifteen students were enrolled.

A further problem was the policy stipulating that educational television courses be developed outside the Extension Service. The director of the Extension Service asked Memorial University department heads to select faculty members to develop courses. According to the Extension Service director, this strategy became troublesome because most faculty members lacked the time, knowledge or television personality required for developing a suitable product. The Extension Service had limited autonomy in terms of content, knowledge and programme design. In short, the Extension Service could not make decisions affecting the structure of a television course.

Memorial University's Extension Service's experiment to adapt course delivery closer to student needs through telephone communication failed. Rather than telephone without charge faculty members who wrote the Extension Service course, students used the opportunity to make general enquiries about Memorial University. To correct this weakness, the Extension Service used off-campus tutors as stand-ins for faculty. Although tutors were required to have at least a bachelor's degree, preference was given to candidates with a master's degree. The students met with a tutor one evening a week, heard two tapes, and discussed them. The tutors collected assignments and telephoned the faculty instructor about any problems. At least once a semester, the latter visited and talked with students at each centre where a course was in session. This adaptation provided invaluable service to students.

The incorporation of tutors provided a level of complexity and coherence the Extension Service needed to become more adaptive. However, the Extension Service was and still is today a department within a structured university. It was destined to remain non-institutional by virtue of its limited decisionmaking authority, reliance on university structures and limited input in programme needs and development.

University of Waterloo

Because the University of Waterloo Correspondence Programme was, much like Memorial University's Extension Service, also a new department within a university structure, it experienced haphazard development. For example, when the Correspondence Programme began in 1968, its mandate was limited to degree courses listed in the University of Waterloo calendar. Furthermore, the Correspondence Programme courses were conducted by traditional Waterloo University academic departments. They had total academic control of the courses in choice of course content, instructors, academic standards, prerequisites, etc., leaving the Correspondence Programme with little autonomy and institutional complexity. In fact, the Correspondence Programme was controlled like a regular faculty, extending from instructor to department, faculty and university senate. Furthermore, lack of autonomy was also evident in student registration policy. Students wishing to enrol in correspondence courses had to meet the same admission requirements as students applying to the University of Waterloo. (Leslie 1979)

Such built-in restrictions gave Waterloo's programme limited complexity to serve special needs, practically no coherence to define its own rules and operating procedures, little decisionmaking autonomy in areas such as instruction, enrolment, administration and territorial rights of service, and little power to adapt to meet changing needs.

According to Leslie (1979), the academic control of correspondence courses resided with the University of Waterloo department offering the course. The department chairman selected the professor, operator, tutor and grader. The operator prepared assignments and examinations for the course, marked the examinations and was responsible for the overall operation of the course. The tutor prepared model solutions for assignments while the grader marked assignments. Although these units helped meet student needs, their control did not lie with the Correspondence Programme, but with the department chairmen.

Overall, the Correspondence Programme could be considered a university appendage (department) designed to serve an alternative delivery system. It was afforded little formal institutional structure to control the development or instruction phase. Yet, according to Leslie (1979), the University of Waterloo distance education structure, in ten years, had grown to be the largest university-level correspondence programme in Canada. Its popularity was linked to its courses, consisting of taped lectures with accompanying lecture notes.

Athabasca University

A major development in Canadian distance education occurred in 1970 with the establishment of Alberta's Athabasca University. Originally it was built to alleviate the University of Alberta enrolment pressures by being a conventional university offering innovative undergraduate programmes in arts, sciences and education. In 1972, plans were changed by provincial order-in-council which 'empowere[d] and authorize[d] the Athabasca University Interim Governing Authority to undertake a pilot project for the production, testing and application of learning systems, to provide study programmes in the arts and sciences leading to an undergraduate degree and for the application of technology and new procedures to improve educational opportunities for adults in general'.

Athabasca University received a revised mandate from the provincial government which redefined its operational model by allowing students to enter and withdraw from the university at any time and by establishing a policy of self-pacing and self-directed study. Not only did it receive full autonomy to operate within its own territorial jurisdiction in non-traditional education, but in 1975 an Alberta order-in-council granted it permanent status as an undergraduate degree-granting institution.

In terms of complexity, Athabasca University developed a number of integrated units to meet different demands. For example, home study courses were designed by course teams consisting of contracted subject matter specialists, instructional designers and editors. One of these people assumed additional duties as course manager. As the university struggled to produce courses more quickly, many subject matter experts were retained on a part-time or consulting basis. (Shale 1982)

Over time, Athabasca University integrated and expanded its units by hiring full-time academic staff and contracting part-time tutors to mark assignments and organise seminars, discussion groups and/or workshop sessions. A student development services unit was established to give students advice on career and organisational planning; and a library services department was set up for reference materials. Instructional development, editorial services and media services units were also set up. This organisation provided sufficient complexity to meet distance education needs and provided the university with operational autonomy within distance education. By hiring personnel with specialised technical training experience, Athabasca University was able to attain suitable coherence.

The operating units were to be responsible to three vice-presidents, who were answerable to the chief academic and administrative officer. When the university was given permanent status, it adopted a unicameral governance system in which its governing council, consisting of twenty-three members assumed the powers and duties of a conventional board of governors with respect to financial and administrative matters, and of a general faculties council/senate with respect to academic affairs. The chairman is appointed by the provincial government, and twelve public members are appointed by the minister. Five academic staff and one support staff are elected by the respective groups and one member represents the students.

This administrative structure proved to be complex and was adaptive. It resulted in a distribution of responsibility to make it more accountable. In particular, responsibility for academic affairs was delegated to an academic council consisting of a broad representation of staff. According to Daniel and Smith, 'the university adopted the unicameral governance structure in the belief that concentrating the responsibility and authority for both academic and administrative affairs in one body would allow the institution to respond in a more timely and concerted manner to service demands placed on it.' (in Shale 1982:51)

Athabasca University's autonomy was shaken in 1980. In that year the provincial government's minister of advanced education and manpower, without input from the university, announced that the university would be moved from Edmonton to Athabasca, a town of 1,800 people, 145 kilometres to the north. The move shook the organisation's internal coherence as the university president resigned and staff became embittered. (Shale 1982) Considerable time and energy was consumed to accommodate the new legislation. Also the unicameral system of administration created coherence problems. As Shale described it:

> Pressures had existed within the University for some time to separate academic and administrative affairs, and the conflicts of interest inherent in the unicameral system were apparent every year when terms and conditions of employment were being negotiated. However, the nascent schism opened widely under the pressure of circumstances that have presented the University with a challenge equal to those it has met in the past. (1982:52)

Although Athabasca University had all the ingredients to become a mature institution, paralysis set in with the provincial government's decision to usurp its autonomy. Internal conflicts created by external political demands interfered with Athabasca University's institutional growth.

TVOntario

A delivery support agency which became a dominant player in Canadian distance education was the Ontario Educational Communications Authority. An act of 26 June 1970 provided for a new agency to absorb the functions of Ontario's educational television branch. The provincial government anticipated increased involvement in the development of educational television by representatives from public school, university and adult education.

The authority was provided with a broad mandate such as the right to 'acquire, publish, distribute and preserve whether for a consideration or otherwise, such audio-visual materials, papers, periodicals and other library matter as relate to any of the objects of the Authority ... engage in research in those fields of activity consistent with the objects of the authority'. (Waniewicz 1979)

To ensure that the OECA would not duplicate existing services, an elected board developed a sound structure which became the basis for interorganisational co-operation: 'To utilise electronic and associated media to provide educational opportunities to all people of Ontario where the use of such media will complement the educational opportunities being offered by other agencies, or, alternatively, will provide educational opportunities not otherwise available to such persons, and further to co-operate with other organisations in attaining social and educational goals.' (Waniewicz 1979)

In brief, the OECA's scope of operational autonomy was designed to include:

1. broadcasting in English and French;
2. educational design servicing;
3. consulting servicing on the use of OECA;
4. community development activities;
5. educational communications research;
6. policy contributions on educational communications; and
7. cable system services to remote communities.

In 1974 the OECA established a network of transmitters and named it TVOntario.

The OECA was to receive its operating grants from the ministries of culture and recreation, education, and colleges and universities. Each grant is based on OECA's intent to support a ministry objective. Hence the OECA's autonomy became restricted by the requirement that it respect the objectives of the various granting ministries. It strived to retain more autonomy and complexity by generating extra resources through co-production, sales activities and requests for federal grants.

OECA's autonomy and coherence were restricted by the requirements of a federal order-in-council which set forth the qualities of educational programming. Its staff was directed to follow operating procedures which met the requirements of these orders. Further, the board was to be accountable to the Ontario legislature.

The board consisted of thirteen members chosen by the lieutenant-governor in council. It incorporated advisory committees in finance, compensation, extension of service, management and goals and objectives. Its organisational complexity was further served with the establishment of five regional councils whose members were nominated by independent nominating groups and approved by the board members.

To be adaptive in decisionmaking, the board has always invited input from groups like researchers; statutory, special and *ad hoc* committees; and provincial councils which deal with the needy. However, OECA still has very little control over programme content and instruction. It was designed to be a specialised agency serving distance education organisations. Built-in checks were designed to ensure that OECA did not move beyond the original intent.

Télé-université

In Quebec, the creation of the provincial ministry of education in 1964 was followed by the secularisation and expansion of education. Part of this innovation led to the establishment of the Université du Québec in 1968. Further, in 1972 Télé-université began distance education services. However, as with so many other distance education organisations, its decisionmaking capacity was restricted.

Télé-université's educational territory was defined on the basis of discussions and surveys conducted before its establishment. Its mandate was to fill an important vacuum left by the conventional universities. For example, due to a lack of service in the co-operative movement, Télé-université was entrusted with the education of the economic, social and legal aspects of Quebec's co-operatives.

Yet Télé-université was governed by a body of representatives from different campuses of the Université du Québec. Télé-université's important decisions had to be ratified by each of the Université du Québec campuses rather than being subject to its own processes. In 1974 the thorough revision of Université du Québec's administrative structure led to Télé-université's becoming one of ten units making up the Université du Québec network. Subsequently it received the same decisionmaking autonomy as the nine campuses.

But, in terms of complexity, Télé-université was institutionally immature. For example, it was not permitted to build a permanent academic staff. A provision dictated that optimal use of Université du Québec's existing staff be maintained to help Télé-université maintain flexibility in selecting courses. (Daniel and Umbrico 1975)

In 1974 Télé-université assumed responsibility of the PERMAMA (PERfectionment des MAîtres en MAthématique), a Université du Québec programme, intended for secondary school teachers. Télé-université was authorised to manage the programme, because it had no permanent course team, lacked poor quality of teaching and had a falling enrolment. Télé-université's answer was to address the complexity and adaptiveness factors of organisations by establishing 'moniteur-animateurs'. Their role was to distribute bulk course materials to respective learning groups; invigilate examinations, operate the television playback equipment, supply feedback to the course team and help each group work efficiently. The introduction of the 'moniteur-animateurs', establishment of a permanent PERMAMA course team and other re-arrangements of the programme brought an increase in enrolment.

Télé-université coherence was tested when the 'moniteur-animateurs' tried to cast themselves in the role of instructors and teach courses. According to Daniel and Umbriaco (1975), their lack of qualifications led to failure. Although there was an apparent need for group instructors, Télé-université did not have a suitable structure to provide them. The formal institutional response did not adapt itself to the need for on-site instruction.

Télé-université's organisational arrangement was closely defined in that it was not intended to encroach on the domain of schools, CEGEPS or other provincial universities. It was envisioned as completing a system in which it has a part with other institutions.

ACCESS ALBERTA

In 1973, the Alberta government followed Ontario's example by establishing the Alberta Educational Communications Corporation, commonly referred to as ACCESS. Its principal role was to provide delivery technologies such as satellite transmission, digitalisation, teletext, videodisc multiplexing, video-taping and radio transmission.

ACCESS was composed of a programme services division which included higher and further education, early and basic education, programming, field services and project management; a production division; a technical services and distribution division; an administration and research division; and special projects and information services. This structure was designed for programming activities in the following: early education - 20% (pre-school and parents); basic education - 40% (grades 1-12); higher education - 15% (formal postsecondary education); further education - 25% (beyond school age and the responsibility of other departments).

Like the OECA, ACCESS was built to be interorganisational: 'The principal role of the Alberta Educational Communications Corporation is complementary to the total educational enterprise within the province of Alberta ... The role of the Corporation is to provide services which support the educational enterprise.' (ACCESS 1982:23)

The corporation was not complex enough to be charged with content of education and methods of presentation. This responsibility was assigned to the provincial department of education and the department of advanced education and manpower. The corporation's clearly defined territory of operation was to provide programming services, production services and acquire educational materials.

In terms of autonomy, the guideline for ACCESS was that:

> The Canadian Radio and Television Commission requires that the Corporation be independent from the provincial government in order that the provisions of Order-In-Council 1972-1569 be met. The purpose of the guidelines for the AECC, while recognising the need to preserve the operational independence of the Corporation, is to assure that those decisions related to education are consistent with the objectives of agencies which have legal responsibility (or are held accountable by the public) for curriculum design, development and implementation. (ACCESS 1981:23)

If this guideline were added to the federal cabinet restrictions enumerated in 1972, there was little room for ACCESS gaining adequate institutional autonomy, complexity and coherence to become a distance education institution.

BUNTEP

In the mid-1970s, Canada experienced a surge of culturally defined distance education activities. This was especially apparent in native Indian education. One of the foremost of these was the establishment in 1974 of the Brandon University Northern Teacher Education Programme (BUNTEP) to achieve the following goals:

1. to deliver postsecondary services to people in the isolated northern communities who traditionally have not the opportunity for such experience.
2. to develop a system of delivery of services utilising all available resources wherein
   a. the community and participants are directly involved in the design, content and conduct of the system, and
   b. the participants are trained to satisfy people services needs through employment in the public sector.
3. to develop innovative techniques for delivery services in the north.

These goals provided BUNTEP with a degree of autonomy, adaptiveness and territorial rights to develop delivery services for a specific cultural group. To achieve this mandate, BUNTEP's administrative complexity was organised around the associate dean of education, Brandon University. Next, the director of BUNTEP was responsible for programme development, field service and community liaison/student affairs co-ordinators. To meet local needs, BUNTEP adopted a service structure comprised of travelling professors, centre co-ordinators/administrators and centre advisory committees.

BUNTEP's establishment was funded by Brandon University, which received funds from the Manitoba government. The BUNTEP was not given the autonomy to acquire its own funds directly from the senior source (federal government).

Although at the time of conception BUNTEP did not formally meet the criteria of a distance education organisation, it did have significant components of a programme which were faithful to distance education design. BUNTEP must still be considered a Brandon University department with unique goals and identifiable territory.

CONFERENCE ON CANADA AND THE OPEN UNIVERSITY: TEACHING AND LEARNING AT A DISTANCE

In March 1974, the executive director of the Association of Atlantic Universities led a conference in Ottawa on Canada and the Open University Concept. It was sponsored by the Association of Universities and Colleges of Canada and the Science Council of Canada. Some points made at the conference specified distance education's institutional development. For example, according to Holmes (1974), the Canadian experience of producing distance education course materials was unsophisticated and inconsequential. It lacked the complexity and coherence evident in the British Open University. When asked whether Canada could support a national distance education institution like the Open University, Dr Holmes answered:

I would see enormous resistance ... to transferring 150,000 students to a 'national' university or to building a new enrolment from scratch. Enrolment for an open university at a provincial or regional level would be unlikely to climb beyond 40,000 ... My conclusion, then is that the Open University as such is not particularly needed in Canada and wouldn't work, even if it were needed. My conclusion applies whether the Open University is projected into a national Canadian context or is thought of in regional or provincial terms. (Holmes:34-5)

When the discussion focused on correspondence courses, a course co-ordinator from the University of Ottawa described two myths that needed to be destroyed: that correspondence courses are inferior, and that traditional university education is accessible to all. Teaching at a distance can be ideal, she said, for brilliant and for dull students, since both can learn within broad limits at their own rate.

The conference's concluding statement reflects distance education's need for greater adaptability:

An Open University such as that in Britain would be wasteful and unnecessary. But openness, egalitarianism, wider access are needed. We need to upgrade adult education in Canada, using facilities of the Canadian Broadcasting Corporation, the universities and colleges, and the National Film Board. We need more experimental programs, such as the one at Trent University for groups of retired individuals. More specifically we need a two-fold thrust. One component would be general interest programs, for example, on inflation, the limits to economic growth. This component would include correspondence courses, with the opportunity for students to phone to instructors. Such general interest programmes could be a culturally cohesive force across the nation.

BRITISH COLUMBIA INSTITUTE OF TECHNOLOGY

The British Columbia Institute of Technology (BCIT) was established in 1964. However, more important, a department of distance education was formally created in 1974. Its priority was to develop programme materials for forestry, business, health and engineering courses. But course development was primarily the responsibility of regular BCIT faculty. Only on rare occasions did the distance education department in operation with BCIT content-specialists build courses. When needed, the distance education department contracted course development to local course writers.

In the service/delivery operations, the distance education department lacked the organisational complexity to serve British Columbia students adequately. For example, if students needed to use educational hardware such as video/audiocassette players or microcomputers, they had to visit the BCIT campus. In 1980 BCIT provided hardware facilities in the Downtown Education Centre, Vancouver. Still, out-of-town students were inconvenienced.

Although BCIT's distance education department depended primarily on print (97 per cent of all materials) and provided limited student access to hardware, course tuition was almost three times the equivalent for on-campus students. (Ruggles *et al*. 1982) This income plus an operating budget of one per cent of the BCIT general budget helped pay for tutors, counsellors, library services and programme development and servicing.

Of greater relevance to the history of Canadian distance education was BCIT's landmark involvement in the Hermes satellite experiment. In 1977 the distance education department became a key player of STEP (Satellite Tele-Education Programme). It was allocated eight one-hour transmissions to present combined documentary and live multi-station discussion series on forestry (Robertson 1981). The Hermes educational experiment became the forerunner of the ANIK-B satellite trials initiated in December 1978 in co-operation with selected British Columbia colleges. BCIT delivered a number of televised credit courses using one-way and two-way audio-teleconferencing.

The satellite experiments highlighted significant institutional factors. According to Robertson:

> BCIT staff realized that the traditional division of staff into departments based on discipline or function while suitable for teaching fulltime students, was not well organised for handling the Hermes project and future educational telecommunications services on a regular basis. The BCIT project planners wished to gain experience in satellite technology and in co-operative project administration. They believed the BCIT departments generally behaved autonomously enough that experience gained internally might be transferable to later dealings with autonomous educational institutions in Western Canada. The departments invited to participate were the Audio-Visual and Broadcast Communications departments which had full responsibility for programme production, the Forest Resources department which provided funding and project co-ordination. It is interesting to note that although the twenty or so staff who worked on the project were part of a relatively small 450 member faculty and shared a connected three-building, four-storey complex, and most had been on staff for at least four years, the majority did not know the name or normal role of most members of the group. (1981:138)

The experiment threatened the organisation's internal coherence whereby individuals with different allegiances became involved within one group. Rather than work as a cohesive unit, the staff operated as autonomous individuals. Further, Robertson noted:

> Some observations are worth noting because educational institutions and government departments tend to combine carefully defined hierarchical structures with a paradoxical freedom of action for individuals, neither of which often make sense or reflect good human relations. Competition is more common than co-operation. (1982:140)

When BCIT received provincial programming responsibility for the ANIK-B project, it invited six colleges which traditionally competed for government funds and new programme authorisations to participate. BCIT's dean of continuing education along with the senior staff of five colleges established the project's technical requirements, operating structure and a detailed project plan. To overcome problems of coherence and autonomy, the following collective agreement was reached:

1. that all decisions involving the basic structure of the project, priorities, and proposed actions involving all participants be made collectively;
2. there would be no unilateral action by any members of the group;
3. the colleges would have first refusal on one receiver station each and would designate the station location within their regions;
4. the colleges would each decide to what extent they would support the project in their region;
5. that BCIT would act as a central co-ordinating agency for the dissemination of technical information, preparation of group advertising, evaluation of overall projects, teaching of courses, solving of routine operating problems, operation of courier systems, preparation of detailed project plan, and communication of special needs to DOC and the Ministry of Education;
6. the colleges would handle local publicity, registration, fee collection, facility preparation, data collection assignment distribution, and general classroom support;
7. both BCIT and the colleges would award course credits, report student statistics, set fees, set priorities, and document activities;
8. BCIT would list courses available for telecasting to the colleges and the colleges would select according to their needs and scheduling constraints; and
9. each institution would appoint staff members to co-ordinate local administration, evaluation, and satellite equipment installation and operation. (Robertson 1982:141)

These guidelines were intended to be a framework for efficient interorganisational activity. Overall it established a complex set of interorganisation relationships to meet project demands. However, again institutional concerns surfaced. The colleges became concerned about their autonomy and their educational territory. BCIT and college faculties felt threatened by the importation of instruction from a central studio. A threat to internal coherence resulted whereby

they wished to alter their normal collective bargaining relationships with institutional administrations and become more directly involved in the local project operating terms. The institution administrations felt this to be an unreasonable request since in no other operating aspects of their institutions did the union have a special role. (Robertson 1982:143)

In summary, the Anik-B experiment provided BCIT and other British Columbia colleges an opportunity to build a complex structure adaptive to technological changes. However, internal conflicts and search for autonomy by member organisations limited the success for a unique interorganisational structure.

POST HERMES EXPERIMENT: CANADA WIDE

Outside British Columbia, the Hermes satellite experiment included Carleton University, Memorial University and the Université du Québec. The post

University, Memorial University and the Université du Québec. The post 1977 Hermes Experiment findings were that: (1) there was no increase in educational effectiveness; (2) most participants found activities satisfactory; and (3) satellite exchanges were less congenial than face-to-face contact for the same purposes.

The Carleton University experiment featured several institutional difficulties. According to Daniel (1978), exchanging courses between agencies was administratively complex, requiring constant co-ordination between sites, resulting in such problems as the unavailability of textbooks, inconsistency in marking assignments and poor student recruitment. A major goal for the satellite experiment was to make distance education more adaptive. It was intended to assimilate new technology with distance education or:

1. answer a primary need;
2. blend with technology in use and developments under way;
3. integrate personnel into the regular institutional structure and train properly;
4. help the institution invest some of its own resources in the project and give it high visibility;
5. allow different departments to collaborate in using the technology and that transfer to the other institutions is easy; and
6. evaluate the use of technology.

But Daniel's (1978) concluding statement on satellites and distance education featured the improbability of meeting the major goals:

Although governments are prepared to make new technologies available to education for experiments at little cost, it is a fair assumption that an operational system would have to pay at least real technical costs. An attempt has been made to identify these costs for two hypothetical education satellite networks in Canada ... Although the costs ... are not large compared to existing budgets for education, there will be no move to make such investments and set up the interinstitutional organisation required unless the result answers a clearly felt need. Even were such networks created by a national policy decision they would, like much previous education technology, wither on the vine unless there proved to be a need for them.

NORTH ISLAND COLLEGE

In 1975, another noteworthy development in distance education appeared in western Canada. North Island College became one of the fifteen regional colleges established by the British Columbia provincial government to provide distance education to residents within the college region. (Ruggles *et al.* 1982) A regional advisory committee recommended that North Island College use non-traditional delivery systems to provide educational opportunities for students. This learning system was designed to be open with respect to place, time and student entry and to provide self-paced mastery learning independent of instructor, campus and schedules. At this time North Island College became the only non-campus based community college in Canada.

At the beginning, North Island College was too small to have sufficient institutional coherence. For example, the college council decided that, because of North Island College's size, it could not produce its own learning materials, but rather it would purchase them from Coastline Community College in California, the BBC, the Open University and Athabasca University. As a result, North Island College was unable to meet unique regional/cultural programme needs and demands.

North Island College's structural complexity consisted basically of fourteen learning centres throughout its region, each one with a local tutor. Because there was a lack of tutors specialising in certain subject matter, the ones on staff became multi-dimensional generalists. As a result, North Island College was unable to integrate its tutors into specialised units of instruction. In 1976, North Island College reached an agreement with Athabasca University leading to dual student status, an available source of university level materials and automatic accreditation to a Canadian public university. But independently, North Island College lacked the complexity to be a full-scale distance education institution.

OPEN LEARNING INSTITUTE

In 1976 the British Columbia ministry of education established three commissions to consider British Columbia's postsecondary educational system. All three commissions recommended an increase in the availability of educational and training programmes and, in 1977, an *ad hoc* planning department recommended establishment of a new institution to co-ordinate the development and delivery of distance education in Adult Basic Education, Career/Technical/Vocational programmes and university disciplines. This led to the creation of the Open Learning Institute. (Kaufman and Bottomley 1980)

The Open Learning Institute (OLI) was charged with developing programmes to meet the full spectrum of the educational needs of the adult population and to do so in a manner that would allow students to study part-time in their own homes. Originally, OLI was faced with the sequential development of over one hundred university courses. To build the complexity and enhance its autonomy for generating its own resources, OLI set up course development teams consisting of a course writer, course consultant, instructional designer, editor, visual designer and 'pilot students'. The plan was also to link advisers to students. To establish a greater sense of coherence, OLI selected advisers on the basis of their experience in student service settings, experience as distance education students, graduate level courses in counselling, and suitable personal qualities. Such requirements made it possible for advisers to inform students on planning, registration and financial assistance. Tutors were appointed based on their experience, teaching ability and subject matter expertise.

Regional advising centres were established throughout British Columbia. They were intended to provide a support system for OLI students, facilitate access to continuing education and ensure that the community they serve is aware of OLI and its program.

The advising centres served university credit programmes in history, psychology, sociology, English, geography, economics, mathematics and biology; career/technical/vocational programmes in construction, motel, restaurant, small business and office management and industrial supervision; and Adult Basic Education courses for high school graduation. These offerings, along with appointments of appropriate personnel, provided OLI with the complexity, autonomy and adaptivity needed to address the needs of its client group.

To help eliminate external conflicts with other organisations OLI was designed on a policy of interinstitutional co-operation. For example, library facilities were/are shared with Simon Fraser University, laboratory facilities were/are shared with community colleges, some joint programmes development was initiated with Athabasca University and Simon Fraser University, and research was undertaken with North Island College and Athabasca University.

To become increasingly adaptive, OLI integrated a number of smaller units and established a department of educational technology in 1981. The main functions were: (1) providing information, training and assistance to programme areas on the use of educational technology; (2) consulting with programme areas on matters of instructional design; (3) developing and maintaining a course evaluation system; (4) developing and maintaining a tutor evaluation system; (5) co-ordinating OLI research and exploration of a new areas; and (6) supporting courses under control.

OLI's organisational complexity, autonomy in developing its own model of operation and legitimate authority to sustain it, intra- and interorganisational coherence and adaptiveness to changing needs of students and technology, provided the organisation with a sound basis for institutional development.

SYMPOSIUM ON DISTANCE EDUCATION 1978

On 5 September 1978, Simon Fraser's Faculty of Education and Continuing Studies sponsored a milestone discussion on research and development activities relevant to distance education. A large number of issues relevant to institutionalisation were discussed by prominent international distance educators. Some of these were: (1) the distance education system should be capable of operation anywhere where there are students, free faculty members from custodial type duties, offer students and adults wider choices, provide opportunities for individual student differences; (2) the mission of the system should be clearly stated. Who determines policy? Is there hostility of professors towards open learning? How do you neutralise the opposition? What collaborations are desirable and feasible with other universities?

KNOWLEDGE NETWORK OF THE WEST COMMUNICATIONS AUTHORITY

The Knowledge Network of the West Communications Authority was created by the British Columbian provincial government as a non-profit society under the Societies Act 1980. The Knowledge Network was designed to become an inter-organisational educational telecommunications authority whose major role was to assist existing distance education organisations through development and distribution of programmes by means of satellite and cable TV. The Knowledge Network received autonomy, in the development, co-ordination and delivery of educational materials. This mandate, however, led to some overlap in distance education activities with other provincial organisations like BCIT's Department of Distance Education. As expected, some territoriality disputes had to be negotiated.

Overall, Knowledge Network's structure provided for interorganisational input at the levels of policy, programmes and operations; for example, the colleges and institutes' working group, whose membership was composed of individual delegates appointed by the principal of each organisation, reported to a network board through a network official. There were and still are today, working groups for the universities and the health service.

As a separate entity, the Knowledge Network's autonomy was designed to be restricted. The board of directors involved at the policy level was designed to include college principals, university deans, and representatives from the provincial ministry of education. The ministry of education provided funding for the salaries of distance education co-ordinators located at the colleges, and to cover the costs of learning centres for use of classroom facilities, support services and so on. (Ruggles *et al.* 1982)

In terms of complexity, the Knowledge Network's educational services was designed to include three essential components. These were telecourses, teleseries and interactive programming. The components were an innovation to meet the needs of British Columbia students.

CONSORTIA ON DISTANCE EDUCATION 1981-2

Recognition of institutional problems in distance education were formally addressed in 1981, with the birth of the Western Canadian Committee on University Distance Education. Meetings with western university representatives were held in Regina and Richmond, 1982 to answer major questions concerning economic, technical, educational, political and social/cultural aspects of distance education. (Mugridge 1983) Concerning autonomy the major point of discussion was the need to collaborate on responses to political pressures. Adaptability included the perceived need to initiate changes in distance education activities for particular societies. Complexity involved concerns about improving distance education organisations' responses to demands made by wider student needs. From a broad conference perspective the delegates attempted to build greater coherence amongst agencies so that they can better address external conflicts with governments, and arrive at consensus over delivery modes and programme designs.

Representatives from the Universities of Calgary, Athabasca, Lethbridge, Alberta, Victoria, Regina, Simon Fraser, British Columbia, and the Open Learning Institute, discussed distance education programme and course development, means of instruction, provision of services to students, marketing, methods of evaluation and research, and management of distance education programmes. In short, the issues discussed impacted institutional factors such as complexity (faculty, services), autonomy (politics, resources, pedagogy), coherence (goals, means, present and future external and internal conflicts, territory) and adaptation (responding to technical, social and economic changes).

On 27 April 1982 the representatives of the attending western Canadian universities decided to establish a Western Canadian Committee on University Distance Education. The objectives were:

1. the encouragement of member institutions to co-operate in:
   (a) the sharing of information about programme offerings, pro-

gramme plans, and delivery systems;

(b) the sale and exchange of course material according to the terms and conditions of use as specified by the source institution(s);

(c) the planning of new programmes and courses;

(d) the facilitation of the transfer of credit among institutions and the exploration of mechanisms through which to address other problems of credit transferability;

(e) the joint utilisation of common course offerings; and

(f) the exchange and secondment of staff among institutions;

2. the encouragement of economies in the use and distribution among institutions engaged in the development and delivery of distance education; and

3. the provision of a forum for the consideration of common problems facing institutions engaged in the development and delivery of distance education. (Mugridge 1983)

TODAY

The historical developments in Canadian distance education provide a backbone for today's numerous courses designed and delivered by a variety of organisations and agencies. Although major benchmark developments were described, numerous more small scale events occurred to provide Canada with an extensive distance education network. Today most of Canada's universities and colleges offer credit and/or non-credit courses by distance. Modern technological advances are used in distance education programme delivery. Some examples are audio/video/computer conferencing, and cable and satellite communication systems; private organisations also participate in earnest. Distance education today is a serious education process. However, the various organisations are far from being full-scale institutions.

CONCLUSION

As can be seen from the description, Canada's distance education history is saturated with an outgrowth of departments, organisations and agencies, all of which had little institutional authority. The result is a national potpourri in which distance education service centres have self-defined, sustaining images of institutional maturity. They have unique organisational structures with differing degrees of institutional complexity to serve client needs. They have differing degrees of decisionmaking autonomy in terms of defining goals, mandates and operations. They have differing degrees of coherence resulting from varied territorial limits of operation, interorganisational functions and external/internal conflict solution. Finally some centres are more adaptive to changing technology, student needs and political climates than others are.

Today one finds a collection of services under the general heading of Canadian distance education. For example, some sources are referred to as correspondence or extension departments/services, some are telecommunications authorities, some are programmes, some are institutes or universities and others are delivery systems. Yet each is considered a distance education player. With today's prevalent mood of education restraint, undoubtedly some centres will be cut, some realigned, some redefined and some reduced in size and mandate. This would hinder even more the ideal of distance education institutions becoming effective instruments of stability, responsiveness and legitimation in Canadian education.

REFERENCES

Access (1982) *Annual Report*, Edmonton, Alberta Association of Universities and Colleges of Canada (1974) 'Conference on Canada and the Open University: Teaching and Learning at a Distance: Proceedings', 28-9 March, Ottawa, Ontario

Carefoot, J. (1982) 'The Birth of a Western Canadian Committee on University Distance Education: Proceedings of Meetings', Saskatchewan: University of Regina

Clark, D., S. McKibbin and M. Malkos (eds.) (1981) *Alternative Perspectives For Viewing Educational Organisations*, San Francisco, Far West Laboratory

Conger, D.L. (1974) *Canadian Open Adult Learning System*, Prince Albert, Saskatchewan: Department of Manpower and Immigration

Daniel, J.S. (1978) 'Satellites in Distance Education: Canadian Experiments on the Humes Satellite', International Council for Correspondence Education, Advance Papers Vol. 1, New Delhi, India, 8-15 November

Daniel, J.S. and M. Umbriaco (1975) 'Distance Study in French Canada: Télé-université', *Teaching at a Distance*, No. 4, November

D'Antori, S.G. (1982) 'Distance Education in Canada: The Need for an information Data Base', Toronto, Ontario: Ryerson Polytechnical Institute

Eisenstadt, S.N. (1966) *Modernisation: Protest and Change*, Englewood Cliffs: Prentice Hall

Gwyn, S. (1972) *Film, Video-tape and Social Change*, St John's, Newfoundland

Huntington, S. (1973) *Political Order in Changing Societies*, New Haven, Conn.: Yale University Press

Kaufman, D. and J. Bottomley (1980) 'The Open Learning Institute: University Programme Development', (A Working Paper), April

La Polambara, J. (1968) *Interest Groups in Italian Politics*, Princeton: Princeton University Press

Lee, George E. (1975) 'Memorial University of Newfoundland Exterior Service' (A Working Paper), January

Leslie, J.D. (1979) 'The University of Waterloo Model for Distance Education', *Canadian Journal of University Continuing Education, 6*

Mugridge, I. (1983) 'Consortia in Distance Education: Some Canadian Ventures', Open Campus, Occasional Papers, Victoria, Australia: Deakin University

Riggs, F. (1964) *Administration in Developing Countries: The Theory of Prismatic Society*, Boston: Houghton Mifflin

Robertson, W.D. (1981) 'Regional Co-operation in Satellite-Delivered Interactive Instructional Television - The British Columbia Experience, 1977-1980', ASPESA Forum 81 Papers

Robins, R.S. (1976) *Political Institutionalisation and the Integration of Elites*, Beverly Hills: Sage Press

Ruggles, R.H., J. Anderson, D. Blackmore, C. LaFleur, J.P. Rothe, and T. Taeriem (1982) *Learning at a Distance and the New Technology*, Vancouver, B.C.: Educational Research Institute of British Columbia

Shale, D. (1982) 'Athabasca University, Canada', in G. Rumble and K. Harry (eds.), *The Teaching Universities*, New York: St Martin's Press

Smith, W.A.S. and B.L. Snowden (1983) 'A Review of Distance Education in Ontario Universities', Toronto, Ont.: Council of Ontario Universities, April

Government Policies

John F. Ellis

Government policies in Canada which affect distance education - where they exist and such as they are - emanate from the governments of the provinces and territories, not the federal government. The fathers of confederation, representative of regional interests as they were, relinquished control of many matters to the new federal authority but not education. The conduct of education was seen as central to the maintenance of religious and cultural values. Lower Canada, in particular, being predominantly French and Roman Catholic, feared the homogenising consequences of a school system which might come to be dominated by the more populous English and Protestant Upper Canada. Obviously then, Canada has not one but twelve educational systems, one for each province and territory.

Not unexpectedly, therefore, the conduct of all aspects of education- including distance education - differs somewhat from one part of Canada to another. Each province or territory has its own statutes and forms. In some, for example, responsibility for all aspects of education from pre-school to higher education is vested in a single ministry. In others, educational responsibilities are shared in ways that make greater or lesser sense. Some, for example, have separate ministries for school-age and adult learners; others make the logically difficult distinction between education and vocational training, assigning certain responsibilities in the latter case to a ministry of labour. Still others attempt to differentiate aspects of early childhood education, assigning kindergartens to one ministry and daycare centres to another. Almost all have different financial arrangements for dealing with the educational concerns of religious, ethnic and other groups.

Nevertheless, despite an almost endless array of minor differences from one jurisdiction to another, the day-to-day activities of ministries, schools, colleges and universities across Canada are very similar. The curricula of schools and universities, for example, are, with minor exceptions, dictated by factors which transcend regional interests. Similarly, and again with minor exceptions, the procedures are more similar, region to region, than they are different. Names and titles may differ but functions do not. Parliamentary government, ministerial responsibility, a central civil service, and some degree of local control are universal.

Even though each province and territory has the nominal control and responsibility for education within its boundaries, however, the federal government has a more than passing interest and involvement. In fact, the various educational systems across the country simply could not function were it not for the bewildering patchwork of federal transfer payments and grants. The research activities of university professors, for example, are funded primarily from federal agencies. The teaching of French to English-speaking children and the teaching of English to immigrants are paid for by federal dollars because, as the provinces argue, bilingualism and immigration policies are federal initiatives with educational consequences. Vocational training is clearly related to federal manpower policies and thus, both levels of government agree, federal funds can flow in this direction. In any case, and here the argument is strained by both in the interests of expediency, training can be differentiated from education and thus the constitutional prerogatives of the provinces in education are not breached.

Communications and telecommunications are similarly fraught with federal-provincial wrangles which will have increasing relevance for the conduct of distance education. Radio, television, telephone, micro-links, satellites and the like are federal responsibilities even though the provinces claim certain rights. Thus, the use of these media by provincial authorities requires negotiation, which at times can be convoluted and acrimonious. To illustrate, the use of the Canadian Broadcasting Corporation (CBC)'s capabilities for a given province's educational programme poses almost insurmountable policy problems. Given that the CBC network is at present the only one with near universal coverage, the use of radio and television as components of distance education activities is inhibited. Admittedly, some of the wealthier provinces are developing and expanding their own networks, but universal accessibility to radio and television signals other than through CBC is some time away.

In brief, the federal-provincial constitutional division makes for an untidy business at best. In 1867, 'education' was synonymous with the public school system and, thus, did not need to cross provincial boundaries. Today, however, much of education reaches across boundaries and relates to a national agenda even though the conduct of formal education, at least, remains the jealously guarded prerogative of each province.

Predictions

Two predictable statements can be made about government policies for distance education in Canada. First, there is no national policy for distance education; in fact, for constitutional reasons, there cannot be one. Thus, national goals such as the removal of regional disparities or the furtherance of human resource development cannot be addressed by a central authority as they are by distance universities in Great Britain and Indonesia. This is not to say that there is no federal involvement in distance education institutions. There is; but it is indirect and piecemeal. It is indirect in the sense that general tax transfer payments reach the provinces, are laundered in the pool of general revenue and ultimately reach the distance education institutions. It is piecemeal in the sense that federal funds for research, vocational training, second-language instruction and the like can flow directly to provincial institutions because they fall outside the constitutional definition of education.

A second general statement can be made concerning government policies in distance education. It is this: there is little similarity in distance education across the provinces. In some, notably Alberta and British Columbia, there is considerable activity. In others, including the most heavily populated provinces of Ontario and Quebec, activity is modest. In still others, the Atlantic Provinces and the northern territories, there is virtually no involvement in distance education.

Some would differ with the foregoing, citing as evidence the elaborate and extensive programmes of educational outreach present in virtually all regions of the country. Professors at Memorial University, Newfoundland and at the University of Manitoba, for example, offer courses in numerous small communities in their vast provinces; and instructors at North Island College in British Columbia use storefronts, mobile laboratories and class-rooms to bring learning opportunities to residents scattered along the fjords of their region. But the generalisation holds if we define distance education as a form of educational outreach having three essential characteristics: the use of comprehensive and carefully prepared and mediated instructional materials; the provision of feedback to learners by appropriate means; and no reliance or minimal reliance on face-to-face interaction between teachers and learners. Thus, the establishment of remote campus centres, or the practice of having instructors fly to distant communities to teach classes indeed bridge educational distance but they are not, technically, distance education. And neither is educational television when it is used for casual or informal viewing and is not linked to the other necessary conditions.

Government Policies

Government policy, in distance education as in other matters, must often be inferred from the perceived actions of governments. These, in turn, normally derive from statutes, their attendant regulations and the interpret-ation of both, typically by civil servants. Thus, if one defines a policy as a reasoned statement of government intent, one might assume that a clear path could be traced backwards from a perceived activity of government to a definitive statement of intent issued by the responsible political official. But this seems seldom to be the case for several reasons.

For one thing, it is sometimes difficult to determine when the public utterance of a politician reflects government intent and, even when it does, intent can change in the light of public reaction. For another, statutes are normally cast in rather general language and typically include aspects of permissiveness or provide discretionary powers to various operating levels. Thus, an action undertaken by an agency might involve activities which were not even visualised by the government which enacted the statute. For example, the Universities Act of British Columbia makes no mention of distance education and yet the three public universities have such prog-rammes. For another, the general language of a statute is made operational by rules and regulations or by orders-in-council, both of which are actions of a cabinet with neither requiring the assent of the full legislature. There are occasions when these involve decisions and actions not visualised in the intent of the original legislation. And finally (though not exhaustively), the interpretation of statutes and regulations by civil servants may or may not be in accord with a government's intent. It is likely to be consistent with the language of the document in question, but here again, language may not necessarily capture intent. All of this is to say that it is seldom easy, and often impossible, accurately to delineate government policy in distance education.

It should come as no surprise that government policies in distance education, at least as these are reflected in statutes and regulations, are few and far between. What might surprise some as they read other chapters in this book is that so much is occurring with, seemingly, so little official

27

policy. Perhaps, in some subtle way, this reflects a Canadian tendency to administer by muddling through. It may even argue, even if indirectly, for the virtues of an unwritten national constitution, such as was the case in Canada until recently.

This is not to say, of course, that distance education activities take place outside a legal framework. Rather, it is to note that the laws which govern and enable them are general rather than prescriptive.

Institutional Arrangements

There are three kinds of institutional arrangements under which distance education functions. First, the ministries of education of the six largest provinces offer correspondence instruction to school-age children. Second, a number of universities and colleges offer distance education courses and programmes as adjuncts to their more central concern. The three universities in British Columbia and Waterloo University in Ontario are examples. And third, three provinces have institutions which use distance education methods exclusively. These are the Télé-université du Québec, Athabasca University in Alberta and the Open Learning Institute of British Columbia. The legal framework for each of the three categories is somewhat different.

The ministry-operated correspondence divisions operate within the context of the schools act, whatever its precise title in the particular province. Little direct mention of correspondence activities appears in these acts but all or most provinces have accompanying rules, regulations and established practices governing this form of instruction. All insist that face-to-face and correspondence education employ a common curriculum and apply common standards. All recognise correspondence as a legitimate extension of a provincial responsibility to provide a basic education for all children, in this case, for those geographically isolated.

Universities and colleges which offer some (typically a small minority) of their programmes by distance education do so under provisions of their particular universities or colleges acts. The acts are silent on the question of distance education but empower boards and senates to make various kinds of educational provision for their students. Typically, the courses and programmes offered are the same as those offered oncampus and are subject to the normal forms of academic quality control. In brief, these activities are undertaken at the initiative of the institution and not because of a legislative initiative by government.

The third category of arrangement - the creation of a free-standing distance education institution - has required direct government action in each of the three existing instances. The courses of action taken by the three provincial governments differed slightly but all used existing legislation, in the main, to achieve their ends. In the case of the Open Learning Institute of British Columbia, for example, the government established the institution by order-in-council under authority of the already existing Colleges and Provincial Institutes Act. Aside from enacting a minor amendment to the Universities Act empowering OLI to grant degrees, no new legislation was required. Speeches made by the minister at the time of this action might be considered government policy but they have not been cited subsequently as such. Parallel events in Alberta and Quebec were not greatly dissimilar.

One could generalise quite safely in saying that the introduction of distance education activities in Canada has occurred with a minimum of direct government policy, political fanfare and public controversy or comment. This stands in contrast to the establishment of institutions like the British Open University, Sukhothai Thammathirat Open University in Thailand and Universitas Terbuka in Indonesia. One can only speculate on the reasons for this difference. Perhaps it can be accounted for by the fact that the Canadian ventures were very small by comparison. Perhaps it resulted from the national scope of the British, Thai and Indonesian institutions in contrast with the more narrow provincial scope of the Canadian ones. Whatever the reason, considerable numbers of Canadians are enjoying the benefits of distance education and there is little disagreement that the programmes are of acceptable quality. The proportion of university level students studying by this method in Canada will probably never reach the proportions found in South East Asia and in Great Britain simply because Canadian provinces have made relatively lavish provision for campus study. Nevertheless, studying at a distance is an increasingly acceptable alternative for certain groups of students and will likely continue to be so.

CONCLUSION

Is there a need for new, clearer or more detailed government policies for distance education? In my opinion, the answer is 'no'. The Canadian practice of statutory permissiveness has more advantages than disadvantages. Distance education in its present form is still relatively new, much has yet to be learned about its optimal functioning, and new possibilities are emerging as the influence of new technology becomes more pervasive. Had government policy been more detailed, it could well have set faulty directions which would be difficult to change. As it is, distance education programmes and institutions have been permitted to evolve within broad legal frameworks, controlled at times by the discretionary actions of politicians and civil servants. Current arrangements are far from perfect, but improvements are more likely through a continuation of current practices than through the enactment of more intrusive government policy.

The Future of Open Learning

Glen M. Farrell and Margaret Haughey

Börje Holmberg has defined distance education as follows: 'Those teaching methods in which, because of the physical separateness of learners and teachers, the interactive as well as the preparatory phase of teaching is conducted through print, mechanical or electronic devices.' (Holmberg 1981) This is a necessary but not sufficient definition. Necessary because providing learning opportunities to people without the physical presence of an instructor has been shown to be both effective and efficient in many parts of the world, and it will become increasingly pervasive. Insufficient because it does not capture the larger context within which distance education has flourished. That context is one which is best described by the term 'open learning' which implies an 'opening up' of traditional education systems through the combination of telecommunications technologies and the more traditional print formats to meet a broad range of individual and institutional needs, using delivery networks that are developing at the institutional, regional, national and international levels.

The underlying thesis of this chapter then is that the future of distance education lies in the evolution of open learning systems. This evolution has, of course, been going on for some time, arguably back to the itinerant teacher, Socrates. Some of the more recent milestones, however, include:

the development of correspondence education, which permitted access to the formal education system using the public postal network;

the use of radio which, in Canada, was exemplified by such Canadian Broadcasting Corporation (CBC) programmes as the 'Farm Radio Forum';

the evolution of teaching machines which, while not addressing the geographical barriers to access, did encourage independent learning; and

the rapid emergence in more recent times of computer and telecommunications technologies which has opened an enormous number of opportunities for open learning.

Most of these innovations in the delivery of education evolved in order to increase access to educational institutions for those who were geographically remote. That will continue to be an important goal; indeed, an increasingly urgent one as telecommunications technology removes the geographical constraints and unleashes demands on the educational system by those who have previously not been served. What our experience has demonstrated, however, is that there are many who are not geographically remote from educational institutions who use the open learning systems that have evolved because, for them, it overcomes other constraints, such as family and work responsibilities.

The paradigm depicted in Figure 1 illustrates the evolution of open learning delivery systems. Traditional models, referred to in Quadrant A of the paradigm, can be characterised as being primarily dependent on the physical presence of a teacher, with the instruction conducted in a fixed physical facility such as a school or on an institutional campus.

The type of learning system typified in Quadrant B is again primarily dependent on the physical presence of an instructor. As transportation systems developed, however, so did the capability of teachers to meet students at locations remote from the 'home campus'. Indeed, the early history of extension programmes at many North American universities is replete with programmes which used the itinerant teacher model, with the instruction in the community and utilising a variety of local facilities.

Distance education as described in Quadrant C is defined as learning which is not dependent on the physical presence of an instructor and which does not occur at a fixed location. The earliest, and still most pervasive, example is correspondence education. More recent examples include the use of telecommunications technologies such as radio, television and computer formats delivered through both land-based and satellite networks.

The learning strategies employed in Quadrant D-type activities are developing because of the emergence of technological delivery systems. For example, during the 1960s, there was experimentation with closed circuit television programming on an intra-institutional basis. As computer technology developed so did the use of computer-assisted instruction and computer-managed instruction through interinstitutional as well as local area networks. Further, as learning materials are developed for Quadrant C-type learning systems, it is being recognised that they are, for the most part, applicable to the needs of learners studying in a conventional school or campus environment. The result is that new educational materials will be developed to meet learning needs in a variety of contexts. The geographical location of the learner will become less important.

Figure 1: The Evolution of Open Learning Systems

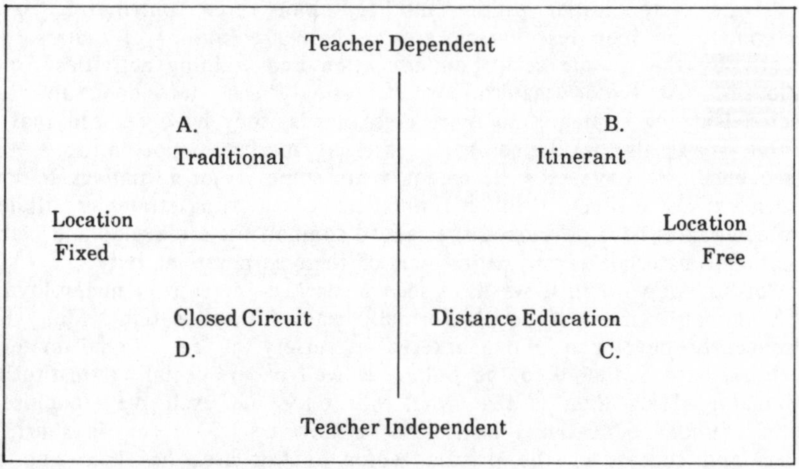

Evolutionary Forces

There are a number of forces contributing to the evolution of open learning systems. Some of these have already been mentioned, such as the increasing demand on the part of the public for enhanced access to educational opportunities and the emergence of new forms of telecommunications technologies. Educators are, therefore, much less reluctant to adapt these technologies to education.

One of the more profound forces at work, however, is the fact that, at least in North America, the concept of education as a lifelong process is becoming firmly embedded in our society. For both social and economic reasons, as well as the fact that knowledge once gained is becoming obsolete at a faster and faster rate, learning throughout one's lifetime is no longer an optional activity. Moreover, we find that demands are being placed on the educational system by people who did not avail themselves of educational opportunities during their youth. Access to these opportunities is very rapidly being seen as a right and that, in turn, is manifesting itself in the political priorities of our society.

Another force at work in this evolution results, curiously enough, from the downturn in the economies of the western world. With education, as it has traditionally been provided, taking such a major share of national and provincial budgets, politicians are attracted to opportunities to reduce costs while, at the same time, respond to the increased demand. Open learning systems with the variety of delivery models they include, taken together with the economies of scale that are possible, provide, therefore, an attractive scenario to governments. As a result, we are likely to see much more leadership from governments regarding the emergence of open learning systems than we have seen in the past. Whereas previously it was more often the case that innovation in learning systems occurred because of the commitment and enthusiasm of particular individuals, now, because of the political imperatives at work, there has recently been a flurry of activity on the part of governments examining distance education and open learning systems. This is particularly evident in third world countries, many of which are developing open learning systems and are looking to the developed countries for input.

Private sector initiatives are another major force contributing to the development of open learning systems. There are billions of dollars spent annually by the private sector on education and training activities for its employees. As these organisations increasingly use more open and self-directed learning strategies to meet these needs, they have realised that the learning materials developed have external market opportunities. As a consequence, we have seen in recent years some major initiatives to make these materials available through sophisticated marketing strategies. Indeed, some companies have developed specialised components to develop and market educational materials as an integral part of their corporate activity.

Concurrent with this, we have seen a marked increase in unemployment and underemployment of people formally trained in education. Many have consequently developed and marketed a variety of educational materials which are also available to the public as well as to specialised institutions. The major effect then is that what was once the exclusive franchise of publicly-funded educational institutions is now no longer so. In short, the efforts and success of the private sector in this area has had, and will continue to have, a major effect on more traditional educational institutions in terms of their involvement in open learning activities.

Support Needs of Open Learning Systems

The emergence of open learning systems will bring with it a variety of needs for student and institutional support which hitherto have not been recognised or at least have not been given priority. One of the more obvious will be the need to create a network of community-based learning centres. In addition to the technical hardware which such centres will need to contain in order to access the telecommunications delivery systems, the centre will also need to provide tutorial support, general information, and educational counselling. In short, this support will be necessary to orient people to the process of open learning. This is a need which is already being identified by many writers and researchers. The basic message is that people need assistance in adjusting to these new learning strategies. Through the community-based learning centre, the same range of student support services will have to be provided as are available to the student of conventional school or campus-based institutions.

Another need which has already been identified, but not given much priority, will be for the development of credit banks through which learners can accumulate course credits from a variety of educational providers in order to earn a particular credential. Traditional educational institutions are likely to be hard pressed in the future to maintain the degree of autonomy which they have had in the past, in so far as recognising and granting credit for course work earned from another institution. Another component of the need for credit banks will be an increasing emphasis on the evaluation and accreditation of experiential or non-formal learning. Individuals acquire a great deal of knowledge through participation in the plethora of non-credit seminars, courses and workshops which are part of their work or a result of personal initiatives. People also learn from the experiences they encounter as part of their daily life. Increasingly in the future, educational institutions will be asked to devise ways of measuring, and subsequently accrediting, such learning in order to permit the formal educational process to complement the knowledge and skills that people have already acquired.

The development of open learning systems is already creating a need, and in some jurisdictions a demand, for increased co-ordination and co-operation among educational institutions. This is manifested in a variety of ways. We already have examples of institutions entering into various consortia arrangements in order to approach collectively the task of curriculum planning and materials development *vis-à-vis* open learning. Where this has occurred, two results are obvious. The first is the rationalisation to some degree of institutional roles. In British Columbia, for example, the provincial universities and the Open Learning Institute, working through the Open University Consortium, have agreed to focus on different types of programmes to be delivered through open learning systems. Such consortia also provide a mechanism through which faculty instructors of different institutions can plan a particular course or programme. The need for this type of collaboration at the planning stage of course and programme development will intensify in the future, and it is likely that institutions which are unwilling to participate in such procedures will find themselves on the sidelines of any substantial involvement in the open learning systems which emerge.

Issues Arising from the Evolution of Open Learning Systems

Just as the emergence of open learning systems creates a variety of needs which must be met in order for such systems to be educationally effective, so do they give rise to some difficult issues which will require resolution. These issues encompass matters pertaining to instructional design, administrative models, and institutional and political jurisdiction.

One of the more philosophical of these issues concerns the type of learner who is likely to be served. Detractors of the increased use of technology express a fear that the educational system overall will become far more elitist than it is, that, far from meeting the learning needs of those segments of society which are disadvantaged, gaps will be widened. Those on the other side of the argument point to the increased flexibility which the emergent technology provides in terms of the opportunities for innovation in instructional design and state that, with the provision of adequate support services, such students can, in fact, be better served. Somewhat related to this issue is the question of how much private sector involvement should be permitted. In other words, where should the line be drawn between the provision of education for the purpose of making a profit and that which must be made available to meet the social and economic needs of our society and, therefore, has a legitimate claim on public support?

On the question of public support and responsibility, the issue is already arising in Canada as to the political jurisdiction of responsibility. Satellite footprints, for example, do not recognise political boundaries, and it is now theoretically possible for students in a very broad geographic area to take the same course from a single institution in a particular province. This is likely to become a particularly difficult issue in the future as governments, at both the provincial and national levels, grapple with the task of sorting out fiscal responsibility for these initiatives while, at the same time, wanting to protect their jurisdiction over education in order to achieve particular economic and social objectives.

Another issue which is very closely related concerns the question of institutional ownership of students. Many postsecondary educational institutions derive their public funding on the basis of some type of enrolment formula. As a result, it is in their interest to maximise enrolment at their particular institution. Such an objective is likely to be at cross-purposes with the increased flexibility and availability of learning opportunities which are made available through open learning systems.

Several issues also arise from the standpoint of instructional design. One of these has to do with the socialization of students studying for a professional credential through an open learning process. The traditionalists argue that only by having students physically together for a period of time, usually several years, can a sense of professional ethics and commitment to a particular philosophy of the profession be developed. On the other hand, there is the argument that such socialisation can better occur if students are learning within their community and the organisation in which they will be working.

As instructional designers have an increasing variety of learning formats with which to work, their sophistication in choosing the best format through which to communicate a particular type of knowledge or skill, and to match that to the specific characteristics of the learners, will need to be enhanced. This will require a much greater effort in evaluation and research. The question as to who should undertake this activity and who should pay for it is likely to be a lively topic of debate in the future.

SUMMARY

In discussing the future of distance education we are in fact discussing the future of education itself and the entire range of activities and age groups it represents. The perspective argued in this chapter is that learning is, and is now being recognised as, a lifelong process that will see individuals more and more learning through the use of materials in a variety of formats, that permit them to integrate this activity with their other roles and responsibilities. This process, taken together with the networks that are developing to plan and deliver these educational 'products', is called open learning.

Section 2: CURRENT PRACTICE

Course Design and Development

Kate Seaborne and Arlene Zuckernick

The process of production of distance education materials is commonly described as the 'course design' process. It is akin to the preparing and presenting content in traditional curriculum design, which is part of teacher training. (Posner and Rudnitsky 1983) The two differ chiefly in that the design and development process usually involves significant input in varying degrees from more than one academic specialist or content expert. It is also the case that production expertise figures prominently in the design and development of distance education courses. (Feasley 1983)

The terms 'course design' and 'instructional design' are used interchangeably to describe the processes involved in course design and development. However, within this definition, there is a wide variance in the practice of distance education by institutions across Canada.[1] No single approach dominates. Current practices range from the 'deluxe' model which is the creation and hallmark of the Open University of Great Britain to a minimally structured process.

Throughout Canada, the practice of distance education is eclectic. The tendency of almost every institution involved in a programme of distance education is to adapt and refine components of selected models in order to install a system appropriate to the needs of its particular clientele. However, while institutions may elect to combine and reorganise these in innovative ways, the components themselves remain the basic ones of curriculum planning and design. A traditional university or college preparing to adopt a distance education strategy may find itself employing a fundamentally different approach to programme planning and design than that of the more common, classroom-based practices. The deployment of institutional resources for the development of a 'non-traditional' programme or course often necessitates increasing the visibility of common developmental tasks such as the identification of potential students, the choice of instructional models, and the determination of appropriate media for the delivery of content. How these tasks are undertaken, or indeed whether they are undertaken, can provide some insight as to the degree to which an institution is committed to its distance education programme. An appreciation of the overall significance of each of the components of the course design process can elaborate one's understanding of distance education in Canada. An emphasis on the role of course development as a measure of institutional support for a distance education service must be kept in perspective. It is but one indicator, albeit a key one, in assessing an institution's commitment to distance education. Of equal importance is the delivery system employed and the administrative arrangements supporting it. These are the structures through which the student maintains contact with the institution.

The analysis presented here describes the institutions only in terms of their overall course design and development. This description is pursued in isolation from the remainder of the distance education system. Since no dominant approach is apparent, a comparative analysis of general categories is presented.

In Canada, there are three distinct categories of educational organisations undertaking distance education course development. Most numerous by far are the traditional campus-based universities and colleges, where distance education is a marginal, or at best, integrated, small-scale function within the larger organisation. Examples of this category are found in every province.

The second category includes those few institutions dedicated to the development and delivery of distance education. These include the Open Learning Institute of British Columbia, Athabasca University in Alberta and Télé-université in Quebec. Distance education is the *raison d'être* of these institutions.

Organisations in the third category might be characterised as associated educational institutions: the educational media authorities and professional associations with a national student/client focus. Prominent among these are TVOntario, ACCESS Alberta and the Knowledge Network, as well as such associations as the Canadian Bankers Association and Certified General Accountants.

Although many Canadian universities make a commitment in principle to distance education, it is often unrealised, particularly at traditional universities. What appears to be lacking in these institutions are the resources to undertake distance education development. For instance, at the University of Calgary, as well as at Laurentian University, although senior administrators have publicly emphasised the importance of distance education, this emphasis has not yet resulted in the establishment of structures and the allocation of human and fiscal resources to carry out course design and development. In many of the traditional institutions, the faculty perception of academic freedom is another factor in the limited development of distance education.

An important factor in course design and development is the way in which educational organisations perceive their mandate to serve the student. In Canada, some are limited through legislation to serving students within a small community; others work actively to draw upon a national student body. Those universities who perceive their primary responsibility as the service of their local communities, in fact do not undertake any significant programmes employing distance education methodologies. Face-to-face instruction remains the most economic approach. Other institutions focusing principally on the local community include most of the community colleges undertaking distance education. However, North Island College in British Columbia and Seneca's Open College in Ontario are notable exceptions to this localised perspective.

In many provinces, however, such factors as the location of the universities, often hundreds of miles from students' homes, as well as the size of the province and its population distribution, have prompted many institutions to engage in distance education activities. For instance, in British Columbia, Manitoba and Newfoundland, the major universities have such a focus.

In contrast, there are institutions which determine their responsibilities regionally and employ distance education as the means to serve this wider student body. The University of Ottawa, for example, provides courses in English and French to the area around the national capital region and is currently exploring the possibility of offering these courses to a national, Francophone audience. Other institutions also regard themselves as providers of distance education nationally. These are principally the educational media authorities and the national professional associations. Occasionally, the universities also fall into this category; most prominent among these is the University of Waterloo which provides credit courses to students across the country and has done so for years.

The third factor which determines an educational organisation's approach to distance education is the strategy it chooses for the delivery of content. Strategies for content delivery can generally be described as following either a dominant media approach or a multi-media approach. There is no question that in terms of the traditional educational institutions, as well as in the dedicated institutions, print is by far the most prevalent format world-wide. (Holmberg 1985) On the other hand, the educational communications authorities tend to focus on an approach based on broadcast television. Other instances of a single media strategy include the use of audio cassette as the primary vehicle for content delivery. The University of Waterloo employs the greatest use of audiocassette courseware in Canada. And, as a result of the lower cost of telephone technology, there is an increasing acceptance of audio-teleconferencing as a means to deliver distance education courses. The University of Calgary, Memorial University, and the University of Ottawa as well as the Telemedicine Group in Toronto are principals in demonstrating the effectiveness of this technology.

By contrast, institutions employing a multi-media approach to delivery can be organised into two camps; those who use two or three media but tend to rely on one, such as print, and those who are 'true' employers of a 'multi-media' strategy. The Open Learning Institute is an example of the first category. Although their materials are predominantly print-based, they include in their course packages a sizeable amount of audio and the institute is now placing emphasis on broadcast television. The University of Waterloo provides another example of this approach. This institution has worked successfully with a combination of audio cassette and print and is now turning its attention to use of computers as a delivery technology. Simon Fraser University in British Columbia relies on a print base, but provides television support for a growing number of credit courses. TVOntario maintains a broadcast television emphasis but is working to incorporate a greater use of print and audio material.

Among the traditional universities practising a true multi-media approach are Wilfrid Laurier in Ontario and the Universities of Regina, Saskatchewan, Victoria, and Manitoba. In the Atlantic provinces, the new Atlantic Consortium as well as Memorial University in Newfoundland follow this practice of choosing a range of media.

THREE APPROACHES TO COURSE DESIGN: THE PLANNING STAGE

Leading researchers in the field of distance education, including Borje Holmberg, have identified some common features in the development and delivery of distance education. (Holmberg 1985) The planning stage generally involves programme and course identification, often in conjunction with a needs analysis of potential audiences. The course development phase varies widely from institution to institution in its approaches to instructional philosophy and design. Course development may involve systematic preproduction planning, production in a variety of media, and formative and summative evaluation. The existence of a distance education support structure within the institution is often considered an important element in the development process.

The definition of a course, however, varies. In a traditional university or college system, a distance education course is analogous to the credit course given on-campus. At a dedicated distance education institution, the definition of a credit course is determined by the governing body but it tends to parallel that of a traditional university. In an educational media authority, practices may vary considerably. For instance, in the case of the Knowledge Network, credit courses are delivered through the media authority but are developed and accredited by a traditional educational organisation, such as a college or university, or a dedicated institution such as Athabasca University or the Open Learning Institute. At TVOntario, this model is reversed. There, the course is developed by the educational authority with the assistance of academic advisers and, on completion, is offered to colleges and universities in Ontario for accreditation and then made available for sale across Canada and internationally.

The definition of a non-credit course varies by institution. Credit-free courses offered by means of distance education can include everything from a one-episode television programme to complete print and audio packages such as those developed by the continuing legal education societies for professionals in the various provinces.

In most institutions, credit courses are developed by programme and therefore the needs of the curricula determine the courses to be developed. There are exceptions to this approach where, for example, the institution is working on an *ad hoc* basis with respect to credit course selection, such as at the University of Regina and Mount St Vincent University. At a dedicated distance education institution, the course selection is almost entirely programme-based. Educational media authorities tend to select courses based on 'market' needs. Courses designed by them for credit and developed in this way are brokered to traditional institutions.

Responsibility for the selection and development of non-credit courses is generally left to individual continuing education units in universities and colleges. In many institutions, however, academic departments or faculties play a judicial role in the selection and development of non-credit projects. In a few cases, non-credit courses, often leading to a certificate, are grouped into formal programmes. The Canadian Bankers Institute is affiliated with universities in various provinces in such an arrangement. All institutions engaged in distance education recognise the importance of the needs analysis process, but implementation of the process differs. The process of needs assessment or audience identification is common to all the institutions in this study, and within these institutions, the units identified with the development and delivery of distance education perceive themselves as being responsible for identifying the audience for a particular course or programme. This assumption of responsibility for needs identification is a traditional component of the programme planning process within continuing and adult education. It is generally the case, as well, that the continuing and adult education operation within which the distance education unit is housed, is administratively responsible for recovering the costs incurred in the development of distance education courses and courseware.

The strategies employed in identifying a target audience vary among institutions. If, for example, an institution is determining whether to develop a credential programme for distance education delivery, a needs assessment employing questionnaires or interviews may be conducted with professional groups planning their own educational needs, or with training officers associated with business, industry or the public. This approach serves to identify needs and to promote audience awareness of the proposed programme.

In other cases, the needs assessment may be undertaken simultaneously with the initial delivery of a course. This approach uses the course as a pilot and involves a written survey testing the audience's readiness to accept the content and format. The University of Lethbridge is presently using the method to conduct a needs analysis of their proposed programme in nursing.

Another approach to needs analysis involves responding to requests for courseware from special interest groups. For example, the University of Manitoba has negotiated a contract with the department of national defence to provide a correspondence programme for Canadian servicemen in Europe. In another situation, the Canadian Correctional Service has contracted with Simon Fraser University to provide a degree completion programme by correspondence. Surveys of potential target groups are also undertaken in the first stage of planning. The certificate programme in computer-based information systems developed by the University of Victoria serves as an example of this strategy.

Institutions across Canada apparently do not share a common philosophy as regards design of distance education. Those dedicated institutions tend to have developed the most comprehensive models of instruction which they provide to their content specialist or the course author. To facilitate the course development process, the Open Learning Institute has created both a coursewriter's manual and model blueprints.[2] In its formative years, Athabasca University has used the Personalized System of Instruction (PSI). (Coldeway 1982).

Within the traditional institutions, the approach to instructional design is rather more eclectic and ranges from humanistic to behavioural. For the most part, however, the process is 'course-author sensitive'. The model adopted by the University of Waterloo illustrates one perspective of the process of course design. Here, the course author is solely responsible for the design of the course, although he or she is required to work within the constraints of the dominant media, that is, lectures recorded for distribution on audio cassette.

Another approach to course design, course-author sensitive, involves the distance education specialists assisting in the evolution of the design of the course as at the University of Victoria and Memorial University. However, most institutions in Canada have adopted an intermediate approach, wherein the distance education units offer advice and consultation on course design when required to do so, and provide administrative support for the production of materials.

DEVELOPING THE COURSE

The degree to which a systematic approach to designing the instruction has been introduced and accepted within an institution can provide a useful focus for discussing the course development process in distance education. Within the postsecondary context in Canada, instructional design generally combines frameworks developed for public school curriculum amended to accommodate current adult education theory. (Smith 1983) The move toward incorporating principles of 'androgogy' into the instructional design process appears to be a determined, albeit low key, goal of distance educators. The incorporation of such concepts as 'learner control' and 'experiential learning' in the design of distance education is gaining credence across Canada. In key institutions, a systematic model of training has been incorporated. Both Athabasca University and the Open Learning Institute were major proponents of clearly-formatted systematic approaches to development in their initial stages of growth, parallel to those employed in industrial training.

Within Canada, a significant element in course design is the course team. The team, comprised of specialists in content, instructional design and production, is dependent on a carefully prescribed working relationship, if it is to succeed in producing a course. Mason and Goodenough clearly elaborate on the conditions required for successful course teams at the Open University of Great Britain. They conclude that 'it is by no means a rigid model, and has been adopted to fit different personalities, different subject areas and different views on teaching methodology.' (Kaye and Rumble p.112)

Across Canada, most institutions, whether traditional universities, dedicated distance education institutions or other educational organisations, have established a support group of some kind to provide faculty with instructional design assistance and project management in the development of course materials. These units vary greatly in their authority to influence and direct course development. For instance, at the University of Saskatchewan, the project team includes two key members, the faculty member and an instructional design specialist from a centralised unit who provides advice on course development and manages the project's evolution. At the University of Victoria, the project team is generally comprised of three individuals, the faculty member acting as content specialist, an instructional design consultant and a project manager. The associated education institutions, particularly the educational media authorities, make use of a more elaborate and job-specific project team. As Ken O'Bryan describes the model, a single team may include as many as nine functions, exclusive of the technical crew, some undertaken by more than one individual. (O'Bryan 1983)

Where a course or project team exists, the major elements contributing to its productivity appear to be the desire to reach decisions by consensus and success in team building. There is no question that, within traditional universities, the faculty member maintains a high degree of academic autonomy and control over the course content. However, the extent to which the practice of distance education is perceived as a legitimate one by the faculty as a whole, along with the degree of credibility accorded the central unit providing instructional design and management support, will determine the dynamics of the project team.

In most traditional educational institutions, the project team is based within the continuing education unit. However, an interesting exception occurs at Wilfrid Laurier University which has established an independent agency, the Telecollege, to co-ordinate and produce distance education courses. Faculty are drawn from the university to work with staff from the Telecollege.

To illustrate the steps in the course design process, it is instructive to examine the ways in which various institutions approach the task, particularly as they relate to the role of the distance education unit. Most institutions in Canada tend to employ the same basic steps. These include conducting a needs assessment or market survey; exploratory discussions between the academic specialist and the other members of the course team about the nature of the course; selection of media; completion of administrative arrangements including copyright agreements and faculty contracts; evaluation and revision of course materials. How these steps are undertaken provides a basis for comparing a variety of approaches.

If the institutions of higher and distance education in Canada were arrayed on a continuum designed to illustrate the degree to which the distance education unit can influence the development of course design and academic content, three degrees of influence might be discerned, ranging from low to high. Using this continuum, institutions in the low influence group could be described as delegating all or almost all responsibility for instructional design and content to the academic specialist involved. Conversely, a distance education unit with high influence tends to have incorporated in its pattern of operations a number of opportunities or check points where suggestions can be made regarding the design of the content. To illustrate the various approaches, institutions representative of low, middle, and high degrees of influence are examined.[3]

Both the University of Waterloo and the University of Saskatchewan employ a low influence model of course development. However, between these two institutions, the interpretation of low influence differs widely. At the University of Waterloo, the course design and development process is essentially delegated to the content specialist. At the onset of the course development, process, a member of the administrative unit associated with the distance education programme (Part-Time Studies) meets with the content specialist to outline the production process which includes making audiotape lectures and preparing course notes. Other elements of course design, such as the identification of course objectives and the selection of media, are not included in this phase of discussion. Selection of media has been predetermined at the University of Waterloo because they adopt a format based on audio cassette lectures and print notes. The identification of course objectives and the writing of course materials is left entirely to the instructor. (Leslie 1979)

At the University of Saskatchewan, a course team approach has been adapted whereby the content specialist is responsible for the academic quality of the course and the instructional designer manages the production and evaluation processes. In this close relationship, the instructional designer is also called upon to evaluate the materials in development. Selection of media is largely pre-determined. Historical precedence has dictated print as the principal medium but the university is moving towards the use of audio cassette and teleconferencing to support print.

Both institutions collect evaluation data for the purpose of course maintenance and revision. At the University of Saskatchewan, the designated shelf-life of the material is between four and five years, and at the University of Waterloo, course materials undergo an academic review every four years.

Administrative matters related to course development, such as appointment of faculty and copyright agreement on course materials, are dealt with rather differently at each institution. At the University of Waterloo, content specialists in the faculty of arts work on course development as part of their regular teaching load; in other faculties, the work is done on an extra-to-load basis. At the University of Saskatchewan, the faculty are involved on an extra-to-load basis. Copyright on course materials is held jointly by the university and the content specialist at the University of Saskatchewan; at Waterloo, copyright is held by the university.

Both institutions believe that the particular model they have adopted for the development of distance education courses is cost-effective and permits faculty a personalised role in the process. Waterloo emphasises that their model is particularly successful from an institutional standpoint because faculty consider the distance education courses to be qualitatively parallel with those taught on campus. Each institution does point out that this low influence model will not accommodate a more structured design process.

Memorial University and the University of Manitoba have adopted models in which the administrative units responsible for course development have been encouraged to take a somewhat more active role, the middle influence model. Since the 1930s, the University of Manitoba has produced correspondence courses and print remains the dominant medium for distance education, but the university is beginning to include teleconferencing as a delivery strategy. Twelve teleconferencing centres have been established and courses delivered at these sites include support materials in print and video formats.

At the University of Manitoba, the development process begins with an orientation for the faculty member conducted by the instructional designer. Each project team is tailor-made to fit the specific needs of the content specialist and the requirements of the course. In the early phases, the content specialist and the instructional designer work together to clarify course objectives, although there is no requirement that these be outlined in the course materials.

The content specialist and the instructional designer establish checkpoints for the review of content, usually at the conclusion of the development of each unit. Where teleconferencing is involved, the instructional designer's role changes from one of adviser to one where the designer assumes a greater responsibility for the shape of the course. However, the content specialist is still accountable for all decisions relating to the content, as is the case at Athabasca University.

Memorial University applies distance education methodologies using print, videotape and audio teleconferencing. Two support groups are involved in the development and delivery process. The school of continuing studies is responsible for the administration and delivery of courses and the educational technology directorate is responsible for the development of the media materials: video, print, and audio. Whether the course is delivered in one medium or in combination, the content specialist is provided with some instructional design assistance. However, the degree to which design assistance is provided depends upon the media chosen. If the course is print-based, the faculty member will receive some guidance from the instructional designer or producer but will be expected to work independently for the most part. In this instance, the instructional designer takes responsibility for editing, layout and production details.

The development of a multi-media course, however, includes the involvement, at the preproduction stage, of the academic strategy group, a body composed of faculty and representatives from the school of continuing studies and educational technology. This group is responsible for determining the overall design of the course and for developing an evaluation procedure. The project team takes its direction from the ideas generated by this group.

The choice of a teleconferencing format requires that the content specialist and the instructional designer work together as a team. In this instance, the designer is responsible for training the faculty member for teleconferencing, as well as overseeing the production of print materials and related course content produced in either video or audio cassette form. A project team composed of a producer, a content specialist and technical specialists can spend up to one year on the development of a print and video package. (Mandeville 1982)

At the University of Manitoba, faculty are involved in course development on an overload or release-time basis. Copyright on all materials is held by the university. At Memorial, the content specialist holds the copyright on all print and audio cassette materials, the university retaining copyright on video materials. Almost all faculty at Memorial participate in the process of course development and delivery on an overload basis.

Assessment of distance education course materials at the University of Manitoba includes the administration of a standard student evaluation after every course delivery and, where applicable, the debriefing of tutors. Courses are prepared for a shelf-life of four to five years. Maintenance amendments or small-scale revisions occur yearly. At Memorial University, no formal course evaluations are conducted, but rather content specialists initiate revisions which are adjudicated by the educational technology unit.

Memorial University regards its model for distance education development and delivery to be particularly strong because it allows sufficient time for the development of courses and provides for a distribution of responsibilities. The Memorial University model will require resources and time to develop the full complement of instructional designers and technical specialists needed. The University of Manitoba suggests that the strength of its model comes from the degree of flexibility it permits its academic specialists. For both institutions, the availability of resources to finance the continuing development of their distance education programme remains an issue of concern.

Institutions in which the instructional design unit is able to wield significant influence over the development of course materials tend to be those who have made a significant commitment to distance education, although the model adopted by the University of Waterloo provides a contrasting hypothesis.

The University of Victoria and Wilfrid Laurier University are representative of institutions in which distance education is a significant feature in the university's overall service to students. At the University of Victoria, seven degree and diploma/certificate programmes, concentrated mainly in the professions, are offered by the academic departments through the division of university extension and community relations. The distance education software group provides the instructional and production support during development. Wilfrid Laurier University has established a more formal structure in the shape of the Telecollege as a wholly-owned company.

Funding for the Telecollege is derived, in part, from the university and from revenue generated by fees obtained through registrations. Programme offerings include a business diploma and courses in the liberal arts.

In both institutions, the course development process begins with the establishment of a course team. At Wilfrid Laurier, this group is known as the academic planning team and includes a faculty member, the content specialist, a Telecollege producer, various production specialists and the dean of faculty as chairman. At the University of Victoria, the project team comprises the content specialist, the educational design specialist and the project manager, along with production specialists as required. However, each team differs in its mode of operation.

At the Telecollege, the academic planning team approaches the course design process by defining learning objectives, agreeing to a specific outline for the course, and locating appropriate texts and readings. In most cases, the choice of media includes print and video, although teleconferencing has become another option. When the course objectives and outline have been defined, the content specialist prepares the video scripts or the seminar notes for the teleconference, along with the content of the course book. Generally, the Telecollege develops thirteen 30- or 60- minute video components. The Telecollege directs the production of both video and print. The time involved for course development is approximately seven months.

At the University of Victoria, the first step in course development involves the initiation of a specific project proposal prepared by the project team in co-operation with the chairman of the sponsoring department. Once the project has been approved, the team meets regularly until the development phase is completed. The team works together to establish the course's objectives and outline, select the appropriate media, mix and review all the materials as they are prepared. The media selection will depend upon the nature of the content. Generally speaking, course teams at the University of Victoria try to combine several media in each delivery design. The average length of time for course development is twelve months. At both the University of Victoria and Wilfrid Laurier Telecollege, copyright of course materials is held by the institution. The content specialists at the University of Victoria are employed on a release-time model. At Wilfrid Laurier, the content specialists are employed similarly.

Course maintenance and evaluation are established components in the overall design process at both institutions. Every course delivered by each institution is evaluated by the students and the information is used to determine whether the course can be maintained with minor or major revisions. At the University of Victoria, courses are planned for a shelf-life of three to five years. The revision process at the Telecollege is dictated jointly by the content specialist and the head of the college after a review of the evaluation. Generally, the marketplace determines the shelf-life of courses produced by the Telecollege.

The Telecollege model permits a flexible response to the marketplace because it stands apart from the university's traditional structure and bureaucracy. The staff consider it a cost-effective model since only a core of professional and technical staff are required to maintain its operation. The University of Victoria believes its model to be a workable one because it encourages a team approach to the development and delivery. The content specialist, together with the educational design specialist and the project manager, operate by a consensus to achieve their goals. The positive effects of this integration of academic and administrative specialists have been felt throughout the institution, improving the visibility of non-traditional instructional techniques.

In both institutions, the limitations imposed on the chosen models are principally those connected with financial constraints. Additionally, each institution feels hindered to some extent by a lack of opportunity to engage more fully in research designed to explore options in distance education.

As institutions across Canada continue to practice distance education, the various approaches to course design and delivery have raised a series of questions: will the increased visibility and acceptance of distance education bring about a decrease of flexibility in course design or in the delivery mix, or is it the case that the institutionalisation of distance education will result in a more cost-effective product?

Questions regarding the appropriateness of various instructional systems are being addressed in many Canadian institutions. Key issues among them are:

what level of interaction is best suited to the Canadian students' need?

what is the most effective way to integrate the content specialist into the enterprise? (Riley 1984)

how should the content specialist be rewarded?

what modes of evaluation will prove the academic quality of distance education courses?

what combination of media best suits specific course content?

what are the appropriate roles for the new communications technologies, including the microcomputer?

The decrease in resources available to postsecondary institutions for traditional as well as distance education programmes raises concerns about the setting of priorities. At the macro-level, there are questions about the decentralisation of distance education: should every institution with a commitment to distance education also create a production facility to address this commitment? Can the course development process be centralised? At what level and by whom? There are questions about the academic quality of programmes and individual courses as institutions and student groups increase their demands on distance education. Issues such as these are being considered not only within individual institutions, but by groups of institutions in both formal and informal arrangements.

TRENDS IN COURSE DESIGN AND DEVELOPMENT

Across Canada, the commitment to distance education is becoming more apparent as provincial governments reallocate resources to support these developments. The establishment of structures for interinstitutional collaboration is also evidence of the growing belief that distance education can be an effective alternative to traditional campus-based learning. The role of the private sector as underwriters of distance education at the postsecondary level is becoming more important. These trends are appearing as pressures increase to provide cost-effective education to scattered student groups.

Institutions are experimenting with ways to integrate the use of computers in both the design and delivery processes. The dedicated institutions, as well as educational media authorities, such as TVOntario, are leading this movement. Innovative projects are encouraging the use of computers as a course development tool. Distance education courses utilising computer-assisted instruction are being offered across Canada. (TVOntario 1984) The advent of communication satellites and the development of audio-conferencing technology have prompted institutions, either independently or in consortia, to become more innovative in their course design and delivery efforts. Indeed, the decreasing cost and growing dissemination of home video technology (VCRs, videodisc players) is prompting a number of institutions to consider the use of educational videocassettes as viable. Canadian educational institutions may be inclined to follow Great Britain's lead in the design of distance education materials for videocassette. (Bates 1984)

Consortia for the sharing and joint development of courseware is a significant trend among postsecondary institutions in Canada. The Inter-Universities North in Manitoba, a co-operative venture of the University of Manitoba, Brandon University and the University of Winnipeg, has been operating successfully for a number of years. In British Columbia, the Open University Consortium and in the Maritimes, the Atlantic Consortium are recent developments. The universities in Ontario have formed a committee on distance education to promote co-operation. Formal and informal arrangements like these may promote strategies for sharing course development and materials acquisition. The establishment of computer databases and common calendars will facilitate the sharing process. Canada has made a significant contribution to the field of distance education by demonstrating that it is viable to produce low-cost, instructionally-sound materials in a multi-media format for small groups of remote learners. In this country, the course design process is in a developmental phase where each year sees major refinements being made to a decentralised, learner-responsive system.

NOTES

1. The authors have not attempted, and in no manner claim to have completed, a comprehensive survey of Canadian institutions involved in distance education.
2. Open Learning Institute blueprints provide a detailed plan for all aspects of course design and production - thus the adoption of architectural terminology.
3. By this consideration of degrees of influence, no judgement is implied regarding the institutional commitment, either in principle or practice, to the enterprise of distance education.

REFERENCES

Bates, Anthony (ed.) (1984) *The Role of Technology in Distance Education*, Croom Helm, Beckenham, Kent

Coldeway, D. (1982) 'Recent Research in Distance Learning' in *Learning at a Distance: A World Perspective*, Athabasca University/ICDE, Edmonton

Feasley, C. (1983) *Serving Learners at a Distance: A Guide to Program Practices*, ASHE-ERIC Higher Education Research Report #5, Washington, D.C.

Holmberg, B. (1983) *Status and Trends in Distance Education*, 2nd. ed., Lector Publishing, Sweden

Holmberg, B. (1985) 'On the Status of Distance Education in the World in the 1980's - A Preliminary Report on the Fernuniversitat Comparative Study', ZIFF, Gesamthoschscule-Hagen

Leslie, J.D. (1979) 'The University of Waterloo Model for Distance Education', *Canadian Journal of University Continuing Education*, 6

Mandeville, M. (1982) '*A Man's Reach Should Exceed His Grasp': Distance Education and Teleconferencing at Memorial University*, Memorial University, St John's

Mason, J. and S. Goodenough (1981) 'Course Creation' in A. Kaye and G. Rumble (ed.), *Distance Teaching for Higher and Adult Education*, Croom Helm, London

O'Bryan, K. (1983) *The Project Team in Instructional Television*, Corporation for Public Broadcasting, New York

Posner, G. and A. Rudnitsky (1978) *Course Design: A Guide to Curriculum Development for Teachers*, Longham, N.Y.

Riley, J. (1984) 'Problems of Drafting Distance Education Materials', *British Journal of Educational Technology*, 13 October

Smith, R.M. (1983) 'The Learning How to Learn Concept: Implications and Issues', in *Helping Adults Learn How to Learn*, R. Smith (ed.), Jossey-Bass, San Francisco

Production, Storage and Distribution

John Bottomley

One of the immediately apparent contrasts between a distance learning institution and a conventional one is in the relative proportion of the operation given over to the support functions of production, storage and distribution. It is possible to gain the impression that the activities of a distance learning institution are analogous to those of an industrial plant rather than those of an educational institution. This, along with other factors, has led Peters (1965, 1973) and others (Keegan 1980) to argue that distance education should be regarded as an industrial form of education. I have elsewhere argued that the analogy is to be treated as, at best, unproved (Bottomley 1982) and have not adopted it as a framework for this paper. Keegan (1980) is undoubtedly correct, however, in asserting that activities like job scheduling, warehousing, postal and media dispatch are characteristic functions of a distance-learning operation.

In this chapter, I shall consider the general principles involved in ensuring that these characteristic functions are performed efficiently within the context of a case study of the activities of the Open Learning Institute. Significant changes in operational procedures have taken place as a result of technological advances in the last few years. These I discuss as well as pointing to likely opportunities that will soon emerge as a result of future technological advancement.

BRITISH COLUMBIA AND THE INSTITUTE

The Open Learning Institute (OLI) was created by order-in-council of the provincial cabinet under the authority of the Colleges and Institutes Act in June 1978. Simultaneous amendment of the Universities Act empowered the institute to award first degrees in arts and science. Since that date the institute has developed, acquired and offered over 190 courses in three broad programmes; the university programme, career/technical/vocational programmes, and adult basic education programmes. Credit enrolments have grown from under 2,000 in 1979-80 to over 15,000 in 1984-5. Approximately 17,000 credit enrolments are expected in 1985-6. Course materials typically consist of in-house-developed course manuals, instructional units and assignments, textbooks purchased from commercial publishers, reprints of journal articles, instructional audio tapes and, in some cases, instructional videotapes, equipment packages and laboratory kits.

The institute is the only educational institution in the province solely concerned with distance education. Other institutions, however, play a significant role. Most important of these is the Knowledge Network, the province's educational telecommunications authority, which operates a number of telecommunication networks including a broadcast/cable educational television channel. The three provincial universities are all involved in different ways with distance education and are members, along with OLI and KNOW, of the Open University Consortium of British Columbia. The consortium makes it possible for a student to enrol in courses offered by any member institution and to use the credits towards a credential offered by any of the institutions. Several colleges and institutes also offer some distance education courses, often using the services of KNOW and materials produced by OLI. The geography of British Columbia has had a significant impact on the manner in which all the institutions have offered distance education programmes. (Ellis and Bottomley 1979) Canada's most westerly province, British Columbia has an area approximately seven times that of England. In North American terms, it is equal in size to the combined area of Washington, Oregon, California and Idaho. With a total population of 2.5 million, of which 1.5 million live in the two major metropolitan areas, Vancouver and Victoria, it is very sparsely populated. The northern half of the province, with a size three times that of England, has a population of less than 100,000. Easy movement is further hampered by a harsh winter climate and the presence of six mountain ranges each with peaks in excess of 2,500 metres. If courses are to be available to all provincial residents, very few demands can be placed on a student to attend face-to-face sessions at a specified location. It is over 2,000 miles by road from northwest British Columbia to Vancouver!

THE PRODUCTION OF PRINT MATERIALS

The goal of the print production system at the Open Learning Institute is simply stated: it is to transform edited authors' manuscripts into illustrated, typeset printed materials as quickly and cheaply as possible and to ensure that these materials can be easily and cheaply revised as necessary. In order to achieve this goal, the institute has in place an electronic publishing system that produces an average of 12,000 new pages per year and prints approximately 15,000,000 pages per year.

Upon receipt from the course writer, manuscripts are entered via keyboard into the editorial system. This consists of MASS 11 software running on a Digital Equipment Corporation VAX 11-750 minicomputer. Once entered, a manuscript is edited and instructionally designed by a course designer working in co-operation with the course writer, a content area expert consultant, a graphic artist and, if necessary, a media producer. With the exception of the graphic artist and the media producer, the roles of these personnel will not be discussed in this paper.

Upon completion of the design process, a course manuscript is electronically transferred to the production system. Typesetting and page make-up is performed using Xerox 8010 Information Processors (Stars) on an Ethernet Local Area Network. The transfer is accomplished through translating, via an in-house developed translation programme, MASS 11 documents into Xerox 860 documents and transferring these to an Ethernet File Server via VAX on the Net software. This process maintains full format integrity for all but the most complex scientific and mathematical material. How such materials are dealt with will be discussed later.

Typesetting and page layout are performed by five page make-up technicians using Xerox Stars. This system provides an interactive WYSIMO-LWYG (what you see is more or less what you get) display and a basic technical graphics capability. The technicians can see the page as it is designed and create required business and simple technical graphics on the screen. Space is left for graphics that cannot be created on the system and the document paginated. Laser-printed proofs are subsequently proof-read and corrected. Corrected proofs are then sent to the originating course designer who indicates any necessary further changes, upon completion of which laser-printed 'galleys' are sent to paste-up for the insertion of graphics not generated on the system. Following paste-up, documents are forwarded to the print shop for reproduction.

A standard 8 1/2" x 11" loose-leaf, two-sided, three-hole-punched, shrink-wrapped format has been adopted for course manuals, instructional units and assignment files. Seventy-five per cent of materials are printed using two offset perfecting presses. Materials with very short print runs and with no half-tone illustrations are duplicated electrostatically and make up the remaining 25 per cent of the total produced.

Paralleling the typesetting, proof-reading, correction process is the graphics production process. As already noted, a graphic artist works in co-operation with a course designer, course writer, etc., in the design of a course. A graphic artist is assigned to each course as it is developed who is responsible for the identification and design of all illustrations. These may be photographs, illustrative drawings, technical drawings or illustrative diagrams. If use is to be made of an existing illustration, copyright permission is obtained. Illustrations requiring creation are the responsibility of the graphic artist who will, in many cases, produce the needed material but who will also make use of contract photographers, specialist graphic artists or, in the case of machine producible illustrations, a page make-up technician. All artwork must be corrected, approved and be available for inclusion in mechanicals by the time the textual material arrives in the paste-up department.

As noted earlier, the MASS 11 system cannot easily be used for the editing and subsequent transfer to production of advanced mathematical and technical material. Until recently, such material was typeset using the TEX typesetting system resident on a main-frame computer at the University of British Columbia. Proofs printed on a laser printer were manually edited, corrected, graphics were stripped in, and the document reproduced. This method of production proved time-consuming and expensive and, hence, such material is now produced in-house using a Star terminal as an input and editing device as well as a page make-up device. This method of production, still in its infancy, promises to reduce turnaround time and costs although, by its very nature, mathematical typesetting is a complex and expensive activity.

The system presently in place is very efficient for a number of reasons, including: (1) manuscripts are only keyed into the system once. This not only saves the time involved in rekeying but avoids the necessity of proof-reading the entire document upon rekeying. As a result the institute only employs four proof-readers; (2) editorial changes are made electronically, an editor making the changes as he or she goes without having to pass on the information to a second person. Given the flexibility of electronic editing, a course designer can experiment with a variety of structures for a given segment of a course before selecting the most appropriate. This is of great enefit to designers seeking to design instructional materials of the highest quality; (3) page layout is an interactive WYSIMOLWYG process with the result that far fewer typographic or layout problems occur than is the case when a code-based non-interactive system is used. Most errors are corrected by the technicians before they are sent to proof-reading. This significantly reduces the time required for proof-reading and the correction of errors, with improvements in both turnaround time and the total amount of time required to complete a document; (4) the use of the Star terminals to produce tables, charts and simple technical graphics reduces the demand for hand-drawn art; (5) the production of mechanicals in the paste-up department has been reduced to simply inserting non-machine-produced graphics and the placement of otherwise complete pages on printing flats; and (6) the adoption of a standard format for most materials has allowed the institute to equip the printshop to be maximally efficient at the production of a standard item. Items requiring non-standard formats, the use of more than two colours, perfect binding, etc. are usually printed on a contract basis, as their total demand does not justify the capital cost of equipping the printshop so as to be able to produce a wide range of materials.

As noted above, the system is productive and efficient. In total, only 22 personnel are employed to typeset, illustrate, lay-out, proof-read, paste-up, print and finish the print materials produced at the institute. Recent technological advances, however, have made it technically, and perhaps economically, possible to become even more productive. The major system enhancements now possible are listed below, following which is a discussion of the possibilities of adopting a true demand printing operation.

It is evident from the foregoing discussion that the least technologically-assisted processes involved in the design and production process are initial manuscript entry, the creation of graphics and the creation of mechanicals. At the present time, the system in place is enhanceable in a manner that will address all these aspects of the process. What is not evident at this time is whether the capital investment required can be justified, given the increases in productivity that would be realised. The institute is actively considering all these possibilities and is hopeful that, over the next few years, a true demand print operation will be in place, which would be, to the author's knowledge, the first such operation in any distance learning institution.

One of the most time consuming and hence expensive activities at the institute is manuscript entry. Approximately 17,500 pages of original manuscripts are received from course writers each year. All these presently require keyboard entry. Of these, over 65 per cent have either been typewritten or produced on a word processor. The majority of the latter had been produced on a personal computer, like IBM PC or Apple, or one of the major word processing systems, such as Wang, Xerox, Micom or AES. Of the 25 per cent received hand-written, almost all are of an advanced mathematical or technical nature for which no practical word processing means exists. At the present time, it is possible to acquire equipment to enter the 75 per cent produced by typewriter or word processor without the necessity of keyboarding. Two possibilities exist: (1) through the use of an intelligent character recognition device and (2) through the use of a media conversion system. I shall briefly discuss the possibilities presented by these two devices.

An intelligent character recognition device is in effect a second generation optical character recognition device (OCR). Such a device is capable of recognising, with the aid of an operator, any consistently produced printed symbol in any font and of digitally storing it for future manipulation. The manner in which it works is as follows. An operator trains the machine to recognise each letter, number, symbol, etc. in a given font by confirming that the machine's guess as to what a given symbol is is correct or is what the operator specifies it to be. Once a given printed symbol is identified as P, L, a comma, 3 or whatever, the device will remember what it is and will henceforth recognise the symbol as such and store it. Given this capability and the fact that the device can output into almost any word-processing format specified, an operator will be able to scan original manuscripts into the system at speeds of up to ten times those attainable through keyboarding. Experience indicates that most well-typed or word-processed documents should be enterable at speeds of up to sixty pages per hour with almost total format integrity. Given in excess of 13,000 scanable pages per year to be entered at the institute, it is likely that a scanner will be acquired in the very near future. At present, the Kurzweil 4000 is the only such device.

An alternative method of entering word-processed documents while maintaining format integrity is to use a media conversion device. Several systems are available on the market, all of which allow an operator to enter a document stored in a particular format, Wang, Micom, Wordstar or whatever, and to output the document into a different specified format. In the case of the institute, the desired output format would be MASS 11. The advantage over an OCR device is that they require less operator intervention and are much faster, but have the disadvantage that they require the acquisition or development of a separate translation and formatting programme for each translation required, i.e., a different programme is required to convert a Wang document to a MASS 11 document than is required to translate an Apple II document to a MASS 11 document. An additional disadvantage is that such a device is of no use in handling manuscripts produced on a conventional typewriter. At the present time, it appears that the institute would be better served through the acquisition of an OCR device rather than that of a media conversion device. This would not be the case, however, if the institute were in a position to specify that manuscripts be produced on one of a specified list of word processors. For institutions with in-house course writers a media conversion device alternative would likely prove advantageous.

It is inherently more difficult to electronically produce, modify and store graphical material than it is textual material. It has only been within the last three years that systems have been developed that address the problems associated with incorporating graphics into textual material. Two aspects of the problem need to be discussed separately: (1) how to generate electronically a higher proportion of needed graphics and (2) how to enter, manipulate and store graphics that cannot be machine generated, i.e., existing illustrations, photographs and illustrations too complex to allow machine generation.

The first problem, how to generate electronically a higher proportion of illustrations than is presently the case, can now be addressed. Two distinct types of illustrations now produced by hand can in fact be electronically produced. These are complex technical graphics, for example, exploded diagrams of gear boxes, complex electronic circuits, detailed maps, etc.; and illustrative drawings requiring artistic imagination such as a view of the Roman Senate in session, the scene of the Battle of Crecy, etc. The first type of illustration can be produced on the present Ethernet/Star system in one of two ways: either by the use of CAD software or through the use of technical drafting software. Both types of software are now available for use at Star terminals. Both have advantages and disadvantages with regard to the use required of them by the institute but both will allow for the generation of required illustrations in a form immediately integrateable with textual material. Which will provide the greatest benefits is not immediately obvious and requires a detailed cost-benefit study. This is presently underway.

The second challenge, that of producing artistic illustrations directly on the system, can also be addressed, albeit to a lesser extent than is the case with technical graphics. Software is presently available for the Star that will allow for 'freehand drawing'. This is limited, however, to the creation of line drawings with block shading. Although this will undoubtedly allow for the creation of a considerable number of presently unattainable illustrations, it does not represent the availability of a true 'electronic palate'. Such systems exist but are not immediately integral with the Star/Ethernet system. Although it is theoretically possible to develop in-house translation programmes, this is a formidable task and one that cannot likely be cost-justified for an institution with production volumes such as those of OLI. It is likely that, for the forseeable future, such illustrations will still need hand generation. It is possible, however, to store and manipulate such illustrations electronically in the same manner as pre-existing illustrations, through the use of a digitising scanner.

A digitising scanner is a device that allows for the electronic storage, manipulation and subsequent output of pre-existing line, free-hand and half-tone art. Such devices work through the division of the image to be scanned into pixels, minute subsections of the image. Typically, scanners reduce a piece of artwork into a series of rectangles measuring from 1/300 by 1/400 of an inch to 1/800 by 1/1,200 of an inch; each square inch of the image is divided into between 120,000 and 960,000 tiny rectangles. Each rectangle (pixel) is stored as one of up to sixteen grey-tones: white, black or one of fourteen tones of grey in between. Once stored, it is possible to crop, change contrast, change the size, etc. of each of the pixels and produce the output image which is either produced on a laser printer or a digital typesetter. Such devices are expensive as the data storage requirements for even a 4" x 5" illustration are formidable. (Twenty square inches represent a minimum of 2,400,000 pixels, each of which can assume one of 16 grey-toned values.) Even given efficient data-compaction algorithms, memory requirements are enormous if a system is to be able to handle simultaneously dozens of illustrations. Such systems do, however, exist; one of which, available through the Xerox corporation, is Ethernet/Star compatible and several of which could be integrated into the system through the development of integrating software. Which, if any, of the available options is cost-justifiable awaits the conclusions of a detailed cost-benefit study.

It is probably obvious from the foregoing discussion that if the previously-discussed enhancements are adopted, the role of the paste-up department disappears, for it will be possible to electronically integrate all textual and illustrative material and output these either via a laser printer or a third-generation digital typesetter. Given this possibility of electronically generating and storing entire documents, on-demand printing becomes possible. What is on-demand printing?

An on-demand print system is a system that allows for the electronic, rather than physical, storage of complete documents and for their subsequent electronic or conventional reproduction. (*Canadian Printer 1982*) If the enhancements to the system previously discussed are implemented at the institute, then such a system is possible. Entire courses will be stored electronically and reproduced either via laser printer or typesetter and conventional electrostatic or offset reproduction. This makes a system at least theoretically possible that would allow for the total electronic processing of student registrations and dispatch of materials. Assuming the existence of a touch-tone telephone available to a student, soon to be universal, the system would work as below.

A student would phone the institute's registration number, indicate via the telephone number pad whether he or she was a new student (this would allow for the generation of a new student number if one was required), indicate via the pad their name, address and telephone number if he or she is a new student and indicate the courses required and specify via the pad their credit card number. Another technology soon to be available, voice recognition computers, will make the collection of this information much more efficient for the user. When this information is received, the computer system could automatically instruct a production volume laser printer to generate a complete copy of the in-house print materials required, with the student's name and address printed on the back cover. Once produced, this could be shrink-wrapped and dispatched to the student. Simultaneously, mailing labels for such items as text-books, equipment packages, etc. could be produced, as at present, in the warehouse and these items dispatched. The savings in the cost of manpower and in the rental or maintenance and amortisation costs of storage space are obvious. Whether these would offset the capital cost of systems development and equipment acquisition will depend on the relative costs of labour and capitalisation associated with any given institution. The Open Learning Institute is studying such trade-offs but it is not at the present time apparent whether the implementation of such a system would be cost-effective. It remains, however, in high labour cost markets, an intriguing possibility. If major savings can be effected, the possibility exists for the redirection of employees to more directly productive activities without any increase in costs.

THE PRODUCTION OF NON-PRINT MEDIA

As already noted, the institute uses audio and video materials in many of its courses. As is the case with print materials, some of these are institute-produced and some are acquired from other educational institutions. Institute audio materials are all distributed on audiocassettes and with very few exceptions are produced in-house. A wide range of materials are produced: interviews, integrated audio-graphic packages, language tapes, illustrative sketches, etc. A small recording and editing facility exists at the institute which is staffed by two full-time media producers, one full-time editing/recording technician, a part-time maintenance technician and a part-time duplicator operator. Professional performers are used on a contract basis in all productions requiring something other than an expert interview. A digital recording and editing capability has recently been installed which allows for the extremely quick editing of most of the types of material produced.

The system of development and production parallels that of the graphics department. As each new course is developed, the course writer, course designer and media producer determine whether a media component is required. If the decision is to produce such a component, the media producer is responsible for hiring a contract script writer, for working in close liaison with the course designer to ensure the audio and print components of the course mesh together properly, for the hiring of contract performers as needed, for overseeing recording sessions and for the post-recording work required to produce a master tape. Once the master tape has been approved by the course writer, course designer and course consultant, it is duplicated as needed on the institute's in-house bin-loop duplication system, packaged in a cassette, labelled and boxed for storage and subsequent dispatch to students. To date some 150 instructional audio tapes have been developed. Approximately 20,000 tapes were duplicated in 1984-5, a number projected to grow to 30,000 within the next three years.

The institute makes use of both videotapes and broadcast video in its courses. Broadcast material is transmitted over the Knowledge Network. Two principal types of material are broadcast: instructional materials acquired from elsewhere or developed by the institute, and live interactive sessions developed by the institute. All broadcast materials are also made available to students in a videotape format so that they can watch them when convenient. Several courses are supported by videotape materials that are not broadcast over KNOW.

The institute has no in-house video production facilities or staff and relies on the use of facilities and expertise available on a contract basis. In some cases the producer's role is filled by one of the institute's media producers but this is not necessarily the case. To date the institute has not been extensively engaged in video production and has relied on acquiring suitable material from other institutions such as the British Open University, the Coast College Consortium and the International University Consortium. The future looks bright, however, as the technologies of video, laser disc and computer-aided instruction converge to allow for the production of CAI courses with integrated video and audio components all stored on one or more laser discs. The potential for using such courses in scientific and technical courses is enormous and may well revolutionise the manner in which such courses are delivered.

THE STORAGE AND DISTRIBUTION OF DISTANCE LEARNING MATERIALS

The goal of any storage and distribution facility is to have materials in stock when they are required and to minimise the volume of stock required to do this. Several factors complicate the attainment of this goal: the institute is dependent on outside suppliers for many of the items required for its courses, for example, textbooks, equipment, lab kits, etc.; the product leaving the warehouse is a course whereas warehouse stock consists of individual items, up to thirty of which are contained in any given course; and students can enrol at any time and require the almost immediate dispatch of course materials. Good physical organisation and an efficient inventory control system are required in order to meet the goal.

The institute warehouse consists of 10,000 square feet equipped with both narrow aisle racking accessed by an order picker and with conventional racking accessed by a fork-lift rack. Space is provided for the bulk storage of individual items, for the storage of made-up course packages and for the quick access storage of individual items. Materials need to be stored in all three ways so that the turnaround time required to ship different types of order is minimal. A staff of eight are responsible for all warehouse operations, for all institute shipping and receiving, for the internal institute mail service and for the operation of the institute's mail-order bookstore. In 1984-5 on a total of 20,000 packages were dispatched as were over 220,000 pieces of letter mail. The mail-order bookstore will gross over $450,000 in 1985-6.

All aspects of warehouse operations are integrated by the in-house developed VAX 11-750 based inventory control system. All items stored in the warehouse are assigned an item number. A given course consists of a set of specific items and once packaged becomes itself an item. Item receipts and shipments are recorded on line and so the system provides a perpetual record of stock levels. Desired item stock levels are calculated by the system using demand, projections, the historical variation in demand and item acquisition lead items. The level specified is calculated so that, given the known variability of demand, needed items will be in stock 95 per cent of the time. The system automatically produces lists of items that fall below the desired stock level. The system is thus designed to ensure that the level of stock is sufficient to meet demand but only just so. This minimises total storage requirements and thus space requirements. This 'just in time' principle is strictly adhered to with in-house produced items but is sometimes violated with items acquired from outside sources. This is particularly true with regard to textbooks. Whenever possible the institute will buy sufficient copies of a text to last the lifetime of a course once notice is received that the text is to go to a new edition. This results in increased storage and carrying costs but is usually cheaper than revising an existing course to accommodate the changes in a required textbook.

Orders to ship items, courses, individual texts, etc., are entered by an authorised originator at a computer terminal. The system then automatically generates a shipping order and shipping label which are printed in the warehouse. Once the shipment has been confirmed as shipped, the system automatically adjusts the stock level in the inventory records.

CONCLUSION

At present, it is possible to support a continuous enrolment distance learning system with efficiently produced and distributed materials at a per student cost that is well below the costs typically associated with face-to-face instruction. Recent and anticipated technological developments will allow for considerably increased efficiency in the near future. Demand printing and 'just in time' inventory management systems will ensure that maximum use is made of available resources. In an era of declining educational resources, efficient distance education institutions are well placed to become even more significant members of the educational community. Provided capital investment is undertaken only on the basis of rigorous cost-benefit analyses so that new systems are truly more cost effective, the future looks bright. Such analyses will need to be independently conducted by each organisation, because what is a good investment in one context may make little sense in another. The goal is efficient service. The means of attaining it are many.

REFERENCES

I would like to acknowledge the useful criticisms of H. Fischer, K. Baresh and T. Lilly, all of the Open Learning Institute and of K. Pridmore of the Xerox Corporation.

Bottomley, J. (1983) Review of *Learning At A Distance: A World Perspective*, J.S. Daniel, M. Stroud and J.R. Thompson (eds.), Athabasca University, International Council for Correspondence Education, Edmonton, 1982, in *The Canadian Journal of Higher Education, 13*
Canadian Printer, (1985) Special Report on Electronic Publishing, September
Ellis, J.F. and J. Bottomley (1979) Problems and Opportunities Associated with Developing and Operating a Distance Education System, presented at the British Open University Conference on the Education of Adults At A Distance, Birmingham
Keegan, D. (1980) 'On Defining Distance Education', *Distance Education*, 1
Peters, O. *Der Fernunterricht. Meterialen Zur Diskussion Einer Neuen Unterrichtsform*, Weinheim: Beltz
Peters, O. (1973) *Die Didaktische Struktur Des Fernunterrichts. Untersuchungen Zu Einer Industrialisierten Form Des Lehrens Unt Lernens*, Weinheim: Beltz

Student Support Services

Ethelyn McInnis-Rankin and Jane Brindley

This chapter describes the nature of and need for student support services; needs of adult learners; how organisational forms of distance education affect staffing of student services; case studies of student services operations at Open Learning Institute and Athabasca University; technology used to deliver student support services; and trends across Canada in the delivery of student support services to distance education students.

Student support services encompass a broad field, particularly in distance education. Support systems vary from institution to institution. In this chapter, we look at a wide range of services including admissions, registrations, records, examinations, information services, advising, counselling, instructional support and student advocacy. Some institutions offer only some of these services, while others may provide all of them but separate them administratively.

Before we describe individual services we shall look at the rationale for providing extra support to students.

RATIONALE

Student support services have long been regarded as an indispensable, although perhaps a peripheral, component of traditional campus-based postsecondary education. In distance education, certain support services, particularly advising, counselling and student advocacy are only beginning to be seen as an important part of the learner's educational experience. For many distance education institutions, the goal is to have the learner become as independent as possible. Consequently, much emphasis has been placed on developing learning packages which enable students to work on their own, with a minimum of contact with the institution. Unfortunately, most students lack the experience to adapt readily to a totally andragogical system. (Coldeway 1982:91) As Smith and Small (1982:137-9) point out, 'external studies will, by definition, continue to be essentially a form of independent study but should never be a sentence to solitary confinement.'

In addition to looking at the difficulties which the learning system presents, it is important to examine the type of learner which distance education institutions generally attract. The majority of distance learners are adults. Although it was once thought that adult learners could be largely self-sufficient, there is now a large body of distance education literature which suggests otherwise. As well as being older than the traditional campus-based student, distance learners differ in other ways. In general, they have a greater variety of educational backgrounds, from less than high school to a university degree. Their most recent educational experience may be some years past. As well as being new to distance education, their study strategies may be rusty, inappropriate or non-existent. In most cases, distance education students are studying part-time and are engaged in other full-time activities, often paid employment. Their role of student is only one among many. The potential for conflict between the demands of their studies and those in other areas of their life is great.

Each prospective student approaches an educational institution with a goal, however fuzzy, or with certain benefits in mind. Morgan, Taylor and Gibbs (1982:103-6) described this as the learner's 'orientation to study'. They described three main types of orientation, personal, vocational, and academic, which affect the way students view their studies. To the extent that students end up in courses and programmes which fulfil their prior expectations, they find themselves more or less satisfied with their learning experience. Isolation from the institution and lack of understanding and information about the educational system lowers the students' chances for a desired match.

Once a student is in satisfactory courses, there is no guarantee that studies will go smoothly. Students can run into a variety of problems, including those to do with course content and/or design, administrative systems such as examinations, their ability and study skills, and changes in their own circumstances. Again, isolation from experienced peers and institutional support personnel who could help aggravates the situation.

In summary, the distance learner's need for a variety of student support services can be well justified. Support services can personalise and humanise the distance teaching systems. While the academic part of the institution tends to focus more on content, support services tends to focus student services staff work towards facilitating each student's full development.

WHAT ARE STUDENT SUPPORT SERVICES?

Registry Functions

Admissions: Admissions includes those policies and procedures which provide for students' entry into postsecondary distance education: admissions policies and academic qualifications can be considered an institution's most important expression of educational philosophy. Although admissions policies vary amongst postsecondary educational institutions offering distance education programmes in Canada, most policies can be categorised as either open or selective. Athabasca University and Open Learning Institute are examples of institutions with open admissions policies. At Athabasca University, the only formal entrance requirements are that a student be at least 18 years old and a resident of Canada. OLI requires that students be Canadian citizens. Universities in Canada that offer distance education programmes usually offer two options to students: regular admission and admission as an adult or mature student. Under regular (selective) admissions requirements, the students' application is evaluated on the basis of previous educational qualifications. The student must meet the university and/or individual faculty prerequisites. Persons of a mature age who do not possess the minimum admissions requirements may apply as adult students. In addition to previous educational records, mature applicants usually must supply a statement about the educational goals that they hope to meet through entrance to a university programme. These applications are considered individually.

Regular admissions policies require applications for admission to be completed by a predetermined date, for example, 2 July for a fall session. Application for admission and registration in courses are two separate procedures in selective admissions policy. In open admissions policies, the admission and registration process is combined in one procedure.

Registration and Records: A student is considered registered in a distance education course once the chosen courses have been approved and a tuition payment is received. Course registration and intake dates for distance education students vary from continuous to fixed. Universities such as Acadia and Athabasca operate on a year-round continuous registration system. The University of British Columbia and Open Learning Institute have six intakes per year. Some institutions such as Simon Fraser University and the University of Waterloo operate on a tri-semester system with three intakes per year. Other institutions maintain two intakes per year, for example, September and January. Queen's University offers correspondence course intake in the September (Winter) session only.

Records information is generated from the admissions and registration forms. A common course of information is required: name, age, sex, citizenship, mailing address, previous educational experience (where required), transfer credit evaluation, programme and/or course goals, course enrolments and grade attainments. The trend is for these record systems to be computer-managed.

Examinations: At the end of most credit distance education courses, students are required to write a final examination. Examination dates may be flexible, (for example, Athabasca University) or in most other instances are scheduled at fixed dates. For example, the University of Waterloo examinations are scheduled on a Saturday at the end of each term at examination centres across Canada. Students in isolated areas are required to make arrangements for their own examination supervisor or proctor.

Institutions vary in their policies for supplemental examinations. There are no supplemental examinations at Open Learning Institute and the University of Waterloo. At these institutions, to improve a grade, students must register in the course. Grades are released on an average of four to six weeks after examinations. A final grade is usually determined by a weighted averaging of the grades for all assignments and examinations.

Information Services

Distance learners require information about the opportunities available throughout the entire postsecondary system, not simply what an individual institution can offer. Often their needs are such that no single institution can meet them all. This type of contact with a prospective student is often similar to short-term academic advising, where specific and sometimes complex questions must be answered before a student can determine whether or not a particular institution is an appropriate learning resource. Information can be provided on a wide variety of topics including educational requirements for specific occupations, availability of certain courses, programme requirements, financial assistance, or registration procedures. Often specific publications are developed to meet students' informational needs.

Advising and Counselling

The definitions of advising and counselling are problematic because these two functions are seen differently by various institutions. As well, there is overlap between advising and counselling both in the skills required of staff who perform these duties and the purpose of each function. Both advising and counselling are performed in order to help the students meet their objectives, cope with their environment, and acquire self-understanding. For the purpose of this paper, we shall attempt to define advising and counselling separately.

Advising: Advisory services are more prevalent in distance learning than counselling services. In general, advising can be said to be more problem-centred than person-centred. The adviser imparts ideas and direction, and obtains and confirms information, usually in response to a direct request. Most frequently, advisers are concerned with the students' need for information, their choice of programme and courses, and their need for special services, such as financial aid. The adviser also plays a role in acting as the buffer between student and institution, by explaining administrative procedure or acting as an advocate on the student's behalf.

There is some overlap between admissions and advising, in interpretation of programme regulations and giving course advice. Advising goes beyond the role of the admissions office in programme planning by taking into consideration the student's needs and objectives in pursuing a programme of studies. Not all of the student's needs may be met by one institution. In this case the adviser may also play the role of educational broker by introducing the student to courses elsewhere. Advising offices may even set up a referral network with other institutions and facilitate this process.

Advisers may also play a role in assisting students with study strategies: time management, reading and study techniques, and approaches to writing different types of examinations. This is distinct from diagnosing and providing counselling or referral for students with particular learning difficulties. The latter activity is usually carried out by someone with more specialised skills.

Advisers generally have postsecondary education and experience in teaching or helping roles with adults.

Counselling: The purpose of counselling within an educational setting is one that has been debated many times. Heffernan (1981:115) states: 'Counselling is conceived as a less direct process, one that is aimed at self-discovery, developing confidence and making personal choices.' In this paper it is defined as helping students or prospective students to acquire self-understanding, relate effectively to their environment, and make personal decisions, all in an attempt to foster their development towards self-directedness. The counselling process, as opposed to advising, is more person-centred than problem-centred. In general, institutions have been slow in realising the worth of counselling in the distance education setting. However, adult learners face a myriad of personal and social problems in returning to education, including role conflicts, financial pressures, learning difficulties and confusion about their goals. The counsellor's role is to help the student assess their situation and alternatives, and to teach decisionmaking and goal planning skills. In order to do this, they need a special set of skills and knowledge: interpersonal, diagnostic, and theoretical.

Counsellors, because of their professional background and extensive contact with students, are uniquely qualified to make a contribution to institutions concerned with programme and course development. Other activities usually carried out by counsellors are service evaluation and institutional research.

Student Advocacy

Most staff who provide services to students perform a student-advocacy function in one way or another. It bears special mention because of its importance in the distance education setting. Students are not only isolated from the institution, but also from one another. They may be unaware of students who face difficulties with the institution similar to their own, and are not in a position to form effective lobby groups. Staff who work with students regularly can take forward individual complaints, and can press for institutional change when necessary.

Tutoring/Instructional Support

Tutors are defined here as the people whose interaction with the student is based on a particular course. They give support with the course content and administrative matters, and provide the human voice amongst the printed materials. Their functions include marking and commenting on assignments, discussing course content and assisting with course evaluation. They may also be involved in organising laboratory sessions, seminars, or discussion and self-help groups. Tutors are subject-matter experts for the particular courses they facilitate and have similar qualifications to staff teaching at campus-based institutions.

VARIATIONS IN STUDENT SUPPORT SERVICE ROLES

The nature of student support services in distance education depends on philosophy, funding and organisational structure. Student services design within dedicated distance education institutions such as Athabasca University and Open Learning Institute has been greatly influenced by the organisation and philosophy of the Open University in the United Kingdom. As new institutions in the 1970s, OLI and AU each designed a student support system with tutors and student advisers/counsellors to meet the needs of distance education students. Detailed case studies for these institutions are described in the next section.

Different student support roles have been developed by other institutions. Télé-université, a distance teaching institution which is part of the network of the University of Quebec has developed a unique staff role in the delivery of student support services, the 'animateur'. This term is difficult to translate, but the role roughly corresponds to that of a facilitator. The animateur may organise workshops for small groups of students on a regional basis. (Caron 1982:145-8) The animateur may also support teleconference links between students. The animateur's role differs from that of the role of the tutor in that the animateur is usually a non-academic specialist. This role does not seem to be duplicated in any other distance education programme in Canada.

At the University of Western Ontario, a 'peer-counselling'/community representative system has been established to assist in developing an information and support system for off-campus and distance education students registered with, or seeking admission to the University of Western Ontario. Area representatives exist for Sarnia, St Thomas and Owen Sound. The representatives are paid a modest monthly stipend for their activities, which include proctoring of examinations, maintaining an information material supply and distributing calendars and brochures. Community representatives exist for Aylmer, Sarnia, Kincardine, Port Elgin, Woodstock, Thamesford, Simcoe, Tillsonburg, Thedford and Owen Sound. Industrial/institutional representatives exist for GM Diesel in London, Firestone Steel Products in London, Ford Assembly Plant in Talbotville, 3M in London, Aylmer Ontario Police College, Brantford Police, Sarnia Police, Goderich OPP, and hospitals in London, St Thomas, and Brantford.

The role of community representatives has been identified as a person willing to discuss problems of university courses with students; knowledgeable about and willing to pass on information concerning the academic channels and contacts on campus; interested in sharing personal experience regarding managing university courses or programmes with students; willing to help identify strategies for academic planning and B.A. programme progression; willing to give the faculty of part-time and continuing education feedback on issues that relate to off-campus centres; and able to communicate between student and Part-Time Continuing Education as an ombudsman.

Representatives come to campus for informational and development meetings twice a year. The organisation of the representative network was undertaken by the director of part-time studies in June 1983 and was delegated to the mature student adviser in June 1985.

The title of 'tutor' as an academic resource specialist is common across Canada. However, the nature of the role and responsibilities varies according to the organisational structure. For example, at Simon Fraser University in British Columbia, the tutor/marker for the Directed Independent Study (DISC) programme may be the course author, another university faculty member, or a graduate student. In the University of British Columbia's Guided Independent Study programme, the courses are developed by full-time faculty members who then agree to act as course tutor for the first year of the course. Thereafter, they act as supervisor, if not the tutor, for another four to five years. Since faculty members are full-time university staff members, they must balance their university duties with the responsibilities of their distance education commitments.

In distance education departments within larger institutions, the role of adviser is subsumed by administrative staff who usually handle the bulk of the information enquiries and advice to students prior to enrolment. If problems arise, administrative staff act as the intermediary between the student and the institution.

COLLABORATION WITH OTHER INSTITUTIONS

Incentives for collaborative relationships in the delivery of distance education range from financial reasons to political pressures. Resources which can be shared include staff, facilities, materials and equipment, budgets and administration. Although there are numerous examples of institutional collaboration in the area of course development, there are fewer examples of collaboration in the area of the provision of support services in distance education in Canada. One new organisation which was designed to collaborate in the field of distance education is the Open University Consortium of British Columbia. The consortium was created by Patrick McGeer, Minister of Universities, Science and Communications in September 1984. The member institutions consist of the University of British Columbia, Simon Fraser University, the University of Victoria, the Open Learning Institute and the Knowledge Network. The function of the consortium is to ensure that students can obtain credits from the offerings of member institutions and other accredited institutions towards the completion of an 'open' degree; co-ordinate needs-assessment procedures and programme planning; ensure evaluation of programmes and methods of delivery; acquire rights to materials produced outside British Columbia; and advertise and promote jointly the programmes offered by the member institutions.

The Open University Consortium makes it possible for students to combine classroom-based and home-study courses from all member institutions in order to obtain a university degree. The degree offered is that of the Open Learning Institute. All students are registered only as OLI students, and all formal students records are maintained by OLI. The delivery institution is responsible for mailing course packages, selling textbooks, and related matters. OLI is responsible for providing advising services such as information-giving, programme planning and financial aid through its existing adviser network.

Another example of support services collaboration is that of North Island College in British Columbia and Athabasca University in Alberta, whereby Athabasca University provides degree programmes to students who are dually registered at North Island College and Athabasca University. North Island College provides all tutorial and support services to students in their region who register in Athabasca University courses.

New initiatives in the area of interinstitutional collaboration are taking place in Ontario. A review of distance education in Ontario as part of the commission on the future of the universities of Ontario resulted in the establishment of a committee on distance education by the council of Ontario universities in 1984. The committee has outlined the following objectives: to facilitate the exchange of information about institutional activities in distance education; to co-ordinate programme planning; to initiate interinstitutional credit transfer policies; and to develop mechanisms for co-operation among universities and between universities and other organisations in the development of course materials and delivery services. (Burge, Wilson and Mehler 1984:53)

CASE STUDY: ATHABASCA UNIVERSITY

Athabasca University is a distance education institution which has an open admissions policy and year-round registration. Most of its students are working adults who study part-time in their own communities. The 1984-5 enrolment was approximately 8,600. Students are located in all parts of Canada; about 75 per cent are from Alberta. Approximately 60 per cent of the student population are female, about 70 per cent are between the ages of 25 and 44.

During 1974, the central offices of Athabasca University relocated from Edmonton to a new permanent facility in the town of Athabasca, about 100 miles north of Edmonton. Regional offices were opened in Fort McMurray in 1977, in Calgary in 1980, and in Edmonton in 1984. Athabasca offers baccalaureate degrees and transfer programmes in both liberal and applied studies. Currently, three-year degrees are available in administration, arts and general studies.

The academic support service for students is the tutor system. Tutorial Services employs about 160 part-time tutors who assist students with course content and administrative matters, and to add some individuality to the printed course materials. Tutorial Services is managed by two full-time co-ordinators who report to the directors of studies. Individual tutors report to the course co-ordinator for the course which they tutor. Tutors work part-time usually out of their own homes.

When students register, they are informed of the name, address, telephone number, and schedules of their tutor. The tutor is advised of each student's name, address and telephone number, and usually contacts the student first. Students may telephone their tutors toll-free during specified hours each week from anywhere in Canada. Tutors have qualifications similar to teaching staff in any university. They are knowledgeable about the academic content of the course, and have previous teaching experience; they mark and comment on assignments, and discuss examinations, course content, and strategies for understanding the material, either by telephone or letter.

At Athabasca University, the term 'student services' refers broadly to those professional and support staff members providing information, and advisory and counselling services. Student Services has always played a fairly central role at Athabasca University. The Student Development Services unit (now Student Services) was created not simply as a service unit within a self-contained university, but as a service which functioned as a system-wide entity. The unit provided services for the institution such as recruitment and outreach, and a wide range of information, advisory referral, and advocacy services for registered and prospective students. In the early days, the unit also performed the admissions function for the university and assisted with transfer credit assessments.

The major goals were to promote the development of students' ability to plan their lives, careers, and education, set realistic goals, and study effectively. In setting these goals, the unit acted on certain beliefs about the student body. The first of these is that adult students, like their younger counterparts on campus, need and want help in setting goals, planning programmes, defining objectives, and improving learning skills. The second is that the same barriers that keep our students from participating in traditional education prevent them from using services which they need. The third belief is that these services can be provided at a distance.

The Student Development Services' mandate became more focused. The admissions function was taken over by the registry, and when a public affairs office was created, the recruitment and outreach function was given away with some relief, as it had always been viewed as being somewhat in conflict with the unit's student advocacy function. During the formative years, approximately the first four, the unit did not hire professional counsellors or perform any services which require the expertise of a psychologist. The need for such services became apparent as the unit's mandate became more focused in the direction of providing a full range of advisory and counselling services, including learning assistance. At this point, the titles of professionals in the unit were changed from 'Student Planning Adviser' to 'Counsellor'. The qualifications necessary were raised to a level consistent with other institutions, i.e., professional qualifications. At the same time, a full-time learning psychologist was hired to diagnose and remediate learning difficulties; another professional was hired to co-ordinate all of the student information programmes and publications; three new counsellors were recruited; and the name 'Student Development Services' was shortened to 'Student Services'. Some new services were added over the next couple of years: financial aid and awards; learning assistance; orientation; and special services for handicapped students.

When the move of the central offices from Edmonton to Athabasca was announced, a plan for regionalisation was developed which included decentralisation of Student Services and some services of the Registry. Major regional offices in Calgary and Edmonton have counselling, advising and registry staff; a smaller centre in Fort McMurray has advising and registry staff. These regional offices provide services for students in the surrounding area. Students in all other parts of Canada are served by the central office in Athabasca. Student Services staff in the central office report to a director of student services; regional staff report to directors of their respective regions. The directors of regions are also responsible for academic programming, and may or may not have a student services background. Although there are no direct reporting lines from the regional offices to the director of student services, the director is formally responsible for ensuring a consistent level of service across the regions. To this end, service guidelines have been developed and there are still regular staff meetings (usually teleconferenced) of all advising and counselling staff. Central office staff also participate in recruitment and training of new regional office staff, and there is co-operation between offices on joint projects. The organisational model is not without problems and is heavily dependent on the co-operation of all staff.

The first part of the Guidelines for Provision of Student Services at Athabasca University describing the role, place, and function of Student Services is reproduced below.[1]

The Role of Student Services at Athabasca University

The student services group helps students and prospective students clarify their goals in seeking postsecondary education, helps them meet their educational needs and provides support and information to give them the best opportunity for success. The group has defined its role after studying the needs and motives of the adult learner and modifying its approach from experience and evaluation.

The services provided are an integral part of the educational process at Athabasca University. The student services group has two general concerns regarding student development: the promotion of growth along a broad spectrum to support students in realizing their full potential not only as students, but in all areas of their lives, and to assist students experiencing difficulties to achieve the progress of which they are capable.

The group staff members also, through their professional background and extensive contact with students, are uniquely qualified to make valuable contributions to university committees concerned with program and course development.

The Place of Student Services at Athabasca University

A. The term 'student services', in general, refers to those professional and support staff members providing information, advisory and counselling services for Athabasca University. At present, these members work out of regional offices, reporting to the Director of Regions, and at Student Services in Athabasca, reporting to the Director of Student Services.

B. Central Student Services is a distinct organizational unit responsible and reporting directly to the Vice-President, Learning Services.

C. The Director of Student Services is responsible for ensuring that all student services and policies are equitable and consistent across the regions.

Functions

The functions and delivery mechanisms listed below have been developed in recognition of the nature of Athabasca University and in response to students needs. Within the limits of its resources, the student services group responds to the changing needs of the institution and its students by adding or modifying specific services, or by modifying the proportion of staff time devoted to various services. Changes are made carefully, following evaluations of needs and impacts. Evaluation of service is an important and continuous function.

The student services group has a central office in Athabasca, with regional staff in other locations in the province. Functions and delivery mechanisms may differ from one geographical location to another, depending on the student group being served and the capability of the particular office. The central office takes more responsibility than other offices as a clearing house for information and packaged program-support materials and with the administration of such programs as Orientation, Writing Competence Tests and the Math Skills Questionnaires.

Whenever possible, the student services group attempts to develop counselling materials suitable for distance delivery for high-demand services. These materials can be used in whole or in part, with counselling support provided either face-to-face or at a distance, to either individuals or groups.

A. Direct Services to Students:

Information Services (a) The student services group provides career and educational information to students and prospective students and is an educational broker that provides information on courses and programs at Athabasca University and other institutions. (b) Student publications that provide information and assistance to students and prospective students include the *Student Handbook*; *Athabasca University Magazine*; *Pegasus*, a literary magazine of students' work; *Awards and Financial Aid Handbook*; and orientation guidebook; and a series of self-help booklets.

Counselling (a) Individual - provides assistance with educational, career, financial, personal and social problems. Based on individual interviews, counselling may involve appropriate and ethical use of psychological tests. (b) Group - establishes programs to prepare students for home study and to help them overcome specific problems, develop skills which will aid them in their study and other areas of their life, and relate their study to their life goals.

Study Strategies Assistance Helps students develop such study techniques as time management, exam-taking strategies and approaches to reading.

Academic Preparedness and Referral Provides assessment and referral services to students unsure about their level of preparedness for university work. Students can receive from counsellors or other professional staff individual feedback about their results from such assessment tools as a Writing Competence Test or Math Skills Questionnaire, and referral to an appropriate Athabasca University course or to remedial courses and services offered by outside institutions.

Financial Aid Ensures that each student has the opportunity to take advantage of financial aid programs. Assistance is provided with financial planning and study scheduling.

Student Awards Ensures students are rewarded for excellence, and are able to take advantage of existing scholarship and bursary programs. Student Services administers more than 150 awards of approximately $32,000 in total value.

Occupational and Educational Information Resource Centre materials are available to support counselling, study strategies assistance, assessment of academic preparedness and to aid students in choosing and preparing for careers. Resource cntres are established in regional offices as student numbers warrant.

B. *Indirect Services to Students:*

1. Consultation services to AU staff (in particular, tutors, co-ordinators, and registry) in their general dealings with students and in the case of an individual student, only with their permission.
2. On the request of, or with the permission of a student, consultation with students and their 'significant others' to improve student-familial relationships.
3. On the request of, or with the permission of a student, consultation

with co-operating institutions or private agencies (especially in the case of 'special needs' students) which may bear some responsibility for particular students. (See Section V., C.)

C. *Services to the University:*

1. In-service training and information sessions for staff of the university and co-operating institutions.
2. Participation in institutional program and course development.
3. Administration of the Alberta Universities Writing Competence Test for transfer to other universities.

D. *Research:*

1. Research which may improve services to students. This includes such topics as identifying student characteristics, need for services, assistance to academic units in the design of studies concerned with student progress and program effectiveness.
2. Evaluative research, which examines the effectiveness of existing services.
3. Research related to individuals' professional interests within the scope of helping services.

The remainder of these guidelines also addresses minimum qualifications of staff, professional development, workload, code of conduct, compensation, and status of staff within the institution. Although there have been some major changes in student services with a more focused role, an expansion of services, and regionalisation, the basic purpose of the unit, and the assumptions upon which it was built have not changed. The major focus is still to provide a form of student development not provided by tutors or course packages to ensure that the student has the best possible opportunity to obtain the benefits they seek in pursuing further education.[1]

CASE STUDY: OPEN LEARNING INSTITUTE

The Open Learning Institute was established by the British Columbia provincial government in June 1978 under the College and Provincial Institutes Act, with additional authority under the Universities Act to grant a Bachelor's degree. It was created to provide educational opportunities for the large number of British Columbians who were unable to attend traditional institutions because of work or domestic commitments, geographic isolation or physical disability.

Since the institute first enrolled students in September 1979, there has been steady growth. The 1984-5 enrolment was approximately 15,000. The majority of students (96%) are located in British Columbia. Approximately 56% of the student population are female; 45 % are between the ages of 21 and 30; 31 % are between the ages of 31 and 40.

OLI offers baccalaureate degrees; programmes of study in career, technical and vocational areas; and programmes of study in .adult basic education. The distribution of students between the main programme areas in 1984-5 was as follows: uiversity programmes, 33%; career, technical, vocational programmes, 43%; adult basic education programmes, 24%.

A wide range of administrative and educational resources have been set up to support the entry and continuing progress of OLI students.

Admissions

The institute grants admission to any adult Canadian citizen irrespective of educational attainment. 'Adult' is defined as anyone aged 18 or over. The admissions process is simple and straightforward. The application form requires only that students give basic information such as name, address, phone number, age, sex, citizenship, and the titles of the course(s) for which they wish to register. Staff in the admissions area screen all incoming registrations for potential study problems such as the number of courses undertaken exceeding the amount of study hours available, or enrolments in courses which require prerequisites. Registrations which indicate the potential for study problems are referred to a head office adviser for a follow-up telephone call or letter.

Admissions staff also maintain waitlists for limited enrolment programmes and courses that require equipment which may be in limited supply, like biology and electronics. For specialised programmes such as Graduate Nurse Refresher and Dental Assistant which have admissions requirements, admissions staff mail information packages and collect the prerequisite documents.

Students transferring credit from other postsecondary educational institutions receive an evaluation of their transfer credits towards an OLI Bachelor of Arts, Bachelor of Arts in Administrative Studies or Bachelor of Arts in General Studies degree programme. For students transferring from other institutions, the institute has adopted liberal transfer credit policies. Candidates seeking a degree may transfer up to 75 per cent of the credits required, provided such credit derives from a recognised college or university. Similar practices are followed in the career, technical and vocational areas. At the Grade 12 levels, the institute is guided by ministry policies.

Registration and Student Records

After the students' fees have been collected, the information on the registration forms is transferred into the computerised student records system (DETREMS). Biographical, course, programme and transfer history is created for each student and is available on-line. New and returning students are sent a computer-generated welcome letter containing the following information: tutor(s') name, address, and OLI phone number and office hours; the phone numbers for advising assistance; instructions on procedures for examination application; and an examination application form.

Computer labels are generated which are sent to the warehouse to initiate the shipment of course materials to the students. At the close of registration, computerised student lists are sent to the tutor indicating the names, addresses and telephone numbers of students assigned to the tutor.

Registration takes place every two months. The fixed intake sessions are January, March, May, July, September and November. Three-credit courses are designed to be completed within a four-month semester. The maximum amount of time students are allowed to complete their course work is six months. If students need more time, they must re-register and pay tuition fees again. Although the six-month option is a popular option with OLI students, analysis of statistics has not shown any increase in completion rates since the introduction of this option.

Examinations

The institute requires a student to successfully complete a final examination in all credit courses. Examinations are scheduled every two months within fixed dates, usually over a week-end. To avoid excessive travel by students, a province-wide network of examination centres is in operation. Centres are organised using local educational and community facilities. In the April 1985 exam session, 1823 exams were scheduled at 58 regular examination centres; 145 'special arrangements' were made, the majority of these being for students living outside of British Columbia. OLI also organised exams in April for 52 UBC correspondence students. UBC correspondence students living outside the lower mainland are scheduled to write examinations with OLI students as part of Open University Consortium arrangements.

The DETREMS system takes care of examination centre booking and schedules. It automatically issues examination confirmation letters to students and registration sheets for examination invigilators. Examinations are sent to specified tutors for marking. Once examination marks have been entered, student transcripts are produced and mailed to students. This process usually takes from four to six weeks.

Advising Services and the Role of Regional Centres

The philosophical assumptions underlying the OLI advising service are very different from those of the Athabasca University student services. There is no counterpart to the Athabasca University counsellor role at the Open Learning Institute. Although the majority of the advisers at Open Learning Institute have graduate counselling psychology degrees, this specific qualification was not a prerequisite for the position of adviser. Advisers with counselling degrees were hired for their communication skills. The emphasis in the adviser role at the Open Learning Institute is on information-giving, academic advising, liaison and promotion, and administrative activities.

In the original proposal for a student advisory service at OLI, Paterson (1979:1) recommended the establishment of regional centres in the major communities of the province. The centres' responsibilities would be to:

1. Act as an information source for enquiries. Distribute printed materials and brochures. Activate appropriate local media resources for advertising and publicity, and establish working relationships with regional educational, professional and service organisations.
2. Administer an advisory service for potential students. Assist in course selection, transfer credit and advise on institute policies and regulations.
3. House and distribute information and learning materials and equipment.
4. Act as a referring agency to the central office for all necessary matters relating to student, programme and institutional concerns beyond local office capacity.
5. Advise the institute on problems and prospects within the region and advise on appropriate measures or initiatives to be taken.

In this first description of the duties of the regional adviser, there was no mention of a student support function (although this function was later added to the initial adviser job description). It was anticipated that once the student was settled efficiently into the system, the regional adviser would have infrequent contact with the student. The student's principal source of support would be the course tutor(s).

As the institute enrolments grew, so did the number of students assigned to advisers. When student loads grew to 600-700 per adviser, the advisers' role began to change. Regional advisers had little time for enrolled student support functions (for example, pro-active student contact) due to the demands of meeting the rapidly increasing volume of prospective student enquiries, and of mounting various promotional activities. As a consequence of cutbacks in the 1984-5 budget, a reorganisation of advising services was undertaken. In 1985-6, students who registered with OLI were no longer assigned a permanent adviser according to a geographic region. Instead, students were directed to contact the student services head office in Richmond for any information relating to records, examinations, financial aid or admissions. Three regional advising centres were disbanded. For the remaining three centres in Kelowna, Prince George and Victoria, the main focus of activities became promotion, liaison and recruitment. Since the student records files and the staff handling the transfer credit evaluation functions were located in the Richmond head office, programme planning responsibilities were shifted to the advisers in the Richmond office.

The majority of the Richmond advisers' duties now consists of responding to student information, academic advising, programme planning and policy enquiries. Most of the advising contacts are with prospective students. The underlying assumption is that enrolled students will not need the ongoing services of an adviser (except for programme planning) once they have become established distance learners.

In order to deal with the demands of increasing student enquiries and enrolments, and a decrease in the regional advising staff, a temporary paraprofessional position was created in 1984-5 in the Richmond advising office. The duties of the information clerk consisted of handling the growing number of telephone enquiries which required general information contained in the institute calendar.

Tutors

Each OLI programme division employs tutors on part-time   six month contracts. This has enabled the institute to maintain the flexibility necessary in a rapidly growing institution. About 120 tutors were under contract in 1984-5, and of those, the majority were employed full-time by other educational agencies: universities, colleges, institutes, school districts.

There are 8 tutors in the university programme area who are retained on part-time 12-month contracts. These senior tutors are involved both in tutoring and in programme development, evaluation and revision of courses. Additional duties are to maintain contact with the other tutors in their discipline. Tutors work primarily from their homes, maintaining regular contact with students by telephone and through the mail. They are required by contract to initiate one introductory telephone call to each student. Most tutors telephone students at least three times during a course: an initial welcoming call, a mid-course checkup, and a pre-examination discussion. Students are encouraged to telephone tutors whenever problems arise, and tutors are encouraged to call students whenever students appear to need additional motivation, help, or advice. Some students request a check-up call every two or three weeks to keep them moving on the course. Some tutors request that students telephone them every two or three weeks to report progress. The level of student-initiated telephone calls varies in each course.

Normally, tutors are in contact with only one student at a time. Often, the same information has to be repeated to several students in sequential telephone calls. Teleconferencing can provide a way to make this sort of tutoring task more efficient. It holds the potential for reducing the sense of isolation felt by many students as it can provide an opportunity for students to hear from others in the same course or from those with similar concerns. Although teleconferencing is used more extensively by Athabasca University than Open Learning Institute tutors, it is recognised at both institutions that there are many topics which may be usefully discussed by a tutor and individual students or students at a group site through a teleconference. Some examples are:

a. discussions to introduce the course and explain how to proceed with the first assignment;
b. discussions to make corrections in course materials or to update course information;
c. discussions to examine a specific assignment in a course;
d. discussions to examine one of the problems faced by many students in the course;
e. discussions following a television course presentation on an educational television network;
f. discussions to summarise and review the main points at the halfway point in the course;
g. discussions to exchange opinions on the course and motivate students to keep working;
h. discussions to develop a group feeling among course participants;
i. discussions at those places in a course where tutorial augmentation is needed by all or many students;
j. discussions preparing for the examination to explain the examination format, review main points, answer student questions, discuss techniques for writing the examination, motivate students to perform well, and reduce student anxieties; and
k. discussions among students themselves to provide mutual support and advice for each other.[2]

At the Open Learning Institute, face-to-face meetings between tutors and groups of students are rare. Teleconferencing provides a means for tutors to communicate beyond the written comments and one-to-one phone calls which are normally used. (*OLI Tutor Orientation Manual*, Open Learning Institute, 1984)

Annual tutor workshops are held in Richmond for tutors from all three programme areas. Since many tutors are at a distance from the institute, OLI subsidises the cost of accommodation and meals for tutors who live out of the lower mainland in order that they may participate in discipline meetings and professional development activities. In 1985, the professional development portion of the tutor conference allowed attendance by anyone interested in the field of distance education.

TECHNOLOGY USED TO DELIVER STUDENT SUPPORT SERVICES

Print

At most institutions across Canada, the primary medium used for delivery of distance education instruction is print. Student support services in distance education are delivered by mainly print, telephone and in-person contacts. Print support for students includes materials such as student information publications, for example, newsletters, magazines; student handbooks, for example, orientation; non-credit career counselling courses, for example, Prep 001, OLI; self-administered diagnostic tests, for example, mathematics; programme planning information and other print information on such topics as study skills and exam preparation.

Audiocassettes

Audiocassettes are used in a variety of ways in distance education in Canada. The correspondence delivery mode of instruction at the University of Waterloo is by audiocassette tapes. Each student who signs up for a correspondence course receives a learning package comprised of lectures on audiocassettes together with accompanying notes, exercises, problems or essay topics. In most institutions, however, audiocassette tapes are used as resources to supplement and enrich the print learning package.

In the delivery of student support services, some institutions use audiocassettes as a vehicle for communication between the tutor and students. Tutors at the Universities of British Columbia and Waterloo may occasionally prepare a tutorial tape with comments for distribution to the entire class of distance students.

As Feasly (1983:30) has stated, 'Audiocassettes have several advantages: they are readily available, relatively inexpensive, and portable and students can stop and replay them at will.' This flexibility plus the added personal touch of a human voice makes audio tapes a popular option in the provision of tutorial support services. Audiocassette tapes are used in the delivery of advising and counselling services by Athabasca University. Their *Student Services Orientation Guidebook* (1983) is supplemented by an audiocassette tape. On this tape, four students registered at Athabasca University talk about their experiences as adult distance education students. In addition, self-help audiocassette tapes are available on loan to AU students on such topics as fear control and relaxation procedures. These tapes help deliver counselling services to those students who are not able to visit a regional centre.

Telephone

The telephone is used extensively in distance education in Canada as a fast, effective communication link between students and tutors, advisers/counsellors and administrative staff. The delivery of tutoring and advising/counselling services by telephone requires good communication skills. An extensive communications course for tutors was developed at Athabasca University. New tutors receive copies of the workbook designed for the course, and are expected to familiarise themselves with the information and maintain an ongoing self-evaluation of telephone contacts. New tutors at the Open Learning Institute receive the Tutor Orientation Manual. It includes print and audio material on telephone techniques. The manual is designed as a self-directed learning package.

Miskiman (1984:4-7) has outlined the factors important to telephone counselling in distance education. The counsellor (and tutor) in distance education has to rely on auditory cues such as voice tone, tempo and inflection; voice quality and speech attributes; and language syntax and semantics in order to initiate and enhance communication effectiveness in telephone contact.

Teleconferencing

Three main types of teleconferencing are commonly in use in Canada. These include audio teleconferencing, video teleconferencing (visual image) and computer teleconferencing (information processing). The types most often used in the delivery of student support services are audio teleconferencing and video teleconferencing.

There are a number of Canadian postsecondary institutions using audio teleconferencing for the delivery of instruction. Some examples are Memorial University, and the Universities of New Brunswick, Ottawa, Western Ontario and Calgary. Some examples of institutions using forms of teleconferencing to deliver student support services follow.

Teleconferencing at the Open Learning Institute is used to supplement individual tutorials. Participation by students is optional. Topics include course content, assignments and exam preparation. In a research project conducted by Heselton (1985), the characteristics of OLI students most likely to join teleconferences were found to include those who had enrolled for longer-term, more specific reasons; who had taken more courses; students who were younger than forty years old; and who were male. Students were most likely to join teleconferences if they could do so by telephone from their own home.

Video teleconferencing is used in the DUET system (Carl 1983:187-9) at Mount St Vincent University in Nova Scotia. DUET (Distance University Education via Television) uses cable television and video teleconferencing to deliver both distance education and to support students by providing the opportunity for interaction amongst students at the receiving centre and interaction with the instructor at the broadcast classroom. Each receiving centre has a television and a telephone which is connected directly to the broadcast classroom at Mount St Vincent University. The broadcast classroom contains speakers for the telephone lines so that the instructor and students on campus can hear and speak with the students at the receiving centres.

Simon Fraser University has used computer conferencing as tutorial support for students enrolled in EDUC 473, Designs for Learning: Reading course during 1985. Each student in the course was loaned a Hayes modem. Students had access to microcomputers within the school system. The students dialed to the Simon Fraser University computer using Datapac and then had the opportunity to interact via computer with the professor and other students. The intent of the computer conference was to simulate the on-campus small group tutorial which is approximately one-third of the student contact hours. The advantages of computer conferencing were twofold: the medium was available when the student was free; and the cost was less than audio teleconferencing would have been.

The University of Alberta has also successfully used a micro-to-main-frame procedure to deliver a distance education course, Education Curriculum and Instruction 501, in 1984. (Kirman and Goldberg 1985) In the fall of 1985, it was made available to students anywhere in Canada serviced by the Datapac system. Since the Computer Assisted Distance Education Telecom-munication (CADET) system contains a bulletin board function for group discussions, and an electronic mail system for private communications between participants, student support functions are served by this system of delivery.

Broadcast Television

Access Alberta, Knowledge Network, TVOntario, Radio-Québec and the Quebec Educational Television Network are educational television networks in Canada which have been involved in the delivery of educational services in their respective provinces. Support services for distance education students have included live television broadcasts supported by interactive telephone talk-back for student-instructor discussion on topics related to broadcast telecourses. In addition, specific programmes have been developed for distance education students such as the Fall 1985 Knowledge Network telecourse, 'Effective Study Techniques' developed by North Island College. This type of programme plays an important complementary role to the counsellor or adviser in the delivery of student services in distance educa-tion.

Videotex

The Canadian system of videotex, Telidon, is used by the University of Guelph to provide services to students. The University Career Planner, a self-paced instructional tool, assists students to pick courses in Biology. Course requirements and entry requirements are listed, and the planner is equipped for on-line registration. The University of Guelph utilises the Grassroots database (a Telidon service in Saskatchewan, Manitoba, and Ontario, that has information of interest to farmers) in Winnipeg to provide Telidon services. (Rosen:45-6).

SUMMARY

This chapter has discussed student support services in distance education in Canada, and has described in detail student services operations at Athabasca University and the Open Learning Institute. The following points were made:

1. student support services include such functions as admissions; registration and records; examinations; information services; advising and counselling; student advocacy; and tutoring/instructional support;

2. the distance learner's need for a variety of student support services can be well justified on the basis of student profiles;

3. support systems and services for distance learners vary from institution to institution in Canada;

4. some institutions share the delivery of student support services through collaboration in the form of special agreements or consortia; and

5. technologies used to deliver student support services are print, telephone, teleconferencing, computer conferencing, audiocassettes, broadcast television and videotex.

This chapter has described a range of student support services. Some institutions in Canada offer only some of these services; others may provide all of them but separate them administratively. A trend in student support as well as instruction is the growing interest in the use of technology in order to provide delivery of services to the distant learner.

NOTES

1. These guidelines were adapted from the *Guidelines for Canadian College and University Counselling Services*, published and distributed by *The Canadian University and College Counselling Associaiton*, David L. Jordan, President, 1982.

2. OLI Tutor Orientation Manual. Open Learning Institute, 1984

REFERENCES

Burge, Elizabeth J., Joy Wilson and Audrey Mehler (1984) 'Communications and Information Technologies and Distance Education in Canada', *New Technologies in Canadian Education, 5*

Carl, Diana R. (1983) 'Creating a Duet: Using Video and Video Teleconferencing to Meet the Needs of the Community', *Programmed Learning and Educational Technology, 20*

Caron, Simon (1982) 'Student Support at a Crossroads', *Learning at a Distance*, J.S. Daniel, *et al.* (eds.), Athabasca University/International Council for Correspondence Education, Edmonton

Coldeway, Dan (1982) 'What Does Educational Psychology Tell us About the Adult Learner at a Distance?', *Learning at a Distance*, J.S. Daniel, *et al.* (eds.)

Feasly, Charles E. (1983) *Serving Learners at a Distance: A Guide to Program Practices*, ASHE-ERIC Higher Education Research Report No. 5

Heffernan, James (1981) *Educational and Career Services for Adults*, Lexington Books, Toronto

Heselton, Norine G. (1985) 'The Future of Teleconferencing at British Columbia's Open Learning Institute', unpublished M.A. Thesis, Simon Fraser University

Holmberg, Börje (1977) *Distance Education; A Survey and Bibliography*, Anchor Press Ltd., Essex

Kirman, Joseph, and Jack Goldberg (1985) *The CADET Project: Computer Assisted Distance Education Telecommunication for Post Secondary Education in Alberta: Final Report*, University of Alberta

Miskiman, Donald (1984) 'The role of Counselling in Distance Education', paper presented at the 1984 Western Regional Conference of the Canadian Association of College and University Student Services, Vancouver, British Columbia 22 March

Morgan, Alistair, Elizabeth Taylor, and Graham Gibbs (1982) 'Understanding the Distance Learner as a Whole Person', *Learning at a Distance*, J.S. Daniel *et al.* (eds.)

Paterson, John C. (1979) 'Student Advisory Services: Regional Centres-Functions and Staffing', unpublished paper, Open Learning Institute, Richmond, British Columbia

Rosen, Thelma (1984) 'Communications and Information Technologies in Canadian Universities', *New Technologies in Canadian Education, 4*

Smith, Kevin D. and Ian W. Small (1982) 'Student Support: How Much Is Enough?', *Learning at a Distance*, J.S. Daniel *et al.* (eds.)

Learner Characteristics and Success

Dan O. Coldeway

The question of whether distance education is a viable form of teaching and learning no longer arises. There are examples of distance education worldwide and reports indicate that the majority of institutions have experienced some success. Looking more closely, there are reports of students completing degrees, receiving credit in traditional and non-traditional subjects, and studying largely independently at a distance from the formal centre of education.

The distance education literature is replete with success stories: distance educators feel they are doing something important for their constituency and doing it successfully. This paper will attempt to examine claims of success more closely. What are the criteria for success? What type of students are having success? Finally, perhaps the most interesting question, is there ample evidence that distance educators can claim success in their efforts? The focus of this paper is on distance education in Canada. However, it is highly unlikely that the analysis of Canadian distance education success would differ greatly from an analysis of any other country. Of course the results are complicated by governmental and societal involvements with education at all levels, and those factors differ greatly within Canada, as well as between Canada and some of the developing nations interested in distance education. Success, not unlike beauty, is in the eye of the beholder. The problem is one of definition, measurement and interpretation. This paper will attempt to address these factors.

DEFINING SUCCESS IN DISTANCE EDUCATION

Few institutions involved in education at any level have the luxury of creating their own definition of success. In most cases it is a three-way mixture of input from the institution, the chief funding agent (in Canada, usually the government), and the student. To make the issue even more complicated, the criteria used by each of the three differ from institution to institution and in many cases from time to time within the same institution. The ratio of contribution that forms the final definition is also subject to local and time differences. Success, therefore, is very difficult to define and discuss without knowing the details of the three inputs described above.

The problem of defining success is not unique to distance education. Conventional educational institutions are continually under fire from all three input sources: the recent outcry about the lowering of standards in US and Canadian colleges and universities is a good example. Even a small percentage of university graduates without the ability to write or basic mathematical skills gets the attention of those concerned with success.

With the understanding that success will never have a universal definition, it is possible to discuss some of the more standard measures of success used by educational institutions and reported by educational researchers. Some of the more popular examples are:

1. student achievement measures (for example, course marks, final exam marks, etc.);
2. overall level of achievement within a programme or curriculum (for example, overall grade point average for students completing a degree, aggregate scores of students finishing a programme, etc.);
3. percentage of the total student enrolment completing a programme or curriculum;
4. student satisfaction with the course, programme, or curriculum;
5. follow-up measures of student success after course, programme or curriculum completion (for example, getting jobs, going to graduate school, etc.);
6. rate of course, programme or curriculum completion (for example, time to degree, etc.); and
7. cost measures (for example, cost per student per degree, etc.).

This list focuses primarily upon the student. According to it, success is largely a measure of what students do. There are, however, other indicators of success that have less to do with what students do. Some examples are listed below:

1. the range of course, programme or curriculum at an institution;
2. the availability of innovative or unique offerings (for example, women's studies or native studies, courses particularly suited to specific groups, etc.);
3. the method of instructional delivery (for example, courses available on or off campus, courses offered at a variety of times during the day and night, etc.); and
4. the availability of services other than those connected with instruction (for example, student counselling, recreation programmes, etc.).

For many institutions, particularly those involved in some form of innovative education, the list grows longer. Some examples are listed below:

1. reaching previously disadvantaged groups of students (for example, adult learning, prison programmes, etc.);
2. giving people an opportunity to enrol who otherwise would not have that opportunity (for example, open admissions, continuous course start dates, flexible pacing, etc.);
3. innovative grading systems (for example, mastery learning, criterion referenced testing, etc.);
4. providing interdisciplinary courses and programmes; and
5. giving credit for a wide range of previous educational and life experiences (for example, credit for experiencial learning, etc.).

It is not inconceivable that an institution would find all the items on the above lists important and many institutions could easily add to the list items which represent efforts they are committed to.

It can be argued that the first problem in defining success is one of constructing a list of indicators and attempting to determine the importance of each item on the list.

DEFINING THE CRITERIA FOR SUCCESS

How do you know success when you see it? Many educators can answer that question for any given item on their list, but few educators agree on the criteria. Excellence at one institution may be average performance at another. Significant numbers of high marks at one institution or within one course may be viewed sceptically in the absence of information about what those marks represent. The criterion of success for the administrator may differ from the instructor's perception. It is not uncommon for the student to define the criterion of success as simply getting through the course and recovering from the experience, never mind meeting objectives and high scholarship.

The lack of reliability and the resulting questions about validity of the criteria for success make the job of evaluating the indicators of success extremely difficult. The problem manifests itself constantly as my colleagues and I attempt to determine whether or not Athabasca University is successful. Athabasca University is committed to allowing anyone over the age of 18 to enrol in its courses, regardless of academic background, location, etc. That statement alone raises a whole series of questions about the indicators, criteria and measurement of success. For example, it would not be unreasonable to expect that an open admission policy would attract students who are not attracted to conventional universities. Given that, the following questions arise:

1. Do the students who enrol differ significantly from conventional students? In what ways?
2. What percentage of the student population is representative of this different type of student? Does that difference represent a major difference from the special programmes sometimes offered at conventional institutions?
3. Are these unique students having the same level of success in courses (for example, achievement, satisfaction, rate of completion, etc.) as their more conventional counterparts?
4. Is it necessary to treat these unique students different in order for them to have the level of success you have defined or is typical for conventional universities?
5. Looking over all of the above, are you satisfied with the result and if not, what can be done about it?

This level of analysis can be done for the entire institution or within the confines of a given course or concentration. Often the answer to such questions provides information that sets the criteria for success (as opposed to defining the criteria in advance and measuring the degree to which those criteria are met). For example, our data suggest that age, sex, location and previous academic experience have little to do with course completion. Given that, it seems as if our open admissions policy is working, that we are successful. However, other data indicate that only 30 per cent of those who enrol finish courses and only a small percentage of those who finish go on to take another course. Perhaps we are less successful than we thought. Would we feel better if the number was 50 per cent? On the other hand, overall enrolments are growing steadily. Given declining enrolments reported over the past few years at conventional institutions, we must be successful. But less than 30 per cent of those enrolled appear to be seriously headed towards finishing a degree at Athabasca University and a majority of those awarded degrees in previous years took most of their courses at institutions other than AU. Maybe increasing enrolments is really the beginning of failure rather than a measure of success.

As is apparent from the above discussion, defining the criteria for success is difficult. As was mentioned earlier, success can often be as much a function of the values and attitudes of those doing the questioning as it is a function of existing standards of educational excellence. Awarding one degree, certificate or diploma to a student who did most of his/her course work at your institution and would not otherwise have had the opportunity, can represent a significant level of success even in the context of 10,000 enrolments, 30 per cent completion rates, and only a small number of students demonstrating the motivation to complete a programme.

THE STUDENTS' DEFINITION AND CRITERIA FOR SUCCESS

Sam Postlewaite, a significant figure in the development of audio-tutorial instruction, once said that 'students are a lot like people.' That statement implies that students require and will use a variety of techniques to match their own style and reach their own goals. Institutions are just beginning to realise that they will also define their own criteria and definition of success.

The matrix shown in Figure 1 is an attempt to describe success from the student's viewpoint. The matrix suggests that students will fall into a block and the aggregate of students will indicate the result of any course or programme. It is up to the institution to determine what they consider to be successful members in each box.

Figure 1: The behaviour, satisfaction, curriculum level matrix

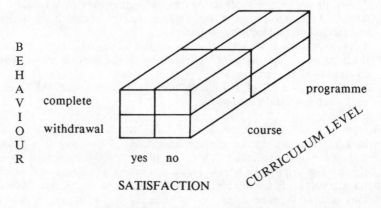

CURRICULUM LEVEL MATRIX

The matrix can also represent other values about success. Figure 2 shows the same matrix with different measures on the axis. Again, it is possible to imagine that students would define success differently than a given institution.

Figure 2: The behaviour, satisfaction, curriculum level matrix with marks as a behavioural factor

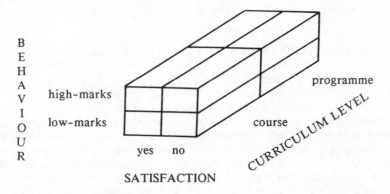

CURRICULUM LEVEL MATRIX

The effect of the success matrix in defining institutional levels of success would depend largely upon the relative numbers that appear in each of the boxes. For example, if the percentage of students who withdrew from courses with a sense of satisfaction that their needs were met was significantly higher than the ones who withdrew and did not feel satisfied, the institution could view that result as acceptable (i.e., the institution could assume that students who withdrew satisfied benefited from the institution, perhaps even learned something either about their ability or what they wanted). On the other hand, if a large percentage of students were withdrawing from the programme after completing courses and reported being satisfied, it would call into question the need for the programme rather than simply offering courses students were interested in taking.

Although the adult learning and development theorists have been talking about the interaction between learner needs and learner behaviour for years (Knox 1980; Knowles 1970), the issue is rarely at the forefront of conventional educational institutions' thinking about success. In contrast, this interaction may prove critical to distance education, especially institutions that cater to adult, part-time students and/or have open admissions policies.

Many adult learning theorists and educators view success in individual terms; that is, success is measured and defined by what happens to the individual adult learner. Given that definition, a successful programme or course must be able to recognise the individual's needs, background and ability, and help the learner use those factors to grow and learn. Hence the need for an 'androgogical system' which encourages and reinforces self-directed learning, as opposed to a pedagogical system in which the learner is only the recipient of content and instruction that is determined and delivered by someone else. Success is therefore a multi-level result. If the

However, some have questioned the importance of self-directed learning and the degree to which the learner should have control of instructional factors conventionally controlled by instructors and institutions. Finally, it is possible to measure the degree to which learners become self-directed and the impact that has on their personal and professional goals. Self-directed learning sounds almost ideal as a concept, but we lack a large enough cadre of self-directed learners to determine the short- and long-term importance of that concept and whether it is worth maintaining or encouraging in our educational institutions and systems.

THE CHARACTERISTICS OF DISTANCE LEARNERS

A majority of Canadian distance learning efforts were designed to attract and support a clientele which was not being served by conventional institutions. Unlike some of the massive distance education efforts by developing countries which are using distance educational techniques and tools as a means of providing basic education for students, Canadian efforts are usually complementary to conventional approaches to education. Again, Athabasca University and the Open Learning Institute of British Columbia are excellent examples. Both Alberta and British Columbia have well established universities and a network of colleges and technical schools, which offer a wide range of programmes and have recently become extremely flexible in allowing adult, part-time students to participate. Through flexible scheduling and admission requirements, these institutions have become accessible to a wide range of people. Why then did distance education develop as an option in these provinces?

One answer to this question is related to the geographical distribution of potential students and the growing importance of providing government-supported services to them. It is clear that both Alberta and British Columbia have residents spread over an extremely wide area. A network of regional colleges was established to provide postsecondary opportunity but it soon became clear that such an approach still had drawbacks. First, the cost of regional colleges and expanded universities is extremely high. Second, once in place, such institutions often develop conventional scheduling, admissions and instructional policies which do not meet the needs of many of the people in their region. Third, the range of courses and programmes that can be supported by a particular institution is also limited by budget and available expertise. Finally, to many leaders in government and education it became clear that many people in large urban centres were not being served by conventional institutions and their approach to education. What appeared to be needed was a complementary system that would appeal to the people who could not or would not be served by conventional institutions.

The implementation of this complementary, distance education system has resulted in a unique clientele. Given that the curricula at a majority of Canadian distance education institutions are similar to the curricula at their conventional counterparts, the clientele attracted to distance learning differs from the clientele at conventional institutions. For example, the distance learners at Athabasca University are older than conventional undergraduate students. Most are not in a position to become full-time students.[1] It is clear that distance education serves a unique population of learners. That population tends to have a wider range of educational background, a wider range of prior educational experience (i.e., have attended more postsecondary institutions before enrolment in distance education), have a wider range of academic ability, and demonstrate a wider range of demographical and personal characteristics (for example, age range, sex ratio, family situations, work experience, etc.).

A review of the institutional reports from a large sample of the distance education colleges and universities in Canada reflects the view that the population is extremely varied and more heterogeneous than conventional college and university student populations. This is especially true with respect to age and previous work and educational experience. As will be discussed in the next section of this paper, it is also important to note that the amount of information about distance learners is limited and many institutions do not have data reflecting the characteristics and success of their distance learning population.

LEARNER CHARACTERISTICS AND SUCCESS: WHAT DOES THE DATA INDICATE?

In an effort to expand the data base on learner characteristics and success (which currently represents only a small percentage of the distance education literature), a letter was sent to a long list of people involved in distance learning (primarily at the postsecondary level) across Canada. This letter requested internal documents, working papers or even a summary of statistics addressing this issue.

Although almost everyone on the list replied, most of the responses indicated that data were not available. In some cases data collection was continuing and simply not ready for circulation. However, in the majority of cases there were no data available and apparently little effort being made to encourage the collection of data reflecting learner characteristics and success.

Based on the above, the reader should be wary of the summary of data presented in this paper and any conclusions drawn from those data. Moreover, as has been pointed out previously (Coldeway and Spencer 1980) there are a variety of ways of analysing data, measuring success, and reporting summary statistics reflecting completion rates and achievement levels. This problem is often magnified by the innovative nature of many distance education efforts. Such programmes are often eager to demonstrate success in order to survive and many of the conventional measures of success do not reflect the service these programmes provide to a unique clientele. Failures do not make good press and are therefore not available for inspection.

The lack of empirical support for the design, expansion and/or overall evaluations of distance education in Canada is clearly represented by the three major publications on distance education in Canada over the last six years. In 1979 a special issue of the *Canadian Journal of University Continuing Education* published a series of articles on distance education in Canada. With the exception of some general enrolment statistics at the University of Waterloo presented by the director of the correspondence programme at Waterloo, James D. Leslie, there was a notable lack of data presented. (Leslie 1979)

By 1983, perhaps as a response to Dennis D. Gooler's paper outlining a model for evaluating distance education programme (Gooler 1983) which also appeared in the special 1979 edition, the amount of published data grew. In another special issue on Canadian distance education, this time published in *Programmed Learning and Education Technology*, authors began to report some results. Richard Lewis reported achievement scores for students learning French on television (Using 'Sesame Street' segments to teach French) and talked about how teachers reacted to the programmes. (Lewis 1983) Unfortunately, the results had more to do with the effective use of educational television in the classroom than with distance education. Nevertheless, the data were impressive and suggested that potential distance educational delivery systems were capable of teaching effectively.

In another paper in the special issue of *Programmed Learning and Education Technology* (1983), Lamy and Henri (1983) report some general statistics on completion rates and learner characteristics obtained from the Télé-université. They report that most of the students (60%) come from regions in Quebec that have no university services. The average student was a woman 35 years of age, who already had a university degree. Most of the female students were teachers and a large percentage of the total enrolment were also teachers. They also report completion rates but fail to correlate completion rates with any of the student characteristics reported. They do mention that students who completed one or more than one course have a much higher probability of programme completion, and also indicate that there was no evident relationship between the number of failures and drop-outs and the estimated difficulty of the course.

The third publication on distance education in Canada appeared as an article in the *Canadian Journal of Higher Education* (1984). In a special article entitled 'University Distance Education in Canada', Smith, Daniel and Snowden (1984) review the contemporary distance education scene. Although they present some rather firm conclusions, they report no data nor refer to any. Without providing references, they suggest that 'evidence suggests that when an institution sets the pace of study, provides structure through scheduled events and deadlines and reinforces achievements on a unit by unit level, students are much more likely to succeed'. Although much of the conclusion makes intuitive sense, the lack of empirical support presented makes that conclusion rather difficult to accept. Moreover, they offer no firm definition of success against which their conclusion can be judged. They do, however, argue that decisions over matters like pacing, deadlines, and the general management of student learning is more a function of institutional values than the guidance by empirical research.

The published results over the last six years on distance education clearly reflect a bias towards non-empirical decisionmaking on the part of most institutions and programmes. It appears that the lack of empirical data only serves to encourage that trend to continue. Nobody appears willing or able to do the research needed to answer even basic questions about learner characteristics and success. It should be noted that such a trend is not solely a Canadian result, but appears world-wide. (see Coldeway 1982)

COMPARING THE SUCCESS OF DISTANCE LEARNERS BETWEEN INSTITUTIONS

Institutional boundaries have always been obstacles to researchers interested in comparing the effects of various institutional practices and policies. Distance education institutions are no exception. Few studies have systematically compared the effects of institutions on the behaviour of learners.

Working in conjunction with project REDEAL at Athabasca University (Coldeway 1980), Gail Crawford conducted a study which compared the completion rates of students at three institutions. (Crawford 1980) All three institutions (Athabasca University, the Open Learning Institute and North Island College) were using the same course package and delivering it according to institutional practice. Because all three institutions share common views on student admission (open admissions policies), the results indicate that student characteristics between institutions were similar: open admission tends to encourage a wide range of students and that students at all three institutions had a wide range of background, educational experience, reasons for enrolment, etc.

The measurement of completion rates between the three institutions yielded some interesting differences. The completion rates at the Open Learning Institute were more than twice (58% of the students completed) those at the other two institutions (Athabasca University and North Island College, 20% and 25% respectively). Although the completion rates at AU and NIC may have increased over time by up to 10 %, the results clearly indicate that the Open Learning Institute delivery system and policies were more conducive to course completion.

An analysis of the institutional variables which might influence completion rates indicated that pacing policies were probably the major difference between OLI and the other two institutions. OLI required a fixed start and end date for the course while the other institutions had a much more flexible start and end time. This factor influences student behaviour in two ways. First, only students who can meet the start and end dates tend to enrol in the course. The 'contract' between the institution and the student under this more strict pacing policy is clear: you begin at Point A and finish at Point B. Students who, for whatever reason, do not feel they can meet that schedule are not attracted by the course. Quite the opposite is generally the case with a continuous enrolment policy and 'go at your own pace' guidelines. Students can be attracted to the course simply because of the course content and are not put in touch with the course contingencies until they have already committed themselves. In other words, they may not be aware of what is required of them until they begin.

The second factor which influences completion rates under a stricter pacing schedule is the schedule itself. Students are less likely to procrastinate when deadlines are clear. Getting behind schedule makes it even more difficult to generate energy to continue and the flexible pacing system provides little guidance and encouragement to a student who has not worked on the course for a week or two. Our recent analysis of students who do not complete courses at Athabasca University clearly indicates that a large percentage of the non-completion group never really got started in the course. If the non-starts are eliminated from the statistics, the completion rate jumps significantly.

The importance of motivation in course completion is also demonstrated by several studies conducted at Athabasca University. Coldeway and Spencer (1980) analysed data from several courses offered by Athabasca University and attempted to correlate the performance of students in these courses with various demographic and personal factors about the students obtained from questions answered by students upon enrolment. None of the demographic or personal factors predicted course completion. However, the actual behaviour of the learner after enrolment was a very good indicator of eventual completion. Students who completed the first unit in the course had a good chance of completing the course and students who had demonstrated the ability to complete distance learning courses previously also were much more likely to complete a second course.

The above results are also consistent with results reported by Télé-université. (Landry 1982; 1983) Their results also indicate that most non-completers were first time enrollers. However, their data also indicate that previous college and university experience was a predictor of course completion.

A recent study at Athabasca University examined, in detail, the factor which account for course completion. (Saraswati 1985) Again none of the personal or demographic factors were significantly related to completion.

In summary, the results suggest several important factors related to learner characteristics and success. First, distance learners tend to be a very heterogeneous group. Second, course completion does not tend to be a function of personal or demographic factors, but does appear to be influenced by motivational variables, many of which are directly related to the pacing and completion policies of the institution. Third, the actual behaviour of the learner after enrolment is one of the best predictors of course completion. Learners with demonstrated skills in independent learning have a much greater chance of completing the course even if the pacing contingencies are less strict. Fourth, the total number of non-completers is greatly influenced by the total number of students who never get started in the course. The non-start population is a significant and important factor in overall course completion rates. This explains the tendency of many institutions to eliminate non-starts from the statistics reported on completion rates under the assumption that non-starts are simply people with an interest in the institution rather than students (i.e., students are people who do work in the course). Finally, institutional reports indicate that students who complete courses perform well in the course. The failure rates, although difficult to calculate and compare across institutions due to differing grading policies, appear to be extremely low.

THE FACTORS WHICH INFLUENCE LEARNER SUCCESS

Figure 3 presents a model for looking at the factors which influence learner success. The model suggests that there are four major factors which influence the learner. For a given learner the importance of any one factor may override the importance of another. For example, a learner who must complete a course in order to meet degree or job related requirements may be influenced more by the factors in Box B than by any other factor. On the other hand, the data suggest that the factors in Box C may be critical to all learners and may often override other factors in terms of course completion. There is also evidence which indicated the importance of factors in Box D. (Williams 1980; Peruniak 1980; Coldeway and Spencer 1982)

It is important to note that all factors work together to influence the eventual success of the distance learner. Moreover, as was discussed earlier in this paper, course completion may not be the only or the best measures of success for a given institution, learner or course. Viewing success as a function of the multitude of factors may prove important in better understanding success in distance education. Conventional measures of success may not be as applicable to the distance education environment and the growing popularity of distance education may require that institutions become sensitive to the difference between that method and conventional ones.

Figure 3: The Factors Which Influence Learner Success

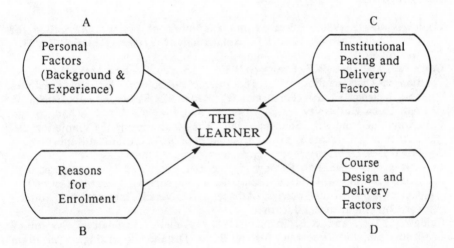

CONCLUSION

Although various forms of distance education have been going on for many years in Canada, the popularity and sophistication of distance education has steadily increased over the last twenty years. Perhaps it is too early to expect a significant and meaningful learner data base to be developed and analysed systematically. Moreover, there are few outlets for published experimental and evaluation efforts in Canada and this type of behaviour has tended to take a back seat to the efforts of developing courses, enrolling students, securing funding and establishing credibility.

The existing data base does speak to the importance of distance education with respect to reaching new clients. There is little doubt that Canadian distance education efforts have made access to educational opportunity possible for a wide ranging population of previously disadvantaged learners. Furthermore, the continued funding and growth of most Canadian distance educational institutions provide some evidence that they are meeting the needs of enough of their learners that the institution can be viewed as successful. What remains to be accomplished is the understanding of the details of that success, how it is specifically achieved for a given learner population and what it represents for future planning and development of innovative approaches to education.

NOTES

1. There are a number of distance learners who use the flexibility of the distance educational system to fill gaps in their full-time programmes conventional institutions. Although they are generally counted as distance learning students by their distance educational institutions, it is more accurate to describe them as students at another institution.

REFERENCES

Coldeway, D.O. (1980) 'Research and Evaluation of Distance Education for the Adult Learner: A Brief Explanation of Project REDEAL', *ICCE Newsletter*

Coldeway, D.O. and R.E. Spencer (1980) 'Factors Affecting Learner Motivation in Distance Education: The Interaction between Learner Attributes and Learner Course Performance', REDEAL Research Report No. 9, Athabasca University

Coldeway, D.O. and R.E. Spencer (1980) 'The Measurement of Completion and Attrition in Distance Learning Courses', REDEAL Technical Report No. 8, Athabasca University

Coldeway, D.O. (1982) 'A Review of Recent Research on Distance Learning', in J.S. Daniel, M.A. Stroud, and J.R. Thompson (eds.) *Learning at a Distance: A World Perspective*, Athabasca University/International Council for Correspondence Education

Coldeway, D.O. and R.E. Spencer (1982) 'Keller's Personalised System of Instruction: The search for a Basic Distance Learning', *Paradigm Distance Education, 3*

Crawford, G. (1981) 'Student Completion Rates Under Three Different Pacing Conditions', REDEAL Research Report No. 12, Athabasca University

Gooler, D.D. (1979) 'Evaluating Distance Education Programs', *Canadian Journal of University Continuing Education, 1*

Knowles, M.S. (1970) *The Modern Practice of Adult Education: Androgogy Versus Pedagogy*, New York, Association Press

Knox, A.B. (1980) *Adult Development and Learning*, San Francisco, Jossey-Bass, Inc.

Lamy, T. and F. Henri (1983) 'Télé-université: Ten Years of Distance Education in Quebec', *Programmed Learning and Educational Technology, 20*

Landry, F. (1982) 'L'Horaire de Travail des Etudiants et des Etudiantes dans les Certificates Chem et Ches de la Télé-université', Rapport de Recherche, Télé-université

Landry, F. (1983) 'Les Etudiants qui suivent un Seul Cours à la Télé-université', Bureau de la Recherche at du Developpement Pedagogique, Télé-université

Landry, F. (1983) 'Les Etudiants qui suivent un Seul Cours à la Télé-université', Bureau de la Recherche at du Developpement Pedagogique, Télé-université

Leslie, J.D. (1979) 'The University of Waterloo Model for Distance Education', *Canadian Journal of University Continuing Education, 6*

Lewis, R.F. (1983) 'Using Canadian Sesame Street Segments in Elementary Classrooms to teach French', *Programmed Learning and Educational Technology, 20*

Peruniak, G. (1980) 'Seminars as an Instructional Strategy in Distance Education', REDEAL Research Report No. 6, Athabasca University

Saraswati, D.K. (1985) 'An Analysis of the Performances of Successful Students in a Distance Education Course', personal communication

Smith, W.A.S., J.S. David, and B.L. Snowden (1984) 'University Distance Education in Canada', *Canadian Journal of Higher Education, 14*

Williams, V. (1980) 'Research and Evaluation of the Tutor Skills Program', REDEAL Research Report No. 4, Athabasca University

Research in Canadian Distance Education

Jocelyn Calvert

'Continuing education can set models for the university of the future.'

(Bernard Shapiro at the annual conference of the Canadian Association for University Continuing Education, London, Ontario, 1984)

'Distance education will be the primary mode of university education in the future.'

(Tony Bates, UKOU, at the Newthink Conference, University of British Columbia, Vancouver, 1984)

Distance education is a central element in the 'revolution of rising expectations in continuing education'. (Guinsberg 1981) The last few years have seen rapid increases in programmes and enrolments across the country and the adoption of new technologies for development and delivery of courses. (Smith *et al.* 1984) To some, distance education holds promise as a cost-effective way to deliver education to scattered populations. To others who espouse traditional approaches, the term 'distance education' is a contradiction in terms.

The opinions of both supporters and detractors about many aspects of distance education are based largely on intuitions, unsupported assumptions and casual observations. As Gooler stated the problem:

Distance education advocates and adversaries ... tend to argue their claims relatively free of data. Thoughtful university faculty and administrators are thus confronted with the task of sorting through claims and counterclaims in an effort to make intelligent decisions about whether, or how best, to adopt a distance education program for their institution. (1979:43)

Although many advances in knowledge have been made since these words were written, important questions remain. Those of us committed to the idea and practice of distance education must realise the importance of documenting, analysing and evaluating every one of our cherished beliefs if our enterprise is to achieve its potential.

The questions and issues surrounding distance education are diverse and numerous. On the educational side, we are concerned with defining student populations and designing appropriate curricula, with instructional design and academic quality, with the provision of student support services, and with choices among communications technologies. On the administrative side, we must address the economics of distance education, the design of institutional structures and their staffing, and the marketing of programmes and relationships among institutions. Distance education is not a single subject but a type of system, and we should encourage researchers from a broad range of disciplines to apply their special knowledge to the questions we face. The study of distance education must be interdisciplinary or multi-disciplinary.

THE ENVIRONMENT FOR DISTANCE EDUCATION RESEARCH

While distance education is by no means confined to public academic institutions, it is these, with their research traditions, that we might reasonably expect to address the central questions concerning distance education. The question is whether the climate of our universities is conducive to distance education research. To begin with, our academic institutions are not noted for their systematic self-analysis or for defining goals and evaluating achievements as they relate to the educational needs of society, except perhaps in the production of statistics for provincial governments and Statistics Canada. Pedersen and Fleming commented, 'Cynically, it could be suggested that not only are universities unclear about where they are going, but they are at least equally unclear regarding what they are doing while they are getting there'. (1981:5)

Not only do our academic communities fail to examine their own structures and processes, but there is also evidence that they do not value such research. Review of research funded by such national granting agencies as the Social Sciences and Humanities Research Council indicates that educational research in general is seriously under-represented. (Andrews and Rogers 1982) Furthermore, according to Pedersen and Fleming, 'the study of continuing education is perceived by faculty as an area of endeavor which is academically second-rate'. (1981:7) Since distance education is usually treated in the broader context of continuing education, the implications must be that first-rate researchers normally will not be attracted to the study of distance education and, when they are, they may have difficulty obtaining financial and institutional support.

Academic institutions have also tended to devalue the activities of the continuing education divisions that administer their distance education programmes, treating them as marginal to their central purposes (Devlin 1982) and according them a status that is 'questionable at best'. (Pedersen and Fleming 1981:7) Their role clearly is not seen as research-oriented, since only half of the professional staff in continuing education units hold faculty appointments, only one-third have doctoral degrees and half engage in no research whatsoever. (Bains 1985) Bains also noted that the vast majority of graduate degrees held by adult educators are in fields other than adult education.

Having thus created marginal units with few resources, excessive workloads, low status and, in many cases, a requirement to be self-supporting, the academic community can, not surprisingly, justify denial of academic respectability on grounds summarised by Pedersen and Fleming:

... the failure of students (of continuing education) to conceptualize this applied area adequately; a lack of success by continuing education personnel to define their campus role properly; the absence of professional identity for this group; a dearth of quality research in this field; considerable variability in the range and standards of graduate programs across the country; and, the ever-present differences in disciplinary perspectives between academics and adult educators. (1981:7)

While the discussions cited here refer to continuing education in general, there is no reason to believe that there exists a better research climate for distance education or that the issue facing distance education are being addressed adequately through research. Ljosa (1980) observed that the bulk of research derives from three sources: strong institutions with large research units, scattered individuals with a special interest in the field, and specially funded major projects. Coldeway (1982a) identified shortages of funding, publication outlets and researchers in his review of recent research. Calvert commented on the practical difficulties of carrying out research programmes:

Distance educators, the ones who know their systems well, usually are newcomers to the field and have their roots in other disciplines; even when they do have solid research skills, they still must 'retool' for this new research area. Furthermore, the emphasis in distance education systems is on doing, not contemplation; most people in the field are administrators carrying a heavy workload. When special research units are established, they generally serve administration and focus on practical day-to-day issues. (1984:1)

Not surprisingly, reviewers with an international perspective typically have been critical of the quality and quantity of research (Childs 1969; Ljosa 1980), and some have commented further that most of what is written is not research at all. (Coldeway 1982a; Calvert and Timmers 1984; Moore 1985) Moore, in a presentation to the European Home Study Council, stated the situation:

We have to admit to only a handful of good projects which produce reliable, generalisable and useful information, a fair amount of work worth giving attention to (but only with great caution because of its weak method), and a massive volume of amateur, unsystematic and badly designed research producing information of very little general value. (1985:36)

Canadians, who have reported relatively little research, have been prolific in their accounts of what they do in their programmes and institutions but often provide few details about effectiveness. This type of reporting may be useful in describing the dimensions of systems and suggesting new approaches, but it also has the potential danger of according apparent legitimacy to questionable assumptions and practices.

However discouraging this account may sound, such constraints need not be a deterrent to research activity (see, for example, Ingalls 1982, and his description of how Mount St Vincent University multiplied its outside research grants by 4,000 per cent in 9 years). They do suggest, however, that we look for simple and economical ways of addressing questions. To do so would not even be bucking the trend in social science research. Trent (1984), who documented a 25 per cent decline in social science research funding between 1974 and 1980, noted that 'Canadian researchers have had to adjust their research style to accommodate low levels of funding.' He also called for attention to be focused on the development of 'effective problem-oriented applied methodology'.

DEFINING A RESEARCH AGENDA

The Research and Development Committee of the newly established Canadian Association for Distance Education (CADE) carries, as one of its terms of reference, a mandate 'to define basic and applied research needs as they pertain to distance education in Canada'. Elsewhere, in a section concerned with the establishment of a research inventory, the committee identifies priorities: 'with special emphasis on technology (equipment and devices), curriculum development, and teaching and learning'. Publications by Canadians also suggest that at least two of these topics, new technologies and teaching and learning, are central preoccupations and are logically the major candidate for intensive research. In fact, since most discussions of technology focus on its application to teaching and learning, the conclusion can be drawn that Canadian distance educators, reflected in the CADE terms of reference, are concerned primarily with aspects of the instructional process.

In this chapter I would like to recommend a broader approach, the recognition of all of the issues and concerns surrounding distance education and the encouragement of any well-defined research projects that promise to address these issues. Administrators faced with justifying funding for programmes not only wish to know how effective their programmes are in the academic sense and how they can be improved, but also need information about efficiency and organisational matters in a system that, in some of its forms, changes the nature of teaching and of the institution. Bains (1985) was critical of the fact that many adult educators do not have formal training in adult education, but this is not necessarily a disadvantage. Because the study of distance education is a multi-disciplinary enterprise, researchers with backgrounds in economics, business administration, psychology, sociology, geography and a variety of other disciplines may fruitfully apply their own perspectives to the outstanding questions (see, for example, Schell and Thornton's 1985 application of an exchange model to the study of student commitment to media programmes).

Organising the distance education literature into a useful set of topics is a confusing task. Student demography, learning styles, tutorial systems and dropout, for example, may be treated as discrete topics, but they are also interrelated and may be dealt with in the same research paper. Figure 1 puts many of the elements of distance education in a framework designed to assist conceptualisation.[1]

Elements are construed as input, process and outcome variables. Input variables are those characteristics of the environment or of the student population that must be taken into account in the design and running of a distance education system. Process variables concern decisions made about development and delivery. Outcome variables are the products of a distance education system that may be used to assess effectiveness and efficiency.

The design of research, or of a system for that matter, generally proceeds from left to right. We may use information about learning styles (an input variable) in the design of tutorial systems (a process variable), or we may directly measure the relationship between learning styles and student dropout (an outcome variable) or between different tutorial systems and student dropout. In a different type of example, institutional policies may influence the choice of instructional media, thereby affecting the cost of the system.

This conceptual framework makes no reference to theories, paradigms or models for a simple reason. Virtually every element can be connected to a body of literature or a research methodology in some discipline. For every question we choose to address, something exists that can inform our study. The only problem is to know where to look or who to ask. Analytical discussion papers (for example, Coldeway 1982b; Vazquez-Abad and Mitchell 1983; Thompson 1984; Howard 1985) are important precursors to effective research on some topics, as are discussions of appropriate research methods (for example, Minnis 1985). In other areas, where straightforward practical questions are at issue, careful observation and reporting may be all that is required.

Figure 1: Conceptual Framework for Distance Education Research

INPUT VARIABLES	PROCESS VARIABLES	OUTCOME VARIABLES
Student	*Development*	*Student*
educational background	curriculum	enrolment
perceived needs	development model	academic progress
motivation	design of instruction	academic
learning style	media	performance
study environment	course workload	use of materials
System	pacing	and services
national requirements	production procedures	dropout
institutional policy	*Delivery*	*System*
financial resources	recruitment methods	development
technological resources	academic support	efficiency
human resources	formal feedback	cost
geography		effectiveness
		acceptance in the
		system

However, whether we are addressing theoretical issues or simply attempting to answer simple practical questions, we should keep in mind another of Moore's observations: 'I believe the convention of reporting previous research as preface to current research is too neglected today, and many of the projects which are reported would have benefited if more effort had been put into grounding them in that way.' (1985:37)

This criticism is offset by an editors' note to a recent article containing twenty-seven references: 'The writer provided a much more extensive bibliography than that published here. As editors we culled it. The list is still extensive enough to provide access to the wider reading the author listed.' (Howard 1985:185)

Lists of variables in a conceptual framework illustrate the range of topics that research may address. However, a review requires consolidation. In the following sections, I draw primarily from Canadian sources to present a selection of general subjects that Canadian distance educators have identified as worthy of attention. This broad, issues-oriented approach ensures omissions, particularly since I have relied primarily on the published literature. It also requires illustrations based on unsystematic observation, since little or no research has been reported on some of the topics. Limitations of space have also precluded linking Canadian work to the international literature. By taking this approach, I am applauding the recent spate of reviews and research exemplified in a recent issue of *Distance Education* (1985:2) where five articles by Canadian-based writers are published. Four are conceptual papers and one reports research.

STUDENTS AND CURRICULA

While it may be unfair to ignore provincial correspondence programmes which have been teaching large numbers of primary and secondary students for many years, the clientele which has brought distance education to prominence is the adult learner who is prepared to enrol in some type of formal part-time education, whether credit or non-credit. The task distance educators face is to identify appropriate target groups, determine the special requirements of these groups and develop appropriate curricula and delivery methods to meet their needs, and market them effectively. Canadians have not reported the detailed sort of market analysis and follow-up conducted by the Netherlands Open University (van Enckewort 1984, 1985), but two examples illustrate approaches to planning for new institutions and new programmes.

Ellis and Mugridge (1983), in their case study of the Open Learning Institute, reported the use of census data, provincial enrolment data, the experience of other distance education programmes and at least one specific study to estimate the demand for different types of programmes defined by the institute's mandate. Three-year follow-up data attested to the validity of many of the predictions but produced a few surprises. Curtis and Bakshi (1984) conducted a market survey by mail to determine the demand for a natural resources planning and management programme, sampling employers, educators and two types of prospective student. An interesting feature of this study is the observation that the various groups and subgroups responded differently to questions about need and usefulness and the type of credential that should be offered. These studies illustrate the complexity of needs assessment and, in the case of the latter, the possible danger of basing decisions on input from a single group. They also provide specific information about the type of student who has been, or might be, attracted to distance programmes.

Demographic data are often reported in published descriptions of programmes and collection and dissemination of this kind of information can assist others who are looking for guidance in programme planning. However, we should be cautious in drawing conclusions from isolated sets of statistics. In Canada there is a broad range of distance programmes that can be expected to enrol different types of students. We also have a plethora of institutional systems, instructional strategies, delivery methods and marketing techniques, all of which may be reflected in enrolment profiles. In fact, because of this diversity, Canada may provide the most fertile ground in the world for teasing out the influence of different factors on student participation.

LEARNING AT A DISTANCE

The object of distance education is student accomplishment, defined variously as persistence, performance on assessment measures, satisfaction and achievement of long-term goals. Research focuses on two general topics, learning styles and their implications for the design of instruction, and the motivating effects of instructional systems. A related interest, most often expressed by detractors, is the academic quality of education in a system where student and teacher do not necessarily meet face-to-face (although Moore 1985, implied, tongue in cheek, that this issue might have been laid to rest in 1929).

Theory and research on learning at a distance have drawn from both behavioural and cognitive paradigms. Project REDEAL, a multi-faceted research project carried out at Athabasca University, focused on the 'management and motivation' of distant learners (see Coldeway 1982a, for an overview) and tested the effects of a number of interventions on student persistence. Among these were immediate test feedback (Coldeway and Spencer 1982), paced instruction (Crawford 1980), optional seminars (Peruniak 1984) and contact between institution and student (Peruniak 1983). In an unrelated study, Scales (1984) investigated the relationship between student- and tutor-initiated telephone contact and persistence in a course. This approach is summed up by the statement that 'contingencies of reinforcement are important for adult learners who are volunteer participants in the learning environment'. (Coldeway 1982b:92)

Some writers have taken a less mechanistic approach in addressing the need to provide interaction while fostering the development of independent learning skills. (Daniel and Marquis, 1979; Forsythe 1983; Daniel 1983) Attention to intrapersonal variables leads naturally to consideration of individual differences in dependence (Thompson 1984) and how knowledge about learning needs and styles can guide instructional design and study skills programmes. (Burge 1984; Fales and Burge 1984; Howard 1985) Clearly, research in this area must draw heavily on the already substantial literatures in adult development, adult learning, instructional design and cognitive psychology. How these bodies of knowledge can be translated into effective course design and effective delivery systems is the important question.

TEACHERS AT A DISTANCE

Distance teaching in Canada follows either an extended system model whose goal is to recreate the classroom experience or a transformed system model in which the elements of the teaching process are broken down and restructured in new formats. The extent to which the job of teaching at a distance requires special adjustments by instructors depends on the teaching model employed.

The extended system takes the lecture or seminar to students in remote locations by means of some form of communications technology and, in some cases, duplicating campus instruction is a primary goal. (Ellis and Chapman 1982) While this may involve little more than the recording of lectures on audiotapes (Leslie 1979), most often teaching is interactive, providing direct communication between instructor and groups of students. It therefore takes place at fixed times with continuing faculty involvement and in some cases it also requires fixed classroom spaces at the remote sites.

Of any form of distance education, extending the classroom to remote locations most resembles traditional face-to-face instruction. It demands the least adjustment of teaching philosophy and teaching practice on the part of faculty. However, the introduction of any form of mediating technology requires an instructor to learn new skills to use the technology and compensate for missing cues. (Forsythe 1983) When he analysed his experience with audio teleconferencing, Jeffery (1983) reported personal experiences and the results of student evaluations. Burge *et al.* (1984) evaluated a coast-to-coast workshop and suggested some important features required for successful teleconference instruction. Catchpole and MacGregor (1984) commented on the characteristics of successful live-interactive telecourse broadcasts.

In the second model of distance teaching, the transformed system, the instructor's voice, literally speaking, is no longer the primary guide for students' study, and teaching becomes a two-step process. Subject matter is presented in different instructional formats, often guided by formal principles of instructional design. The base is generally print, but it may be supplemented by audiotapes, audiographics, videotapes and more sophisticated technological media. If elements of the extended classroom are included, they are not the central feature of instruction and, where they are optional, students may choose not to participate. (Peruniak 1984)

In course development, the first stage of this model, the central issue is how to develop effective courses efficiently. Effective courses result from the application of principles of learning and motivation and on the appropriate selection of media. Efficiency, from the teaching perspective, means keeping time and conflict to a minimum. These concepts are set in perspective when we consider that producing instruction for distance education requires from two times to three hundred times more academic time, depending on the medium, than preparing for classroom instruction. (Sparkes 1984) It is also a new experience for most faculty who are accustomed to face-to-face teaching with few resources and without collaboration or interference. Canadians have written little about the course development process except for some descriptions of institutional practices and some prescriptions for course development planning. These provide some suggestions about what we should look at more closely.

The obvious first step in course development is to define the instructional possibilities and establish procedures for decisionmaking. Rogers (1982) and Vazquez-Abad and Mitchell (1983) have described systems models for planning that take into account a variety of input and process variables. Implicit in a system approach is the requirement for technical assistance with course planning, design and production. Smith *et al.* (1984) marked acceptance of instructional design approaches in distance education as a new achievement in university teaching, and Fales and Burge (1984) suggested that the smallest acceptable course team consists of subject specialist and instructional designer working in partnership. Timmers and LeCouteur (1985) reported successful collaboration of course writer, course designer and academic consultant using flexible, microcomputer-based course authoring templates and electronic transmission of documents. Among the benefits they cited were substantial time savings, ease of revision and general goodwill fostered by the process.

This rosy picture is clouded slightly by other observations. Smith *et al.* commented that relations between academics and instructional designers may sometimes be difficult and that 'the courses produced as a result of such co-operation are (not always) of optimum quality.' (1984:80) Crawford and Crawford (1984) noted tendencies for course writers to relegate instructional designers to the role of cosmeticians for finished manuscripts and for institutions to evolve design formulae based on rigid application of a small set of principles. It appears that, on the one hand, we need to develop techniques and institutional strategies for managing academic course developers to ensure that acceptable standards are applied; this may involve, in part, a question of power. On the other hand, we must also try to encourage a flexible approach to design that accommodates different learning requirements and adapts to new technologies; this involves, in part, continuing study and experimentation.

The extra effort required in the development of distance education courses pays off when the same materials can be used to teach any number of students at any number of different institutions. The creator of the course need not be involved in delivery, and the tutor who deals with students 'ceases to be the master of the content and must become the guide, mentor and catalyst to aid the student's journey through a pre-structured or open-ended learning experience'. (Forsythe 1983:163) Communicating with distant students requires special skills for which training may be provided. (Williams 1980; Cochran and Meech 1982; Sturrock 1983; Kaufman 1984a) This is an area that would benefit from further attention by researchers.

Forsythe emphasised the positive side of distance tutoring and stressed that lifelong learning systems may increase opportunities for instructors. However, there are other aspects to tutoring that should not be ignored, and several descriptions of Canadian tutorial systems provide background for an assessment (for example, Daniel and Meech 1978; Salter 1982; Lamy and Henri 1983; Ellis and Mugridge 1983; Sturrock 1983). First, tutors often are isolated not only from their students but also from their institutions and one another. Second, while they may have impressive academic qualifications, tutors usually are part of a category of worker that has been growing in the Canadian labour force: the part-time employee who works for low pay without benefits. Third, when modern distance education makes heavy use of electronic systems for administration, with concomitant ease of data gathering, tutors may be subject to more monitoring and management than their campus-based counterparts (see, for example, Coldeway 1980, and Scales 1984). Finally, fixing in advance the instructional materials on which students are evaluated restricts the freedom of tutors to modify, elaborate and disagree, all normal functions of an academic.

These conditions may be perfectly acceptable to people who, through family or career considerations, are not looking for full-time employment and the rewards of classroom teaching. They are also classic elements that contribute to alienation from work. Calvert (1982) found few symptoms of such alienation in a study conducted during the early days of Open Learning Institute. However, more research is required to ensure that we are not establishing unsatisfying job ghettos for teachers while expanding flexible learning systems for students.

SUPPLEMENTARY SUPPORT SERVICES

Campus-based students have access to bookstores, libraries, academic advisers, counsellors and learning assistance programmes, but there is little research on what services are provided for students studying at a distance, how services are best provided and to what extent students use them. In one study of use, the majority of students reported that they had not consulted an adviser about their academic programmes or learning problems. (Durward and Durward 1983) A recent unpublished survey of library services offered by Canadian institutions for off-campus students found wide varia- tions in support. (Slade and Webb 1985) Elsewhere are descriptions of a regional advising system (Meakin 1982), a tutor-adviser approach that provides assistance with both course content and study skills (Salter 1982), and an audio-tutorial programme to assist students with reading and study skills. (Howard 1985) Miskiman (1983, 1984) has written about concepts relevant to distance education counselling. Research in this area should establish what students feel they need, how and how much they use services when they are provided, and in what ways the needs and behaviour patterns of students in distance education programmes differ from those of on-campus students. All three are important considerations in effective decisionmaking.

TECHNOLOGY FOR INSTRUCTION

The greatest bulk of Canadian publications in the field of distance education consist of descriptions of the use of telecommunication technologies for instruction. Canadian educators clearly have been experimenting enthusias- tically with a range of media and found them appealing. Such enthusiasm is not surprising when we consider that telecommunications substitute most often for travelling faculty who formerly delivered lectures to small groups of students in distant communities. More students in more places can be served and this, in fact, is how the extended system operates. It has the advantage of bringing groups of students together with an instructor and the disadvantage of restricting the location and time for educational interac- tions. Shobe (1983) has given an overview of current technologies, some criteria for selection and a substantial bibliography. Burge, Wilson and Mehler (1984) provide another review of communications technology in Canadian distance education.

Perhaps more challenging than the question of how to use telecommuni- cations to extend the classroom is the issue of how to use new technology in the transformed system. Daniel (1983) reversed an earlier position that computer-assisted instruction and other forms of programmed feedback lack interactive qualities, citing Baath's (1982) report that students not only benefited from, but actually preferred, carefully constructed computer feedback on their work. Audiographic exercises, videocassettes that the student can stop and start as required, microcomputer programmes and videodiscs linked to computers are some examples of technologies that can provide rich educational supplements for independent learners (see Bates

1984a, for descriptions of available technologies with assessments of their advantages and disadvantages). Garrison criticised as extravagant our most commonly used electronic medium in distance education, the student-tutor telephone conversation, and advocated abandonment of 'the restrictive view that interaction is mediated person to person communication'. (1985:238) I record this comment despite the fact that some of the statements in this paragraph contradict his broader thesis that computer-based instruction is the only technology that can simulate interaction. We need to explore further the meaning of interaction in learning systems.

OTHER USES OF COMPUTER TECHNOLOGY

Smith *et al.* commented that computers are used most in Canadian distance education not for instruction but 'in institutional recordkeeping and in the text processing aspects of preparing printed course materials'. (1984:80) Bates (1984b) relegated computer-assisted learning to fifth-place standing when he predicted the relative importance of different roles for the computer in distance education over the next ten years. More important, in his estimation, are the use of computers for administration, communications (between students and tutors and among staff), course production and student assessment. While we have not produced research on this subject, Mugridge (1985) has described institutional uses of computers in distance education and Kaufman (1984b) has addressed the subject of computer communications. Timmers and LeCouteur's (1985) course development illustration suggests a specific area for research.

INSTITUTIONAL POLICIES AND STRUCTURES

Smith *et al.* (1984) have described the different models for distance education found in the Canadian postsecondary system. These models encompass two types of institutional structure, distance teaching programmes in campus-based institutions and autonomous distance teaching institutions. While the issues facing the two are not entirely the same, both face organisational challenges with the expansion of distance education that are quite new to postsecondary education. Research can identify areas where policies are needed and suggest appropriate structures.

According to Smith *et al.*, 'distance education operations usually need to be highly centralised and require a much more directive style, analogous to that needed to operate say a high technology factory'. (1984:79) In a campus-based institution where the classroom model is still considered to be the norm, faculty may not enthusiastically support the goals of expanding the role of distance education and using modern technologies for development and delivery. They may also see centralisation as an erosion of their traditional authority over instructional matters. Even when they are supportive, questions about such things as teaching credit for development and delivery of non-traditional forms of instruction and the ownership of instructional materials must be resolved. Analysis of obstacles and successful models could contribute to the solution of this sort of question.

Autonomous distance teaching institutions whose mode of teaching is clearly defined avoid some of problems faced by campus-based programmes and are more likely to physically resemble the 'high technology factory' referred to above. However, the four Canadian institutions operating primarily at a distance (Athabasca University, Télé-université, North Island College and the Open Learning Institute) have created organisational models quite different from campus-based institutions and in some ways from one another. Perhaps the time has come to evaluate these models and draw some conclusions.

RELATIONSHIPS AMONG INSTITUTIONS

Crawford and Crawford (1982:183) surveyed the Canadian landscape and concluded that 'most distance education is developed within single institutions and with few exceptions, with neither knowledge of, nor consultation with, other institutions. The pattern is one of competition rather than cooperation.' They argued that economies of scale are essential to the provision of diverse and sophisticated programmes and services, and recommended that providers of distance education join forces in an interactive educational network to facilitate development and delivery.

Communications has improved nationally and regionally in the last few years. The Canadian Association for Distance Education links distance educators across the country. Regional mechanisms for information gathering and exchange have been established in the Maritimes, Ontario and Western Canada. While enthusiasm may account for some of this traffic, outside pressures cannot be discounted. The establishment of the Western Canadian Committee on University Distance Education was propelled by concerns expressed by provincial governments and university presidents 'over potential duplication of effort in the field of distance education'. (Mugridge 1983b:27) In a further development, the government of British Columbia has established an Open University Consortium, consisting of the four public degree granting institutions and the educational communications authority, to foster co-operation, minimise duplication and ensure availability of a range of university programmes throughout the province. (Yerbury 1985) On a smaller scale are examples of collaborative course development projects (see Mugridge 1983b, for some examples), a joint student status agreement between a community college and a university (Hart 1981), and increased sales and purchase of courses among institutions.

The goals of collaboration and co-operation are to increase educational opportunities, improve access, share technological resources, avoid duplication of effort and minimise total costs. While exploring different strategies, we should also be assessing the mechanism we are experimenting with, the obstacles we encounter and the effects of our efforts. Research can suggest where policies are required and also what policies are appropriate. In a minor example, Calvert (in press) assessed obstacles to course sharing among institutions and concluded that institutional barriers are at least as influential as academic barriers. The Western Canadian Committee on University Distance Education is currently surveying member institutions to determine institutional policies on course ownership and copyright, and preliminary results suggest considerable diversity. If this survey leads to some type of standardisation or to the revision of policies that prevent sale or purchase, one of the obstacles will have been overcome.

ECONOMICS

Financial considerations pervade every aspect of distance education, yet to date there has been only one Canadian article on the costs of distance education, Snowden and Daniel's (1980) comparative analysis of the cost of a small, autonomous distance teaching university. Smith *et al.* (1984) noted the expectation that the comparatively high cost of developing distance education materials is offset by low marginal costs for delivery once an optimum number of students has been served. However, they also cautioned that Canada's low population and fragmented educational system mitigate against the economies of scale that could make distance education truly cost effective. This is an area where more information is required.

Also important are the relative costs of different teaching methods, different types of programmes (especially those requiring special equipment and resources), and open enrolment systems with their higher than average dropout rates. Finally, we should not ignore the cost to students of studying part-time at home while remaining employed compared to giving up work and relocating for full-time study.

SUMMARY AND CONCLUSIONS

Canadian distance educators have described their systems in considerable detail and are moving towards move conceptual approaches and research, particularly in the area of student learning. However, many important subjects have received little critical attention and the climate for distance education research is not particularly congenial. Recent efforts to promote communication and co-operation among institutions hold considerable promise for the systematic definition of some organisational and administrative issues and their resolution. In addition, the Canadian Association for Distance Education is exploring ways of fostering research communication, focusing on the establishment of a journal, the development of a bibliographic database, and national teleconferences. All of these were recommended by Trent (1984) as ways of encouraging social science research.

If current enthusiasm is to bear fruit, our institutions must also look at the ways in which they can assist research endeavours. Some possibilities include establishing facilities and information access for distance education research, granting time to administrators for research activities, and providing mechanisms and encouragement for faculty members in different disciplines to apply their knowledge and skills to this applied area. Finally, we need to develop top quality educational programmes in this field and ensure that they are accessible to working practitioners as well as full-time students.

NOTES

1. I am indebted to Dr Weerayoudh Wichiarajote of Ramkamhaeng Open University in Thailand who suggested this method of conceptualising distance education variables at a meeting in Penang, Malaysia, in 1984.

REFERENCES

Andrews, J.H.M. and W.T. Rogers (eds.) (1982) *Canadian research in education: A state of the art review*, Social Sciences and Humanities Research Council of Canada, Ottawa

Baath, J.A. (1982) 'Experimental research on computer-assisted distance education' in J.S. Daniel, M.A. Stroud and J.R. Thompson (eds.) *Learning at a distance: A world perspective*, Athabasca University/International Council for Correspondence Education, Edmonton, Alberta

Bains, G.A. (1985) 'A profile of adult educators in Canadian universities', *Canadian Journal of University Continuing Education, 11*, 12-26

Bates, A.W. (1984) 'Selecting and designing low-cost media for distance education', Ziff Papiere 53, FernUniversität

Bates, A.W. (ed.) (1984) *The role of technology in distance education*, Croom Helm, Beckenham, Kent

Burge, E.J. (1984) 'Adult learning principles and distance learning design: Bridging some professional distances', *Open Campus, 9*, 7-25

Burge, E.J., J.M. Roberts and M.W. Waldron (1984) 'Audio-teleconferencing in continuing education: A case study with implications', *Canadian Journal of University Continuing Education, 10*, 20-31

Burge, E.J., J. Wilson and A. Mehler (1984) 'Communication and information technologies and distance education in Canada', *New technology in Canadian education, 5*

Calvert, J. (1982) Tutoring in the most industrialzed form of education, Paper presented at the annual convention of the American Educational Research Association, New York

Calvert, J. (1984) A perspective on distance education research, Paper presented at Working Group Meeting on Distance Education Research, Universiti Sains Malaysia

Calvert, J. (in press) 'Facilitating inter-institutional transfer of distance courses', *Open Learning*

Calvert, J. and S.F. Timmers (1984) A research agenda for distance education, Paper presented at the annual conference of the Canadian Association for University Continuing Education, London, Ontario

Catchpole, M.J. and A.A. MacGregor (1984) 'British Columbia's Knowledge Network: Macro and micro perspectives on the use of television in educational delivery', in L. Parker (ed.) *Teleconferencing and electronic communication III*, University of Wisconsin - Extension, Madison, Wisconsin

Childs, G.B. (1969) Report of the Chairman of the Committee on Research, Proceedings of the 8th International Conference, International Council for Correspondence Education, Paris, 40-58

Cochran, B.R. and A. Meech (1982) 'Training telephone tutors', in J.S. Daniel *et al.* (eds.), *Learning at a distance*, 143-8

Coldeway, D.O. (1980) An examination of tutor management strategies for use in distance education, REDEAL Research Report #2, Athabasca University

Coldeway, D.O. and R.E. Spencer (1982) 'Keller's Personalized System of Instruction: the search for a basic distance learning paradigm', *Distance Education, 3*, 51-71

Coldeway, D.O. (1982a) 'Recent research in distance learning', in J.S. Daniel *et al.* (eds.), *Learning at a distance*, 29-37

Coldeway, D.O. (1982b) 'What does educational psychology tell us about the adult learner at a distance?' in J.S. Daniel *et al*. (eds.), *Learning at a distance*, 90-3

Crawford, D.G. and G.C. Crawford (1982) 'From realities to plans', in J.S. Daniel *et al*., (eds.) *Learning at a distance*, 182-4

Crawford, D.G. and G.C. Crawford (1984) 'On-line or off-line courseware: the weakest link', *Computers and Education, 8*, 343-8

Crawford G. (1980) 'Student completion rates under three different pacing conditions', REDEAL Technical Report #11, Athabasca University

Curtis, F.A. and T.S. Bakshi (1984) 'Market research for a proposed natural resources planning and management program by home study', *Distance Education, 5*, 93-102

Daniel, J.S. (1983) 'Independence and interaction in distance education: New technologies for home study', *Programmed Learning and Educational Technology, 20*, 155-60

Daniel, J.S. and C. Marquis (1979) 'Independence and interaction: Getting the mixture right', *Teaching at a Distance, 15*, 29-44

Daniel, J.S. and A. Meech (1978) 'Tutorial support in distance Education', *Convergence, 11*, 93-8

Devlin, L.E. (1982) 'Marginality: Some conceptual approaches for university extension', *Canadian Journal of University Continuing Education, 8*, 4-9

Durward, G.W. and M.L. Durward (1983) A telephone survey of distance education students at the Open Learning Institute, Unpublished report, The Open Learning Institute

Ellis, G.B. and R.S. Chapman (1982) 'Academic equivalency of credit courses by teleconverence', in J.S. Daniel *et al*., (eds.) *Learning at a distance*, 276-8

Ellis, J.F. and I. Mugridge (1983) 'The Open Learning Institute of British Columbia: A case study', Distance Education Research Group Papers, The Open University, Number 8; excerpted in *Educational Media International, 3* (1984), 22-32

Van Enckevort, G. (1984) 'Problems of research for a new Open University', *Distance Education, 5*, 72-83

Van Enckevort, G. (1985) 'The Dutch Open University opened: An unexpected success', *International Council for Distance Education Bulletin, 7*, 28-34

Fales, A.W. and E.J. Burge (1984) 'Self-direction by design: Self-directed learning in distance course design', *Canadian Journal of University Continuing Education, 10*, 68-78

Forsythe, K. (1983) 'The human interface: Teachers in the new age', *Programmed Learning and Educational Technology, 20*, 161-6

Garrison, D.R. (1985) 'Three generations of technological innovations in distance education', *Distance Education, 6*, 235-41

Gooler, D.D. (1979) 'Evaluating distance education programs', *Canadian Journal of University Continuing Education, 6*, 43-55

Guinsberg, T.N. (1981) 'From the quagmire to the promised land: The unfinished agenda of university continuing education in Canada', *Canadian Journal of University Continuing Education, 8*, 15-25

Hart, R. (1981) 'Joint student status: An idea whose time has come?', *Canadian Journal of University Continuing Education, 8*, 51-3

Howard, D.C. (1985) 'Reading and study skills and the distance learner', *Distance Education, 6*, 169-88

Ingalls, W.B. (1982) 'Increasing research productivity in small universities: A case study', *Canadian Journal of Higher Education, 12*, 59-64

Jeffrey, G.H. (1983) 'Multipoint teleconference and regular classroom teaching', *Canadian Journal of University Continuing Education, 9*, 18-23

Kaufman, D. (1984a) 'Practice and theory of distance education: Course blueprint', *Distance Education, 5*, 239-51

Kaufman, D. (1984b) 'A computer-based instructional system for distance education', *Computers in Education, 8*, 479-84

Lamy, T. and F. Henri (1983) 'Télé-université: Ten years of distance education in Quebec', *Programmed Learning and Educational Technology, 20*, 197-201

Leslie, J.D. (1979) 'The University of Waterloo model for distance education', *Canadian Journal of University Continuing Education, 6*, 33-41

Ljosa, E. (1980) 'Some thoughts on the state of research in distance education', *Distance Education, 1*, 99-102

Meakin, D. (1982) 'The role of regional centres', in J.S. Daniel *et al.* (eds.), *Learning at a distance*, 157-9

Minnis, J.R. (1985) 'Ethnography, case study, grounded theory, and distance education research', *Distance Education, 6*, 189-98

Miskiman, D. (1983) 'The nature of counselling in distance education', *International Council for Distance Education Bulletin, 2*, 42-3

Miskiman, D. (1984) 'Communication effectiveness in distance education counselling', *International Council for Distance Education Bulletin, 5*, 43-6

Moore, M.G. (1985) 'Some observations on current research in distance education', *Epistolodidaktika, 1*, 35-62

Mugridge, I. (1983) 'Consortia in distance education: Some Canadian ventures', *Open Campus, 8*, 22-9

Mugridge, I. (1985) 'Applications of computer technology in distance education: The case of the Open Learning Institute,' *Canadian Journal of Educational Communication, 14*, 6-7

Pedersen, K.G. and T. Fleming (1981) 'The academic organization and continuing education', *Canadian Journal of University Continuing Education, 7*, 4-9

Peruniak, G.S. (1983) 'Interactive perspectives in distance education: A case study', *Distance Education, 4*, 63-79

Peruniak, G.S. (1984) 'The seminar as an instructional strategy in distance education', *British Journal of Educational Technology, 15*, 107-24

Rogers, K.V. (1982) 'Identifying an effective and efficient distance education system', *Canadian Journal of University Continuing Education, 8*, 37-42

Salter, D. (1982) 'Mobile learning centres in an Open learning system', in J.S. Daniel *et al.*, (eds.), *Learning at a distance*, 154-6

Scales, K. (1984) 'A study of the relationship between telephone contact and persistence', *Distance Education, 5*, 268-76

Schell, B.H. and J.A. Thornton (1985) 'A media course commitment study in a Canadian university: Empirical validation of an exchange model', *Distance Education, 6*, 209-22

Shobe, C.R. (1983) 'Telecommunication technologies and distance education: A report on recent Canadian initiatives', *Open Campus, 8*, 5-21

Slade, S. and B. Webb (1985) Canadian off-campus library services survey, Unpublished report, University of Victoria

Smith, W.A.S., J.S. Daniel and B.L. Snowden (1984) 'University distance education in Canada', *Canadian Journal of Higher Education, 14*, 75-81

Snowden, B.L. and J.S. Daniel (1980) 'The economics and management of small post-secondary distance education systems', *Distance Education, 1*, 68-91

Sparkes, J. (1984) 'Pedagogic differences between media', in A.W. Bates (ed.), *The role of technology in distance education*, Croom Helm, Beckenham, Kent, 207-22

Sturrock, J. (1983) 'Tutor training', *Distance Education, 4*, 108-12

Thompson, G. (1984) 'The cognitive style of field-dependence as an explanatory construct in distance education dropout', *Distance Education, 5*, 286-93

Timmers, S.F. (in press) 'Microcomputers in course development', *Programmed Learning and Educational Technology*

Timmers, S.F. and P. LeCouteur (1985) Microcomputer-based course authoring templates, Paper presented at 13th World Conference, International Council for Distance Education, Melbourne

Trent, J.E. (1984) 'Social science research in Canada: The next step forward/La recherche en sciences sociales au Canada: L'étape suivante', *The Canadian Journal of Higher Education, 14*, 1-8

Vasquez-Abad, J. and P.D. Mitchell (1983) 'A systems approach to planning a tele-education system', *Programmed Learning and Educational Technology, 20*, 202-9

Williams, V. (1980) Research and evaluation of tutor skills training project, Athabasca University, REDEAL Research Report #7

Yerbury, J.C. (1985) 'The Open University Consortium of British Columbia: What are the implications for Simon Fraser University?', *International Council for Distance Education Bulletin, 9*, 43-8

Consortia in Canadian Distance Education

Abram G. Konrad and James M. Small

Distance education is not a new concept. In fact, it is as old as correspondence education - an arrangement which has provided learning for thousands of students in all corners of the world (see, for example, Daniel 1982). Nor is the concept of consortia a recent innovation in postsecondary education as, from the early beginnings of university education in North America and elsewhere, formal arrangements for collaboration between institutions have been quite commonplace. As an example, the University of London, through its external degree programme, forged formal ties with colonial universities throughout the British Commonwealth. In the face of economic constraints, political pressures and technological developments, a new interest has developed in formalising arrangements between universities, colleges and other public agencies to become partners in distance education. This chapter focuses on these arrangements and explores their potential as facilitative mechanisms for distance education.

CONSORTIA IN POSTSECONDARY EDUCATION

Collaboration between institutions occurs at three levels, depending upon the extent of formalisation. Informal agreements and *ad hoc* arrangements which have been beneficial to both institutions result in formal arrangements. The highest level of collaboration is reached when a new structure or organisation is created to manage the mutual interests of the institutions, such as an agency for needs analysis, production and marketing of materials for partner institutions. The concept of a consortium, whether or not the actual term is used, fits the third level of collaboration.

Moore (1968:175) defines a postsecondary consortium as 'an arrangement whereby two or more institutions - at least one of which is an institution of higher education - agree to pursue between, or among them, a programme for strengthening academic programmes, improving administration, or providing for other special needs'. There is also an important element of enlightened self-interest behind the creation of any consortium. Martin (1981) emphasises that if the chief purpose of a consortium is anything other than 'to serve members' needs', the consortium is doomed to failure through misunderstandings and misguided priorities.

Structure

Structurally, a consortium is characterised by a voluntary formal organisation, two or more member institutions, multi-academic programmes, at least one professional administrator, and an annual contribution or other tangible evidence of commitment of members. (Patterson 1977) Academic consortia have taken a wide variety of forms, each adapting itself to its particular set of circumstances, and no single prototype has emerged as the 'one best way'. However, it is possible to group consortia into four categories, as described by Martin (1981):

1. homogeneous institutions serving a specific purpose;
2. heterogeneous institutions serving a specific purpose;
3. homogeneous institutions serving a general purpose; and
4. heterogeneous institutions serving a general purpose.

The homogeneous special-purpose consortium is established by similar institutions to serve one specific need or purpose, such as operating a research facility too expensive for any one partner to maintain. An example is the Marine Science Consortium in Pennsylvania, which, with thirteen member-institutions, operates two co-operative marine stations.

Heterogeneous special-purpose consortia are made up of a mixture of dissimilar institutions which co-operate to provide one special service or serve one particular need. The mixture of institutions in a single consortium may include government or private agencies, universities, colleges - public or private - and others. An example is the Pacific Northwest International/ Intercultural Education Consortium which has a variety of members in three states and Canada. Together, these institutions provide opportunities for faculty and students to study abroad in a variety of programmes.

The homogeneous general-purpose consortium is one in which similar institutions co-operate to provide a wide range of services and to share each other's strengths. This type of consortium is found among small liberal arts colleges as well as among major universities. An example of the former is the Five Colleges Incorporated of New Hampshire which has joint pro-grammes, services, faculty and departments. Examples of the latter are the Inter-Universities North in Manitoba and the Western Canadian Committee on University Distance education. A heterogeneous general-purpose consortium is one in which a mixture of dissimilar institutions and agencies, often in close physical proximity, co-operate to provide a wide range of services and programmes to their clientele. An example is the British Columbia Open University Consortium, which includes the three universities and the Knowledge Network.

The special-purpose consortia do not involve a major portion of the faculty in any of the member institutions. These consortia relate to only *one* portion or department, existing on the periphery of the institutions and making little impact upon them. However, in general purpose consortia, the commitment to co-operation penetrates deeply into the central functions of their members. The total institution is more likely to participate, or at least be affected by consortium membership, and therefore the impact of member-ship is quite substantial.

Membership

Membership in a consortium is, by definition, voluntary. Hence, those co-operative arrangements which are designed *a priori*, or legislated into existence, do not qualify as true consortia. The number of members in a consortium may vary widely, from two or three members to over forty. While there exists no theoretical ideal, size often depends on purpose, location, and other circumstances. Franklin Patterson (1974:12) comments on the size of consortia:

> ... it is difficult indeed for a co-operative effort to be very successful with more than seven or eight member institutions. Co-operative effort involving an institution intensely will by its very nature involve conflict and compromise, and the larger the number of institutions involved, the more diluted (or disputed) the eventual product is likely to be. Where a consortium exists to provide service to member institutions, bigness appears to lead to fragmentation among members.

Member institutions must give some evidence of a long-term commitment to the consortium. Usually, this takes the form of a written agreement. In some cases, this agreement is not fully acted upon, but serves as a public declaration of the willingness of institutional members to co-operate.

Membership fees, where required, may range widely depending on the programme. In cases where grants have been received from government or private foundations, membership fees may be reduced or eliminated entirely. Institutions may be required to designate office space, staff time, or other services as a condition of membership. Often the commitments required relate directly to the funding base and relative wealth of an institution.

Governance and Leadership

The policy and decisionmaking functions in a consortium are usually performed by a board of directors, drawn from each member institution. A full-time officer who reports to the board usually carries out the management of the consortium. Although this is the basic governance model, some variations exist. In special-purpose consortia, the president may designate a department chairman, or another representative, to attend board meetings, reserving the right to be consulted in major decisions. In some cases, especially where the membership is large, an executive committee may make operational decisions, referring only major policy decisions to the board.

Some general-purpose consortia have expanded the governance structure even further. In instances where the executive director's office and staff are not located on an institutional campus, assistant directors may be appointed from academic faculty to serve as consortium representatives on each campus. Such arrangements increase the visibility of the consortium, and improve communication among member institutions.

The executive director of a consortium answers to the board of directors. His tasks may include planning, organising, budgeting, consulting with administrators and faculty members, convening meetings, arranging for the use of facilities and equipment, submitting annual reports, and acting as a liaison with external agencies.

Glass and Allen (1979) indicate the importance of providing adequate leadership for consortia. They argue that the executive director should be a full-time professional with key responsibilities to facilitate communication among member institutions, and to act as a catalyst to speed up the decisionmaking process of the consortium.

Efficacy

It is generally agreed that consortia have been an effective educational innovation in postsecondary education. Theoretically, consortia provide a means of ensuring co-operative programme delivery, cost efficiency, optimal utilisation of existing resources and cross-pollenation of ideas for innovative programme development.

For whatever reasons institutions actually join a consortium, the underlying premise appears to be that, as part of a group configuration, each member is better able to adapt to institutional, economic and societal circumstances. A consortium can enhance the development of services and programmes which would not be possible without a co-operative association of some kind. However, a consortium arrangement in postsecondary education is by no means a panacea for problems facing colleges and universities. Some writers contend that most consortia cannot solve all the problems they purport to address; nevertheless, the literature is fairly consistent in the advantages ascribed to them.

RELEVANCE OF CONSORTIA TO DISTANCE EDUCATION

Distance education, in its simplest expression, is the moving of learning content from an institution to a learner across physical space. The physical space can be between the instructor and learner, as in mediated delivery, or between the main instructional centre of a college and the site of instruction, as in extension delivery. In assessing the potential of consortia to facilitate distance education, the needs of both the agency and the learner must be considered. The requisites for distance delivery can be grouped under eight generic headings (Small and Byrne 1984): (1) logistics, (2) instructional materials, (3) technical support, (4) fiscal resources, (5) academic support, (6) community interfacing, (7) academic credibility, and (8) evaluation. A consortium of institutions set up specifically to support distance education could provide a number of benefits, in respect of each of these requisites.

Logistics

Administrative concerns in distance education arise from the goal of getting the right materials and resources to the right locations at appropriate times. Logistics relates to such basic activities as registering students, collecting fees, mailing or otherwise distributing information, and receiving and returning assignments. It is important to assign responsibility and secure resources to ensure that all those seemingly minor chores are looked after. If not attended to, such details can quickly become the Achilles' heel of distance education. A consortium could have the advantage of economy of scale, so that specialist personnel could routinely handle logistical details. In regions with concentrations of students, local representatives of the consortium could handle administrative concerns as agents for the institutions involved. Distance education students who might otherwise have to deal with several programming agencies would benefit from having all communication and support services emanating from one source.

An illustration of consortia which provide solid logistical supports are the five postsecondary consortia in Alberta. Created in the early 1980s, these consortia provide postsecondary programmes and courses to residents in regions of the province which lie outside of the primary service areas of existing institutions. Best described as heterogeneous general purpose consortia, each with a college, university and technical institute member, these consortia bring the equivalent of full-time programmes to residents in their service communities. (Pickard 1981) Each consortium has a board of directors comprised of institutional chief executive officers or their designates. A consortium co-ordinator acts as director, and one member institution serves as agent for legal and administrative purposes. An advisory committee, appointed locally, provides community input on programme needs. Administrative and programme grants are provided by the provincial government. Each consortium operates an educational centre which serves as a site for registration, instruction and study.

Instructional Materials

Instructional materials which will meet the academic requirements of a course as well as the particular needs of the distance learner must be prepared and packaged. Even greater care may be required in preparing instructional materials for distance education than for on-campus use, where the instructor can make mid-course adjustments based on face-to-face interaction with the students.

The preparation of adequate materials for distance delivery may be rather complex, involving academics familiar with the field of study, instructional systems-design experts, as well as media experts. In the case of television instruction the process may become quite sophisticated and costly, and would be difficult, if not impossible, for one institution to justify 'front end' expenditures. However, under a consortium, arrangement of instructional materials by institutions which specialise in the production of materials in focused areas, and contracting personnel in areas of their expertise to serve on production teams can greatly enhance the development of instructional materials.

The Southern California Consortium for Community College Television, for example, now in its second decade of production, was established to provide televised courses for college credit. 'The Consortium was formally established in the spring of 1970 by eighteen community colleges, most of them in Los Angeles County. By 1975, the number of college members had doubled, and included campuses as far away as San Luis Obispo, Palm Desert, Ridgewest, and Barstow'. (SCCCCT, n.d.:3)

Co-operative effort was required to solve a variety of problems related to the selection of courses, academic advisers, production staff, facilities, and the acquisition of broadcast time. 'Few colleges could maintain the sophisticated level of course production, distribution, and evaluation that is possible through a consortial effort' (SCCCCT n.d.:3).

A recent meeting of representatives of all institutions in the four western Canadian provinces offering university-level courses by distance education gave rise to the formation of a Western Canadian Committee on University Distance Education. This co-operative venture provides for collaboration between institutions ranging 'from the simple exchange of information about a variety of matters through the sharing of expertise to joint development and use of course and programme materials'. (Mugridge

1983:5) The potential for more formalisation by creating a consortium for distance education in Western Canada is clearly evident.

Technical Support

Technical support covers the variety of communication and educational technology employed to package, deliver and provide interactive capability between the instructor and student. Most technical problems can be avoided by acquiring reliable equipment, adequate technical staff and by thoroughly testing the medium before commencing a course offering. Nothing will cause disillusionment faster for faculty and students than a breakdown in equipment. Dedicated lines are expensive and can only be justified by high use. In the case of the Alberta postsecondary consortia, collaboration has justified the rental of lines between each consortium centre and the major sources of instruction, as well as the establishment of teleconference studies.

Fiscal Resources

Acquiring adequate fiscal resources for distance education may be a major problem when distance education comprises a small, hybrid part of an organisation competing with the 'established' delivery systems. Competition for scarce resources within the organisation heightens the problem. An administrator may have a sound basis for obtaining more fiscal resources when greater numbers of students are served through consortia arrangements; additionally, distance delivery may qualify as an innovative or experimental programme for special funding through governments or private foundations.

Special funding from outside agencies is more likely to be obtained by a consortium than by individual colleges. The consortium is an appropriate agency to administer large sums of money because it can manage its resources by drawing on the expertise of several institutions. Sometimes, as in heterogeneous consortia, one member institution may have a specialist role in delivery and thus add considerably to the credibility of the consortium. In Alberta, ACCESS Alberta, the provincial agency for broadcast educational materials and a formal member of some consortia, provides expertise in broadcasting not developed in other consortia members. Such consortia are natural recipients of grants for major ventures in distance delivery. Another source of funds are text-book publishers, who are ready to underwrite course development costs in return for the rights to produce the accompanying textual materials.

Another attractive aspect of funding a consortium rather than an individual college lies in the appearance of equity in the treatment of postsecondary institutions. Thus a funding agency can avoid inferences of favouritism and a series of similar applications from individual colleges when dealing with a consortium.

Academic Support

Academic support for distance education encompasses many of the same services required for on-site delivery (learning resource materials, counselling, instructor preparation and evaluation, etc.). Instructor preparation, especially orientation to distance education delivery systems, however, is important to ensure success in distance education. An instructor who has never conducted a class via a telephone bridge or via television may find it stressful when there is no student feedback. Availability of appropriate support materials to distance students often limits the types of courses that can be offered. The newer forms of communication technology, such as Telidon, provide electronic linkages with data bases that contain learning materials. However, the costs of such technologies may restrict their availability to individual students, unless the college can meet them directly in the course budget.

Consortial arrangements can help to provide the necessary academic support for both instructors and students. Expert staff employed by the consortium can provide guidance to instructors from member agencies and, in the case of smaller consortia with a limited consortium staff, the consortium can maintain an inventory of experts who can be released from their institutions from time to time to provide in-service instruction. The electronic data bases, now in increasing supply, usually contain vast resources beyond the needs of any single course or even institution. However, subscriptions to such bases are often on a long-term rather than casual-use basis. Again, the consortium can subscribe to such bases through which multi-institutional access can be obtained.

There are many Canadian examples of consortial arrangements in support of specific programmes; for example, Guelph-Waterloo (Chemistry); Guelph-McMaster (Philosophy); Ottawa-Carleton (Chemistry); and Emmanuel College, Knox College, Regis College, St Augustine's Seminary, University of St Michael's College, Trinity College and Wycliffe College (Theology).

Perhaps one of the most notable Canadian consortia for academic support is the Tri-University Meson Facility which was established to provide a world-class research facility in medium-energy nuclear physics, accessible to students in Western Canada. With a budget of $25.8 million, 70 professional staff and 298 support staff, TRIUMF carries out excellent research at the forefront of nuclear science.

Community Interfacing

Any distance education undertaking must arise in response to a demonstrated need. Thus, it is critically important for programme planners to know what clientele is to be served. The interfacing of institution and community may be accomplished through a wide range of contacts, perhaps the most important of which are the needs surveys. These should be undertaken at periodic intervals within target communities and should follow a good survey design.

Needs surveys are time-consuming and costly, and if done badly can provide erroneous data and have a negative effect on the population being surveyed. Individuals may be 'surveyed to death' if various agencies conduct needs surveys one after the other. A consortium serving a specific community can guard against this problem by orchestrating major surveys; indeed, in many instances surveys can be made sufficiently comprehensive to serve the needs of member institutions all at one time.

When a programme has been developed, it must be marketed. Educators should not shy away from this requirement since even the most beneficial and polished programme will be undersubscribed unless its availability and usefulness is adequately promoted. Confusion in marketing can be allayed by developing a single comprehensive brochure and by operating one information centre through a consortium.

To a large extent, these activities are evident in the Alberta postsecondary consortia. Inter-Universities North provides another good example of community interfacing by offering university credit courses north of the 53rd parallel through Brandon University, the University of Manitoba and the University of Winnipeg.

Academic Credibility

The academic concerns pertaining to distance education seem to stem from two basic issues: course equivalency and academic standards. The method of establishing credit weight often creates difficulty in equating a distance education course with a traditionally delivered course. (Ellis and Chapman 1982) Many colleges use a time-based formula that employs lecture, lab, field placement or similar form of contact hours to tally credits. These criteria may not be easily transferred to a course packaged, for example, in ten one-hour video lectures with an estimated 35 hours of independent study for a student who may never have direct contact with an instructor. Equivalency criteria based on content and/or level of mastery must be developed for distance education courses.

The fear of loss of credibility of the institution and/or particular courses, when many of the traditional trappings of quality control are not present, adds to the reasons for hesitancy on the part of some educators to award credit for distance education courses. This hesitancy is compounded by the tendency of distance learners to constitute special cases whose needs and backgrounds are not typical of the students for whom campus-based programmes were designed. Often pressure arises to make concessions on admission and other programme requirements beyond what would be considered acceptable on the home campus. For administrators, such arrangements are often 'messy' and confuse established operating and reporting procedures. For academics, the potential erosion of standards may lead to mistrust of colleagues who may be seen as contributing to problems for everyone.

Consortia can do more than simply act as a vehicle for the delivery of distance education; they also can serve as a watchdog agency to ensure the maintenance of standards. Additionally, they can provide a mechanism through which courses offered by one institution can be accepted for credit at another. Examples of transfer of credit through interagency co-operation in the United States abound, The University Without Walls being the best known.

Evaluation

Finally, every programme should be evaluated to determine the extent to which objectives have been reached, at what costs to the institution, and with what long-term effects on institutional operations, effectiveness, and mandate. Distance education is too powerful a mechanism to be accepted uncritically, and some provisions for both formative and summative evaluation should be incorporated into its functioning.

To the writers' knowledge, only one consortium has been established specifically to evaluate programmes. The Council for the Assessment of Experiential Learning (CAEL), later to be renamed the Council for the

Advancement of Experiential Learning, was set up in the United States in response to the need for some controls on the granting of credit for life experiences. Over the years it has proven itself capable of providing evaluative services and standards to its members. A similar national or regional agency could well be established to evaluate the many forms of distance education.

CONCLUSION

This chapter has illustrated some ways by which consortial arrangements between institutions might enhance distance education. Most consortia have been established in response to some specific need, i.e., programme, region or service. The Alberta postsecondary consortia are among the few in Canada that have been given a general mandate to provide distance education to specific communities. Others, such as the Knowledge Network of the West, provide a circumscribed delivery service (i.e., satellite television) to a less specific area (i.e., Western Canada).

Perhaps the strength of any consortium lies not in an attempt to provide all services to all people, but rather in its commitment to perform specific tasks for member institutions which they have difficulty in doing independently. Thus, whenever a consortium is being considered, the question of purpose must be the primary consideration, and potential members who are not fully committed to the purpose should not join the co-operative venture. Nevertheless, there appear to be few limits to the contributions that consortia can play in distance education because its demands are such that few institutions, the British Open University being the most notable exception, have the capacity to do it well on their own.

REFERENCES

This chapter contains material from a paper by the authors entitled 'Consortia in Postsecondary Education' submitted for publication to the *Canadian Journal of Higher Education*, and from an article by J. Small and P. Byrne, 'Distance Education: Some Basic Considerations', *College Canada*, 7 (1983). Both are used with the consent of the authors and publisher.

Daniel, J.S., M.A. Stroud and J.R. Thompson (eds.) (1982) *Learning at a Distance: A World Perspective*, Athabasca University, Edmonton

Ellis, G.B. and R.S. Chapman (1982) 'Academic Equivalency of Credit Courses by Teleconference', in J.S. Daniel, *et al.* (eds.), *Learning at a Distance: A World Perspective*, Athabasca University, Edmonton

Glass, J.C. and E.D. Allen (1979) 'Consortia: Guidelines and Research Needs', *Canadian Journal of University Continuing Education*, 5

Martin, D.M. (1981) 'The Academic Consortium: Limitations and Possibilities', *Educational Record*, Winter

Moore, R.S. (1968) *A Guide to Higher Education Consortiums 1965-1966*, Washington, D.C., U.S. Government Printers

Mugridge, I. (1983) 'Consortia in Distance Education: Some Canadian Ventures', *Deakin University Occasional Papers*, No. 8

Patterson, L.F.K. (1974) *Colleges in Concert*, Jossey-Bass, San Francisco

Patterson, L.D. (1977) *Consortium Directory: 1977* ERIC Document, ED 143299
Pickard, B.W. (1981) 'Consortia: A Means to Improve Access to Postsecondary Education', *College Canada*, Sept./Oct.
SCCCCT (n.d.) *A Second Decade*, Southern California Consortium for Community College Television, Downey, California

Section 3: DISTANCE EDUCATION INSTITUTIONS

Open Learning Institute

Ian Mugridge

The Open Learning Institute of British Columbia (OLI) was established by order-in-council of the government of the Province of British Columbia on 6 June 1978. At that point, the institute was a necessarily general idea in the minds of those connected with its foundation. Seven years later, it has become a well-developed organisation responsible for some sixteen thousand student course involvements per year. This article will attempt to survey the planning and efforts behind these rather bald statements.

OLI began with an advantage over most educational organisations in that the terms of its mission were clearly laid down at the outset. They were very simple and direct: to provide by distance means throughout the province of British Columbia, programmes in adult basic education, in career-technical-vocational areas, and leading to undergraduate degrees in arts and sciences. Thus, the provincial government established an institution supported by provincial funds and directed by a government appointed board, whose sole and specific charge it was to reach at a distance those people who could not or would not take advantage of the existing system of public education in the province. The task which faced the board and its newly-appointed principal, Dr John F. Ellis, in June 1978 was to carry out this mandate and to make a reality of the intention of the provincial minister of education, Dr Patrick McGeer, to provide the means to fill as many gaps as possible in the existing provincial system of postsecondary education. Before describing how OLI planned and began to work, it is important to outline the context into which the new organisation was placed. A full discussion of this can be found in a paper delivered by the principal in November 1979 to the Open University conference on the education of adults at a distance, so that only a general statement is necessary here.[1]

British Columbia, Canada's westernmost province, has a population of approximately two and three-quarter million, spread thinly over almost 370,000 square miles. Apart from Greater Vancouver, with 1.1 million people, and Greater Victoria, with 230,000, only three centres have a population of more than 50,000, while the entire northern half of the province is inhabited by fewer than 50,000 people. This population is dispersed over a province where summer temperatures of 35 degrees Celsius are not uncommon in some areas, and winter temperatures of -35 degrees Celsius are frequent in others; which is divided by three mountain ranges with peaks of over 10,000 feet; and where 55% of the land is categorised as forest. Such factors make any kind of travel difficult and unpredictable for most of the fall and winter. In the early days of OLI, they also meant that the kind of electronic communications used by many distance learning institutions were unavailable and that postal and telephone services provide the only province-wide means of communication.

The public educational system in British Columbia presents a picture of similar diversity. The provincial government funds a total of twenty-three postsecondary institutions: three universities, fifteen community colleges and five provincial institutes. Most of these institutions carry on activities in a variety of areas so that, at least for full- and part-time resident students in the fields covered by OLI's mandate, the opportunities for conventional, classroom learning are already considerable. In addition, some of these institutions are also engaged in distance education of various kinds. One further organisation must be mentioned at this point. For many years, the provincial government has also supported a Correspondence Education Branch (CEB) which had initially been established to provide high-school completion programmes for school-age students whose opportunities for conventional instruction were insufficient for their needs. Because of the absence of similar services for adults, however, the CEB had enrolled increasing numbers of adults and, though to a limited extent, had gone outside the strictly high-school aspects of its work. Into this situation OLI was placed, with a mandate to do what others were doing, though usually by different means, but for those whose needs were not being met by the existing system. Its problem, as simple to state as it was difficult to solve, was to carry out this mandate in the geographical and educational context outlined above.

One of the earliest decisions made by the institute and its board both simplified and complicated this problem and its solutions; but it also seemed - and seems - inescapable to those who made it. The decision was very simple: the Open Learning Institute, however innovative or even eccentric it might turn out to be in some respects, must be regarded as part of an existing provincial system and must therefore work within that system. The institute staff began with a number of other assumptions, among which were the following. Most of its students would be adults in the 25-40 age group. A high proportion of these people would already have part or all of the qualifications they needed and would simply require additional courses to complete or upgrade their existing qualifications. For example, all the community colleges in the province offer two-year university transfer programmes designed to prepare students to undertake the last two years of their degree at one of the provincial universities. Over eighty per cent of students entering such programmes in the ten years up to 1978, however, had not gone on to one of the universities; and it was thus reasonable to assume that some of them might wish to use their earlier work to complete an OLI degree. Similarly, many students have left the universities needing a small number of courses to complete their degrees; and the existence of an OLI degree programme might give such people a chance to finish their degrees, a chance they might otherwise have been denied. Thus, while the OLI degree programme had to have a shape and integrity of its own in order to meet the unique demands of distance students, it must also be designed in such a way as to allow students to transfer in from and out to other provincial institutions with ease.

Similarly, a high-school completion programme which did not meet the standards and requirements established by the ministry of education would be of little use. Further, apprenticeship programmes produced without reference to the provincial apprenticeship board or courses in hotel and motel management which did not meet with the approval of accrediting agencies in the hospitality industry could be bold and innovative, but scarcely credible to the actual or potential employers of those who enrolled in them.

Thus, it was clear from the outset that the existence of OLI and the offering of its programmes could and should add a significant new dimension to public education at all levels in British Columbia and that this would be true not merely in terms of students served or methods of delivery, but also in terms of content and teaching method. But it was also assumed that any developments in these areas would have to come within the context of a provincial system in which the type and form of instruction were usually well established.

It quickly became obvious to the institute's administration, as it has to those of other distance institutions, that their programmes of instruction must not merely meet the standards set by existing programmes in conventional institutions, but also must be clearly demonstrated to do so. The institute was, after all, entering areas where no previous instruction had been done at a distance in British Columbia. This is particularly true in the career-technical-vocational area where the feeling became apparent quite quickly that many people already in the field not only thought, as did many in the universities, that distance education was not as good as face-to-face instruction, but that it was simply inappropriate to think in terms of teaching some subjects at a distance.

Having made a number of basic decisions such as those already outlined, the institute began to develop programmes in the three areas covered by its mandate. The question of offering continuing education programmes was shelved at least temporarily because of the difficulty of defining this area in an instruction where, according to many definitions, everything being offered might be characterised as continuing education, and where little of the subject matter usually thought of as continuing education could be offered at a distance.

Along with the decision that OLI programmes must be designed in order to fit with those already in existence in the province went two others. In a distance education institution, it was vital that the options available to students, while they must almost inevitably be limited, must also be simply and clearly defined. It was further necessary to state these options clearly from the outset so that students entering during the first semester would be able to predict, at least in general terms, the directions they could take to complete the programmes in which they were enrolled. It was thus essential that the programmes to be offered in all three areas should be readily comprehensible to students who had varying educational experience before enrolling.

In a sense, the simplest programme to define was that in adult basic education (ABE). Much of what comes under the umbrella of adult basic education in British Columbia is, in fact, not basic education at all, for it is concerned with providing high-school completion programmes for those who have been deprived of them. Most British Columbia school districts mount programmes in this area as part of the Dogwood Certificate provision, a scheme by which individual school districts are allowed to offer high-school programmes to those whose education has been interrupted and whose certificates are signed by their district superintendent of schools. It was decided to produce an OLI version of the Dogwood Certificate and permission was granted by the provincial ministry of education for the director of the Correspondence Education Branch to act as superintendent of schools for OLI students gaining a high-school certificate. It should be noted here that the first example of substantial and important co-operation between OLI and another agency occurred in those between the institute and the CEB such that agreement was reached early that the latter should now work within the terms of its original mandate and provide programmes only to school-age students, leaving the institute free to serve adults.

It was decided to move towards the establishment of a high-school completion programme in two stages. The first would be the development of a Grade 10 programme which was implemented with the mounting of courses in English, mathematics, science and social studies in September 1979. This approach had an advantage beyond providing the first stage in high-school completion in that Grade 10 is a requirement for entry into, for example, a number of provincial apprenticeship programmes. The courses to provide a complete Dogwood Certificate would follow later. These courses were brought into effect progressively beginning in January 1980, with core or required courses being developed first, followed by optional courses in a variety of areas.

In the career-technical-vocational area (CTV), the problem of establishing a clearly defined and useful programme was rather more difficult. This was the product partly of the almost limitless number of options which seemed to present themselves and partly of the chaotic and almost completely uncoordinated state of teaching in this area. The original proposal for the CTV programmes was an attempt to cut through this unfortunate situation and to present a programme which concentrated on essentials in areas where great need and demand existed in the province. Thus, a matrix of some sixty courses was produced which could be applied either to a general certificate in which students took ten courses in areas which they chose themselves, or to certificates in particular areas which also required ten defined courses.

Some courses such as those in accounting, small business management or effective supervision could be applied to a number of certificates, while others in subjects like hotel and motel management, project supervision or office procedures were designed for specialised certificates. In the development of these courses, extensive consultation was undertaken with representatives of the provincial government and of the industries concerned so that, in pursuit of the institute's earlier determination to provide programmes which met real needs and requirements, acceptance by these bodies could be assured.

The CTV programme began offering courses later than the other two areas because planning for the programme began later. It was, however, brought quickly into operation and the first courses, then 52 in number, were offered at the beginning of the first academic year of operation in January 1980. These were supplemented by a similar number in September 1980 and January 1981.

The third programme area was the undergraduate degree. It was clearly unrealistic to assume that, even though the institute had taken advantage of legislation enabling it to grant its own degrees in arts and sciences, it would be able to offer the wide variety of subjects and courses required by the conventional universities to mount their major and honours programmes. It was thus necessary to define those areas where demand and need existed and which could, at the same time, be offered effectively at a distance. An initial choice of eight disciplines was made of which one, biology, was chosen both because of need and as an experiment to attempt to solve the immense problems of offering a laboratory science in a vast province like British Columbia. The second step in the process of defining the programme was to design a degree structure which would enable students both to transfer their work to one of the existing universities and to pursue a coherent degree programme completely through OLI or using at least some work undertaken elsewhere. Two elements were incorporated into the OLI degree. These were the completion of a general education requirement, equivalent to one year's work out of four and normally undertaken at the beginning of the degree studies, and specified amounts of work in two areas of specialisation during the third and fourth years with preparatory work during the second year. These areas of specialisation, while not providing students with the kind of extensive acquaintance with a discipline which would follow from a conventional university major or honours programme and which would hence allow such students to proceed directly into a graduate programme, were nevertheless designed to give students a solid grasp of the core of their chosen disciplines by requiring six semester courses in each area followed by a semester-length course of directed reading.

These basic decisions about the shape of the degree programme having been made, it remained to define the courses in each of the chosen disciplines which would form its core. The programme director consulted widely on this question and was naturally presented with as many opinions as there were people consulted. Choices were finally made, however, and specific course development began. Initially, three pilot courses were offered in September 1979, all of which were either wholly or largely based on courses which had been developed elsewhere. These were followed by a further sixteen in January 1980, all but one of which had been developed by the institute.

One other aspect of the development of the university programme should be mentioned at this point. One of the most difficult problems in offering university-level courses at a distance in the province of the size and make-up of British Columbia is the provision of library service to students. Clearly, packages of materials sent to students had to be as self-contained as possible; but, equally clearly and particularly for senior level courses, it would be impossible to make all of them so. Some students would have access to college and university libraries, for these institutions have always allowed members of the community to arrange to use their facilities; but, here again, the assumption, born out of experience, was that at least a substantial minority of students would not live within easy reach of a good library. In co-operation with the university librarian at Simon Fraser University, therefore, a scheme was devised to provide library service to students enrolled in OLI university courses. A reference librarian, hired by the institute, would be provided with office space and other necessary facilities at Simon Fraser, would be available by telephone, toll-free, for students to request books, articles and other information, and would then send the requested material or information back to students. This project, begun in September 1979, has now become an integral part of the institute's operation.

Naturally, one of the major problems encountered in the early months of planning was that of the method of course development. In the initial phase of development when the ABE Grade 10 courses and the first university courses were being written, two methods were tried. The four original ABE courses were written by a group of resident course writers who worked together at the institute and were thus able to consult regularly with one another, with the instructional designers and editors, and with the programme director to ensure that the courses were well integrated, written at the required level, and designed appropriately to the needs of the students who would take them. At the same time, the first university-level courses were written by a somewhat different method. Each course was provided with a course writer, experts in their field who, in most cases, taught similar courses at one of the colleges or universities, and a course consultant, another subject expert, normally an experienced teacher and senior academic whose function was to review the material produced from an academic point of view and to ensure that it met accepted standards for the subject and level in question. Each course writer was also provided with an instructional designer and editor whose job essentially was to turn a body of academic material into a good distance learning package. Although both of these methods have obvious and great advantages, it was the latter model which was increasingly followed as the institution moved towards maturity.

Along with the planning of programmes and the development of initial courses went the establishment of the systems required to support their offering. From the beginning, most of the actual production of courses was done at the institute itself, so that print and audio facilities have been set up which will increasingly be able to accommodate the institute's production needs. The registrar's office has established the necessary support systems for admission and registration of students, recording and dissemination of grades and so on. One function of this office requires particular mention. In a province the size of British Columbia, it is clearly impossible, at least at this stage of the institute's development and probably indefinitely, to provide face-to-face contact between tutors and students. Contact is thus normally restricted to written comments on assignments and to regular telephone conversations, since all tutors are provided with an institute telephone on which they may contact students and by which, at least at specified times, students may contact them without charge. One early and continuing assumption was that, however well this kind of tutoring was carried on, however effective and well-motivated students and tutors might be, the kind of contact which they might have would probably be inadequate to serve all the needs of the students. It was thus essential to provide students with a further contact point with the institute, one which would preferably be personal and continue throughout their time as students. The response to this assumption was the advising service. In its first year of operation, the institute established four advising centres in various parts of the province. Each adviser was assigned a number of students for advice on a variety of matters like programme planning, registration, financial aid and problems, not specifically academic, related to the handling of courses. Each student who registered was assigned an adviser who remained with him or her as long as he or she is enrolled at OLI.

To this point, this essay is a revised and shortened version of another written in the early days of the institute to describe the initial planning for OLI and the early implementation of that plan. It is included here so that, as the institute moves into maturity and perhaps into a new and rather different phase of its development, the early assumptions and plans which guided its growth may be compared to the situation which has evolved.

In the five years which have elapsed since the first article was written, major changes have occurred in distance education in British Columbia as they have elsewhere. In particular, these relate to the availability and use of a variety of technologies. An early decision of OLI planners was that no course would include a mandatory television component: access to television was, after all, severely limited in many areas of the province. Progressively, however, this situation has changed until, with the full development of the Knowledge Network, founded in 1981 to deliver educational television programmes throughout the province, more and more use is being made of a resource which is now almost universally available except in the north of the province. Similar developments in other areas have also accelerated the use of computer assisted and managed learning, of teleconferencing, of live interactive television and so on. Such innovations have changed and will continue to change the shape and form of OLI's offerings in ways that are discussed elsewhere in this book.

In many ways, however, the first seven years of OLI's existence have seen not merely steady growth in the range of programmes offered and in the numbers of students served, but also a growing recognition of the value and potential of distance education in British Columbia and elsewhere. In the latter sense, OLI has merely been part of a world-wide development in the use of distance instruction to solve a variety of problems, educational, social and economic. A few examples of this are appropriate. OLI's sister institution in Alberta, Athabasca University, has doubled in size since 1980. The British Open University, one of the world's major and most prominent distance education institutions, has continued its steady growth and acceptance so that it now enrols almost 90,000 students each year. The Australians, long time users of distance education methods at a number of levels, have continued, expanded and made more sophisticated their distance programmes. But the most spectacular advances have been made in the Third World where distance education has increasingly been a solution to the apparently overwhelming problems of educating and training large numbers of people quickly and economically. Two recent examples will suffice: the Sukhothai Thamatirat Open University in Bangkok offered its first courses a year later than OLI, awarded almost ten thousand degrees at its first convocation in 1984, and now has a total enrolment of about 400,000 students; and the Universitas Terbuka in Jakarta opened its doors to first enrolment of 57,000 students in September 1984 and has already seen this increase to about 90,000 a year later.

Figures such as these are impressive and testify to the widespread use now being made of distance education. They also tend perhaps to cast something of a shadow on the achievements of a comparatively small institution like OLI. It has been calculated, however, that the institute, with its current annual enrolment of almost 17,000 students, serves a larger proportion of the adult population of British Columbia than does STOU with its 400,000 in Thailand. Such an observation adds a different perspective from that which comes from the use of pure numbers and even, from the admittedly biased viewpoint of the writer of this essay, shows the progress of the last seven years to be a substantial achievement.

On the basis of the planning outlined in the first part of this essay, the institute has moved to complete the programmes and courses laid down in the original CTV plan, to develop substantial programmes in ABE at the Grade 10 and Grade 12 levels and to come within striking distance of finishing the initial options outlined for the undergraduate degree programme. At the same time, an efficient computerised system has been developed which handles student registrations, records and examinations, and integrates such functions with the storage and dispatch of course materials. This system is becoming widely recognised as a model for other institutions and has already served as the basis for a similar system being designed at Universitas Terbuka, the Indonesian Open University. Efficient, though in the rather eccentric world of course development not always effective, systems of course design have been established and also used as models in other institutions. The systems of materials production are described elsewhere in this collection.

Programme options have been expanded substantially beyond those originally planned to include major developments in the teaching of English as a second language, a project undertaken in conjunction with five other provinces, the addition of a degree in administrative studies and, more recently, substantial offerings in science. Most significant perhaps is the growth of technical and vocational programmes, where new areas of instruction have been added in a wide variety of more practical subjects ranging from nursing and dental assisting to power engineering and heavy duty mechanics.

As these developments have continued, the institute itself has gained increasing acceptance within the province as an agency which can and does make a major contribution to education. Increasingly, it works with regional colleges in co-operative activities; and the establishment of the Open University Consortium of British Columbia has provided an important role in the widespread and co-ordinated offering of degree programmes in the province. At the same time, the institute works increasingly with special groups to fill particular needs which cannot be or have not been met by the traditional system of education. Finally, as this volume goes to press, developments are taking place which will mean the fusion of the Open Learning Institute and the Knowledge Network, as well as the greater co-ordination of distance education activities in the provinces, developments which, it is hoped, will build further on the solid foundations laid down in the last seven years.

NOTES

Mugridge, Ian (1981) 'The Establishment of a New Distance Education Institution: The Open Learning Institute of British Columbia', *Distance Education*, March. (Material from this article is printed here by permission of the editors of Distance Education.)

REFERENCES

Ellis, J.F. and John Bottomley (1979) 'Problems and Opportunities Associated with Developing and Operating a Distance Education System', presented at the Open University Conference on the Education of Adults at a Distance, Birmingham

Athabasca University

Ross Paul

Insecurity and booming enrolments, identity crises and leadership status in the world of distance education, a relocation that could not be justified on educational grounds and first-class new facilities, innovative ideas and a traditional quest for credibility: contradiction and controversy have surrounded Athabasca University (AU) since its inception in 1970. The institution has a colourful history that would be the envy of universities several times its age, and yet the real challenge facing AU in 1986 is to find ways to preserve the best aspects of these dynamics at a time when it has finally achieved the permanence and security that have long been so elusive.

Athabasca University is an open university serving some 8,000 adult students (12,500 course enrolments in 1984-5) in all provinces of Canada with the majority located in Alberta, Saskatchewan and British Columbia. The only admissions criterion is that the student be a Canadian at least eighteen years of age. The primary mode of course delivery is the self-paced home study package, supplemented by a telephone tutor for each course but this is increasingly being enhanced by instructor-paced, in-person or teleconferenced seminars to cater to the needs of rural students in particular. It offers three university degrees: a Bachelor of Arts with a number of programme concentrations; a Bachelor of Administration; and a Bachelor of General Studies, a non-resident, credit co-ordination credential.

As a relatively new field of endeavour, distance education is too often characterised by a tendency to overstate its achievements and to overlook its difficulties. Using Athabasca as a case study, this chapter attempts to avoid this tendency. While some of the highlights of the institution's history are presented here, the focus is on the major issues and problems that have characterised its development. Because the institution has had to work through almost every aspect of its development 'from scratch', its experiences should prove of interest to anyone interested in or contemplating the application of distance education in another institution.

HISTORY

The Beginnings

As is well chronicled in Laurie Hughes's book, *The First Athabasca University*,[1] the evolution of AU deviated substantially from the path originally envisaged by Alberta's government in its January 1970 white paper on postsecondary educational policy.[2] Alberta's fourth university after Alberta and the relative newcomers, Calgary in 1966 and Lethbridge in 1967,

Athabasca was to be located in St Albert, just north of Edmonton. It was created to address the greatly increased demand for university places, but also to emphasise undergraduate education at a time when concern about the rapid growth of the 'multiversity' across the river, the University of Alberta, was at its height. A small *ad hoc* planning group, which included Tim Byrne and Sam Smith, later to become the institution's first two presidents, was established to develop guidelines for the university's establishment. The subsequent choice of Dr Byrne as AU's first president was a logical one, as he had been Alberta's deputy minister of education since 1966 and a driving force in AU's creation.

As Hughes has shown, the life of the 'first' Athabasca University was short. With Peter Lougheed's upset victory for the Conservatives in August 1971, 36 years of Social Credit rule ended and the future of AU was placed, not for the first time, in some jeopardy. A series of political factors combined to challenge the advisability of establishing yet another university in Alberta: postsecondary enrolments actually declined that year, and the new government was committed to a full-scale review of all pending capital projects. Within two months of its accession, the Lougheed government ordered an immediate halt to physical planning for the St Albert site and it looked very much as if the new university would never be established. The next year, 1972, was a grim one, as the small staff continued planning for an institution that might never exist.

Dr Byrne played a pivotal role in maintaining the institution's existence. Particularly because of his success in defusing a difficult situation at Red Deer College early in 1972, he was highly respected within the department of advanced education and by its minister, Jim Foster. On 30 May 1972, Foster accepted the academic plan developed by the governing authority of Athabasca University and approved the development of a small (250-student) pilot project for the institution, although the university was not formally established in its new guise until 20 December 1972.

There were several significant aspects of the early days of Athabasca University that have characterised the institution throughout most of its history: insecurity about its existence and physical location, a high degree of government involvement, a strong but rather vague sense of mission and difference from traditional universities, and a dogged determination to 'succeed despite it all' on the part of a small but dedicated staff. Indeed, it is probably the very adversity and insecurity that have enabled the institution to survive; had it been more established as another residential university in St Albert, the oft-repeated rumour of an imminent takeover by the University of Alberta might have become a reality.

THE EARLY YEARS: 1972-8

The three years of the pilot project, 1972-5, were characterised by much frenetic activity by a tiny staff of about 35. By 1975, the university had developed three courses for about 650 students but it was extremely difficult for the latter to plan or persist, given the uncertainty about the very existence of the institution, let alone what course might next become available.

Nevertheless, the university took on many of the dimensions that characterise it to this day. A perusal of the many planning papers that emerged at that time reveals a strong interest in the non-traditional learner, in home study, in learning theories and their application to instructional design, in interdisciplinary curricula, and in educational technology.

A 1975 project evaluation report[3] prepared for the deputy minister of education by an independent consulting firm validated the university's assumptions about the need for its non-conventional delivery systems, although it urged the university to pay far more attention to problems of motivation and student support. It paid special tribute to the university's commitment to independent evaluation and an ever changing model based on what worked rather than on what individuals' preconceived notions suggested. It concluded with a statement that, in hindsight, was rather ironic: 'we ... cannot help but conclude by wondering if it may not be time to lift the burden of uncertainty from the institution by giving it permanent status.'[4]

While the uncertainty was to persist for nine more years until the 1984 relocation to Athabasca, the government did respond by giving approval-in-principle to AU's establishment as a permanent baccalaureate university in October 1975. This was based on a June 1975 document from Alberta Advanced Education and Manpower (AAEM), *Athabasca University: Proposed Role and Mandate*[5] which recommended a five-year renewable mandate to serve as an open university accessible to all Albertans and offering three-year degree programmes.

The university would emphasise open admissions, personalised learning, a credit co-ordination function, interdisciplinary studies, and new delivery systems; develop university transfer programmes for Keyano (Fort McMurray) and Lakeland (Lloydminster/Vermilion) Colleges; and work co-operatively with other institutions, notably ACCESS and the Universities of Alberta and Calgary, in the development of computer-assisted learning. Significantly, the question of the university's 'permanent' site was left open.

The 'new' university pursued this mandate with vigour and, by July 1977, had developed a clear action plan, *A Framework for Development*,[6] which very closely previewed the university as it has evolved. It was to offer three-year degree programmes in Arts and Science, General Studies and Administrative Studies within which were contained interdisciplinary concentrations. The plan contemplated the characteristics of a 'traditional' university and consciously rejected them. At the same time, it recognised the dangers of trying to establish an institution based totally on responding to student needs. A synthesis of the two approaches was proposed in the form of an undergraduate degree-granting institution that linked a liberal arts core to a 'needs-determined group of applied programmes' and an emphasis on research that was 'applied' rather than 'pure'. The university was to be organised into the two major divisions that remain today: University Services and Learning Services. When the university finally received its charter in 1978, it was well on the road to implementing the plans set out in *A Framework for Development*.

Relocation

Since its inception, AU had been functioning in rented 'factory outlet' facilities in an industrial park in northwest Edmonton. The temporary nature of the accommodation reinforced feelings of uncertainty and hence it is not surprising that the securing of permanent facilities was a major goal for the institution. In the face of recurring rumours of a pending government decision, the university published, in 1977, a set of criteria for the selection of its future site.[7] Among the central criteria were institutional autonomy, proximity to centres of communication and printing, and accessibility to the University of Alberta, mainly for its library and computing services and for the academic staff, many of whom were course writers or tutors at AU. A location near Edmonton was a basic assumption of the document.

On 5 March 1980, with only half an hour's notice to Governing Council Chairman Ken Chapman and President Sam Smith, the minister of advanced education Jim Horsman announced that AU would be relocated to the town of Athabasca, a tiny hamlet of about 1,800 on the Athabasca River, about ninety miles north of Edmonton. While it was subsequently revealed that the decision had been made at the cabinet level over a year earlier while bidding for the university had been a preoccupation of many Alberta towns, the announcement nevertheless came as a severe shock to the university staff.

Before the dust had settled, President Smith and senior council member Ed Checkland had resigned over the issue and most staff were disillusioned that their governing council (AUGC) had not stood up to this 'political' intervention in the affairs of the university. After several stormy meetings, the AUGC agreed to establish a planning commission under the direction of Barry Snowden, Vice-President, University Services. The commission was mandated to study the consequences and requirements of implementing the decision to relocate AU to the town of Athabasca. The 1980 Relocation Commission Report was considered by the AUGC at its first meeting in 1981, on the basis of which it was concluded that the move was feasible given certain government support, notably in such areas as relocation staffing, housing and the establishment of a creditable undergraduate library.[8]

Housing was a particular problem. Rental accommodation was scarce in the small Athabasca community and there were very few houses for sale. Many of the staff had purchased homes in Edmonton during the boom years which coincided with the rapid expansion of the university and would face major losses in their attempts to sell in less prosperous times. To exacerbate the dilemma, property values in Athabasca were somewhat inflated after the announcement, although they returned to more normal levels when the expected boom did not materialise. One major rental housing development was realised with the help of the Alberta Housing Corporation but the market has remained somewhat difficult for most staff contemplating relocation.

At the time of writing (Spring 1985), the university is just completing its first year in excellent new facilities in Athabasca. While 142 (58 per cent) of the original 1981 staff have left the employ of the university since the relocation decision (48 per cent of the professional staff and 58 per cent of the support staff as of 15 May 1985), the numbers are smaller than had been expected, primarily because of the great reduction in employment opportunities from the time of the original projections. Nevertheless, a number of relocated staff were less than delighted with the move and almost one-half of the academic staff took advantage of the one-year daily commuter bus service from Edmonton, which entailed up to four hours travel per day.

Fears about the shortage of support staff have not been realised because the town has supplied some 65 staff members to the university. Although many of these were hired away from local businesses, there is little question that the university has contributed considerably to prospects for employment in the region. This factor has also contributed in some way to breaking down the 'town-gown' conflicts that many had anticipated.

For some, it is incredible that the university relocated at all, and miraculous that it continued to expand at a phenomenal rate during this period. The concentrated importation of so many new staff during 1984 (with almost a 100 per cent turnover in the registry and library) made tremendous demands for on-the-job training, especially at a time when enrolments were booming (up 26 per cent over the previous year). The university made full use of temporary 'parallel staffing' funding to get over this hurdle, but the relative lack of decline in the levels of service to students was mainly a product of the extra efforts of so many staff in coping with the crisis. At the same time, and rather ironically, the generous funding and high staff turnover associated with relocation gave AU an opportunity, unique to universities in Canada in the 1980s, to develop new programmes and to import fresh faces and new ideas, at a time when her sister institutions across the country were dealing with retrenchment and a consequent resistance to change.

SOME CONTENTIOUS ISSUES

Traditional and Non-Traditional Values

Uniquely in Canada, Athabasca University is an open university dedicated to the extension of access to university education to those who cannot avail themselves of opportunities at more traditional universities. One manifestation of this mandate has been an inherent dynamic between traditional and non-traditional values in the debate about the role and priorities of the institution.

Structure and Process: Where open or distance programmes are given by a specialised division within a more traditional institution, the same conflict may exist but it tends to be between the division and the rest of the institution, a frequent issue, for instance, for faculties of extension or continuing education in traditional universities. In AU's case, the struggle has been within, most notably between academic staff members recruited from the mainstream of Canadian universities and others more attracted by AU's commitment to innovation in instructional development and design.

While one should not normally attribute too much significance to a name, it has already been seen how convenient the name 'Athabasca' was to the government when it was searching for a small town for the relocation of the university. The 'university' part of its title may also be of particular significance. Because it was a university by title (and not, for instance, an institute like OLI), Athabasca tended to attract staff from traditional universities, many of whom emphasised the importance of research and academic credibility over the desire to be innovative.

In the earlier organisational modes at AU, the role of the traditional academic was somewhat downplayed. There was almost an obsession with creating an institution which was 'different' and some individuals had opposed calling Athabasca a university for precisely that reason. The co-ordinator of course development, for instance, was not even a member of an academic unit and the instructional developers and editors were also organised into independent units. Between 1980 and 1983, the vice-president of learning services (VPLS) made a number of organisational changes which were intended to break down what he perceived to be an artificial separation among those responsible for course development (the instructional developers and editors), course delivery (regional and tutorial services) and the overall academic programme (the academic co-ordinators).

Two new senior academic administrative positions were created: director of liberal studies, which encompassed social sciences, humanities and sciences, and director of administrative studies. Three managerial posts, co-ordinator of course development and the headships of editorial and instructional development were eliminated and the units absorbed by the two major academic divisions, liberal and administrative studies. The tutorial part of regional and tutorial services was absorbed into the appropriate academic areas and the regional operation was split into the northern and southern regional offices under senior directors. All these changes were intended to delegate more authority from the VPLS to the directors of studies and to ensure that they were in a position to assume full authority for the quality of the university's academic programme in all its facets. Whatever their eventual impact, these changes symbolised, for many staff, a trend away from the non-traditional ideas of the earlier days and a definite shift in the balance of power in the direction of the course co-ordinators (full-time faculty).

The proliferation of delivery systems and the extension of the regional services throughout Alberta and beyond has created new strains on the institution, especially because of the enrolment boom that these initiatives helped to generate. The regional network of more than 60 centres in Alberta and notably the flagship operations in Edmonton, Calgary and Fort McMurray have contributed significantly to the explosion of demands on the central services and the resulting difficulties are often blamed on the regional model. Traditional centralised/decentralised disputes are exacerbated by the sheer number and complexity of delivery modes and locales, and perhaps the most obvious tension is that between those who promote the university's potential to serve new clienteles in new communities and those who have to respond to the consequent demand without compromising the quality of service offered. It is but the latest example of the conflict inherent between the traditional concerns for quality and the non-traditional emphasis on responding to needs. Proponents of the regional model insist that the resulting tension is a healthy one, but all have conceded that the university must do a better job of coming to grips with the rate of expansion its systems can tolerate.

Concerns about the model and levels of service notwithstanding, there is general agreement in the institution that a constantly increasing demand for the university's services is the right kind of problem to have.

Course Development

The 'ideal' model for course development, the principal activity in the early days, was the course team, consisting of a subject matter expert, who might or might not be an in-house academic, instructional designer, visual designer and an editor, one of whom was normally the course team manager. The sources of conflict within course teams have been well documented at other distance education institutions,[9] but several factors exacerbated this at AU. The earliest teams were ambitious and took two years or more to produce extensive courses that proved extremely difficult for students. As the academic staff increased in numbers (because it was a university, it was important to have a subject-matter expert in each main discipline), there was increasing resistance to the power of the instructional developers by academics who resented being told that they didn't know how to teach their own discipline. As key instruments of quality control, editors, too, were often placed in the difficult position of criticising academics' writing skills.

The organisation and management of a course team is a considerable challenge and few aspects of Athabasca's operations are more crucial to the institution's success. While there was always a considerable divergence between theory and practice, as time went on the ideal course team model increasingly gave way to more pragmatic attempts to assemble smaller teams that would work well together. If an academic staff member had a proven record of course development, he or she would be left to get on with the next course with only more cursory checking by an ID and/or editor, leaving the latter staff members principally to work with new or external course authors. While there is little evidence to suggest that this approach has compromised the quality of courseware, there is recent evidence of a renewed commitment to course and programme evaluation that may ultimately challenge this assumption.

One major feature of the original course development system that has been retained is the 'Phase III', that stage when a course proposal is formalised and circulated widely for comment and feedback. This document sets out the objectives of the course, its place in the curriculum, the resources its development will require, and how students will be evaluated. A crucial component is a sample unit which is the best indicator of what kind of final product can be expected. Hence, no one just produces a course: it must be approved after it has been scrutinised by course co-ordinators, instructional developers and other managers and staff. The major difference from earlier days is that it is the appropriate director of studies, rather than a university-wide committee, who decides that a Phase III course is ready for full development (Phase IV).

Governance: Uniquely among Canadian universities, Athabasca retains a unicameral system of governance whereby the 23-member Governing Council[10] serves the tripartite role of board, senate and general faculties council. Until 1981, the governance structure was extremely centralised with the two key committees respectively chaired by the academic and adminis-trative vice-presidents. However, serious efforts have been made since that time to develop a stronger academic council within the formal authority of the Academic Council and its standing committees although it retains final budgetary authority.

These efforts have only been partly successful. Staff have been cynical about the 'real' power of the academic council, given that it can always be overruled by AUGC, the only statutory body in the university and the one with budgetary authority. Academic staff, who make up only 40 per cent of the membership of the academic council, feel underrepresented in a model that is perhaps more reflective of the earlier university. Nevertheless, it is inevitable that the academic council will increasingly mirror the more traditional academic model whether or not a bicameral system of governance is ever adopted.

The evolution of collective bargaining at the university, notably with the impetus of the relocation decision, has also contributed substantially to the drift away from the original non-traditional model. The major responsibility for these negotiations and related contractual arrangements has been carried by Neil Henry, Vice-President of University Services, over and above his regular responsibilities, although the additional workload has been a characteristic for many others as well. A notable development was the 1984 splitting of the professional staff into two categories with respect to promotion: academics (including instructional designers), and professionals (including editors and visual designers). The former group retained the four academic rankings and promotion according to traditional university criteria of scholarship and creative activity, while the latter were reclassified into positions according to negotiated criteria and appropriate salary ranges. While the non-academic professionals still retain benefits often denied them in other universities (such as research and study leave), this split clearly set the traditional academics apart from other professional staff in a way typical of universities but previously unknown at Athabasca University.

Research: The treatment of research at Athabasca University perhaps best illustrates the evolution of the institution over the decade in question. In its earlier days, there was some interest in institutional research but almost no support for the standard disciplinary research that is the hallmark of a university. In fact, some academic staff were explicitly told that they would not have much time for their own research because of their course development and delivery responsibilities. One of these individuals was somewhat shocked to find himself denied promotion several years later because an external examiner had found his publication record unacceptable!

When Stephen Griew was appointed AU's third president in 1980, he brought a strong commitment to disciplinary research to the university and its importance gradually increased during his tenure. A standing academic research committee annually awards funds for staff projects and a new position in the VPLS office was introduced in 1985 to provide more support for research and development. Nevertheless, it would be misleading to suggest that most academics have been hired on the strength of their research records or that the university is now strong in any areas of research. The trend is unmistakable but the institution has a long way to go in comparison to more traditional universities.

The university record on instructional research is similarly uneven, although it probably publishes as much in 'distance education' journals as any single institution, notably through its institutional studies unit. Special government funding yielded a series of research reports in 1980 under the instructional development project 'REDEAL' and, more recently, in 1984, three members of staff were each given half-time release to concentrate their research efforts on the 'non-start' problem (see *Course Delivery* below). There has been no lack of interest in institutional and instructional research at the university, but many efforts have been frustrated by the relative inability of the university's systems to keep up with the rapid growth and sophistication of its individualised course registration requirements.

An interesting offshoot of the research debate is the question of staff time. With students enrolling at the beginning of each month, there is no real beginning or end to the academic year. With no formal classes to meet, academic staff theoretically have more control over their own work schedules than do their counterparts elsewhere, but the rigours of course development, demands for meetings with course teams and tutors, and frequency of telephone calls counteract this advantage. Professional development and research leave are provided for by contract, but the effective academic at AU must have the same time-management skills that characterise its most successful students.

Systems Requirements: These trends can be seen by most as very positive ones: the coming of age of Athabasca University as a credible institution of higher learning. At the same time, the unique demands of a 'distance education' model for integrated systems did not go away and they produced new tensions in the university, especially during a period of sustained and rapid growth.

While professionals working in bureaucratic organisations frequently experience conflict between their professional orientations and the systems requirements of the bureaucracy, the unusual degree of integration required by a distance education institution magnifies this conflict. The usual expectations for process that characterise a university often run headlong into the 'assembly line' demands of the publishing house with its emphasis on teamwork and adherence to deadlines. The academic staff member cannot be left alone in the classroom but depends as much on the effectiveness of course materials, media services, the registry and the regional offices as on the tutors and other members of a course team. It is this interdependency that constitutes perhaps the greatest adjustment for most new academic staff members at AU.

As the university increased in size and complexity, there was increasing reliance on bureaucratic mechanisms to direct and control the operation. The elaborate production system, the complicated registration procedures and all the difficulties associated with tracking individual students on individual programmes made severe demands on the systems, and registry and computing staff in particular had to develop their own models in the relative absence of similar systems in other institutions. Rapid growth and the proliferation of delivery options placed ever increasing demands on the idiosyncratic systems and frequently found them lacking. At the time of writing, the university was embarking on an ambitious and expensive plan to develop highly computerised in-house systems for student records, library acquisitions and circulation, student monitoring, finance, personnel, office automation and course production among others.

On balance, the university has been fairly successful in its efforts to cope with the idiosyncrasies of its highly individualised student systems and highly integrated production processes. It is important to note that almost everything from student record systems to academic degree regulations and computer support systems reflect the uniqueness of the institution's mode of operation and hence have of necessity been created 'from scratch'. There just are not many places like Athabasca University (whether by accident or design).

Course Delivery

While the content of Athabasca University's courses is fairly traditional, its innovation is found in the various models of delivery which it offers in attempts to extend access to a university education. Within this 'open' mandate, however, lie several dilemmas emanating from a commitment to openness within the context of ensuring high standards. Several of these are discussed below.

Open Admissions and the Adult Learner: Athabasca's admissions criterion is singular: age 18 or older. The university is committed to the notion that any adult learner deserves university access regardless of previous educational experience. Merely to leave it at that, however, is to abrogate responsibility and hence to make the open door a revolving one. The literature of adult education stresses the independence of the learner and challenges the 'teacher knows best' pedagogy of traditional education. To carry this philosophy to its logical conclusion, the university would merely provide adult learners with the resources and leave it to them to take advantage of these to meet their personal goals. This is the way it works for a significant minority of AU students, whether they slave for hours over a kitchen table to accumulate enough credits for a degree (surely the hardest way possible) or simply garner the information or knowledge they seek without ever completing a course.

Over and against this, however, is the university's quest for credibility and the maintenance of academic standards. This is not merely an internal concern on the part of academic staff, for it is important to the student as well. A 'correspondence' degree is often suspect in the outside world, and the university must do everything in its power to ensure that its credentials are accepted by other universities and by employers. Especially because the course materials (i.e. the classroom teaching) are printed for all to see, extra care must be placed on course design. Perhaps the indicator that best epitomises the dilemma between not 'spoon-feeding' the adult student and ensuring the credibility of the institution is that of completion rates.

There was a glib assumption in the institution that most courses had a completion rate of 50 per cent or better until a 1980 study by Institutional Studies head, Doug Shale, revealed the overall completion rate at the university to be a mere 26 per cent.[11] Further analysis suggested that the real problem was not completion rates so much as the 'non-start' problem: students who signed up for a course but never completed an assignment and often avoided all contact with the tutor. While some of the 'non-starters' may nevertheless have garnered all they wanted from the course materials, it was clear that many of them were either intimidated by them or never got around to starting, despite their initial good intentions at registration time.

Many efforts have been made to reduce this problem, including designing easier starting units, providing for more immediate feedback, introducing writing competence and math skills tests, channeling all first-time students through the university's counselling service, designing courses on writing skills and critical thinking, and introducing various pacing mechanisms into certain courses. At the same time, the university has been careful to maintain its basic home-study, self-paced delivery mode with registration at the beginning of any month on the premise that it is the resulting accessibility and convenience to the student that is at the heart of Athabasca

University's success. By 1982, the overall course completion rate was 38 per cent[12] and it is anticipated that it will continue to improve with subsequent studies.[13] The completion rates could be much higher, but only at the expense of the very group that the university is designed to serve.

Regionalisation and Outreach: One of the most spectacular changes in the university's mode of operation in recent years has been the emphasis on outreach, the establishment of regional offices throughout Alberta, the increase in co-operative arrangements with colleges and other institutions in many parts of Canada and, above all else, in the delivery of 'paced, enhanced delivery' (PED) courses. In the earlier days, the emphasis was on 'distance education' exclusively, as if any other form of delivery was contrary to the university's mandate. That quickly changed, however, mainly at the instigation of the rural students.

The neophyte to the world of distance education might naturally assume that a university like Athabasca caters mainly to rural students who do not have ready access to universities. On the contrary, the self-paced home study mode of delivery is particularly appealing to the urban student who cannot or chooses not to attend classes at local college or university campuses. He or she opts for the autonomy and control over the learning environment that Athabasca provides.

The rural student, on the other hand, often has no other choice: it is Athabasca University or nothing. Surveys have shown that such students will take home study, but prefer more interactive processes. A 1983 study by Chuck Shobe[14] indicated that rural students ranked 'classroom based' courses as vastly preferable to 'teleconferenced' courses, with home study a clear third. Working with the recently established Educational Consortia in five regions of Alberta and in other areas as well, notably with the native peoples' centres in St Paul, Morley and Slave Lake, Athabasca has developed a network of seminar supported and teleconferenced courses to provide the socialisation and pacing elements lacking in its home study programme. The university has also developed close working relationships with a number of colleges in Alberta, Saskatchewan and the Yukon, and with North Island College in British Columbia, where the college staff and facilities are employed in various ways to enhance the basic home study packages. The day is fast approaching when a full Athabasca University degree programme will be available in a paced, enhanced mode on several college campuses.

Hence, in a very significant way, the emphasis has been on providing access *by whatever means* rather than exclusively by distance education. By 1984-5, approximately 10 per cent of the university's 12,000 plus course enrolments were in seminar supported or teleconferenced modes and the percentage was still increasing, although the various modes of delivery are always an enhancement to and never a substitute for the basic course package.

Educational Technology: There has long been an expectation that Athabasca University would be a Canadian (if not world) leader in the development of educational technology. Television was considered as the primary mode of delivery during the pilot project and deliberately rejected as too expensive and requiring too long a development period. The irony is that the basic educational technology that evolved (specially designed home study materials, support of telephone tutor, flexible registration procedures) has been extremely successful and is increasingly the envy of other institutions venturing into distance education, many of which are far more sophisticated than AU in their use of the electronic media. Nevertheless, the university is seen by many observers to be relatively unsuccessful because it has not had many high profile 'cutting edge' projects.[15]

Where the university has successfully applied new technology to the delivery of its courses, it has been as enhancement to the basic technology described above. This includes the use of television (a number of supporting programmes run regularly on the ACCESS satellite network) FM and side-band radio (via ACCESS station CKUA), audio and videotapes (by mail and in regional centres), audio-teleconferencing (throughout Alberta and Saskatchewan), interactive television and radio, and microcomputer-assisted instruction. As a small institution, AU does not have massive resources to put into experimentation in this area and has been most successful where it has co-operated with other agencies: at the time of writing, the university was considering membership in the new Canadian Centre for Learning Systems, a Calgary-based consortium of educational institutions and corporations dedicated to computer assisted-instruction.

Of particular interest to any distance education institution is the growing interest and use of the electronic media (such as laser videodiscs and computer-assisted instruction) in traditional universities. To the extent that these gradually gain a foothold in these universities (and one should not underestimate the resistance to them in these most conservative of institutions), they will challenge the very rationale of perpetuating institutions given exclusively to distance education: will such places become redundant as all institutions develop the capacity to serve students in their own homes?

Student Support: The Tutors and Student Services: Student Services are frequently without great political power in a university and this is especially problematic in an institution like AU. Whatever the rhetoric of adult education, the university's counsellors and tutors know that its students need a great deal of personal support, advice and information if they are to succeed.

The primary contact people for most students are the telephone tutors who are expected to be information agent, 'pacer', teacher, subject-matter expert, examiner and often personal counsellor to their students. These individuals, who are part-time employees of the university, frequently have very little personal contact with others in the institution (except perhaps by phone), and yet they are at the very heart of the delivery of its academic programme. They often feel neglected, unappreciated and politically powerless. Recent efforts to involve tutors in key areas of decisionmaking, to insist that all course co-ordinators do some tutoring, and to integrate tutorial services into the academic divisions have perhaps addressed this concern but much remains to be done. A tutor association has been formed to strengthen the tutor advocate role in the university.

Student Services is another often underappreciated division which has developed new skills unique to this sort of institution (for example, counselling by telephone) but it cannot possibly provide the sorts of in-person services often expected of it. The proliferation of PED courses in rural areas has encouraged groups of students in all areas of the province to request 'in-person' counselling but the university just does not have the resources to comply. The emphasis has consequently been on training workshops for staff of other helping agencies such as the Educational Consortia, colleges and native peoples' centres, and the development of student 'self-help' and orientation materials for use at a distance. As more and more educational institutions use distance techniques, the unique experience of AU's student services staff will become of increasing interest to them.

Measures of Success: As the institution matures, more and more energies are being put into attempts to measure its success. Until recently, there was so much pressure to develop the basic courses and to relocate the university that there was insufficient energy for this sort of activity.

The university has been well-funded to date and this has perhaps allowed it to postpone confronting the inevitable question as to its cost efficiency. Such studies are now under way but it will always be difficult to compare it to traditional institutions as it is serving many students who otherwise would not have access to a university. The savings on the capital side are obvious, even with the university's new campus in Athabasca, but not so clear on the operating side. The initial investment in course development is high and AU is only now really reaping the benefits of its earlier frenetic activity in this area: the cost per enrolment has been declining steadily over the last few years.

If student numbers are an indication (and they traditionally have been in the university world), Athabasca University is an unqualified success. Its population has grown from 5,000 course enrolments to over 12,500 over the past five years. While the number of graduates has grown steadily each year, the numbers are still small by traditional standards. However, one factor is often overlooked by those who cite the size of the annual graduating class as insufficient return on the investment: a very large number of graduates in other universities in Alberta and beyond would not have been successful without the help Athabasca gave them at some point in their university careers.

THE FUTURE

With the 1985 appointment of Dr Terry Morrison as its fourth president, Athabasca University enters a new era. He inherits a booming institution, one that is firmly established in its new and permanent home and one that faces unparalleled opportunities for expansion and development. Nevertheless, the challenges remain. There was much creativity and innovation in the face of so much insecurity in the past: will the new stability and 'comfortable' rural atmosphere undermine the dynamism that has made AU different and responsive to student needs?

A long range plan approved by the AUGC in 1985 gives some indication of future directions but it inevitably raises as many questions as it answers. Should the university play a stronger social role than it has in reaching out to the disadvantaged? Where will it find the resources to implement plans for four year degrees, graduate programmes and non-credit education? How can the university's research record be improved? What about a residential component or conference centre? Should the institution accelerate its national role? Does Athabasca have a particular role in the north? Will the demand for its courses continue to grow at current rates? If so, will the university be able to find the additional resources that this will require?

Whatever the answers to these questions, Athabasca University in 1985 is a vibrant institution. Many staff are still recovering from the relocation blow; there is a collective insecurity about the institution's research record and viability of its whole mode of operation; but, in the meantime, it is extending access to a university education to more and more students in Alberta and beyond. Where it is not 'the whole answer' (as it is to the individual who scrambles his or her way through 90 credits of courses via home study or PED courses), it is more and more frequently a significant part of the answer. This may be via offering a credit co-ordinated BGS degree or full-time resident programme at a native peoples' centre, helping a nurse get her baccalaureat at the University of Alberta, or simply providing the course that someone needed to enter another institution, get a job or promotion, learn a skill or pursue an individual interest. In the process, it is constantly searching for and often finding new ways to serve students more effectively at a distance.

In one sense, then, nothing has changed. Athabasca University has potential, it is a challenge, it is expanding, it is non-traditional, it is looking for credibility, it is not the same as it was several years ago. As such, it remains one of Canada's most fascinating universities and the biggest fear is that it will become too entrenched in its new environs and lose that capacity for innovation which characterises new and 'different' institutions. Can it become more like other universities without losing that essence? The answer should be clear by 1990.

NOTES

1. L.J. Hughes, *The First Athabasca University* (A[thabasca] U[niversity]), Edmonton, 1980.

2. Robert Clark, 'Postsecondary Education Until 1972: A Policy Statement', Department of Education, Government of Alberta, Edmonton, 1970.

3. L.W. Downey Research Associates Limited, 'The Athabasca University Pilot Project: Report of an Assessment', 24 March.

4. *Ibid*, p. 37.

5. Alberta Advanced Education and Manpower, 'Athabasca University: Proposed Role and Mandate', June 1975, pp. 256-7.

6. AU Governing Council, 'Athabasca University: A Framework for Development', 4 July 1977 (2 volumes).

7. AU Governing Council, 'Criteria for the Selection of a Permanent Site', 4 July 1977.

8. AU, Commission for Relocation Planning, 'Report on Impacts, Consequences and Costs of Relocation', December 1980 (2 volumes).

9. Malcolm Crick, 'Course Teams: Myth and Actuality', *Distance Education, 1*, 2 (September 1980), 127-41.

10. Thirteen public representatives appointed by the provincial government, three *ex officio*: the president and two vice-presidents, 9 elected staff, 1 student.

11. AU, Office of Institutional Studies, 'Course Completion Rates', 22 August 1980 (13 pages).

12. Doug Shale, 'A Study of Course Completion Rates', *Institutional Studies Report 6*, AU, July 1984 (27 pages).

13.   Readers are cautioned not to use these figures for comparison purposes without consulting the Shale paper which discusses the complexities of defining student cohorts and course completion rates at an institution like AU where students are individually registered and self-paced.

14.   Charles Shobe, 'Teleconference Course Evaluation', AU, 3 November 1983.

15.   For representation of the variety of opinion on educational technology within AU, see Ross Paul (guest editor), 'Athabasca University Issue', *Bandwidth*, *2*, 3 (February 1983).

Télé-université du Québec

Patrick Guillemet, Roger Bédard and Francine Landry[1]

In the early 1960s, Quebec was experiencing what is known as the 'Quiet Revolution'. The Province of Quebec proposed a complete reformation of its educational system, with the democratisation of education as its main goal. For the next several years, much effort would be put into establishing a network of primary and secondary public schools in order to cover needs in all parts of Quebec. In 1967, the main objective was the setting up of CEGEPs (Collège d'enseignement général et professionnel) to serve the two functions of technical training and preparation for higher education. All the regions of Quebec were to have their college and there are 47 today.

It was obvious that this democratisation must also be implemented in higher levels of education where Quebec was much in need of modernisation in order to be at least comparable to neighbouring provinces. It must be noted that, at the end of the 1960s, a large proportion of the Quebec population was between 20 and 24 years old, as a result of the post-war Baby Boom.

It has to be kept in mind that with the exception of Sherbrooke, institutions of higher education had always been concentrated in Montreal and Quebec City. It must also be noted that this reform planned that teacher training, until then the responsibility of 'Ecoles normales', would be within the competence of universities.

It was therefore necessary to provide these new students with integration facilities. Accessibility was the main objective, not simply 'for all', but for all in their own regions. In order to fulfil this demand, Université du Québec was established at the end of 1968. Set up by the government, the Université du Québec first organised four campuses: Montréal, Trois-Rivières, Chicoutimi and Rimouski. But, as a result of demand, other institutions were created. Hence, today, the Université du Québec can be considered as a conglomerate, some units with a general and some with a specific mandate.

GENERAL CHARACTERISTICS

History

Télé-université began on 18 October 1972, with the creation of the Commission de Télé-université, dedicated to the creation of a distance education programme in Quebec. It came out of research conducted by Quebec into the role of distance education at the university level, and how to provide university-level distance education which would be as appropriate in its content and reference points as in its methods and organisation.

Télé-université and University Distance Education in Quebec[2]

The Beginnings (1972-4): The 'Commission de la Télé-université which became, in June 1974, the 'Direction générale de la Télé-université, was established as a five-year research and development programme for distance education. The tasks with which it was entrusted included the PERMAMA project, an upgrading programme for mathematics teachers which was subsequently revised and re-organised; the study of two courses dealing with an introduction to the Quebec economy and an introduction to human co-operation; the study of an upgrading programme for teachers of French and second languages (PERMAFRA) created in 1975 and assigned to Télé-université; and a joint study with the Université du Québec of the possibility of giving courses in the remote Outaouais and Northwest region of the province, using the distance education model.

First Successes - First Difficulties (1975-9): Since its creation, Télé-université occupied an ambiguous position within the Université du Québec, and more particularly *vis-à-vis* other general education components of the university. In effect, it had received a mandate to conduct research in university-level distance teaching, whereas other constituents were charged with making university-level education more accessible to the public in each region of Quebec. This notional ambiguity concerning 'distance' and 'accessibility' produced the difficult task of integrating Télé-université with the rest of the units of the Université du Québec. Indeed, it was to characterise mutual relations, despite the possibilities for joint action which were offered.

Télé-université's early years were successful. The first course, offered in 1974, drew 4,965 students; the PERMAMA programme enrolled more than 25% of Quebec's practicing secondary-school mathematics teachers; and the certificate in cultural education CHEM (Knowledge of Man and his Environment), begun in February 1975, had brought in more than 2,000 students by 1977. By 1979, Télé-université awarded its first CHEM certificates and had 13,661 students in its courses. In four years, 32,782 students had been enrolled.

These numbers, however, intensified the active disquiet among other components of the Université du Québec. These divisions, charged with the task of training and upgrading teachers, saw the PERMAMA and PERMAFRA drawing students away from them to Télé-université, a university institution with no faculty in 1974, and not likely to be receiving any under its first three-year plan (1975-8). Their intervention led the Université du Québec's Board of Governors, in the autumn of 1975, to adopt a protocol of association between the constituent units of the Université du Québec and Télé-université. This was followed in 1976 by a rearrangement of their responsibilities for the management of the PERMAM and PERMAFRA programmes and to a decision to evaluate the role and place of Télé-université within the Université du Québec.

A crucial stage was passed on 28 May 1976, when the Board of Governors of the Université du Québec decided to maintain Télé-université as an institution of formal education, but on a limited basis. The university ceased all administration of the PERMAMA and PERMAFRA programmes, as well as joint projects with other constituent units. Télé-université's role was to be embodied in the cultural education programme CHEM, development of which was to proceed along the lines decided by the Université du Québec. On 28 November 1979, the Université du Québec's Board of Governors recommended to the Quebec Ministry of Education the granting of letters patent to the higher learning institution to be known as 'La Télé-université de l'Université du Québec'.

Consolidation and New Problems (1980-3). A new stage began in January 1980 with the Quebec Government's creation of a commission on adult education. This decision effectively delayed the granting of letters patent, Télé-université having always been associated with adult education. On 28 October 1981, the Board of Governors amended the project to grant Télé-université a patent. The new mandate clarified operation in terms of three principal university missions; teaching, research and public service. In this respect, the mandate granted to Télé-université for its public service role supported the mediatisation of teaching in association with other institutions, which harked back strongly to joint projects proposed in 1974.

During this time, Télé-université developed other programmes. In 1981 it offered the CHES (Knowledge of Man in Society) and, in 1983, it brought out the GPT (Work Prospect for Tomorrow), as well as a certificate in computers applied to education. However, new difficulties arose. From 1978 to 1982, between one half and three-quarters of the university's students were teachers engaged in upgrading their professional classification. In 1983, the Quebec Education Ministry withdrew recognition for this purpose from general socio-cultural programmes like CHEM and CHES: a 25% drop in enrolment followed. Furthermore, the certificate in educational informatics placed Télé-université in direct competition with other units in the Université du Québec which had similar programmes, again raising the co-existence question. Agreements with these units led Télé-université to cut back its programme creation considerably, resulting in the loss of an important element of new students who had preferred 'professional' studies and been attracted by the computers course.

New Scope in Development (1984-5). In February 1984, amidst new difficulties, the Quebec Government announced its policy on adult education. The statement recognised Télé-université as responding to the needs of the Quebec public. It proposed the creation of a provincial distance education corporation, for the college and secondary-school levels, to be associated with Télé-université to provide new adult education services. Meanwhile, the university was again trying to define the role bestowed by its patent (as yet ungranted), as well as to define the place of distance education in accordance with education department policy. In this spirit, and endorsed by the Board of Governors, it set forth eight institutional pursuits on 1 May 1984:

-undergraduate programmes of a 'general baccalaureate' nature;
-study of offering a Master's level programme;
-research support for its main line of development in informatics and communications;
-organisation of university-level training activities in co-operation with public and private enterprises, small businesses and organisations,- professional associations, etc.;
-improving distance education techniques;
-developing a computerised course bank ready for distance-mode use;

-co-operation with non-Quebec agencies; and
-co-operation with the Quebec distance education corporation.

Operational Methods

In search of autonomy and its letters patent for thirteen years now, Télé-université has questioned not only its environment, but also its own theory and practices. At its beginnings, it was inspired by the philosophy of the 'open university' as well as by that of the traditional university. Its choice of social and cultural education was rooted in an analysis of the social and cultural preoccupations of the Quebec public, to which it chose to respond with a multidisciplinary approach. Its goal was to democratise learning and not to allow it to be associated with an élitist approach to knowledge. Télé-université's far-reaching early successes justified this vision.

However, the university began to question the quality of its methods. If courses were well prepared at a university level, they were nevertheless taken by students piecemeal, not as part of a comprehensive university programme. Realising that this imperilled its institutional responsibility, Télé-université began to question its teaching practice, which had consisted in mediatising courses and offering them in an appropriate framework but without a professorial staff.

The question arose whether it would be possible to continue to base development on the production and development of courses designed by subject-matter experts from outside the institution, assisted by educational and media professionals belonging to it. Is distance education incompatible with a stable and permanent teaching corps? If so, how is it possible to sustain intellectual pursuits and instil a desire for research; in short, to enable a complete university experience without allowing the material to be taken piecemeal?

A major change was initiated in 1981 with the decision to develop a professorial staff, which would assume responsibility for Télé-université's dealings with students. This decision implied a radical change of perspective towards the operation of a distance education institution. To this point, an 'industrial' concept of training, or the act of teaching, had included planning, designing, production, distribution and evaluation. With the involvement of a faculty, the emphasis turned towards the integration of the teaching function under the sole responsibility of the professor.

These two visions of distance education continued to live together for some time, albeit not harmoniously. In this way Télé-université came to its deepest point of introspection, in terms of its approaches, its educational materials, its operational methods and its organisational structure. By a structural re-organisation which accompanied its new approaches, the university now focuses on teaching and programmes rather than on the methods of producing the materials. This focus includes sections devoted to instruction, student support and educational technology.

The future will show whether this option most profitably combines the demands of industrial or semi-industrial production and those of courses and programmes, which the existence of a professorial staff allows.

Student Clientele

Rapid Advancement: In 1985, Télé-université welcomed 25,000 persons, an equivalent of 2,411 full-time students. However, although these figures reveal its viability, they do not reveal the problems it has had to overcome to achieve such results. Nor do they reveal that problem as yet unresolved: the search for a stable clientele, both in terms of quality and quantity.

In quantitative terms, Télé-université had to learn in its initial years how to absorb its rapidly-increasing enrolment, increasing from 1,300 students in 1978-9, to 2,680 students in 1979-80, to peak at 2,830 students in 1980-2. Consequent on the decision of the Quebec Government, in 1983 the university suffered a 25 per cent diminution to student enrolment concurrent with a tendency away from social and cultural programmes, to programmes of a more professional orientation. Following this decision, Télé-université had no more than 2,150 students. However, thanks to new programmes, in informatics and most recently in administration, it has somewhat recouped its losses; in 1984-5, it had 2,411 students.

Structural Weaknesses

Qualitatively speaking, the university has experienced even more pressing problems. On the one hand, the institution has been dependent upon the enrolment of teachers because of their classification structure. This has been particularly so with the PERMAMA and PERMAFRA cases, as well as with those of CHEM and CHES. As Table 1 indicates, this characteristic serves to explain why the university has made a determined effort to seek a more diversified clientele.

The second major qualitative problem has been the way in which students have approached education at Télé-université. Students are effectively part-time and enrolled, on the average, in one course per trimester. One-half are enrolled in study programmes, but the rest either take piecemeal courses or enrol in short programmes which do not lead to diplomas. In each trimester then, one-half of its students are new. The university reaches many students, who, however have little time. Although these students are satisfied with their courses, they seem to be more interested in specific courses than in continuing programmes. A high turn-over rate results.

Table 1: Principal Occupations of Students in All Courses and Programmes (Winter - 1985)

Occupation	Number	Percentage
Administrators and Managers	343	3.2
Professionals	551	5.2
Teachers	2,013	18.9
Technicians	1,204	11.3
Supervisors	300	2.8
Skilled Labourers	461	4.3
Sales and Office Workers	1,232	11.6
Agriculturalists and Horticulturalists	18	2.0
Unskilled Labourers	245	2.3
Unemployed	1,420	13.4
Unknown	2,848	25.0
Total	10,635	100.0

Télé-université has to make considerable effort each year to attract new students, in the midst of changing needs, passing fads and trends. It is essential to remember that society influences their needs, which appear so impelling and diverse. It is no surprise that the economic crisis of 1983 and the continuous publicity about technological change have brought about a trend towards more professional orientations. Students are opting overwhelmingly for courses and programmes which appear to present the best prospect for employment. Many have thus dropped the social and cultural education offered by the university.

Télé-université has thus had to adjust rapidly to significant fluctuations amongst its clientele, making planning that much more difficult. Since 1983 it has chosen a long-term programme development, parallel with short-term activities. It has, therefore, accepted the challenge in developing long undergraduate programmes in the new communications technologies and the social sciences. This is intended to appeal to a significant part of its clientele which may embark upon distance-education activity stretching over several years, even if the programmes are not, strictly speaking, professional.

The Students: Who are Télé-université's students? What type of studies do they follow? Certain features are invariable: they are Canadian (99%), French speaking (98%), and resident in Quebec (99.5%), even though some courses are given in other provinces and in New England. Other characteristics vary from year to year. A sociological portrait done in 1984 provided the following profile: age - 35 years, 9 months; sex - 57% are female; last degree obtained - baccalaureate (43%); reasons for enrolling - to expand one's knowledge, but 44% unknown; and profession - teachers (35%). The portrait differed somewhat in 1984-5. Male and female students were now equally represented and more than 40% were between 30 and 40. More than 99% were part-time students, and although no professional class predominated, those from the teaching profession accounted for 19%. Their most frequent choice of study was social sciences (47%), only 20% choosing informatics.

Programmes

The Search for Original Programmes: The evolution of the university's programmes reflects the political and social environment, the Université du Québec's Board of Governors and the Government of Quebec. Overall, it reflects the students themselves. The first courses were thus developed in response to directives from the university board: courses on human co-operation and on the Quebec economy, as well as for those related to mathematics and French teachers' upgrading programmes. Course development was more rapid in the last case, since it rested on a homogeneous clientele and on previous educational experience.

The new mandate bestowed on Télé-université by the Board of Governors in 1974 allowed it to develop a cultural education programme, an opportunity to bring together the needs within the social environment and decisions made within the context of the political environment. From this synthesis emerged Télé-université's first internally-developed programme, CHEM, which became the institution's prime mover in development. The decidedly sociocultural approach was strengthened in 1981 with the launching of the CHES certificate.

The university came to an important turning point in 1981 when the Government of Quebec prepared a policy statement on adult education. The three-year plan for 1982-5 was approved by the Board of Governors. Its development centre was to be in the domain of information and communication while its institutional strengths were those of mediated teaching, communications technology and continuing education. The accuracy of this analysis of the needs of adult students in Quebec society was confirmed when the Government of Quebec announced a new policy on teacher classification, withdrawing socio-cultural programmes from the classification scheme. Of the new programmes launched in 1983, the work prospects and informatics certificates, the latter was enthusiastically received, engaging half the student body in 1984.

The attractions of the informatics courses were short-lived, however. Course implementation having been severely restricted, Télé-université is embarking today on a new generation of programmes, of long-term undergraduate development rather than short-term programmes and certificates.

Accomplishments and Perspectives. From 1972 to 1985, then, seven distinct programmes have been offered:

the specialised bachelor's degree in secondary-school mathematics teaching;

the mathematics teaching certificate;

the upgrading certificate in the teaching of French;

the CHEM certificate;

the CHES certificate;

the GPT certificate; and

the informatics-applied-to-education certificate.

Only the last four are still offered, although five more short programmes have been added. These programmes, not exceeding 15 credits, were created from existing courses to respond to a particular limited demand, limited, for example, by the specific needs of a given industry, as in the case of the computerised office management programme. Table 2 gives the numbers of graduates from the various programmes.

Table 2: Diplomas Granted to September 1985

Programme	Total
Knowledge of Man and the Environment: CHEM (Certificate)	4,420
Knowledge of Man in Society: CHES (Certificate)	233
Work Prospects for Tomorrow: GPT (Certificate)	-
Informatics Applied to Education (Certificate)	-
Bachelor of Secondary-School Mathematics Teaching	347
Certificate in the Teaching of Mathematics	110
Certificate of Proficiency in the Teaching of French	274
Bachelor of Arts (Body of Certificates)	47
Bachelor of Administration (Body of Certificates)	2
Total	5,433

Other Programmes

	Total
Short Programme in the Law and Personal Freedom	-
Short Programme in the Use of Pesticides and their Effect upon the Environment	159
Short Introductory Programme in Informatics	64
Short Programme of Introduction to Microcomputers	37
Total	260

Even though the introduction of short courses allowed Télé-université to adapt to rapidly changing conditions, the university was no less inclined to stress longer-term undergraduate programmes with a general bachelor's degree. In 1984, it initiated a baccalaureate programme, drawing from its communications and informatics development, which intended to produce information technology generalists capable of dealing with the new technologies and reconciling users' needs with the requirements of the systems themselves. The development of a second baccalaureate covering the arts and social sciences is also in progress.

Télé-université will continue to enhance current programmes in an effort to make them as attractive as possible. The Government of Quebec's expected policy towards certificate programmes will influence the university's attitude towards them in future programme development. Similarly, it will continue to respond to the need for university-level education on the part of public and private enterprises and organisations, as well as to continue projects in the mediatisation of its courses. Télé-université is considering graduate-level studies (Master's). It is studying the possibility of advanced professional studies by drawing from its relationship with other units of the Université du Québec.

Pedagogical Media and Methods

Télé-université is often thought of only as a 'university of the air'. However, television is only one of the vast array of media, most notably electronic media, which it uses.

Print: As in other distance education settings, print remains the primary instructional medium at Télé-université. Material sent to students is intensively studied for pedagogical and linguistic clarity, of which illustrations are an important element. In some cases materials are sent together with a reference work. In others, like language courses, audio cassettes are included and educational games may accompany mathematics materials.

Television: Television serves to support many course offerings. Small groups may screen videocassette tapes at prearranged meetings or students may view presentations over Radio Québec or the educational channel on cable television. Broadcasts are repeatedly scheduled at different hours throughout the week, and students receive a telecast schedule from the university upon enrolment. Live educational television broadcasts have also interested Télé-université. The university has experimented with several types of television broadcasts combined with an open-line telephone link. These have permitted public debates, discussions, interviews with visiting professors, Telidon demonstrations, debates on themes touching upon courses (which allow indirect publicity), and an actual live enrolment session. Some materials from these activities were later used in regular courses. Thus far, however, no courses have made further use of this technique, whether for enrolment, presentation or teaching purposes.

The establishment of an interuniversity consortium for educational television, CANAL (Corporation pour l'avancement des nouvelles applications des langues) in which Télé-université plays a significant role, bodes well for the future of this approach. Already Quebec's principal universities are linked through a commercial cable television distribution system to the Université du Québec's television network. There have been audio-visual interactive links between Télé-université sites in Montreal and Quebec City, satellite links between all of Quebec's cities, and other broadcasts allowing viewers to follow debates of the Learned Societies. One should also note the heavy use of a television system linking the university's Montreal and Quebec City offices for administrative purposes: television cameras in each city may be controlled by participants in the other city. No use has yet been made of this system for courses, but it may be tested shortly, given the ease and quality of communication it allows.

Information Technology: Computers and communications technology are used in a large number of courses. Since the birth of Télé-université, three programming courses in the LOGO language have been included in the PERMAMA programme. Students learn programming by using a Montreal-based computer via telex terminals. In 1976, the course 'Computers ... aren't Magic' featured the PLATO network, allowing students to create text and graphics from their terminals: several courses have been developed and distributed using such technology. More recently, and particularly since the introduction of the informatics certificate in education, students have been able to work independently on microcomputers, which are capable of linkage to a central processor. Such efforts have enabled students to familiarise themselves with the most popular microcomputers, and through the short office-skills programme, use machines that they will encounter daily in the workplace.

Other experiments have taken the university away from actual courses. Following its association with the VISTA project, it has experimented in mediatising portions of its courses using the TELIDON videotex system, so as to determine the viability of offering courses to students at home. Similarly, two professors are testing the educational properties of videodisc technology.

Télé-université's educational applications of information technology are supported by Quebec's Bureau de télématique, created in 1982. Furthermore, the university is co-operating with the Videotex technical committee established by the Canadian Standards Council, as well as with a committee established by the Quebec Department of Education to derive a five-year development plan for the educational applications of computers.

New Media and Pedagogy. Télé-université expects to profit from the full potential offered by the new technologies, by comprehensively researching them so as to provide students with pedagogical environments which allow the most fruitful interaction with various disciplines. Already it is examining its own educational media practice in light of changing technologies; and it is currently redefining its practices and techniques at the front-end as well as at the administrative levels. The prospect of the electronic university is, for Télé-université, a highly stimulating exercise in imagination and pedagogical introspection. It evokes an image of a university which would combine and enrich the resources offered by print, telephone, television (live and delayed broadcast), videotex and interactive videodisc, and microcomputers linked to educational networks such as UNIPAC (Quebec's university network), EDUPAC (Quebec Ministry of Education), CONSORTEL (Trans-Canada Network) or EDUCOM (USA). Data-base consultation, computer-assisted instruction, telephone teleconferencing, television, computer, electronic mail, and telematics would be set to educational purposes in user-friendly frameworks, shaped to the needs of students, and allowing maximum exploitation of the professional and academic resources.

The Pedagogy of Mediatisation: If the prospect of the electronic university seems as yet remote, it nevertheless lies at the heart of Télé-université's pedagogical *raison d'être*. A course is seen as an integrated system comprising

-content (a discipline or science addressed by the course);
-a didactic approach, i.e. the conversion from a state of knowledge into a process of learning;
-a pedagogical approach, i.e. the strategies and activities of learning;
-one or more educational media;
-some kind of student evaluation; and
-student support and encouragement.

The particular arrangement of these elements for each course may assume several configurations. In certain cases, notably that of second languages, the student receives all the tools and materials for a self-instructional approach and is left on his or her own during the learning phase. More frequently, in addition to the materials (which may include cassettes or refer to video-tape resources), the student may participate in study groups with other students or have tutorial assistance. Computer and human relations courses also have lab components. In a few cases, face-to-face instruction was used. Thus, depending upon the course and the stage of the course, the student may learn at home, in a regional study group or in an appropriately equipped location.

CREATION, PRODUCTION AND DISTRIBUTION OF COURSES

Course Creation

Due to the demands of mediatisation and follow-up support, distance education requires heavy financial resources, as well as a systematic approach. A professor operating 'face-to-face' may rapidly modify his or her course presentation as a function of student reaction during the course. Thus, the creation and production cycle for distance education courses is longer than that in conventional universities. For reasons of profitability, courses must be modified with an eye to the diverse needs of potential students. This is undoubtedly the reason why distance education's course creation and production is so often characterised as an 'industrial' process, even if without reference to any type of industry.

The course creation cycle at Télé-université thus begins with a professor taking charge of a course-creation project and setting up a course-creation team. Under the professor's supervision, the team's first task is to draw up a course presentation dossier, to serve as a pedagogical and technical manual. This dossier describes the course objectives, the course content, the approach intended for the student, student support and student evaluation methods. It describes as well the human resources required, the tasks assigned them, costs, projected media needs and other services that may be required.

The course plan is then evaluated and approved, subject to its academic and pedagogical value, and its material and financial feasibility. Upon approval, the directing professor may proceed to hire the necessary external human resources, thereby getting the course project under way. External human resources are most often professors at other universities, should the course content go beyond the course director's own specialisation. This serves to broaden the director's own perspective, and offers the student the benefit of the finest resources available.

The course creation team varies in size and composition from course to course. However, it always includes a directing professor, assisted as needed by a student support specialist, an educational technologist, subject-matter experts hired as required on contract, specialists in scripting, production, graphic arts, editing, computer programming and, although less frequently, a course implementation agent.

Production and Distribution

Print Materials: Production of print materials begins at the end of design phase. Texts are scrutinised for clarity of language and readability, by the Service de Révision Linguistique. Revisions are performed in consultation with the course director. Specialised personnel carry out all tasks. To lower the cost, however, the actual printing is contracted out. Print materials are intended to cover minimally a three-year period during which no major changes may be carried out. Consequently, teams often wish to test their courses on student control groups or implement them on a limited scale before distributing them widely. Distribution is done by mail, but heavy use is made of private couriers (85% of materials).

Non-Print: Production of audio-visual materials, including software, may at times begin during the design phase, since first drafts of these materials may necessitate design changes, something which is not the case with written materials. For this reason, designers and producers occasionally work with the course-design teams during the design phase.

Télé-université's own personnel produce the audio-visual materials. Since such specialists are scarce, external producers are sometimes hired under house supervision. All technical personnel, however, are hired contractualy, and audio-visual production is supervised by the directing professor, with the assistance of an educational technologist. Software production is quite similar and is done by the telematics department (Bureau de télématique).

Audio-visual materials distribution is done in two distinct but complementary ways. Some materials are sent by mail or courier to student study groups, who meet with a tutor or group spokesperson to view the materials. Thanks to the interuniversity consortium (CANAL), provision has been made for television distribution of audio-visual materials over cable television networks. Certain cable television channels have been reserved in Quebec, specifically for educational purposes. These channels broadcast all day to make the materials available to all students. In addition, Radio Québec broadcasts materials during its off-peak schedule hours, and Montreal has its own UHF channel reserved for educational broadcasting. Finally, Télé-université has occasionally used satellite services to link all cities in Quebec, and it may have access to the Canada-wide channel which broadcasts House of Commons debates. As for software distribution, students receive materials during the computer lab sessions.

The university has had little recourse to existing materials, for two reasons. Available materials in French are scarce and do not meet specific needs. Materials in other languages require such adaptation and translation that costs approach those of producing originals in any case. The one exception to this rule, however, was the use of the 'Ascent of Man' series produced by the BBC, featuring Jacob Bronowski, and already translated into French.

STUDY REGIMES AND STUDENT SUPPORT

Student Administration

Publicity: Each year the university mounts two extensive advertising campaigns to recruit students. The largest coincides with the autumn return to classes and its advertising is published in Quebec's principal newspapers. Other mass advertising is done through a campaign directed at former students as well as at persons having had contact with the university over the previous two or three years. These people are sent a package consisting of a course and programme brochure, together with a current course schedule and registration form.

Other on-going types of publicity support the main campaigns. These include publicity spots on the educational channel, and radio and television broadcasts promoting current course themes. Press conference and kiosks are also used for publicity.

On another level, Télé-université maintains constant contact with potential clients through its liaison with the Federal Quebec Public Services and the private sector, etc., as much to promote its own educational activities as to analyse such organisations' educational and training needs. In addition to all of this, the student services department follows up on all persons who contact the university enquiring about courses and programmes.

Registration: Télé-université accepts individual or group registration at all times; but September, January and May, corresponding to the Fall, Winter and Summer trimesters, are the heaviest registration periods. Individual registrations received after a certain point may be delayed a session in certain courses, but there is no restriction on student enrolment even though equipment constraints may limit the number of students in certain courses.

To enhance access to adults, the university allows those who do not have the minimum university entrance requirements of a 'Diplome d'études collégiales' (DEC), corresponding to 13 years of study held by two-thirds of its students, to enrol, if they are at least 22 years old with pertinent knowledge and experience. Students may enrol full-time (15 credits per session) or part-time (up to 12 credits per session). However, the vast majority of students are part-time, carrying about three credits per session.

Registration fees are $7.50 per session; course fees are $50 for a three-credit course; and $17 per credit for other courses with a $200 maximum. The student is required to pay a $10 fee per course to cover the costs of publication, handling and delivery of course materials.

Meetings and Student Data Keeping

Upon completion of registration, the bringing together of students must begin, due to the scheduling of television broadcasts, computer availability or even students' own scheduling requirements. In the case of students who are completely isolated, a self-instructional approach is chosen supplemented by occasional tutorial telephone contacts. Bringing students together involves hiring resource persons, locating space and circulating audio-visual and software materials, and it is supervised by the student support administration.

Courses involving group registration begin shortly after the forwarding of the registration form. Individual courses begin from four to six weeks after students have registered. Two or three weeks after receiving registration confirmation, students receive their course materials along with a letter containing the steps to follow to begin their course, and a schedule of any study group meetings. All data concerning students' vital statistics and course activities are recorded by computer. The university is currently establishing a data base which will allow the co-ordination of student data with those on resource persons, space availability, and the availability of materials and audio-visual and computer equipment, to completely systematise the operation of the student support centre.

Student support[3]

Support at Télé-université involves teaching support offered the student to help learning. Thus far, it has tested six different support formulae, each of which present certain advantages and disadvantages, as well as each having a limited sphere of application.

Group Discussion: This was the first formula used. About 15 students in the same locality or region are brought together and assigned a group moderator from the same region and conversant with the discipline. Through a series of meetings, students may profit from mutual exchanges and helping each other over difficulties, with or without the moderator's help. Learning activities are occasionally offered.

Telephone Coaching: This has arisen since 1975 due to problems imposed on group meetings by geographical remoteness. Students are put into contact with each other and with the group coach, by telephone and teleconferencing. With several adaptations, this enables the group activities promised.

Small Study Groups: This form of support caters to students' natural tendency to form small groups. Units of three to five students form voluntarily. They take charge of their learning, chose a spokesperson and may have the services of a study 'coach', who helps them get started and handles problems, usually by telephone. By regular contact with the spokesperson or with the students themselves, the coach follows their progress.

Tutoring: Tutors have responsibility for thirty students, whom he or she telephones at least three times. The tutor gives the student 'office' hours, follows their progress and helps them when they encounter difficulties. Students may also contact their tutor when in difficulty.

Combined Methods: The methods described above may be combined in many ways. The most common combination is that of group leadership with tutoring. The student begins on his own with the availability of the tutor, and some weeks later, the tutor leads several sessions, the last synthesising the course. A small group and a tutor may also combine.

Self-Support: In this method the student is left totally to his or her own resources, being guided by the directions included with the educational materials. The student-to-university link is that of the marker who corrects, annotates and returns the student's work.

With the exception of Montreal and Quebec City, where the administrative offices are located, where students may attend their group meetings and where the computer labs are situated, the university does not have a permanent 'campus'. It prefers to maintain a light infrastructure and adapt to changing regional needs. This necessitates a complex logistical effort to ensure that space, materials and equipment meet at the same point when required. For example, no less than 480 of the university's 600 microcomputers are continuously being moved from place to place for course use.

The difficult search for coexistence with other units of the Université du Québec in various regions is not unrelated to the light infrastructure approach. However, two other universities have recently combined with Télé-université to offer university education in the previously deprived Beauce Region of Quebec. This appears to augur well for harmonious co-operation in the future between the university and the regional institutions.

Student Evaluation

Télé-université's student evaluation practices reflect the importance that is placed on the adult student's autonomy. Home-based work and home-based examinations constitute the principal evaluation method. Students either mail work back to the university where it is corrected by tutors, or hand it to the moderator. Computer correction is a feature of some courses using the 'XO' system. This allows a personalised comment for each student response. All student work is returned and includes essays, objective tests, project reports, graded exercises, and course journals. Some types of work are graded while others are sent back only with comments. Work which will be graded is described in the student's course guide and grades used are the five-point scales, A, B, C, D, and E. When marking is centralised for certain courses, the markers are usually regional tutors or specially hired markers.

Evaluation is done according to Université du Québec standards and is part of the learning process. The description of the evaluation and grading method is prepared by the course design team, under the course director's supervision. The evaluation description includes the evaluation instruments, marking methods, provisions for regrading, etc. Evaluation in the distance mode is no easier than in the face-to-face mode. Since it is much more public, however, the rules of the game having been very clearly enunciated beforehand, it is thereby much easier to criticise. At Télé-université, the challenge of excellence is as important as at other distance education institutions.

ADMINISTRATIVE ORGANISATION

Structure and Operation

Télé-université not yet having its letters patent, its legal status derives from the Université du Québec wherein it is represented by the 'Comité exécutif du Président de Université du Québec.' This was set down in 1984 to operationalise the eight announced orientations and approved by the university Board of Governors to enable Télé-université to obtain its letters patent. It structures the university very closely around its three principal activity sectors: teaching and research, communications services, and administration. Around the 'Direction Général' have been placed the operation of the 'Secrétariat général', as well as those of the 'Bureau de la co-opération extérieur' which is occupied with liaison with the Quebec university network, with the marketing of university products and with international co-operation.

Like all organisations, Télé-université has modified its organisational structure over the years, to respond strategically to changes in its environment. The most recent changes were shaped by the university's willingness to equip itself with a more efficient decisionmaking structure, and to affirm the pre-eminence of teaching and research among its activities. The stress has thereby been placed on the maintenance of educational content, rather than on the creation of educational activities. It has also fallen to academic and teaching resources to allow the most flexibility and responsiveness. This reflects the university's determination to plan its development, notably in economic terms, to perform in a more financially stable fashion than in the past. A more stable clientele is one feature of this objective. Finally, the 'Bureau de la co-opération extérieur and the office of upgrading services have replaced the office of mediatisation of teaching.

Besides working out internal regulations and administering pedogogical regulations at the Université du Québec, the sub-commission's principal tasks deal with the development and revision of courses and programmes; conferral of diplomas; organising teaching and research; interuniversity co-operation; and evaluating and planning teaching and research activities.

The third element is the Interinstitutional Co-operation Sub-commission. It is responsible for what its name implies, and for developing a mediatised approach to teaching. However, its importance is subordinated to those of the other two.

Control of Operations

Day-to-day control of Télé-université's activities is performed by the Studies Sub-commission, with regard to academic activities, and by the 'Commission de la Télé-université' which is the ultimate authority. The decisionmaking bodies of the Université du Québec, the Board of Studies and the Board of Governors operate through these.

Institutional research activity also acts as a controlling force. Institutional research has primarily been conducted in concert with researchers from the 'Institute national de la recherche scientifique' (INRS-Education), between 1974 and 1977. In dealt with student characteristics, course quality, the quality of the human resources offered by the university, etc. Certain research activity had been led by Télé-université personnel until 1984, but it was of limited importance. Other research, done on a contractual basis, examined both the university's finance, and the cost of student support.

Therefore, the new university organisation stresses institutional research and development through the creation of a planning and research office, reporting to the 'Secrétariat général' and the creation of an office for economic and financial studies, reporting to the 'Direction des Affaires Administratives'.

Physical, Human and Financial Resources

Télé-université's 1984-5 operating budget, based on an enrolment of 2,400 full-time equivalent students, with a regular staff of 209 employees, amounts to $15,000,000. More than 80 per cent of operating revenue is received from the Government of Quebec, and student tuition accounts for slightly less than 10%. The investment budget itself amounts to $115,000. Télé-université is financed by the Government of Quebec under the same regulations as other Quebec universities, something that has not harmed its development. However, the review of the financing of Quebec universities, which is expected to favour certain levels of teaching, and more particularly long-term and advanced-study programmes in technologically-related disciplines, threatens to handicap the university should it continue to concentrate its teaching activities in certificates and the social sciences.

Human resources are distributed as follows: The Head; 3 senior administrative personnel; 15 middle-level administrative personnel; 27 full-time professors; 49 professionals (including 12 educational professionals); 29 technical staff; and 86 office workers, for a total of 209 regular employees. Teaching and research occupy 95 regular employees, while 50 are attached to management and 44 are attached to communications services. The remaining 20 are shared between other services. The faculty's youth should be noted. In the early days it was expected that Télé-université would develop its teachers in concert with the Université du Québec's network. This proving premature, the university chose to hire staff contractually. It was thus difficult to develop programmes and research, and thereby, credibility; hence the option towards regular faculty since 1981. These professors had to have a well-rounded and comprehensive approach to their discipline. They had to be sensitive to adult education, capable of directing a course team, and informed in the area of mediatisation. They have since become indispensable to Télé-université's development.

With regard to physical resources, Télé-université is centred in Quebec City and Montreal, between which administration is shared. Beyond these administrative locales, where some teaching activity occurs, computer labs have been set up in Quebec City and Montreal for informatics students.

CONCLUSION

Télé-université's 13-year history has provided an abundance of distance education experiences. Counter-pointed by many trials, these have also been the opportunity for as many challenges as the university has been able to meet, with audacity, poise and imagination. But these thirteen years of tumult have also left the university with the desire to continue its life on a more peaceful plane and to transform its trials and errors into gain. It finds itself at a crossroads, and hopes that thirteen more years will not have to pass for it to receive recognition as an adult institution, which deals with distance education for adults.

NOTES

1. This paper was translated from the French by Thomas Wilson, Instructor in Educational Technology, Concordia University.

2. This section is based on 'The Télé-université of Quebec (1972-9)', Marquis and Grenier, Télé-université, 1979. The Open University Conference on the Education of Adults at a Distance, Birmingham, Nov. 1979.

3. This material is borrowed from a paper presented by France Bilodeau, then director of student support services, at the International Council for Correspondence Education Conference held in Vancouver in 1982.

North Island College

John Tayless

North Island College is one of the fifteen community colleges that serve the province of British Columbia. The college was founded in 1975 with the mandate to deliver educational services to the population residing in Central and North Vancouver Island and the adjacent mainland coast.

In anticipation of the college's foundation, a regional advisory committee was established in 1975 to advise the government on what the nature of the new institution should be. This committee produced a visionary statement that has guided the institution to its present day:

> We envision North Island College to be a 'community-based' college providing traditional as well as non-traditional clientele with traditional and non-traditional services through non-traditional delivery systems. This community-based college will analyse the needs of the North Island communities, will join forces with other agencies in meeting those needs, will re-evaluate programme priorities, will take the college to the community, will redirect resources and will set the pace for a new and expanded community college thrust into human services providing lifelong learning to all adults.[1]

To implement this diversified, community-based, delivery model, the college has introduced a system of interdependent individualised learning resources, on-site tutors, and local resources learning centres. With these three elements in place throughout its region, the college has found that it has a particularly powerful support and delivery system that enables it to provide educational services to the most isolated of students. The efficacy of the system is borne out by the population participation statistics, which show that some 28% of the adults in the region avail themselves of college services.

THE COLLEGE REGION

The area served by the college comprises the northern three-quarters of Vancouver Island, the archipelago to the east and north of the community of Campbell River, and the contiguous mainland north to the Bella Coola valley. It is a region of rugged coastlines, deep fiords and high snow-capped mountains hemmed in by the breakers of the Pacific Ocean to the west and the permanent glaciers of the coast range to the east.

The regional population of 110,000 is maintained by an economy based upon logging, with its lumber and pulp and paper derivatives, copper mining, fishing and tourism. The demographic reality of a population exhibiting no economies of scale dictate the locally tutored, open learning system that the college has refined to reach its students.

THE COLLEGE MANDATE

North Island College students enrol in a myriad of courses, for the mandate of the community college in British Columbia is particularly broad. Offered are an academic university transfer programme at the first and second year levels; a college preparation programme; a high-school completion programme; an adult basic education programme that embraces literacy to Grade 12; vocational training programmes; technical training programmes; English language training; and a non-credit continuing education programme.

THE STUDENT

The Canadian population, like that of most countries in the developed world, is an aging population and this is borne out by the average age of the college students, which is approximately 28 years old with more women than men enrolled. Thus the college predominantly serves older part-time students who often have family, community and employment responsibilities rather than younger, single full-time students. Therefore the college's programmes and courses must be accessible to people leading multi-faceted lives of which studying is but a part. It is this problem of access by the adult learner that together with the regional demography has shaped the college methodology.

INSTITUTIONAL METHODOLOGY

The college's operation can be best described as an open learning system composed of well-designed, individualised, learning resources managed by a local tutor, based upon a local learning resource centre, and the whole supported by the administrative resources of the institution. Thus with local tutorial support available to the student, North Island College cannot be described *in sensu strictu* as a distance education institution.

INDIVIDUALISED LEARNING MATERIALS

North Island College is a relatively small institution, thus the decision was made early in its career that rather than write its own courses it would acquire well-designed, well-written materials from other institutions, providing that they were not culturally bound to a particular society. Of particular assistance to the college has been Athabasca University in Alberta. A close and indeed unique co-operative arrangement has existed between the two institutions for ten years, namely that of dual enrolment. When a student enrols at North Island College in a course supplied by Athabasca University the student also fills out an Athabasca University registration form and is then dually enrolled at both institutions. Athabasca University provides the summative grades by marking the final exams, thus fulfilling the role of an external examiner. North Island College tutors provide the local tutorial support and supply Athabasca University with the formative grades. This arrangement has led NIC students to continue their third and fourth year with Athabasca University, thus maintaining the momentum and continuum of their postsecondary education and enabling them to complete their degrees while remaining in their home community.

In British Columbia the college obtains written course materials from the Open Learning Institute. These materials are particularly appropriate as the Open Learning Institute is writing for the British Columbian adult student and thus there is an appropriate fit between the materials and the student. The Open Learning Institute maintains a close liaison with the three provincial universities and indeed many of the courses are written by lecturers from these institutions. The student is also able to continue their third and fourth year of study with the Open Learning Institute and thus obtain their degree while remaining at home.

Courses have also been obtained from the BBC, The Open University, Seneca College in Ontario, Coast Community College in California, Dallas Community College, The University of Maryland and other institutions. Becoming increasingly important, particularly in the sciences and technologies, are complete course materials produced by commercial companies. This particular source of courses will become more and more important the more ubiquitous home ownership of microcomputers becomes.

THE LEARNING/RESOURCE CENTRES

The college operates four types of learning centre, the characteristics of each being defined by the number of registrations it generates. These are generally directly proportional to the size of the community served.

Learning Centres:

Type I	1,000 registrations or more:	3 Centres
Type II	250-1,000 registrations:	3 Centres
Type III	100-200 registrations:	14 Centres
Type IV	Mobile learning centres:	2 Mobile Centres

Total   22 Local Learning Centres

The learning/resource centres (hereafter called the centre) are resource centres in a very full sense. Available to the students in the Type 1 centre are:

1. tutorial services;
2. academic advising;
3. career reference and search;
4. quiet study areas;
5. computer facilities;
6. a modest laboratory;
7. library
  a. reference
  b. journals and periodicals;
8. seminar rooms;

163

9. student lounge;
10. audio-visual equipment including satellite reception facilities and video-players;
11. comprehensive videotape library;
12. business office training equipment;
13. art studios;
14. welding shops (individualised, continuous entry/exit programme);
15. electrical Technology labs;
16. drafting labs;
17. nursing labs;

The Type II centres includes all of the above with the exception of the specialised laboratories. The Type III centre generally consists of a reference library, videotape library, a microcomputer and audio-visual equipment and most importantly a local tutor/adviser. The Type IV centre, the mobile learning centre, is operated by the tutor/adviser and consists of four study carrels, is equipped with a microcomputer and audio-visual equipment and visits its small communities on a set schedule.

The four types of learning centre are considered to be general community resources andit is not necessary to be enrolled in a course in order to make use of their facilities.

When opening a new learning centre the college always endeavours to find a building close to the centre of the community if possible with convenient parking, preferring to follow the medieval approach to the problem of town and gown rather than the more modern campus orientation. The learning centres must be conveniently accessible to students, convenient in not involving any commuting and accessible in not having inappropriate hours of operation. Positioning them in the centre of the community and making their services available from 8:30 a.m. until 10:00 p.m. solves the convenience and accessibility problem.

THE TUTORIAL SYSTEM

The main strength of the North Island College system lies in its tutorial staff. There are four types of tutor in the system and depending upon the particular circumstance, a single staff member may fulfil the requirements of all four. The four tutorial categories are: course tutor, local tutor, general tutor, and marking tutor:

The course tutor is a tutor with a graduate degree in a particular subject who is charged with the institutional responsibility for a particular course within his/her subject specialty. The course tutor is responsible for overseeing all aspects of the course, as well as the evaluation, content appropriateness, pacing schedules, up-dating of the subject matter, tutoring students and acting as the academic course resource to local, central and marking tutors.

The local tutor has expertise in a particular subject and acts as the tutor at the local level for courses within his/her subject speciality and maintains a close liaison with the course tutor.

The general tutor acts as a local course manager ensuring that students receive their study materials, arranges students study schedules, proctors examinations and refers students to course tutors for academic advising.

Marking tutors have a graduate degree in the subject in question and, with the course tutor, grade assignments and examinations.

The tutoring function at the centre is fulfilled in several different ways as dictated by the need of the individual student.

For most courses offered by the college the student has a six-month learning contract to adhere to; however, students are strongly encouraged to enter into a fifteen-week or twenty-week study schedule. For courses with high enrolment in the centre there is frequently a paced group meeting available where the students meet each week as a group and the tutor paces them through in fifteen weeks. These paced options are generally exercised by students taking more than one course. However, the time of the group meeting is decided upon by the students themselves after the first meeting, as the objective of the institution is to remain as student-convenient as possible. Those students who do not wish to avail themselves of the paced options receive individual tutorials and are encouraged to meet with their tutor at least once every two weeks. All tutor/student consultations are noted on the student progress form.

The student advising function at the centre is also carried out by the tutors and this has led to the appointment of the duty-tutor. Each tutor takes a three-hour segment of the day or evening when they are available to answer questions arising from the public and prospective students. These questions are generally concerned with career paths, career ambitions, training opportunities, programmes available at other institutions, prerequisites at other institutions and how they can be met at North Island College and, indeed, how the college can aid them in achieving their stated educational goals. In this manner the centre tutors become true community resources in their own right, filling a general educational role that is not easily duplicated in the traditional central campus setting.

THE USE OF TECHNOLOGY IN COURSE DELIVERY

The necessity to provide educational services to students where there are no economies of scale has led the college to develop innovative uses of educational technology. These include courses offered via on-line, remote computer terminals, microcomputers and the educational TV-communications satellite ANIK-C.

A large number of courses also have integrated into them videotapes and computer exercises.

COURSES OFFERED BY REMOTE COMPUTER TERMINALS, ON-LINE

At present the beginning first-year university level course in the Pascal programming language is available on this system with more courses to follow.

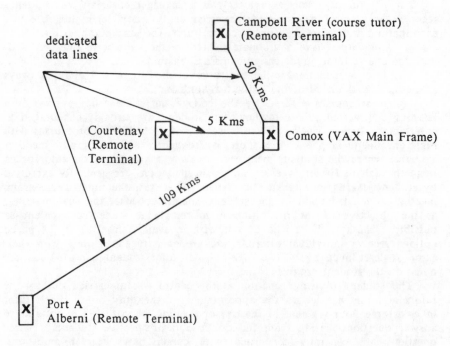

A microcomputer version of these courses is also being written to further distribute the courses to the smallest type II, III and IV learning centres or to students' homes if they have their own personal computer.

COURSES OFFERED USING THE ANIK-C EDUCATIONAL SATELLITE

The college is presently offering a study skills course and two university level courses in English and Psychology via the ANIK-C educational-communications satellite. This is a particularly effective delivery method as the course is delivered direct to the students' home via the local TV cable system.

The courses consist of course texts, study guides, videotapes and interactive tutorial sessions delivered via the satellite. By using their home telephones the students are able to consult directly with the tutor in the television studio. This system demonstrates a particularly effective use of educational television and students served by this system continue to demand that more and more courses be made available to them in this format. The success of the system is emphasised by the more than one thousand students who have now utilised it for their studies. A further use of the system is for general education as the staff of the Knowledge Network of the West in Vancouver, who operate the system, are aware that at any one time some eighteen thousand non-enrolled interested viewers are following the course.

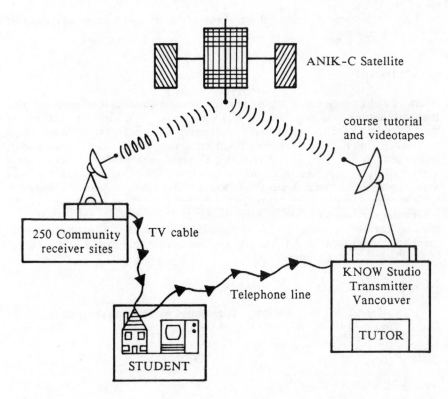

The KNOW television signal is presently being received by 250 communities in Western Canada. The 'footprint' of the satellite includes The Yukon Territory, part of the North-West Territories, Saskatchewan, Alberta and British Columbia.

ADMINISTRATION

To administer this open learning system the college has adopted a management system that consists of the college principal and four central directors. A college board consisting of local citizens drawn from the region served governs the college as appointees of the provincial government.

Operating under the guidance of the principal, the four central directors - bursar, director of programmes, director of student services and management information systems and director of materials - serve as the support system for the learning centre directors and their staff.

While the first three positions are traditional in their responsibilities, that of director of materials is a product of the needs of an open learning system. The learning materials, library resources, videotapes, computer software and hardware, have to be brought together to form the synergism that is the strength of the systems. This requires a professional with a strong background in learning methodology and learning innovation.

At the local centre level, the centre director and the tutorial staff are responsible for identifying the educational needs of their community and working as a team to answer those needs using the wide range of resources available to them.

CONCLUSION

North Island College has designed and implemented a system of open learning that concentrates on encouraging adult access to education by eliminating the systemic impediments of fixed semesters, fixed registration dates, fixed attendance times, fixed locations, fixed class size, fixed entry requirements, fixed group progress and fixed instructional methodology. Continuous entry/exit into courses that utilise individualised study materials and appropriate educational technology has enabled the students to integrate their studies into lifestyles where their formal learning is but a part of the adult responsibilities of family, employment and community contribution. By making learning so accessible, it is then able to become a life-time commitment for the adult, thus making life-long learning a true reality.

NOTES

1. Report of the Advisory Committee to the North Island College Board, Campbell River, March 1975, pp. 61-2.

Section 4: DISTANCE EDUCATION PROGRAMMES

University Programmes

Robert Sweet

This chapter will outline the existing system of distance education at Canadian universities, first in terms of the social purpose of extending educational opportunity to a clientele other than the 18-24 year-old age group which traditionally has been served. Developments in the Canadian postsecondary system from 1970 are described to illustrate how university distance education has come to be associated with the concept of life-long learning and, more specifically, has been directed towards serving adult, part-time students. The second section describes various types of university level distance education programmes currently operating in Canada. For each, a representative institution is discussed, highlighting the essential features of that programme. The section includes discussion of issues associated with the future development of Canadian distance education programmes: the need for continuing student support services to make institutional access and programme completion a reality for older students; the contribution of technology to improved quality of instructional materials and delivery procedures; and the trend towards co-operation among institutions where the development of consortia appears to facilitate accreditation, academic legitimacy and the development of a unique identity for distance education in the Canadian postsecondary system.

THE POSTSECONDARY CONTEXT

In the 1970s, the age structure of the Canadian population caused a dramatic shift in university enrolment patterns. While the number of full-time students from the 18-24 year-old age group steadily decreased, the older 'baby boom' generation entered the age range normally associated with part-time studies and demand grew for improved access to postsecondary facilities. Demographics alone would have caused part-time enrolments to increase. There were, however, additional factors that contributed to higher participation rates among older persons. The most important of these were the impact of technology on the economy and the changing role of women.

As Canada began moving towards a 'post-industrial' society, a workforce possessing specialised, technical skills and knowledge became increasingly important. Technological changes in most occupations were rapidly outdating the knowledge acquired through formal education, necessitating further learning if the employee hoped to advance in his or her career. The post-war investments Canada had made in its educational system combined to produce, by the 1970s, a highly educated population. (Statistics Canada, 1979) As employees, many of these people were willing and able to enrol in further education programmes, and many Canadian companies made available some form of educational leave. However, part-time study was the only real alternative for most fully employed workers with family responsibilities.

One of the more significant social changes of the period was the evolving role of women, both in the family and in the workplace. Two trends became apparent at this time: a preference for smaller families, and increased participation in the workforce, particularly in the professional occupations. Both have resulted in greater financial and personal independence, attributes considered by Belanger, Lynd and Mouelhi (1982) to have stimulated and enabled women to pursue part-time studies for practical and personal purposes.

Based on a consideration of the social and demographic forces that shaped this demand for part-time university enrolment by older Canadians, Tetlow and Taylor (1981) characterised the new, mature-student constituencies as follows:

1. The Mature Non-employed. The principal sub-groups are housewives and retired persons, many of whom are seeking degree completion or personal enrichment courses.
2. The Wage Earners. Many individuals in this category are seeking enhanced skills and an improvement to their career. Diplomas, certificates and degree completion are the goals of most such individuals, although many are enrolling for personal enrichment. A variety of reasons operate to make educational pursuits viable for this group. Generally shorter working hours provide more leisure time to pursue intellectual interests while the availability of paid educational leave encourages enrolment to more applied areas of study. While restricting personal resources, unemployment also acts as a strong catalyst for further learning.
3. The Professionals. Organisations from both the public and private sector are requiring ongoing educational involvement of their employees. In business and industry the 'half-life' of many professionals is less than 10 years because of changes in technology, legal requirements, and an exponential growth in knowledge.
4. The Mobile. Numerous factors have made Canadian families and individuals more geographically mobile. As a result, many of these people find difficulty in completing degrees.

By the end of the 1970s, these groups made up one third to one half of the total enrolments at Canadian universities. The social changes underlying the altered nature of university enrolments led to a redefinition of what constituted equality of educational opportunity. One interpretation was offered by the OECD report on educational policies in Canada: 'the recognition that the right to educational opportunity should not remain confined to the short period of childhood and youth, but should be a life-long recurrent principle, aimed at catching up on lost chances and at opening up new opportunities'. (OECD 1976:39)

Various assessments of the postsecondary situation made in the early 1970s were guided by principles of life-long learning and recommended policies designed to increase institutional accessibility for adults. Two of these analyses were provincial government commissions: the Commission of Educational Planning in Alberta (Alberta 1972); and the Commission of Post

Secondary Education in Ontario (Ontario 1972), known as the Worth Report and the Wright Report, respectively.

In developing the theme of improved access, the Worth Report stressed the potential of recurrent education to expand an individual's skills and thereby improve his life chances. The Wright Report emphasised the need for dramatic shifts in institutional policies regarding student admissions requirements, programme diversity, responsiveness and flexibility and course credit transferability. A focus on the personal development and well-being of each individual is apparent in the recommendations of both reports. Molyneux (1974) summarised their position: 'There is the belief that while education is a social process systematically organized and institutionalised, learning is a personal experience. It begins and ends with the individual and the time has come to invest him with considerable choice in deciding where, when and how he will seek to learn'. (p. 119)

The reports also outlined some specific directions for improved access: a completely open admissions policy; an increase in student financial support; and a means of transferring credits from one institution to another. As well, they strongly promoted institutional innovation as necessary to achieve the goal of improved accessibility. Proposals to found an 'Alberta Academy' and an 'Open Academy of Ontario' illustrate the extent and direction of recommended institutional change. These undoubtedly were inspired by the demonstrated effectiveness of the British Open University (BOU) and represented a 'new delivery system of learning involving use of advanced communications technology'.

Distance education concepts were seen as relevant both to existing social imperatives and the geographic necessity of decentralising postsecondary instruction in Canada. Canada's population of 25 million inhabits the world's second largest country. Most live in cities distributed along the southern border and this is, of course, where the major universities are. Many others live in smaller communities some distance from the metropolitan areas and for them, distance and geography are barriers to higher education.

In the event, neither the Alberta Academy nor the Open Academy of Ontario was established; nor did later developments evolve in quite the form intended by the commissions. The many different channels to further learning advocated in the reports, as well as the emphasis each gave to expanding educational requirements, set a direction for university distance education developments throughout the 1970s.

UNIVERSITY PROGRAMME TYPES

The *Directory of University Correspondence Courses* (CAUCE 1983) lists 27 institutions offering courses through distance. Most of these programmes were established in the past decade indicating the rapidity with which distance education has developed at Canadian universities. As well, the organisational formats of the various programmes continue to evolve in terms of their structure and management style. Despite this fluidity of form, Smith, Daniel and Snowden (1984) have identified five different programme developments: the traditional correspondence courses; and the extension and 'outport' programmes associated with the established universities; the newer 'open' universities, patterned on the British Open University model; and finally, the communication networks designed as broadcasters and distributors of television programmes for sponsoring universities.

Correspondence Courses: First offered by Queen's University in 1889, correspondence courses are the oldest form of distance education in Canada. The Queen's courses were designed for and enrolled elementary school teachers anxious to acquire university degrees. Correspondence programmes today appeal to a more diverse clientele. Courses designed for professional certification and upgrading serve individuals in a wide variety of professions; and these courses are improving in design and growing in number. However, most available correspondence courses are intended for university degree credit in the traditional disciplines and all are recognised equivalents of classroom courses. (CAUCE 1983)

Print materials traditionally have formed the instructional base for correspondence courses and the popular conception of learning by correspondence remains fixed on print materials. Since audiocassettes are just as likely to be the primary vehicles of information exchange in a modern correspondence course, the presence or absence of print materials does not accurately characterise this form. Perhaps the distinguishing feature of correspondence programmes is their reliance on the mails as the primary method for delivering instructional content and, in some cases, of providing the means of teacher-student interaction.

Most representative of the correspondence programmes in Canada is that developed at the University of Waterloo. The correspondence programme began at Waterloo in 1968 with four courses in physics. Six years later, Waterloo had available 111 courses in the areas of Modern Languages, Humanities, Social Sciences, Natural Science and Mathematics. By the 1983-4 academic year, over 300 courses had been developed and nearly 10,000 full-time-equivalent students were enrolled. The scope of operations for that year is further indicated by the 18,882 registrations processed through 435 courses over three semesters. Waterloo's programme has grown to be the largest in Canada and its success has been attributed by Pike (1978) to the 'systematic approach to distance education in which there is breadth of programme and consistency of method'. In the view of the programme's originator, success has followed the application of 'common sense' and the desire to keep development 'simple and relatively cheap'. (Leslie 1979)

There are a number of features unique to the Waterloo model, most of which derive first from the relationship established between the correspondence programme and the various university departments, and second, from the attempt to make the off-campus experience match as closely as possible the on-campus experience of a regular student. The correspondence programme operates as a separate entity within the general university structure. Courses are administered by the programme office which deals with such matters as registration, issuance of textbooks and routine communications with students. While the correspondence programme is an autonomous, and autonomously funded, administration unit, its role appears to be primarily limited to course delivery. Curriculum decision making rests with the different academic departments with whom the correspondence director contracts for courses. In Leslie's (1979) words, 'the academic control of a correspondence course resides with the department offering the course in particular, the departmental chairman is responsible for selecting the professor, operator, tutor, and grader'. (p. 38) The further division of labour among the last-mentioned positions is interesting. The professor prepares only the lecture tapes and accompanying notes while the operator prepares the course assignments and examinations. The operator has the further responsibility of marking the examinations and co-ordinating the overall operation of the course. Tutors prepare model solutions for the assignments and provide relevant comment as feedback to students. Graders mark assignments. Separation of the evaluation and content functions in course development seems unlikely to contribute to improved instructional design of courses. Presumably some measure of communication occurs between professor and operator in the development phase; and conceivably they could be the same person. This would be most likely in the first semester of a new course. Overall, the process is what Pike (1978) termed 'private' in the same sense that traditional, classroom teaching allows the teacher to control completely the content and standards of a course. In any event, the product of this process is a package of 20 audiocassettes containing taped lectures of approximately 40 minutes. The package includes also a set of lecture notes and textbooks; and in certain courses, there are special resource materials such as rock samples, microscope slides and 35 mm. slides.

Underlying this course development process is an analysis of the communication channels in a typical, classroom lecture situation. According to Leslie (1980), these are the *formal* and *informal* visual channels represented respectively by texts, notes, pictures, etc., and the more spontaneous writing that might be made on an overhead or blackboard. There is also the audio channel - what is said by way of explanation and illustration during a lecture. The use of tapes and accompanying lecture notes in the correspondence course is intended to recreate the formal visual and the audio channels of the classroom. The design of these materials is straightforward:

> The actual way that professors prepare one of our taped correspondence courses is that they sit down at a desk with a tape recorder, the formal visual material and a pad of paper. The professor talks into the tape recorder, and can refer the students to various aspects of the formal visual material. The professors can do examples or present written notes using the pad of paper just as they would use a blackboard in a classroom. We tell the professor to imagine that the student is sitting in the room looking over his or her shoulder just as would be the case in an individual tutorial, when you are talking to a student in such a situation, or demonstrate some principle by doing an example. (Leslie 1979:36)

While this description outlines the general form of course development at Waterloo, the nature of the process allows much individual variation and the academic departments undoubtedly have evolved a format for development that best suits their personnel and disciplines. However, it is not likely that an institutional standard could be established or maintained in such a decentralised system.

Tying the correspondence programme as tightly as possible to the regular, on-campus programme results in fixing the starting times and durations for courses as well as the assignment and examination schedules. While this organisational rigidity would seem to disadvantage the mature, part-time student, the enrolment figures indicate otherwise. One obvious advantage of programme similarity is the ease with which correspondence study can be combined with on-campus study. Without problems of accreditation and integration, students can pursue a degree programme with greater ease and intellectual benefit.

One of the less favourable features of any strictly correspondence course is the delay in providing students with instructional feedback. Leslie (1979) reported that turn-around time for assignment marks and assignment comments was at least three weeks. Also, although the comments were put on tape by the tutors and thus could be fairly detailed, they were addressed to the 'class as a whole' and not to any one individual. More recently, Waterloo has experimented with audio teleconferencing and computer conferencing in an attempt to individualise their instruction and feedback. This last mentioned development, if pursued, marks a rather significant policy shift towards technological complexity.

Extension and Outport Programmes

Like the Waterloo correspondence programme described above, extension and 'outport' programmes in Canada are associated with established universities but their first priority is extending educational opportunity to the more geographically distant communities in each province. In pursuing this goal, much faith is placed in the use of electronic communications media. (Smith *et al*. 1984). This is so for those extension programmes offering 'distance education' as opposed to 'education at a distance' instruction. (COU 1985) Where the former conforms to accepted definitions of distance education, the latter refers to off-campus courses using conventional instructional techniques. This 'travelling professor' provision still predominates in the extension departments of many universities. However, the financial penalty of sending faculty to the field as well as the students' demand for home study is rapidly reshaping the instructional planning of university extension departments. (Gallagher-Mullen 1984, Smith and Snowden 1983)

The University of British Columbia. Virtually all of Canada's universities provide opportunities for part-time study through extended day or evening programmes, and most have plans to supplement if not supplant their field services through distance education techniques employing some form of electronic media combined with print materials. The University of British Columbia's Extension Department is an example of a traditional programme augmented by a distance education service. The UBC Guided Independent Study (GIS) Programme offers a limited number of courses in both professional and general studies areas, the latter supporting B.A. and B.Sc. degrees. The courses are built around a core of print materials: the text; a student handbook which outlines administrative; and a student manual containing a study guide, instructor's notes, the assignments, and (optional) self-testing materials. Supplemental materials include audio tapes, and lab kits or books of readings. Some courses are enriched with television programmes broadcast by the Knowledge Network of the West (KNOW).

Course development proceeds along administrative lines that require professors to surrender some of their 'academic sovereignty' in that a blueprint of the course must first be prepared and approved by the GIS Programme staff. As the course is written, faculty collaborate further with an instructional designer in an attempt to apply appropriate design principles and achieve consistency and quality in the final product. The GIS Department also develops print components for video courses, essentially constructing a print 'wrap around' for the existing visual medium. Students are supported through a telephone link to the UBC library and have available the services of a library research and resource person. Of particular importance is the individual telephone access students have to their instructor, which provide rapid instructional feedback as well as encouragement to students.

The use of a variety of media for course delivery is characteristic also of distance education programmes at Memorial and Brandon Universities. These institutions are attempting to provide programmes at extreme distance to small and scattered populations. Each is approaching the use of media in ways that reflect not only the needs of their clientele but also their different institutional histories.

Memorial University: Memorial University of Newfoundland has extensive experience in multi-media distance education. Its first venture into production of televised credit courses was in 1969 when a major effort was made to upgrade the qualifications of school teachers throughout the province. This required development of videotaped lectures at Memorial which then were distributed to learning centres in the field. In the initial stages of this programme, the tapes were supplemented by on-site tutors and by communications with the (Memorial-based) instructor through use of audio-cassettes. The results were less than encouraging: tutors were not academically adequate to the task, and the audiocassette exchanges between students and instructor had too great a turn-around time to be useful. (Roberts 1982) Nevertheless, a beginning had been made and the lessons learned in this early application of media were applied to ongoing developments in the areas of teleconferencing and video production.

Distance education activities at Memorial are supported by a television production unit capable of constructing purpose-made broadcast or videotape television programmes. Broadcasting from this facility has gathered a range of experience that includes but is not limited to credit courses. For example, a responsive, public television service called 'Playback' was instituted in 1978, which allowed viewers in the Greater St John's area to submit to a Memorial broadcast studio technician their telephone requests for specific programmes. While the capability exists to transmit such television programmes across the province to local cable television links, these are too few to warrant immediate development. Memorial was an active participant in the 1975 Hermes satellite field trials. As a result of this experience, two-way interactive satellite transmission is seen as necessary for effective educational broadcasting. (Starcher 1982)

One of the problems in deploying instructional television at a distance is the necessity of relatively large audiences (approximately 300 - 400 persons). In 1977 Memorial began experimenting with audio teleconferencing as an alternative, two-way communication system that could gather reasonable 'class sizes' by linking small groups or even individuals over the public telephone system. Memorial has since established a 4-wire, dedicated network that includes hospitals, vocational schools and other facilities throughout the province. Audio teleconferencing of credit courses was initiated in 1977. Courses in Business, Special Education, Philosophy, and English have since been offered. More recently, telewriters have been used to communicate with students.

Memorial recently embarked upon a reorganisation of its continuing education and extension services, part of which included creation of an Educational Technology Department. Built largely from the old Educational Television section but with overall responsibility for distance education course development, the new department is well able to apply new communication technology to course design and delivery. The rationale and a possible course development process have been outlined by Starcher (1985). The co-ordinating body in this process is the Academic Strategy Group which screens course proposals and advises on the appropriate mix of media for a given course and audience. Since the reorganisation of Memorial is so recent, it is not possible to know exactly how the course development process will evolve. However, the present format for constructing distance education credit courses strongly reflects the previous involvement of Memorial with telecommunications technology.

As outlined by McNamara (1985), the typical media blueprint used in the design of a course would include:

1. a student study guide;
2. books of readings;
3. thirteen televised lectures (1/2 hour each);
4. thirteen audio teleconference sessions (1 1/2 hours per week); and
5. five audio tapes.

With a small and dispersed population to serve, Memorial has always been a leader in the application of technology to distance education, and with reorganisation, seems gearing up to renew that role. A mandate to serve the outport communities located along Newfoundland's coastline requires imaginative use of the video technology with which Memorial has gained considerable expertise. Because of the limited availability of cable systems in the province and the very high costs of satellite communication, it likely will be necessary for Memorial to co-ordinate its future broadcasting efforts with the other universities in Atlantic Canada.

Brandon University: Brandon University has only recently developed a multi-media distance education programme, enrolling its first students in 1983. Its current clientele are elementary and secondary teachers posted to the many small villages that dot the northern part of Manitoba. As well, they enrol a number of Native Indians in teacher-training and teacher-aide courses. These individuals previously had been served directly by university personnel flown in to the remote communities under the Brandon University Teacher Education Programme (BUNTEP) and the Project for the Education of Native Teachers (PENT). Brandon is a relatively small university and these programmes were integrated with similar training and education efforts offered by the Universities of Manitoba and Winnipeg under a co-operative arrangement called Inter-Universities North. Although effective, the BUNTEP and PENT programmes were expensive to mount and difficult to sustain. With limited resources available, Brandon began to develop courses for delivery using a variety of media. Initially, educational video programmes were purchased and print materials suited to the special needs of northern students were wrapped around the videos. Experience with this adaptation process has produced some interesting course development and delivery techniques. Because many of the native students are primarily visual learners and prefer to study within a co-operative learning structure, instructional materials must accommodate these cultural and individual differences. Various mixes of videotapes, 35 mm. slides, and print materials enhanced with visuals have been attempted. Audiocassettes also have been used. More recently, teleconferencing has been employed with some success, although here too adaptations must be made to differences in learning style. (Paulet 1985)

The extension and outport programmes operated by Canadian universities are employing increasingly sophisticated technology in their course design and delivery methods. Memorial and Brandon Universities in particular have employed various media in imaginative ways to overcome problems of isolation and distance in delivering courses.

Open Universities

The criteria for 'open learning' as defined by Mackenzie, Postgate and Scupham (1975) included

1. involving students not adequately covered by conventional educational programmes;
2. offering courses outside the mainstream education provision;
3. utilising learning systems which have some element of newness in curriculum, organisation, course development or delivery; and
4. a concern with student attainment leading to some recognised qualification.

With the possible exception of Memorial, Canadian universities at the beginning of the 1970s had introduced into their programmes few essential elements of the open learning ideal. To those educators who felt a more innovative approach was needed to cope with anticipated enrolment increases (for example, Trotter 1970), the 'open university' concept seemed to offer a particularly effective system. Much of this interest undoubtedly was stimulated by the British Open University's success in extending educational opportunity to mature, part-time students. Despite obvious differences in the educational situations of the two countries, a distance education institution fashioned on the British model was an attractive proposal in at least three provinces.

The Télé-université in Quebec and Athabasca University in Alberta were established in the early 1970s as the first dedicated distance education institutions in Canada. A third such university, the Open Learning Institute, was created in British Columbia in 1978. While the mandate of each was tailored to the particular postsecondary system of the home province, all shared the institutional autonomy so necessary to function as an effective distance education organisation:

... an open university, whilst it may share with other universities the fundamental mission of teaching, research, and public service, undertakes this mission in an entirely different manner. The new teaching/learning system on which an open university is based has repercussions on every other aspect of the operation, from governance, management and leadership to the work of the faculty and the design of physical plant. (Daniel and Smith 1979:64)

The organisational and management aspects of the Télé-université and Athabasca University were outlined by Daniel and Smith (1979) and a similar treatment was given British Columbia's Open Learning Institute (OLI) by Ellis and Mugridge (1983), and Kaufman and Sweet (1983).

When they were first established, a unique characteristic of the open universities was the lack of any formal academic prerequisites for entry. At the same time, it was recognised that concepts of openness and access implied more than expanded opportunity to enter into a university programme. The initial policy statements of both institutions assumed that comprehensive student support services, and well-designed and constructed instructional materials were necessary to provide the non-traditional learner with a meaningful education. (AAEM 1975; Kaufman and Bottomley 1980)

Student Support: The Distance Education Committee of the Council of Ontario Universities recently pointed out that 'accessibility as admissibility' is not really a problem for adult, part-time students. Nearly all universities now have in place some form of open admissions policy for 'mature' students. (COU 1984; Hegel 1981) However, the older student often finds it difficult to persist in his or her studies while maintaining a job and supporting a family. (Pascal and Canowich 1979; Sweet 1985) Attaining a university degree by part-time study requires counselling and programme advice at least as effective as that given students at a traditional institution. The organisation of student support services varies considerably among the three Canadian distance education universities. In general, all are concerned with: providing information on admissions and registration regulations as an aspect of student recruitment; maintaining student biographical records and examination results; and offering individual tutoring, counselling and advocacy services.

In Sewart's (1982) view, the effectiveness of the distance education enterprise rests on the ability of individual tutor/advisers to fulfil the mediating (teaching) function required of home study materials. In Sewart's description of the BOU, mediation includes fostering a personal, supportive relationship between student and tutor/adviser as well as direct instruction in the subject matter of the course. Positive relationships between students and faculty are facilitated at open universities because of the separation of production and teaching functions. This makes possible hiring as tutors and advisers those individuals whose primary interest is teaching and advising students, rather than administration or curriculum development.

Tutoring and advising roles are separate functions at two of Canada's open universities. The Télé-université, for example, has established a student support process based on a non-academic 'animateur', an individual appointed to facilitate student learning and communication with the institution. This is accomplished through such activities as regional workshops and teleconferencing links between students. (Caron 1982) In many ways, the animateur functions as a student advocate. Advocacy is an essential task in distance education where students are isolated not only from the institution but also from one another.

Comprehensive student services are available at Athabasca University. Athabasca's academic support system includes tutors who work and comment on assignments as well as hold telephone discussions with individual students on these and other academic matters. Separate advisory and counselling services are offered through the student services unit. Student services personnel engage directly in student counselling procedures based on an analysis of the needs and motivations of the adult learner. For example, students are helped in clarifying personal goals, defining objectives, planning a programme and improving learning skills. Athabasca provides advice and counselling to individuals at a distance and face-to-face through regional centres. These offices are located in Edmonton and Calgary and offer counselling, advising and registry services. A smaller office in Fort McMurray has advising and registry staff available.

Student support services at the OLI are similar in scope to those at Athabasca, with the important exception of the counselling function. Where Athabasca intervenes to promote student independence through counselling, OLI assumes students possess these attributes. These philosophical differences reflect an ongoing debate in the literature regarding the appropriate level of individual support that should be given the distance education student. (Smith and Small 1982) An informational rather than counselling role for the OLI adviser was first laid out in 1979 to guide the operation of regional advisory centres located in the larger communities of the province. (Paterson 1979) These centres recently were reduced in number as a result of cutbacks in government spending. As a consequence, much of the advisory work now is conducted from the OLI central office. To the extent that it is needed, the task of personal counselling is borne by the academic tutor who is in regular contact with the student by telephone. (Sweet 1982)

Course Development and Delivery Systems: The course development system put in place at Athabasca and OLI were variants of the 'course team' arrangement used at the BOU. At both Canadian institutions the team approach evolved to suit changing organisational demands although the basic idea of the course team process was retained, including the course team structure comprising academics and other professionals with responsibility for the design and construction of a particular course. This team approach to course development ensures that even in small universities the quality of instructional materials is maintained at a high level. (Daniel and Smith 1979)

The production of high quality, team-produced learning packages, print based with supplementary audio and video materials, requires an equally sophisticated delivery support system. The Athabasca delivery model includes an extensive telephone tutorial network, teleconferencing and video transmission through community cable television facilities. The OLI delivery system is similarly configured.

The three open universities are recognised as especially innovative developments in Canada postsecondary education and they have had an impact on the general administrative and instructional life at the established university system. (Pike 1980) The influence of the new open systems has been felt most directly in university course development and delivery arrangements where faculty must accept new roles if they involve themselves in distance teaching at their universities. The team approach to course development demands that content specialists interact directly with instructional psychologists and designers, submitting their work to scrutiny and, often enough, some form of editorial criticism. This process contrasts with the private curriculum development activities of the individual professor who designs his or her lessons for the classroom. Course teams require also that one accepts as essential the educational uses of new communications media, an idea that Smith *et al.* (1984) suggest is not well understood or appreciated by most university faculty members. Positive attitudes toward the value of instructional design and technology are forming among faculty at conventional universities where extension departments are adopting a team approach to course development. Contributing also to this attitude shift is a growing literature on the Canadian university experience with instructional media. (Daniel 1983; Rogers 1982; Shobe 1983)

The Telecommunication Networks

Following establishment of the Open Learning Institute, the British Columbia Government created the Knowledge Network of the West (KNOW). Designed to support the communications needs of the province's educational community, KNOW operates an educational television channel that broadcasts by means of satellite and cable. Intended primarily as a communications carrier and support system responsive to the needs of educational institutions, the network has initiated development of original television productions. (Knowledge Network 1983) As well, KNOW has taken a leadership role in coordinating the educational efforts of the various colleges and universities. For example, a learning systems unit has been formed for the development of training materials and workshops designed to increase educators' understanding of television-based learning. (Forsythe 1983) Comparable organisations have been established in other provinces. TVOntario or TVO (The Ontario Educational Communications Authority) operates a broadcast television channel that reaches all areas of the province. At the same time, TVO has developed and marketed original educational programmes. SASKMEDIA (Saskatchewan) and ACCESS (The Alberta Communications Centre for Educational Services and Systems) provide similar production and distribution facilities and expertise to their respective provinces. As Smith *et al.* (1984) point out, the majority of programming produced or distributed by these organisations is done for the various provincial educational institutions. However, each possesses the capability of developing programmes independent of sponsoring institutions; and in some cases, a sufficiently broad mandate is held to allow independent activity. Network relationships with other provincial education institutions are evolving and, although their final form has yet to be decided, a trends toward collaborative ventures is clearly discernible.

Collaboration has been a consistent theme in Canadian distance education. The impetus towards greater co-operation may be attributed to a number of causes. The long history of correspondence programmes notwithstanding, distance education is seen as a recent arrival on the postsecondary scene and a sense of isolation among its members likely contribute to group cohesion and the sharing of resources and ideas. In fact, the presence of distance education programmes has not always been welcomed by established university faculty. The difficulties in this regard are well documented at two institutions: the Télé-Université in Quebec (Daniel and Smith 1979), and the Open Access Study Plan when affiliated with The Atlantic Institute for Education in Nova Scotia. (Sullivan 1985)

Depressed economic conditions in the country and the resulting restraints imposed on government financial support for postsecondary education have further encouraged collaboration among distance education institutions. (Mugridge 1983; Rice 1985) To the extent distance education depends on costly technology, the start-up costs of a new course are extremely high, although development costs can be offset by large enrolments. Since Canada has few very large concentrations of population, 'economies of scale' do not apply. Sharing development and acquisition costs with others makes it possible for a relatively small institution to operate a quality distance education programme. In a more positive vein, co-operation is fostered by the sense of purpose associated with serving non-traditional students, and by the excitement of exploring new methods of course development and delivery based on advanced communications technology.

With these incentives, distance education institutions have formed a variety of formal and informal alliances. Among the former is the Western Canadian Committee on University Distance Education involving all of Western Canada's universities. Formed in 1982, the committee serves a variety of functions from the exchange of information and ideas to joint development and use of course and programme materials. As Mugridge (1983) has described the arrangement, all partners agreed to the conditions of co-operation but only with the qualification that 'no institution, by assuming membership in this committee, faces erosion of autonomy.'

A formal approach is thought by some to be necessary if the arrangement is to benefit all parties, and endure. (Smith and Snowden 1982) Formal ties have worked well in a number of instances to settle differences in accreditation and integration policies. The British Columbia Open University Consortium provides an example. Created in 1984 at the direction of the provincial government, the consortium's member institutions include The University of British Columbia, The University of Victoria, Simon Fraser University, the Open Learning Institute and the Knowledge Network of the West. The degree is awarded through OLI which also provides the necessary student support services. The consortium members are, however, responsible for delivering their own courses. Numerous informal arrangements have been reached between institutions. These typically are bi-lateral and limited in scope. Rice (1985) describes the informal development of a spirit of co-operation in the Atlantic Provinces Association for Continuing Education (APACUE). Its predecessor, the unsuccessful Atlantic Institute for Education, was created specifically to effect co-operation and was 'viewed with suspicion from the outset'. APACUE was formed initially by administrators of university summer schools in a spirit of comraderie, support, reinforcement and sharing. More recently, members of this organisation have combined their interests in technology and instruction by undertaking a number of distance education and communication activities. Rice (1985:10) suggests that while informal arrangements are not necessarily the best means for everyone to accomplish co-operative ends, they have been effective in Atlantic Canada: 'In this region of Canada, it has been discovered that informal, voluntary arrangements based on trust have been able to accomplish greater co-operation in a few short years than more formal bodies and structures have been able to do in the past century.'

Any institution outside the traditional or mainstream educational system requires a sense of identity if it is to grow and contribute. (Gallagher 1980) In the view of many, university distance education has acquired uniqueness as a result of its 'industrial' organisational structure, and its willingness to adopt the ideas of instructional design and educational technology. (Keegan 1983) In Canada, institutional co-operation may be the distinctive feature of the distance education movement which has greatest influence on the broader educational system.

SUMMARY

The chapter began by discussing the changing composition of the postsecondary student population in Canada. In the face of declining enrolments among the 18-24 year-old age group, the increasing interest of older persons in formal learning has given the universities a new clientele and a renewed sense of purpose. This renewal of spirit is expressed in the alternative provision universities are making to accommodate the non-traditional student. Distance education represents only one alternative. It is, however, a particularly vigorous movement.

As a consequence of current financial constraints imposed by governments, universities are concerned with maintaining academic standards while improving access for greater numbers of people. (COU 1984) Distance education can contribute to the achievement of both goals. Instructional quality at established universities can benefit directly from the various curriculum design and development innovations of distant educators, who also have demonstrated a willingness to experiment with and share in the potential of communications technology. At the same time, distance education programmes are contributing to the process of democratising the Canadian postsecondary system by increasing avenues to university study.

REFERENCES

Alberta (1972) *A Choice of Futures*, Report of the Commission on Educational Planning, Edmonton Government Printers

Alberta Advanced Education and Manpower (1975) *Athabasca University: Proposed Role and Mandate*, Edmonton AAEM

Belanger, R., D. Lynd and M. Mouelhi (1982) *Part-time Degree Students: Tomorrow's Majority?*, Statistics Canada: Postsecondary Education Section, Education, Science and Culture Division, November

Caron, S. (1982) 'Student Support at a Crossroads', in J.S. Daniel *et al.* (eds.), *Learning at a Distance: a World Perspective*, Edmonton: Athabasca University/ICCE

CAUCE (1983) *Directory of University Correspondence Courses,* Canadian Association for University Continuing Education available from The Open Learning Institute, Richmond, British Columbia

COU (1984) *Continuity and Renewal: The Demands of Excellence*, Toronto: Council of Ontario Universities

COU (1985) *First Annual Report*, Toronto: Council of Ontario Universities (Committee on Distance Education)

Daniel, J.S. (1983) *Independence and Interaction in Distance Education: New Technologies for Home Study*, PLET, 20, 155-60

Daniel, J.S. and W.A.S. Smith (1979) 'Opening Open Universities: The Canadian Experience', *Canadian Journal of Higher Education*

Ellis, J.F. and Mugridge, I. (1983) *The Open Learning Institute of British Columbia: A Case Study*, DERG Paper no. 8, The Open University Distance Education Research Group, August

Forsythe, K. (1983) *Learning Systems Report*, KNOW: Annual Report, Vancouver: Knowledge Network, June

Gallagher, P. (1980) *The Culture of the Public College*, Unpublished Manuscript available from Capilano College, North Vancouver

Gallagher-Mullen, E. (1984) 'Teleconferencing: Nursing Education at a Distance, *Canadian Journal of University Continuing Education, 10*

Hegel, E.J. (1981) *Survey of Policies in University - Level Correspondence Programs in Canada and the United States of America*, Saskatoon: University of Saskatchewan

Kaufman, D. and J. Bottomley (1980) *The Open Learning Institute: University Programme Development*, Unpublished Manuscript available from the Open Learning Institute, Richmond, British Columbia

Kaufman, D. and R. Sweet (1983) 'Increased Educational Opportunity for Adults: A Canadian Example', *Higher Education in Europe, 8*

Keegan, D. (1982) 'From New Delhi to Vancouver: Trends in Distance Education', J.S. Daniel *et al.* (eds.), *Learning at a Distance*, Edmonton: Athabasca University/ICCE

KNOW (1983) *Annual Report*, Vancouver: Knowledge Network, June

Leslie, J.D. (1979) 'The University of Waterloo Model for Distance Education', *Canadian Journal of University Continuing Education, 6*

McKenzie, N., R. Postgate, and J. Scupham (1975) *Open Learning*

McNamara, C. (1985) *Personal Communication*, Memorial University

Molyneux, F. (1974) 'International Perspectives' in V. Houghton and K. Richardson, *Recurrent Education*, London: Ward Lock Educational

Ontario (1972) *The Learning Society*, Report of the Commission on Postsecondary Education in Ontario, Toronto: Ministry of Government Services

Ontario (1984) *Ontario Universities: Options and Futures*, Report of the Commission on the Future Development of the Universities of Ontario, Toronto: Government Bookstore

Organization for Economic Cooperation and Development (1976) *Review of National Policies for Education*, Canada; Paris: OECD

Pascal, C. and S. Kanowich (1979) *Student Withdrawals from Canadian Universities: A Study of Studies*, Toronto, OISE

Patterson, J. (1979) *Student Advisory Service: Regional Centres - Functions and Staffing*, Unpublished Manuscript available from the Open Learning Institute, Richmond, British Columbia

Paulet, R. (1985) *Distance Education Manitoba*, Unpublished Manuscript available from Brandon University, Manitoba

Pike, R. (1978) 'Part-Time Undergraduate Studies in Ontario', in R. Pike, N. Mcintosh, and U. Dahlof (eds.), *Innovation in Access to Higher Education*, New York: ICED

Pike, R. (1980) 'Open Access in Canadian Higher Education during the Seventies', *Canadian Journal of University and Continuing Education, 7*

Rice, K. (1985) *Nineteen Steps at a Time: An Atlantic Canadian Approach to Implementing New Communications Technologies In Higher Education*, Unpublished Manuscript

Roberts, A.H. (1982) 'Distance Education at Memorial University', in M. Mandville, *'A Man's Reach Should Exceed His Grasp': Distance Education and Teleconferencing at Memorial University*, Memorial University, St John's

Rogers, K. (1982) 'Identifying an Effective and Efficient Distance Education System', *Canadian Journal of University Continuing Education, 8*

Sewart, D. (1982) 'Individualising Support Services', in J.S. Daniel *et al.* (eds.), *Learning at a Distance: A World Perspective*, Edmonton: Athabasca University/ICCE

Shobe, C. (1983) 'Telecommunication Technologies and Distance Education: A Report on Recent Canadian Initiatives', *Open Campus*, Occasional Papers, Victoria, Australia: Deakin University

Smith, K. and I. Small (1982) 'Student Support: How Much is Enough?' in J. Daniel *et al.* (eds.), *Learning at a Distance*, Edmonton: Athabasca University/ICCE

Smith, W.A.S. and B.L. Snowden (1983) *A Review of Distance Education in Ontario Universities*, Toronto: Council of Ontario Universities, April

Smith, W.A.S., J.S. Daniel and B.L. Snowden (1984) 'University Distance Education in Canada', *The Canadian Journal of Higher Education, 14*

Starcher, D. (1982) 'Educational Television at Memorial University', in M. Mandville *'A Man's Reach Should Exceed His Grasp': Distance Education and Teleconferencing at Memorial University*, Memorial University, St John's

Starcher, D. (1985) *Academic Strategy Group*, Unpublished Manuscript available from Memorial University, St John's

Statistics Canada (1979) *The Changing Educational Profile of Canadians, 1961 to 2000*, Ottawa: Ministry of Supply and Services

Sullivan, K. (1985) *An Evaluation of a Neomobilistic Change in Canadian Graduate Studies: The Open Access Study Plan*, Paper presented to the Canadian Society for the Study of Higher Education, 1985 Conference, University of Montreal

Sweet, R. (1982) *Distance Education: The Personal Response*, Paper presented to American Educational Research Association Conference, New York

Sweet, R. (1983) *Applying Tinto's Model of Student Dropout to Distance Education*, Unpublished Manuscript available from The Open Learning Institute, Richmond, British Columbia

Tetlow, W. and R. Taylor (1981) *Looking Beyond*, Vancouver: University of British Columbia

Trotter, B. (1970) *Television and Technology in University Teaching*, Toronto: Committee of Presidents of Universities of Ontario and Committee on University Affairs

Community Colleges

John Dennison

Before beginning a discussion of the issue of distance education in community colleges, it is first necessary to examine the role and function of a college in the Canadian context. Unfortunately, this is no easy task. All ten provinces support postsecondary educational institutions distinguishable from and often alternative to the traditional universities. The titles associated with such institutions vary among the regions and include 'college' (in British Columbia, Newfoundland, Prince Edward Island), 'community college' (in Alberta, Saskatchewan, Manitoba, and New Brunswick), 'college of applied arts and technology' (in Ontario), 'collège d'enseignment général et professionnel' (in Quebec) and often 'institute' (in several provinces, including Nova Scotia).[1]

Just as their descriptive titles vary, the institutions assume a wide range of mandates, curricular designs, governing structures, and relationships with their provincial ministries, largely reflecting the historical, socio-cultural and economic conditions under which the colleges developed. However, it is also possible to identify a number of significant characteristics which they share. In general, all such institutions were created in a period when the provision of access to educational opportunity beyond secondary school was regarded as an attractive social policy. Consistent with this priority, the colleges promoted an open admissions policy designed to remove barriers to those traditionally denied further education, whether for economic, geographic, academic or psychological reasons. Further, colleges often sought to increase access by dispersing educational opportunity throughout the wider community by establishing satellite campuses in modest facilities and by offering part-time, evening and week-end courses.

Many, though not all, colleges were responsible for defined regional constituencies, or communities, for which they served as cultural and educational resource centres. Indeed, the community orientation of such colleges was reflected through local representation on governing and advisory bodies and in their direct responsiveness to the employment need of community businesses and industries. It is of further significance to recall that most college systems across the country were created and grew into relative maturity within a fifteen-year period between 1960 and 1975. These were the 'golden' years for postsecondary educational development in Canada. It was a period of unbounded faith in the value of further education and governments, enjoying relative economic buoyancy, gave priority to growth and expansion of both traditional universities and new designs in alternative institutions of higher education. The key to government initiative at the time was the much quoted notion of accessibility and its associated theme, the 'democratization' of higher education. In 1960 there were two institutions which might be regarded as public community colleges; by 1980, the total number of such institutions had reached 125.[2]

It was not long, however, before limitations upon accessibility to a college education became a subject of debate in educational circles. (Anisef 1983) While the success of the new institutions in broadening the base of participation in higher education was acknowledged, it became evident that colleges provided educational opportunity for an essentially conventional clientele - those students who could participate in face-to-face instruction, albeit on irregular schedules and often in satellite facilities.

Much of the thrust of new concerns over the question of access has been summarised by Forsyth (1983) in the following passage:

> The notion of a comprehensive community college should be modified and give way to that of a comprehensive community college education. Rather than planning around the traditional comprehensive campus, future efforts need to be directed toward a community system for delivering a comprehensive postsecondary education. The traditional campus should become just one part of this system, complemented by other means (such as media) which do not require the continual presence of instructors and also by neighbourhood satellites, storefront operations, mobile units, limited-purpose centres, work experience, co-operative education, credit by examination or for previous extra-collegiate experience, community library resources, and other community facilities in whatever combination provides access in the most efficient manner. (p. 5)

Inevitably, the recognition that a substantial segment of society could only participate in a college education if barriers of time and distance were removed, led to an emphasis on the concept of distance education as a necessary and desirable component of the programming of a community college.[3] But others have criticised the narrow focus of 'distance' education as a method of programme delivery in the community college sector. While the concept is attractive, implying new ways and new technologies for serving students who cannot, or choose not, to participate in face-to-face instruction, it misses the real point of the exercise, which is to focus attention upon the learner, rather than the instructional format. Crawford (1983) summarised this concern in a recent article in *College Canada:*

> By making the individual the focus of attention, rather than the institution, its delivery system, or its staff, and by deemphasizing the time and location of learning, a new start is possible and is required by the new demands facing postsecondary education. By emphasizing the individualization of instruction rather than the delivery methodology, be it distance education or exotic information technologies, however attractive they may be as 'bait' for special funding!), a number of advantages accrue for both on and off campus applications. (p. 9)

Wing (1983) suggests that the major emphasis in the matter of programme delivery should revolve around the notion of 'open learning'. The latter should be distinguished from distance education in that the focus is upon how a learner may gain access to formal education in a manner consistent with his learning style and living conditions. It implies that learning opportunities should be available to all individuals despite traditional obstacles, among which distance from the classroom is only one. Wing also raises the fallacy of perceiving distance learning and conventional classroom instruction as dichotomous entities rather than existing at opposite ends of a continuum of learning styles, in which the prospective student will choose his own place according to his personal limitations of time, place, programme or technology.

Wing, among others,[4] argues that the comprehensive but conventional community college is structurally unable to adapt to the wide diversity of learning needs in the community, a point of view which invites debate of the feasibility of distance learning as a component of college education. There are several dimensions to this issue, some of which follow.

The Community College Mandate

As outlined earlier, most colleges were designed to serve regional constituencies. While many of the latter comprise large urban areas, several colleges serve widely dispersed rural communities with limited populations. Given the high costs of producing quality course material, the issue of economy of scale must dominate any discussion of the financial practicality of individual colleges becoming involved in the production of their own courses for distance delivery. But production of courses is one matter; delivery is quite another. There are now large numbers of quality courses available which can be purchased by individual institutions. Nevertheless, there are also costs of delivery, both administrative and supportive, which would be assuredly duplicated if all colleges engaged in distance education. At the same time, colleges might argue, with some justification, that such costs are demonstrably less than those of conventional instruction.

While such questions merit debate, the fundamental issue is that community colleges which are designed to fulfil a limited mandate within broadly dispersed population centres are not constituted to embark upon the production and delivery of a wide scale of distance education activities.

Faculty Attitudes

Somewhat related to the issue of the community college mandate is the matter of faculty reaction to the new instructional techniques. Most college teachers have experienced a conventional preparation for their role, whether in universities, technical/vocational schools or industry. Teaching, for them, is very much a matter of face-to-face contact, with students either in a lecture or seminar. Laboratories and workshops involve activities in unison while following a preplanned script. Communication between student and instructor is personal, direct and relatively easy to arrange.

To 'convert' such faculty into a new and distinctly different relationship with students through a distance learning format is a matter of delicate reorientation of role. By far the greater part of community college evolution, while generally more innovative in practice than universities, has been to adjust at a moderate pace to change in clientele and to conditions of employment for its teaching personnel.

To complicate further the issue, community college faculty often regard distance education as a replacement for face-to-face instruction, and respect, with its introduction, the inevitable consequences of staff reduction, if not redundancy. In a recent position statement of distance education, released by the College-Institute Educators' Association of British Columbia (1985) the essential argument is that distance education must be regarded as a 'necessary adjunct', but not a 'replacement' for classroom-based instruction.

Further, the statement includes a number of recommendations, of which the first is the most central:

> The greatest resource for the development of courses in distance education mode is the faculty presently employed in the postsecondary sector. Greater effort should be expended to provide professional development opportunities such that faculty can master distance education techniques in course development and tutorial support. (CIEA 1985)

It is evident that faculty attitudes remain a significant factor in evaluating the feasibility of distance education programming within the community college sector.

The Comprehensive Curriculum

Another factor relevant to the issue is the composition of the typical college curriculum. Colleges have adopted a greater or lesser degree of comprehensiveness in their curricula, in which academic, technical, technological, vocational upgrading and general credit-free community education courses all contribute.

To introduce open learning (including distance education) methodology into such a wide diversity of curricular offerings is a formidable task. While many aspects of the humanities and social sciences have long been available as 'correspondence' courses using essentially print media, laboratories and other clinical activities have limited the availability of pure and applied sciences. The challenge is even greater with technical-vocational programmes and adult basic literacy. In this context it is significant to note the innovative approaches by the Open Learning Institute of British Columbia and by North Island College in the same province, both of which have developed distance based programmes in all curriculum areas, albeit in different formats.[5]

Are there any college programmes which cannot be offered in a distance learning format? With some caveats, and in the light of rapid technological advances, the answer is probably no! The highly practical clinical, laboratory or workshop experiences, so integral to programmes such as dental assisting, heavy-duty mechanics or advanced chemistry, can and are made possible through arrangements with other institutions and industrial/business settings located near the students' homes. Technical aids such as audio and videocassettes, microcomputers and audio-graphics allow for quality learning experiences in activities ranging from adult basic literacy to senior years in baccalaureate programmes. Of interest in this context is the theme recorded in a publication by Tolley (1983) concerning Britain's Open Tech.

Despite all of the foregoing, the assumption that colleges have almost unlimited curricular jurisdictions makes broadly based adoption of distance education a challenge of some magnitude. It is more realistic to explore the notion of colleges playing a 'broker' role in the delivery of distance education programmes which emanate from more specialised sources.

Co-ordination of Distance Education Activities

As the 'new wave' in distance delivery of educational services rolls and strengthens, it is almost inevitable that proliferation and duplication of activities will occur within the postsecondary community (including universities, colleges, technical institutes and specialised tertiary institutions). Equally inevitable are concerns from government and other sources over costs of perceived duplication and the need to 'co-ordinate' institutional enterprises.

However, institutions are understandably reluctant to surrender voluntarily those which they perceive as revenue and status producing operations which place them in the 'centre' of the new technological age. Even more so, colleges hasten to protect enrolments which often form the basis for additional funding.

There are practical problems, even in the most obvious approaches to co-ordination strategies, such as the purchase of quality programmes developed by other jurisdictions. To uncritically adopt a course prepared by another provincial institution, or even from another region, is a dangerous exercise. The time frame demanded to complete the course, the requirements for a recognised credential in another province, even the socio-cultural orientation of the course material, all make for reduced applicability of apparently suitable courses or programmes.

If there is to be effective co-ordination of distance education activities in a given region, certain conditions must be met (BCAC 1984):

1. the mandates and jurisdictions of all affected institutions must be respected, while ensuring that such mandates do not obstruct co-ordination;
2. leadership by the appropriate government agency is essential, although government does not necessarily need to assume the managerial function in the process;
3. the prime beneficiary of any new arrangement must be the potential students rather than the institutions involved;
4. funding policies should provide incentives to encourage institutional participation rather than disincentives, such as lost revenue; and
5. institutions involved should have the opportunity to participate in policy making and in the resolution of disputes.

All of the foregoing suggests that the solution lies in the creation of a provincial level 'authority', initiated by government, upon which all institutions would be represented. The 'authority' would decide questions such as student credit transfer, jurisdictions regarding programme and course development, and the purchase and distribution of software.

An organisational structure, such as the one described above, could go far towards overcoming the limitations of college participation in distance education in the light of their limited resources, human and financial. Colleges would be able to meet the multitudinous needs of their communities through distance learning methods by capitalising on high quality resources available in the particular provinces.

Even the specific mandates of participating institutions in distance learning activities could be clearly defined by a co-ordinating agency, a process which would be to the ultimate benefit of all parties concerned: the institutions, the students and the taxpayer.

Current Approaches to Distance Education in Community Colleges

Across the ten provinces, activity within the colleges with respect to distance education has been somewhat limited, although several factors are contributing to increased entrepreneurship in this area. In a period of financial restraint, governments tend selectively to fund innovative programmes which address new student needs, particularly for job preparation and upgrading, by cost effective methods. Distance learning methodology qualifies under such criteria.

A second factor of increased interest in distance education within the college sector is the availability of course material necessary to supplement new programmes. Quality courses with a Canadian orientation, developed by Athabasca University, the Open Learning Institute, the Télé-université, University of Waterloo, Memorial University and by various provincial public and private agencies for TVOntario, Sask. Media, Knowledge Network of the West and similar organisations, have created a substantial pool of resources which colleges can access.

While it is true that many of the present distance education formats are variations of 'correspondence' type studies, using essentially print media, there is increasing supplementation through newer technology, teleconferencing, and utilisation of resources in other institutions. Indeed, the notion of partnership with more specialised educational and private sector institutions does much to alleviate the constraints upon the colleges noted earlier.

It would be quite impossible and inappropriate to attempt to refer to all of the many and varied experiments in distance education currently found in Canada's community colleges. However, a few examples will provide a flavour of the activity.

The most notable case is North Island College on Vancouver Island, which has adopted an open learning methodology involving correspondence courses, mobile instructional resources, and a variety of technical support materials and delivery system. It is the only college in Canada which is totally committed to this approach, while largely evading the conventional college teaching model. In consequence, North Island's student profile is atypical, as are its teaching faculties.

Grant MacEwan College in Edmonton has developed two programmes which involve a combination of formal distance instruction and clinical practice in established institutions. The programmes, Nursing Upgrading and Extended Care Nursing, also include self-paced learning and extended admission times. Courses are either developed by Grant MacEwan or adopted from Athabasca University. Clinical practice is arranged in hospital settings near the student's home. Parenthetically, it is interesting to note that in distance education, Alberta's colleges appear to be developing programme specialties as their mandate, rather than focusing upon serving specified communities.

In Saskatchewan, community college policy is to adopt a 'broker' role in which programmes and courses from other institutions are made available through college facilities. Kelsey Institute in Saskatoon, for example, offers a Personal Development Worker Programme by teleconferencing, part of which is brokered through Saskatoon Community College.

Recently, the professional organisation comprising continuing educators in Ontario produced a report on the state of distance education in Ontario's colleges. (Knowles 1985) While not all colleges participated in the study, the results revealed a widely comprehensive involvement in the particular instructional methodology under review. It was apparent that individual colleges were developing experience in specific subject and programme areas regarding production, while delivery appeared to involve an impressive degree of co-operative effort. Programmes ranged from ophthalmic assistants, electronics and robotics, and emergency care to fashion design, early childhood education, travel courses and floral techniques.

Another feature of the Ontario scene was the creation of a large number of learning centres by colleges in which a variety of self-paced learning programmes were made available. Such centres reflect, as does the range and scope of distance learning activities, the way in which Ontario colleges respond to the distinctly different needs of their community. For example, Confederation College in Thunder Bay serves an area of 235,000 square miles with a population of 200,000 in 92 centres. Since 1977, Confederation College has provided outreach activities which involve the creation of resource centres in hospitals, libraries and private industry. The centres are used by students to access video and audio tapes and print material. Arrangements are made for students to teleconference with instructors at the college to review their progress and discuss subject matter. The teleconference material remains on tape for use by students unable to attend the resource centre. (Scharf 1983)

With respect to co-operative activities, many smaller colleges draw upon the resources produced by the major centres for the production of learning packages, such as Seneca and Humber Colleges, although co-operative efforts among geographic groups of institutions are also evident.

Colleges view the direct co-operation of TVOntario in the delivery of programmes as a goal which is yet to be fully realised. In this context it is also interesting to note that Ryerson, although not a community college, has created an affiliate, the Open College, with an FM radio outlet which offers courses through three delivery modes, the radio, audiocassettes and traditional correspondence. The Open College provides another resource for delivery of programmes upon which colleges may draw.

CONCLUSIONS

Despite a number of inherent problems, community colleges in Canada are adopting distance education strategies consistent with their mandates and realistic in scope considering the resources at their disposal. Given the limited constituencies to which most colleges are responsible, programme development and delivery on a comprehensive scale by all colleges is hardly feasible on either financial or upon a student population basis.

However, entrepreneurship in programme delivery has become a significant challenge in the 1980s and colleges recognise the advantages of co-operative endeavours with other institutions and with the business-industrial sector. Furthermore, advances in technology and in the development of portable equipment for practical components of courses have done much to reduce costs and further diversify programme and courses. With imminent technological innovations, such as the use of fibre optics, extensive resources for learning will be accessible by more people. Colleges must, and will, capitalise on such resources.

Furthermore, it has become appropriate that governments display initiative in the co-ordination, management and delivery of distance learning, both as the custodian of the education dollar and in their responsibility for the monitoring of new communications technology, such as the satellites and cable systems. Community colleges must, however, play an important role in any management systems which are created; their contribution will be significant, albeit controlled, and consistent with their role.

Colleges were created to serve a learning society well beyond those who had been the privileged participants of the past. Despite their efforts, through open admission, decentralised campuses, evening and week-end scheduling and extensive curricular offerings, the colleges have failed to accommodate a segment of the community who cannot, or prefer not to, use face-to-face instruction. Open learning, a concept which implies the creation of learning opportunities based upon individual student needs and living conditions, constitutes a challenge which cannot be ignored. Despite an uncertain financial future, the colleges must meet this challenge and, in doing so, will surely change the character of their learning resources.

Distance education, perhaps modified, but in creative formats under imaginative and co-operative planning, and with the assistance of sophisticated technology available now and in the future, will assuredly become a regular supplement to classroom instruction in the educational future of Canada's colleges.

NOTES

1. The titles 'Technical Institute' and 'Community College' do not connote consistency in mandate or organisation. Manitoba's 'community' colleges, for example, are provincially-governed institutions with a heavy vocational emphasis.

2. The numbers quoted here refer to public community colleges in the more restrictive use of the term. They do not include provincial institutes or private colleges, as in Quebec.

3. Several articles on this theme appear in *College Canada*, January-February 1983.

4. A number of papers by Denis Wing appear in the Proceedings of the Outreach Seminar, noted in the References.

5. The Open Learning Institute does not meet the criteria for a community college, as argued in this paper. However, an excellent analysis of the development of the OLI appears in Ellis and Mugridge (1983).

REFERENCES

Anisef, Paul (1983) 'Accessibility Barriers to Higher Education in Canada', *Postsecondary Education Issues in the 1980s*, Toronto: Council of Ministers of Education

B.C. Association of Colleges, Distance Education Working Group (1984) 'Models for the Organisation of Distance Education', Unpublished Discussion Paper, Vancouver, B.C.A.C.

College-Institute Educators Association of B.C. (1985) *Statement on Distance Education*, Unpublished, Vancouver, CIEA, June

Crawford, D.C. (1983) 'Old Wine in New Skins?' *College Canada*, 7 (January-February)

Ellis, John F. and Ian Mugridge (1983) 'The Open Learning Institute of British Columbia: A Case Study', The Open University, Distance Education Research Group, Milton Keynes, *The Open University*

Forsythe, Kathleen (1983) 'Bridging the Distance towards 1995', *College Canada*, 7 (January-February)

Knowles, Arthur F. (1985) 'PCCED Study of Distance Education in Ontario's Colleges', Unpublished Report, Humber College

Scharf, C. Ralph (1983) 'Outreach: A Distance Learning Project', *College Canada*, 7 (January-February)

Tolley, G. (1983) 'The Open Tech Programme: A New Initiative for Adults', *International Journal of Lifelong Education*, 2

Wing, D. (1983) 'Distance Education-A Reaffirmation of the Community College', in *Outreach Seminar: Report of Proceedings*, Vancouver, BCAC

Wing, D. (1983) 'Outreach--An Integral Function of any Postsecondary Institution', in *Outreach Seminar: Report of Proceedings*, BCAC

Public Elementary and Secondary Schools

Norman McKinnon

The objectives of this chapter are to describe briefly the origins of publicly-funded distance education in Canada at the elementary- and secondary-school levels and to provide information about what currently is happening across the country. In addressing these objectives, discussion of current trends, future directions and sample projects are included. A major theme is the evolution of distance education from its modest beginnings in the early decades of the twentieth century to its present status as a respected and valued alternative to traditional in-school education. A second theme is the response of the provinces to the challenges and opportunities presented by technology. References to distance education pertain to pre-tertiary levels of learning unless otherwise specified.

THE BEGINNING AND PRESENT STATUS OF PROVINCIAL DISTANCE EDUCATION SERVICES

Canada's first publicly-funded distance education service started in 1919 in the province of British Columbia in response to a lighthouse-keeper's request for elementary-school courses. During the 1920s, five other provinces initiated services: Nova Scotia (1921), Alberta (1923), Saskatchewan (1925), Ontario (1926) and Manitoba (1927). A polio epidemic in 1939 served as a catalyst for New Brunswick's involvement; and Quebec joined the field in 1946. Presently, eight provinces offer distance education services; and two-Newfoundland and Prince Edward Island - and the federal territories do not. Students in Newfoundland and Prince Edward Island usually enrol in New Brunswick's service, while students in the Yukon register with the British Columbia Correspondence Education Branch, and the Northwest Territories use Alberta's Correspondence School. The government of Newfoundland recently formed a committee to study the feasibility of creating pre-tertiary courses for that province.

Most of the services, with the exception of Quebec's, Nova Scotia's and New Brunswick's, started by providing elementary-school correspondence courses for isolated or ill students. Not surprisingly, this first occurred along the coastal regions of British Columbia and then on the Prairies where outpost regions, sparsely populated with settlers, traders and trappers, could not justify the creation of schools. In Alberta, for example, the minister of education, disturbed by the plight of ten children living in an area too poor to form a school and with no access to formal education, decided these children should receive lessons by mail. That decision led to the creation of the Alberta Correspondence School (ACS), a school that has since grown to a staff of over 180 serving almost 30,000 students.

The creation of Saskatchewan's correspondence school resulted in part from ACS's existence. Settlers in Saskatchewan living near Alberta's border wrote to the Saskatchewan department of education enquiring about the availability of correspondence courses and requested permission to enrol their children in the ACS if courses were not available. At that time, Saskatchewan's department of education employed an energetic, enthusiastic woman named Catherine Sheldon-Williams who had been conducting an unofficial 'school by mail' as a follow-up programme for youths released from a boys' detention home. She campaigned vigorously for a correspondence school. She used the needs of the settlers as expressed in letters and reports, as well as her own interest in and dedication to correspondence education, to convince the decision makers to provide education by mail to remote sections of the province. Since its inception in 1925, the Saskatchewan Government Correspondence School has served approximately 425,000 students.

The modest beginnings of distance education in Western Canada are typical of the beginnings in other provinces. Isolated or ill students and a dedicated teacher (or small group of teachers) committed to serving such students were the basic ingredients in the early models of publicly-funded distance education in Canada. In many ways, the first correspondence teachers needed as much of a pioneering spirit as the settlers who lived in remote parts of the country and who struggled to survive. The teachers often provided the total service with little professional or clerical help. In Saskatchewan, for example, Miss Sheldon-Williams worked alone for two years in a small, second-floor room in the legislative building preparing lesson sheets and performing clerical work. In this sense, she was not unique, for similarly devoted teachers in other provinces working in less than ideal conditions laid the foundations of distance education in Canada.

As the various services became established, they broadened their programmes to include secondary courses. (Exceptions to this pattern, as noted earlier, occurred in Quebec, Nova Scotia and New Brunswick: Quebec's service focused initially on vocational training for secondary trade schools and community colleges; Nova Scotia started at the technical college level; and in New Brunswick, the service was initiated for students in junior and senior high school.) Over the years, the mandates of most services changed to meet the needs of new clients. For example, British Columbia's service evolved from its original purpose of serving isolated or ill students to a more diversified group of clients that currently includes in-school students, especially in small schools who need courses not offered by the school or unavailable because of timetable conflicts; out-of-school school-age students who are working; and adults seeking vocational or interest courses. Since the development of the Open Learning Institute (OLI), British Columbia's Correspondence Education Branch has reduced its service to adults and encourages them to use OLI.

What evolved in British Columbia is typical of what developed in other provinces: a gradual expansion of service to meet the needs of children, adolescents and adults. The success of the provincial institutions has created a demand for their learning materials by local school boards, for use of curriculum resource materials in adult drop-in programmes or in alternative schools. The present status of publicly-funded distance education is that of an established service encouraged and supported by governments and recognised by an increasing number of educators as a viable educational alternative. In 1985, approximately 250,000 Canadian students, ranging in age from five to ninety-two years, participated in publicly-funded distance education courses designed, developed and delivered by the provinces. From a modest beginning, provincial distance education services have provided educational access and opportunities to hundreds of thousands of students. The future presents many opportunities for the services to play a leadership role in curriculum implementation, instructional design refinements and technological innovations.

CURRENT TRENDS AND FUTURE DIRECTIONS

Current Trends

Eight major trends are significant. These are:

1. an increased use of technology;
2. a commitment to interprovincial co-operation in programme development and course sharing;
3. an emphasis on developing courses suited to adults applying for secondary-school courses;
4. a growing demand by school boards and school districts for distance education materials to support, complement or supplement school programmes;
5. a decentralisation of service in some provinces;
6. the emergence of new clients with specialised needs;
7. a heightened awareness of public profile and the importance of projecting a professional corporate image; and
8. a commitment to improve distance education through innovation, technology, and experimentation.

These items represent a composite of what is occurring around the country but the degree to which these trends are evident or significant varies. A brief elaboration of each trend follows. Technology has dramatically affected distance education in two ways: the first concerns the computerisation of the office; the second is the use of the technologies in programme development, delivery and evaluation. Large services such as Ontario's (over 80,000 students) initially automated their administrative, enrolment and record-keeping functions in 1979 and then began to experiment with educational uses of the technologies. Automation of time-consuming office tasks followed by educational applications of appropriate technology is the general pattern of services as they move towards the office of the future and search for educational applications of technology. Specifically, the provinces are experimenting with the telephone, audiocassettes, television, videotape, videodisc, and computers. For example, Ontario and Alberta are using the telephone for student tutorials and limited experiments in teleconferencing; language courses in British Columbia, Alberta, Saskatchewan, Manitoba, Ontario and Nova Scotia incorporate the use of audiocassettes; Quebec and Manitoba successfully use television and videotapes in a computer course that teaches about computers; Ontario is developing an Adult Basic English Course on videodisc; and five provinces - Alberta, Saskatchewan, Manitoba, Ontario and Quebec - are experimenting with various forms of computer-managed and computer-assisted instruction.

An important accord among the provinces that facilitates learning and sharing is a commitment to interprovincial co-operation. The co-operation is based on a philosophy of sharing ideas, courses, innovations and, by doing so, reducing development cost. The cost factor is a critical one in all provinces, but especially in New Brunswick and Nova Scotia where the economic bases and the student numbers are significantly smaller than in the larger and wealthier provinces such as Ontario and Alberta. Interprovincial co-operation is evident in three ways: the sharing of existing courses; the distribution of new courses to the other services; and joint funding of programme development.

Joint funding first ocurred in 1981, when six provincial services - in British Columbia, Alberta, Saskatchewan, Manitoba, Ontario and Nova Scotia - and the Open Learning Institute (OLI) agreed to participate in an English as a Second Language (ESL) project. The seven participants shared the costs and the OLI agreed to develop and produce the course and to provide master copies to the participants for use in their provinces. Despite the problems of co-ordinating the project among such a diversified group, the course became a reality in 1984. After a year of implementation, the early results indicate that the course is accomplishing its objectives: students are learning to use basic English to communicate in everyday situations. The development of a second ESL course requiring similar co-operation is planned.

A different kind of co-operation involves the sharing of existing courses among the provincial services. As each province has designed its curriculum to meet the needs of its residents, it is often difficult for one province to use material from another without rewriting or redesigning it. There are, however, some courses developed in one province that fit the curriculum requirements of one or more of the other provinces or can be adapted to do so. When this occurs, it makes economic sense to share. Examples of such sharing included Nova Scotia's use of British Columbia's elementary courses, Saskatchewan's German courses, and Ontario's secondary-school French courses; Ontario's adaptation of British Columbia's mathematics courses for use in Grades 4 to 6; and Manitoba's and British Columbia's acquisition and use of Ontario's secondary-school French courses. Such sharing results in considerable savings in development costs.

The third example of co-operation ocurred in 1984 when the provinces agreed to provide one another with copies of all new courses which they produced. Not only does this create an exchange of ideas on methodologies, instructional design and graphic innovations, but it also furnishes curriculum material that may be used with or without modification to fit a programming need. Clearly, interprovincial co-operation saves money and stimulates ideas. The importance of this will become more significant and more valuable as technology becomes more integrated into the services. In the future, the high cost of developing computer-based courses, for example, will deprive some provinces of the technology unless course sharing or joint funding projects exist. Despite the differences in curriculum requirements in the various provinces, sufficient common or core curriculum exists among the provinces and provides numerous opportunities to share exemplary material. The trend towards interprovincial co-operation and sharing is a healthy one that should elevate and improve the educational experience offered to students and reduce development costs.

The trend towards continuing education and lifelong learning has produced a sharp rise in the number of adult students returning to full- or part-time learning. Since the 1920s, many adults have chosen the distance mode for their education because of its flexibility. In the past two decades, however, adult learners have used distance education in increasing numbers and have affected the direction of some services. Ontario and Quebec, for example, primarily serve the adult student, and both provinces are designing programmmes for the adult learner. Responding to the needs of the adult student, however, raises an important issue. The issue is the need to design courses specifically for adult learners and to incorporate adult learning principles into the materials; the challenge inherent in the issue is to provide appropriate in-service training for staff to deal with the adult learner. Distance educators will need to become more cognizant of how adults learn and how to teach adults at a distance. A side effect to increased adult demand is the decline of programme development at the elementary level: provinces like Saskatchewan and New Brunswick are allocating development funds to the secondary-school level where greater demand exists. New Brunswick offers course for Grades 7 to 12, and Saskatchewan provides courses to high-school students and adults. Quebec's current mandate has two directions: to produce manuals for trade schools and institutes of technology, and to provide an extension service for technical education via distance education.

Greater involvement in the regular school system is reflected in a number of ways. Small schools, for example, in British Columbia, Manitoba and Ontario, are able to offer a broader curriculum and to overcome timetabling conflicts by using distance education courses. Night schools, summer schools and adult continuing-education departments are finding distance education materials to be valuable alternatives for many of their students. Teachers, too, have found the material useful for independent study activities and as teaching resources; these in-school uses have great growth potential, especially in the area of computer-based materials. British Columbia, Alberta, Saskatchewan, Manitoba and Ontario have procedures whereby in-school students under certain conditions may enrol in courses. Saskatchewan and Manitoba offer a unique service in which students register through a school and use the correspondence school lesson materials under the guidance of a local teacher. The teacher corrects all assignments and assesses achievement for promotional purposes. Promotions are granted by the school authorities. This model is quite apart from the traditional distance education service offered to school-age students attending school and to students not in school. But it does illustrate how a traditional service can be tailored to meet the needs of a non-traditional distance education clientele. The evidence suggests that the schools are an important market for distance educators and that the use of distance education learning materials in the schools will continue to expand.

Decentralisation of service is not a widespread trend but it is occurring in British Columbia, Alberta and Ontario. British Columbia has established a satellite centre at Fort St John to serve the needs of four school districts in that area, an experiment discussed in detail in the last section of this chapter. Alberta operates an information, counselling and enrolment centre in Edmonton and will likely open one in Calgary. Ontario sells its courses to school boards and the boards take on the responsibility of delivering the courses to schools.

In the 1980s, new clients with specialised needs came to the attention of distance educators. Besides a growing immigrant population needing ESL, the upgrading needs of adults, the widespread existence of illiteracy, the lack of basic life-survival skills and the burgeoning numbers of senior citizens offer new directions and challenges.

Distance education is becoming high profile, and concerns about corporate image naturally follow. Anniversary ceremonies, outreach programmes, awards/scholarship programmes, newsletters, pamphlets, displays at conferences, news releases, mottoes and, most important, visually attractive learning materials that provide a quality education are consciously becoming part of some services' efforts to project a positive public profile and professional corporate image.

One key factor in image is the impression created through the service to the client. There is a widespread commitment across the country to provide efficient, fast service in order to counter criticisms of long delays in lesson returns and enrolment procedures. Automated enrolment procedures are being used or are being established, and the telephone is being used for experiments in providing course information, tutorials and feedback. Computer-managed marking has successfully reduced course completion time for many students. There is clearly an effort to use technology and innovation to improve the service and quality of the education offered. Specific examples of projects that address this issue will be briefly mentioned in the last section of the chapter.

Future Directions

The major future directions are: commitment to research; computer-conferencing; electronic mail; computerised learning centres; and computer centre networking.

Research has played a small part in provincially funded distance education. It primarily serves the needs of local decision makers, and is not disseminated widely. That, however, is changing. A chair of research and development has been created in Ontario, and other provinces are giving research activities a higher priority. A research network to communicate and share research findings among the different services has been formed. Plans are being made to produce a publication to disseminate research results more effectively among the services and to other distance educators. An objective of the research network is to produce quality reports and articles that contribute to the literature from the pre-tertiary perspective.

Computer-conferencing, electronic mail and resource-based, computerised learning centres are other intriguing developments. Computer-conferencing and electronic mail will enable the teacher and the student to communicate with each other in a more flexible and rapid manner. The learning centre will give less privileged students access to resources and computers they might not otherwise have available to them. The learning centre concept can take many forms. The design favoured by Ontario is one that creates a place which students can visit and use. The centre will be filled with resources and computer-based learning programmmes. An extension of the centre is a network that can be used to download programmmes from the centre to designated sites, similarly equipped, in libraries, schools, shopping plazas, community centres and, eventually, individual homes. The network is the distant future: the learning centre is the near future; it is scheduled to be operating at Ontario's Independent Learning Centre (ILC) in late 1986.

PROJECTS

Decentralisation of Service

One decentralisation project in British Columbia is an attempt to improve its service to small secondary schools. Piloted in 1984-5, the project aims at helping schools cope with multi-programmming class situations where student numbers are small and resources are limited. The Correspondence Education Branch provides courses to schools, and the marking is done on-site by one teacher. The advantage to the student is the immediate feedback from the on-site teacher; the advantage to the teacher is the availability of lesson materials to cope effectively with the multi-programmming needs of a range of students within one class. Eighteen schools and approximately 1,000 courses are involved.

Another project is an arrangement with the school board at Fort St John to handle all secondary correspondence services for four northern school districts. In effect the school at Fort St John functions as a satellite centre to British Columbia's provincial service in Victoria. The objectives of this activity are to provide faster service to the 700 students who are participating and to test the premise that bringing the service closer to the client will result in improved performance. British Columbia's evaluation of its decentralisation project is in progress.

Adult Basic Literacy and Adult Basic English

The illiteracy rate in Canada is approximately 23 per cent. In Ontario, one out of every five adults has less than nine years of formal schooling. Unfortunately, the majority of these adults are functionally illiterate. To assist those adults who need training in basic English skills, the Independent Learning Centre is developing two courses, Adult Basic Literacy and Adult Basic English.

The basic literacy course integrates visuals, audiocassettes and print, and is designed for the adult who cannot read or write. An indispensable feature of the course is the need of a family member or friend to be a volunteer tutor, without which a student will not be able to do the course. The basic English course, on the other hand, is designed for adults who have some reading and writing skills; it is written at the Grade 4 to 5 reading level. The learners work independently but are supported with audiocassettes and telephone tutoring. The data generated from these two courses during 1986 will be useful in evaluating the strategies used in instructional design, the effectiveness of using audiocassettes and telephone tutoring, and the role of volunteer tutors in serving the needs of adults with limited skills in English.

Videotex

In the early 1980s, the Alberta Correspondence School participated in the distance education field trials of Telidon, the Canadian videotex system. It involved using the Telidon system as a delivery vehicle for a Grade 12 introductory course in mechanics. The instructional component was delivered through print material and the student response component via Telidon. The lesson assignments were prepared in a multiple choice format, and the students indicated their response by entering numbers on a keypad. Students received immediate feedback on answers and further explanation and remedial exercises if required. The report on this project is a useful planning document for those interested in assessing the viability of videotex as a delivery mechanism in distance education.[1]

Computer-Managed Instruction

Both Manitoba and Ontario have conducted successful CMI in small schools. Manitoba's correspondence school, in partnership with the University of Manitoba, developed a senior physics course to run on the Commodore series of computers: the software consisted of a set of lesson discs, a teachers disc and individual student discs. The computer is used to direct the students' learning. Students are able to proceed at their own pace and instant feedback is provided. The pilot programme in three small rural schools received enthusiastic praise. Research is continuing with the goal of making the physics course available to schools at the end of the testing period.

The Ontario experience focused on a computer-managed basic electronics course for small schools; it developed as a joint project between the Independent Learning Centre (ILC) and the Ministry of Education's Computers in Education Centre. The purpose of the project was to provide electronic education to small schools that did not have an electronics teacher on staff. The ILC developed the course material, the audiocassettes, a student manual, a facilitator's manual and the CMI software. The school board provided a qualified teacher, who was trained to be a facilitator, and a properly equipped room. An electronics expert was available in the community. The teacher/facilitator in the classroom could get emergency assistance through telephone links with the course author and the ILC. The pilot study in one school proved so successful that the programme expanded to four schools in 1984-5, a CAI component was developed, and a second course in digital electronics was prepared and is being tested. When the pilot studies are completed, the two electronics courses will be available for purchase.

Television

Project OCTOPUCE, through the collaboration of the Quebec Direction des Cours par Correspondance and TVOntario, combined television, printed learning materials and computer-assisted marking to provide practical information on microcomputers to students, parents and teachers. OCTO-PUCE was televised four times between 1982 and 1984. The programme attracted over 24,000 registrants; it is now available on videocassette. A second TV series called OCTOGICIEL is designed as a continuation to OCTOPUCE.

In January 1986, Manitoba introduced a computer literacy course designed to use TVOntario's *Bits and Bytes*, the English language predecessor to OCTOPUCE. Optical scanning is used to process answers and each student receives a computer printout of the results.

Computer-Managed Marking

Computer-Managed Marking (CMM) has proved to be cost- and time-effective in a number of projects. Saskatchewan started in 1983 to plan CMM of objective-type assignment questions for implementation in September 1986. As a result assignments in all new courses have been designed so they can be partially or entirely computer scored. This approach leaves Saskatchewan a number of options in its use and assessment of CMM as its service becomes more and more computerised. A high-school power mechanics course offered by Manitoba uses objective-type questions which are computer marked. Answers are optically scanned and an error analysis is performed by the computer. Computer-generated teaching loops provide remedial instruction for incorrect answers. Without CMM, Quebec's processing of the huge enrolment in OCTOPUCE would have been extremely expensive; it will continue with CMM in OCTOGICIEL. CMM of a law course in Ontario proved to be successful in generating higher completion rates at less cost than in a traditionally marked version of the course. A probable future direction in most education institutions will be to expand the use of the computer in scoring and evaluating students' assignments.

Computer-Assisted Instruction

Ontario is developing a series of computer studies courses for use in schools. Students who take these courses will do so because of timetabling conflicts or insufficient enrolment to warrant the school offering them. Many schools will use the courses as a resource or supplement to their computer studies programme.

CONCLUSION

Publicly-funded distance education services at the elementary and secondary-school level are involved in many initiatives to use technology effectively and to improve the quality of education they provide. By continuing to work together to share experiences and materials, they have the potential to make a significant contribution to distance education and to the distance learner.

NOTES

1. Planning and Research, Alberta Education, 11160 Jasper Avenue, Edmonton Alberta, T5K OL2.

REFERENCES

Alberta Education (1985) *Alberta Correspondence School Calendar, 1985-6*, Barrhead, Alberta Correspondence School
Correspondence Schools Association (Canada) (1982-5) *Newsletter*, 4 vols., Barrhead, Alberta Correspondence School

Thirteenth Annual Conference 18-21 September 1983, Montreal, Direction des cours par correspondance

Correspondence Schools Association (Canada) (1984) *Proceeding of the Fourteenth Annual Conference 16-19 September 1984*, Barrhead, Alberta Correspondence School

Manitoba Department of Education (1984) *Correspondence Courses 1984-5*, Winnipeg, Correspondence Education

Nova Scotia Department of Education (1985) *Correspondence Courses 1985*, Halifax, Nova Scotia Institute of Technology

Ontario Ministry of Education (1985) *Correspondence Education 1985-6*, Toronto, Independent Learning Centre

Province of British Columbia, Ministry of Education (1984) *Correspondence Education 1984-5*, Victoria, British Columbia, Correspondence Education Branch

Private Correspondence Schools

Christopher Hope

BACKGROUND

In 1984 there were 39 private schools licensed in Canada by provincial governments to provide distance educational services. It is estimated that these schools served over 25,000 Canadian students in over 500 different courses and subjects. The private schools offering distance education complement the publicly-funded sector by providing services that are not available through provincial systems or by providing the same services in a more convenient or superior way.

Free enterprise activity can be counted on to provide the best and the worst of any product or service. However, in the case of education, the private sector does not operate in a free environment but in a provincially regulated one, and hence private schools offering distance education range from the very best schools to schools that are merely satisfactory. These satisfactory schools meet the minimum provincial standards as outlined in the various trade schools acts and regulations.

This is important, as these regulations define the type of school and type of distance education permitted. The general rule is that, if owners are to open and operate a new school or advertise a private distance educational institute in a province, they are required to be licensed.

Part of the process of registering is to become bonded. This means that schools are required to post a $1,000 to $50,000 bond with the provincial licensing department. The amount of the bond depends on the province, number of students to be enrolled and the fees charged. The bond is a financial guarantee. The bonding company requires the owners to co-sign (guarantee) the bond, making them liable if it is called. To be able to co-sign it, they would have to have assets necessary to back its face value.

Bonding is an important part of the registration process. It provides the administrator with the means of settling a dispute in the student's favour. It provides protection for students when a school fails to provide quality education or succumbs to market forces and closes down, and allows for the reimbursement of the fees. This means that students who enrol in private schools offering distance education are not only financially protected but also have the provincial administrator to turn to in case of a dispute.

The final part of registering is the approval of the contract and the printing of the refund regulations on the back. Since these business standards vary from province to province, the school either needs a number of contracts or one complex one.

This chapter will describe the licensing process for a private school and describe the trade associations that work with provincial governments on the regulations that govern the industry. We shall then look at the industry leaders and the courses they offer, including a list of all private schools licensed to offer distance education, a partial list of courses offered through the private sector, and the names of three publications that provide detailed information on individual schools.

THE LICENSING PROCESS

The requirements vary greatly from province to province. In some cases managers are required to complete forms, post a bond and attach the provincial refund regulations to their contracts prior to opening. In other provinces, the managers are required to demonstrate that employers are going to accept their graduates for employment. One province requires the managers to have their material vetted and literally endorsed by experts within the province.

Managers who wish to register in more than one province are sometimes surprised that provincial governments in their educational administration duplicate work completed by one another. The regulations encourage temporarily disheartened students to discontinue their courses and seek refunds, as the sooner they discontinue the more refund they receive. The formulas, based on the number of assignments completed, are set up to force graduates not only to pay for their course but also the course overheads of the students who withdraw. Schools have to double their intended fees once they start using any of the refund regulations. This is one of the reasons why private schools must charge so much for their correspondence courses.

Schools that are provincially licensed have credibility and provide safeguards for Canadians who may have enrolled in a course and have not been able to finish. The regulations provide schools with a government-approved format on which to run their institutions and offer their courses.

PRIVATE POSTSECONDARY SCHOOL TRADE ASSOCIATIONS

Private schools have formed trade associations to upgrade the industry and advise provincial governments on updating regulations. The main associations are: the Association of Canadian Career Colleges (ACCC), the Private Career Education Council (PCEC) of Ontario, the Private Career Training Association (PCTA), Manitoba Association of Career Colleges (MACC), the Council for Private Vocational Schools (CPVS) in Quebec and the National Accreditation Commission (NAC), Canada's national accreditation agency for private career colleges. Each association has its own character and each association provides essential services to the schools it serves. Schools who have serious commitments to excellence in education support these associations.

Association of Canadian Career Colleges (ACCC)

This association has 47 private career college members of which 10 per cent are involved with distance education. However, many of the schools use self-paced learning in the classroom which is the application of correspondence education to the resident format. The association holds an annual convention and has a newsletter called *The Communicator*.

The examination services division provides monthly examinations across Canada in some 40 separate subjects. Students who write these examinations become eligible for the ACCC certificate, a national educational benchmark by which all private school students are judged. Twice a year all participating schools meet to discuss procedures and curriculum development and share knowledge on texts and procedures. The ACCC schools co-operate with one another. For instance, distance education students may use them as centres for writing supervised examinations or, in case of a mail strike, they may use the ACCC schools as drop-off points for their assignments. By joining the ACCC, a school-owner can tap into the wealth of knowledge and experience of other successful private-school owners, both resident and correspondence.

The Private Career Training Association (PCTA)

This British Columbia association is perhaps one of the most active of the associations, with meetings every two weeks. It has 47 members. PCTA also has an annual convention, and keeps its members up to date with news sheets. PCTA is active in representing the interests of the industry at government level.

The Manitoba Association of Career Colleges (MACC)

This Manitoba association has 18 members and is active in the representation of the industry in that province. It provides the opportunity for co-operative advertising and works closely with provincial education authorities in developing and maintaining educational standards.

The Private Career Educational Council (PCEC)

This Ontario association has 67 members. It co-operates with the provincial government by providing information on industry requirements. PCEC and the Ministry of Colleges and Universities hold an annual joint two-day professional development seminar for the industry. Day One is for managers and owners; Day Two is for teachers.

It has an annual convention combined with its AGM in Toronto. Four to six times a year PCEC issues a publication called *The Bulletin*. This publication carries the minutes of the monthly board meetings, together with minutes of meetings with government departments, both federal and provincial. Two or three times a year PCEC also holds social events for members and their families.

The Council for Private Vocational Schools (CPVS)

This Quebec association has 24 members. It is active in providing a forum for its Quebec schools.

The National Accreditation Commission (NAC)

NAC is the national accreditation body for private business and technical schools, both resident and distance education systems. It is devoted to excellence in education, and provides a system through which both private resident and private distance educational schools can become accredited.

PRIVATE SCHOOLS OFFERING DISTANCE EDUCATION

We shall now look at a selection of schools that each, in its own way, provides Canadians with the best in privately funded distance education. These schools will be ICS, McGraw-Hill Continuing Education, Granton Institute of Technology, Westervelt Business School, Aviron, Hume Publishers and Heathkit/Zenith.

ICS Canada Ltd.

Founded in 1890, ICS has been a pioneer in career education through guided independent study, as well as providing training to business and industry for more than ninety years. In addition to serving over 15,000 Canadian students, ICS clients range from individually-owned enterprises to multinational corporations, utilities and government bodies. Over fifty of the Top One Hundred companies, as rated by *Canadian Business Magazine*, have used ICS facilities and services to achieve their training objectives. ICS has its headquarters in Montreal, providing services to students in every province in Canada. All students have unlimited use of the ICS toll-free 'Dial-a-Question' telephone service to ask questions of their instructors.

ICS Canada Ltd. has many programmes including Accounting, Aircraft Mechanics, Animal Science, Appliance Servicing, Art, Auto Mechanics, Bookkeeping, Business Management, Carpenter Builder, Computer Programming, Drafting, Diesel Mechanics, Electrician, Electronics, Fashion Merchandising, Firearm Repair and Maintenance, Fitness and Nutrition, High School Diploma, Hotel Restaurant Management, Interior Decorating, Motorcycle Repair, Secretarial, Small Engine, TV Servicing, and Wildlife Forestry Conservation. ICS Canadian Ltd. is also involved in many aspects of distance education including the use of interactive videodisc technology.

McGraw-Hill Continuing Education Centre

This is the private vocational school division of McGraw-Hill Inc., the largest supplier of educational text material of its kind in the world. McGraw-Hill offers courses by home-study diploma programmes through NRI (National Radio Institute) established in 1914. Courses of study offered by correspondence are Automotive, Television/Audio Servicing, Communications, Electronics, Marine Electronics, Aircraft Electronics, Mobile Electronics, CB Radio, Digital Electronics, Industrial Electronics Technology, Basic Electronics, Microcomputers and Microprocessors, Small Engine Repair, Servicing Electrical Appliances, Air-conditioning, Refrigeration, and Heating with Solar Technology. McGraw-Hill's Canadian headquarters are in Scarborough, Ontario. NRI has enrolled over one million students world-wide, and the success of NRI's method is attributed to the 'hands on' teaching system using the tools and kits supplied with every major course. All texts, kits, tools, and test instruments are included in the price of the course and become the student's property. McGraw-Hill is also active in supplying Canadian industry with stand-alone distance education study modules that train students in separate topics of technology.

Granton Institute of Technology

Granton was established in 1934 and today, with over 400 correspondence courses, offers the largest range of programmes available from any Canadian private school delivering distance education. Granton's headquarters are in Toronto, where it has been at its Adelaide Street address for over a quarter of a century. The Granton system of education is based on three components. First, students are supplied with published text material for reference, together with a Granton study guide. Second, students are supplied with a telephone number that they can use to call the school collect, and have their questions answered. Third, students are supplied with submission forms for mailing in assignments. Students learn from the text material, complete their assignments as outlined in the study guide, then mail their work to their tutor. The assignments are evaluated (under the Granton 24-hour turn-around policy) and returned to the student. On completion, students are awarded certificates for single subjects and diplomas for complete programmes.

Granton's most popular courses include Accounting, Advertising, Appliance Servicing, Aircraft Mechanics, Auto Mechanics, Bookkeeping, Business Management, Commercial Art, Cosmetology, Drafting, Electricity and Electronics, Engineering and Technology (licensing and certification examination preparation for Civil, Chemical, Electrical, Electronics, Industrial and Mechanical Division), Early Childhood Education (ECE), Aesthetics, Fashion Merchandising and Design, Forestry, High-School Diploma, Hotel/Restaurant Management, Journalism, Law Enforcement, Legal Assistant, Library Science, Medical Secretary, Medical Terminology, Nurses' Aide, Photography, Psychology, Shorthand, Social Work, Travel Counsellor, Typing, and Veterinary Assistant. With over 400 courses, Granton has the flexibility to meet the needs of its students wherever the demand arises.

Granton is the first and only Canadian-owned private school offering distance education to be accredited by the National Home Study Council in the United States.

Westervelt Business and Travel Schools

Westervelt, established in 1885, is made up of two schools, Westervelt Business School and Westervelt Travel Institute. Although the business school is restricted to resident training, the travel school offers a distance education component. Westervelt Travel Institute is located in London, Ontario and is certified by the Canadian Institute of Travel Counsellors. It has a one-year resident programme and a combination resident and home-study programme. The combination programme consists of 24 lessons of home study followed by seven weeks of intensive in-school training. The distance education component of the training was introduced in 1973. Westervelt is associated with Lougheed Business College of Kitchener, Ontario.

Aviron Technical Institute

Aviron was established in 1937 and is located in Montreal. Aviron provides both resident and distance education, its distance education component followed by a residence requirement of two to six weeks. Aviron education philosophy is based on providing published textbooks and workbooks. The majority of assignments are in multiple-choice format which is particularly suitable for the subject matter in which they specialise. Aviron concentrates on automotive and trade level courses, including Auto Engines, Electrical Systems, Diesel Mechanics, Auto Transmissions, Auto Disc Brakes, Auto Collision, Auto Air-conditioning, Auto Maintenance and Troubleshooting, Auto Suspensions and Steering, Welding Skills and Practice, Welding Technology, Refrigeration and Air-conditioning, Plumbing Installations and Design, Fundamentals of Electricity, Basic Electricity and Electronics, Electrical Construction Wiring, Interior Electric Wiring, Blue Print Reading, Graphic Arts, Carpentry, Machine Shop Operations, Photo Technology, Upholstery. Aviron also has a travel agency course. Aviron is licensed in the province of Quebec. It has an active export business with some 2,000 students in the Caribbean.

Hume Publishing

Hume Publishing is one of the fastest growing distance educational companies in Canada. It was established in 1974. It offers four courses: Successful Investing and Money Management, Advanced Successful Investing and Money Management, Successful Real Estate Investing, and Successful Business Management. The first three courses have a final test that is mailed in for correction. All courses are state-of-the-art correspondence courses. The course material is presented in magazine format and is mailed regularly to students. Hume uses extensive press and direct mail advertising to introduce Canadians to its instructional material. Students can call in for help and advice. Hume provides Canadians with contemporary distance education.

Heathkit/Zenith Educational Systems

The Heath Company was established in Canada in 1954. It first offered home learning courses in 1964 and, since then, has become one of the leaders in the industry. The home learning system used is self-contained, with the exception of a final test that is mailed in for grading. Many public and private correspondence schools use Heathkit/Zenith course material to supplement their own training. The company is not licensed in any province, since it is a purveyor of education and does not offer a qualification. Heathkit/Zenith has seven main course groups with 36 different topics. Fundamentals of Electricity/Electronics (DC Electronics, AC Electronics, Semiconductor Devices, Electronic Circuits, Test Equipment, Electronic Communications), Digital Technology (Digital Techniques, CMOS Digital Techniques), Microprocessor/Microcomputer Technology (Microprocessor Technology, Microprocessor Interfacing, Voice Synthesis, 6809 Microprocessor, Microprocessor Applications, 16-Bit Microprocessor), Computer Programming (CP/M Operating system, MS-DOS, Assembly Language, BASIC, Microsoft BASIC, Pascal, FORTRAN), Advanced Electronics (Operational Amplifiers, Active Filters, IC timers, Phase-Locked Loops, Opto-Electronics, Fibre Optics, Passive Circuit Design, Transistor Circuit Design), Industrial Arts (Soldering, Concepts of Electricity, Printed Circuit Boards, Concepts of Electronics, Automotive Electronics, Automotive Ignition), Robotics Technology (Robotics and Industrial Electronics, Robot Applications).

Students may purchase the state-of-the-art distance education material either with or without the accompanying kits. Heathkit/Zenith's contemporary approach to distance education is yet another alternative available to students in the private sector.

CONCLUSION

Private correspondence courses provide a viable alternative to the courses provided by the departments of education of provincial governments. Private schools offering distance education are licensed, bonded and use provincially-approved enrolment contracts carrying provincially-specified refund regulations. Private schools that are committed to excellence in education support a number of trade associations that have been instrumental in obtaining financial benefits for private school students that were once only available to students of the funded sector. As governments cut back on educational budgets, private sector schools offering distance education expand to supply the need and continue to grow.

PRIVATE SCHOOLS LICENSED BY PROVINCES TO PROVIDE DISTANCE EDUCATION SERVICES

The following list of private schools offering distance education is consolidated from information supplied by the various provincial administrators, including the provinces in which the various schools were licensed and the trade associations, in brackets, that they support:

AMJ Electronic College, Alta., Ont. (PCEC)
Art Instruction School, B.C., Ont.
Aviron Technical Institute, P.Q. (ACCC, CPVS)
Canada College, Ont.
Canadian School of Tax Accounting, B.C.
Canadian School of Travel, B.C.
Canadian Securities Limited, N.S.
Canadian Security Research, B.C.
Career Canada Limited, Ont. (PCEC)
Century Business Academy, Ont.
Columbia Academy Radio, TV, Recording, Alta., B.C.
D & R Tax Centre, Man.
Electrolysis Educational Institute, Ont. (ACCC, PCEC)
Granton Institute of Technology, Alta., B.C., N.S., Ont.
(ACCC, MACC, PCEC, PCTA)
H & M Professional Training Institute, Alta.
Huett, Ayres Beghara Limited, Alta.
Hume Publishing, B.C., N.S.
ICS Canada Limited, Alta., B.C., Man., Nfld., N.B., N.S., Ont.,
P.E.I., P.Q., Sask. (ACCC, MACC, PCEC, PCTA)
International School Haute Esthetique, Ont.
Investigation Science Canada, Ont. (PCEC)
K & D School of Taxidermy, Man.

Karen Hall Careers, N.S., Ont. (PCEC)
Lorman Institute, Ont.
Mann Career Training Ltd., Alta., B.C.
McGraw-Hill Continuing Education, Alta., B.C., N.B., Nfld. N.S., Sask., Ont. (PCEC)
Merv Orr's Transport School, Ont.(PCEC)
National College, Alta., Ont. (PCEC)
National Institute of Broadcasting, Alta., Ont.
New Skills Vocational School, Ont.
Participation Transport Training, Ont.
Practical Business Institute, Ont.
PTL Truck Driving School, Ont.
Radio, Electronic, TV School, Ont. (PCEC)
Rapid Results School, Ont.
Sales Training School, N.B.
School of Canine Science, Ont.
Shaw Home Study College, Ont. (ACCC, PCEC)
U & R Tax Schools, Alta., B.C., Man.
Westervelt Business School, Alta., N.S., Ont. (ACCC, PCEC)

SELECTION OF SUBJECTS OFFERED BY PRIVATE SCHOOLS LICENSED TO PROVIDE DISTANCE EDUCATION IN ONE OR MORE PROVINCES IN CANADA

A
Accident Investigation, Accounting, Advertising, Agribusiness, Aesthetician, Air-Conditioning and Refrigeration, Aircraft Mechanic, Animal Sciences, Announcing (Radio and TV), Appliance Servicing, Art (Commercial, Fundamentals), Automotive Servicing

B
Bar Training, Basic Electronics, Blueprint Reading, Bookkeeping, Building Construction, Building Contractor, Building Estimator, Building Maintenance, Business Administration, Business Management

C
Carpentry, Carpentry and Building, Cabinet Making, Ceramic Technology, Clerical, Communications Electronics, Computer Programming, Computer Technology, Cosmetology, Culinary Arts

D
Data Processing, Degree Courses, Dental Office Assistance, Dental Office and Chairside Assistant, Dental Office Procedures, Digital Electronics, Diesel Engines, Drafting, Dress Making and Design

E
Early Childhood Education (ECE), Electrician, Electrolysis, Electronics (Various), Electronic Design Technology, Engineering (Chemical, Civil, Electrical, Electronic, Industrial, Mechanical, Professional License, Structural), Export-Import

F
Fire Control and Technology, Firearm Repair and Maintenance, Forestry

G
Gemology, General Record Keeping

H
Heating and Ventilation, Homebuilding and Remodeling, Hotel Operations and Management, Hotel-Motel, Housing Management

I
Import-Export, Industrial Electronics, Income Tax, Interior Design, International Freight Forwarding, Investigation and Security

J
Journalism

L
Landscaping, Library Science

M
Machine Shop, Management (Accounting, Small Business, Traffic), Marketing, Mechanical Courses (Motor), Medical (Laboratory Assistant, Office Assisting and Procedures, Office Procedures, Records and Terminology, Transcription), Metallurgy, Microcomputers/Microprocessing, Motel Operation, Motorcycle Repair, Motor Mechanics

N
Navigation

O
Office Practice and Management

P
Paste-Up (Graphic Arts), Petroleum and Gas, Personnel Management, Photography, Plant Technology, Plumbing, Power Plant Engineering and Operation, Professional Microcomputer Technology, Pump Technology, Purchasing, Psychology

Q
Quality Control

R
Real Estate, Receptionist, Record Keeping, Refrigeration, Retailing, Restaurant Management

S
Salesmanship, Secretarial (Executive, Medical), Shorthand, Small Engine Repair, Social Work, Solar Technology, Statistics, Stationary Engineer, Stenography, Surveying and Mapping, Systems Accounting (Computer), Systems Analysis and Design

T
Taxidermy, Telecommunications, Television Copy-Writing, Television Servicing, Textiles, Tractor-Trailer Training, Travel Careers, Travel Counsellor, Typing

U
Upholstery

V
Van Customising, Video/Audio Technology, VCR Technology, Veterinary Office

W
Welding (Various), Window Display, Word Processing, World Tourist Destinations

Z
Zoology

PUBLICATIONS PROVIDING INFORMATION ON PRIVATE SCHOOLS OFFE ING DISTANCE EDUCATION

Registered Private Vocational Schools. Ministry of Colleges and Universities, Toronto, Ontario. This publication provides the names and addresses of private schools and the list of distance education courses they offer. The publication is free on request.

Directory of Approved and Recommended Schools and Courses. The Private Career Education Council, Suite 718, 130 Adelaide Street West, Toronto, Ontario. The publication is free on request.

Distance Education: Canadian Courses by Correspondence. Career Services Branch, Alberta Manpower, 2nd Floor, Sun Building, 10363 - 108 Street, Edmonton, Alberta T5J 1L8. $6.00.

Section 5: USE OF TECHNOLOGY

New Technologies in Distance Education

Charles R. Shobe

The phrase 'distance education technology' conjures up visions of computers, laser beams, satellites and videodiscs linked by switched microwave networks and flashing optical fibres in an educational Promised Land. However, in Canada and throughout the world, an overwhelming majority of distance education is still conducted by correspondence methods. Where audio, video or microelectronic communication technologies are used, they almost invariably complement or supplement core, print-based course materials.

The Directory of Distance Education in Ontario recently published by the Ontario Ministry of Agriculture and Food, Rural Organisations and Services Branch (Gray and Watson 1985), identified an impressive range of Ontario distance education courses and programmes offered by an even more impressive array of agencies. It also presents a convenient framework for estimating the relative emphasis given to various technologies in the current practice of distance education in Canada. Among the 52 institutions and agencies identified in the directory were 11 universities, 11 colleges, 11 private vocational schools and 19 other organisations. Collectively these institutions offered more than 100 diploma and certificate programmes including at least 14 degree programmes and nearly 300 additional individual distance education courses. All 52 providers used 'written study materials' as their primary delivery vehicle, with 29 identifying print as their only instructional medium. Audiocassettes were named as an important complementary instructional medium by 14 institutions, while videocassettes were mentioned by only 8 agencies. Broadcast strategies (radio, television and cable systems) were employed by 5 organisations, but distance education via computer was mentioned by only 1 college. Four institutions named other media including slides/filmstrips, kits and audio teleconferencing. Fibre optics and videodisc technologies were not mentioned by any of the agencies. Printed material accompanied by audiocassettes was the most common media combination mentioned by institutions using two or more delivery media. Only 11 organisations, 9 of them universities, reported the use of more than two media for distance education.

Although these figures are not rigorously quantitative, they undoubtedly reflect the proportionate use of various media for distance education in Canada in 1985. If similar figures were available for 1975, they would certainly reveal a much smaller number of distance education providers, almost all of which were exclusively correspondence institutions, with perhaps two or three notable exceptions.

Since the mid-1970s, however, there has been a world-wide explosion in the availability and variety of distance education services, with Canadian technological research and development in this area outstripping that of most other nations. Indeed, the geography and demography of Canada have historically challenged visionary Canadians to test the ability of new technologies to meet the nation's communication requirements generally, and specifically to support teaching and learning at a distance. In recent years, as in the past, Canadian educators have been especially adept at responding to those challenges.

HISTORICAL PERSPECTIVES

Whether the technology was 'print and penny mail' (1880s), radio (1920s), television (1950s) or computers and satellites (1970s), Canadian educators have consistently been among the early adopters of emerging technologies for distance education. The introduction of correspondence study for selected arts and science courses by Queen's University in 1889 (Queen's University 1979), soon after the introduction of generalised postal services (penny mail), is arguably one of the earliest examples of a concerted public or private sector distance education service. It is also noteworthy that the Queen's University correspondence programme has been available without interruption since its inception.

Early Educational Radio Services

In 1925 and 1926, H.P. Brown of the University of Alberta Extension Department arranged for broadcasts of lectures from the University of Alberta by the fledgling private radio station CJCA in Edmonton. The success of this informal educational service led to the funding and establishment (through a delightful piece of subterfuge on the part of the Extension Department) of radio station CKUA to broadcast music, adult education programmes and school broadcasts for specific curricular instruction (for example, French language instruction). When an epidemic closed all Edmonton schools in 1936, CKUA radio undertook to broadcast school lessons to children in their homes. (Lambert 1963)

Between 1925 and 1936, similar independent developments in the use of radio for both classroom and home-based study occurred in virtually every province of Canada. These initiatives depended almost entirely on the interest, initiative and success of local educators in persuading private broadcasters to allocate free time for school-related instructional programmes. In 1938, however, the newly established Canadian Broadcasting Corporation began to allocate time to school broadcasts on its provincial network in British Columbia. This service spread to the prairies and maritime provinces during the period 1938-41 and by 1942 a strengthening programme of school broadcasts was being carried nation-wide by the CBC, impelled to a significant degree by a strong lobby from rural teachers and parents. Although it was not developed explicitly as a distance education service, the impact of the national school broadcasts on home-bound learners and isolated rural children has been regarded as very significant over the years.

Another early Canadian radio service has also served as a model for educational broadcast services in some developing countries. The telephone 'talk-back' format developed by the CBC initially for its important, informal educational radio series entitled 'Farm Radio Forum' and used also with some school broadcasts, is now widely used in developing countries to add an interactive element to public educational broadcast initiatives. (Jenkins and Perraton 1978)

Early Experiments with Educational Television

Following the introduction of television services in Canada in 1952, the first Canadian experiments with nation-wide educational television were conducted by the CBC in 1954 and 1955 (Lambert 1963). These experiments were intended in part as visual supplements to the national radio school broadcasts but more important, they served as a research vehicle for examining teacher and student reactions to instructional television. Those initial reactions, with certain reservations, were generally favourable.

In 1959, a private television station, CJON-TV in St John's, Newfoundland, provided free air time - about four hours per day for three weeks - to provide educational services to children studying at home during an extended school closure resulting from a polio epidemic. These lessons were prepared on very short notice and follow-up evaluations by the Newfoundland Teachers' Association found them to have a number of shortcomings. Nevertheless, many students, parents and teachers acknowledged the generally beneficial nature of the service and commented on its success in interesting and assisting children with their school work. Although this service was short-lived, it did underline the potential of educational television to deliver basic education services at a distance to a dispersed population.

In the late 1950s and throughout the 1960s, educational television continued to develop provincially rather than nationally, reflecting the fact that education is constitutionally a provincial responsibility, while communications policy governing television broadcasting is a federal one. Although the early 1960s saw some additional initiatives in the use of national television for school broadcasts, most activity in this area has come from provincial educational communications agencies and local television stations, or educational broadcast and cable consortia.

Taken as a whole, these early experiments with educational radio and television broadcast identified issues that remain a part of the debate over the design and use of educational broadcast services. These key issues include programme length relative to student attention span; restrictions on utilisation arising from differences in broadcast schedules and classroom schedules; the use of teachers or actors as presenters; the appropriateness of a particular medium to course content; and the relative emphasis on production values versus content scope and depth. Such debates undoubtedly originated with the first educational radio and television programmes, and some of them may never be resolved to the satisfaction of both educators and broadcasters.

Short-Wave Radio

There are indications that, during and after the Second World War, the Canadian Armed Forces and the Government of Canada employed instructional teleconferencing and short-wave radio broadcasting for staff training. Very little information seems to have been collected or made publicly available on these early activities. If today's events are any indicator, however, one can speculate that such applications have been widespread, as the armed forces in Canada and elsewhere are often the earliest and most intensive adopters of new technologies for personnel training and communications functions.

The New Technologies

The years 1970-5 can be said to divide the era of educational communications into the 'new' and the 'old'. Before 1970, educational radio and television broadcasts were available in the home and, towards the end of the era, both audio and videocassettes and cassette players began to be commercially available at a reasonable cost for home study. Of course the old standbys of film, slides and filmstrips were also available, but they were somewhat expensive and inconvenient in the 'at-home' context of distance education programmes.

Since 1970, and due in large measures to the enormous advances in microelectronics that have given rise to dramatically increased capabilities while radically reducing costs, the array of transmission devices and learning station hardware has continued to increase and diversify. Not only were new technological delivery systems developed, but also old technologies have been refined and reworked to permit new applications. Even more important, convenient multimedia systems and interactive technologies began to emerge.

During that era, several new agencies - the provincial Educational Communications Authorities - were established to optimise the use of media and new technologies in support of both conventional and distance education. New institutions were also created exclusively to provide innovative distance education services. New industries and research and development agencies were established to advance the applications of communications technologies for business, industry, entertainment and education. As the revolution in communications and media technologies progresses, it is evident that these technologies and applications are merging into a integrated, multipurpose system. Information technologies are becoming an essential adjunct to virtually every aspect of living and the impacts on education in general and long distance education in particular will be especially significant.

M.G. Ryan has reported on research in the early 1970s by the Canadian Department of Communications (DOC) on the administrative and training applications of audio teleconferencing. (Ryan 1975) These studies were partly a response to teleconferencing initiatives under way elsewhere in North America, and partly applications research undertaken prior to the introduction of a radical new telecommunications system for Canada.

Telecommunications Satellites

In 1972, with the launch of ANIK-A into geostationary orbit, Canada became the first nation in the world to deploy a nation-wide, satellite-based telecommunications system. (Ruggles et al. 1982) With the joint launching in 1976 by Canada and the United States of the Hermes satellite, a new era in research and development of educational broadcast services was born. Following Hermes were ANIK B and the ANIK C and D series of Canadian communications satellites, each of which in a variety of ways has expanded the scope of educational broadcast services in Canada. (Bottomley 1981; Forsythe 1982; Ruggles et al. 1982; Shobe 1983a)

Canadian educators have been experimenting successfully with satellite delivery systems since the launching of the Hermes satellite in 1976. Beginning in that year, the University of Quebec used direct video broadcasts, interactive audio conferencing and facsimile transmission to provide access for isolated students to campus-based library resources, master's level credit courses in education and non-credit professional development programmes. (Daniel *et al.* 1978) The University of Western Ontario and Memorial University of Newfoundland used one-way video with two-way audio conferencing to provide continuing medical education and medical consultation services to isolated health care personnel. (House *et al.* 1981, 1982; McNamara 1978; Ruggles *et al.* 1982) In an international distance education experiment, the Faculties of Engineering at Carleton University in Ottawa, Ontario, and at Stanford University in California used audio teleconferencing in conjunction with digital video compression, video multiplexing and slow-scan video techniques to exchange graduate-level engineering courses. (Daniel *et al.* 1978; Guild *et al.* 1976) More recently, Memorial University has acquired a low power portable TV transmitter which it is able to transport to rural centres. The 'instant' community television broadcast service is used effectively for community-wide communication (three-to-ten-mile range) and community education programming that complements Memorial University's community development approach to continuing education. This regional broadcast telephone talk-back process presents some intriguing regional distance education possibilities.

Beginning in 1977, Hermes was used by the British Columbia Institute of Technology to deliver forestry-related training programmes from the Provincial Educational Media Centre in Burnaby, British Columbia, to five portable receiving sites scattered across that province. (Bottomley 1978; Ruggles *et al.* 1982) In 1978, additional experiments with instructional television were conducted in British Columbia on ANIK B, and in 1979, six postsecondary institutions in that province committed themselves to regular satellite delivery of courses. (Ruggles *et al.* 1982)

The most important outcome of the British Columbia experiments was the establishment of the Knowledge Network of the West (KNOW) Communications Authority. KNOW is now funded by the Ministry of Education as an educational communications utility to operate and maintain central studios and uplink facilities and to assist institutions with acquisition, development, distribution and promotion of television-based courses. (Forsythe 1982) The KNOW signal, originally transmitted to ANIK B from an uplink in Vancouver, is now distributed via ANIK C and can be received throughout British Columbia and in the parts of the Yukon Territory, and in western regions of Alberta and the Northwest Territories. Local distribution occurs mainly via coaxial cable systems; but participating institutions and many individual homes have special equipment (TVRO) that enables them to receive programmes directly.

TVOntario has also been heavily involved in research and development of satellite-based educational television services. Experiments in 1978 with a live two-way television programme involving TVOntario and a California educational cable system were followed in 1979 with direct broadcast experiments in conjunction with the Department of Communications (DOC). By 1984-5, TVOntario was providing educational television services to more than 90% of Ontario residents by satellite-to-cable, satellite-to-low-power rebroadcast transmitters, and satellite-to-TVRO systems. Of particular interest is the ongoing funding programme of the Ontario Ministry of

Northern Affairs to assist small communities with the installation of low-power rebroadcast transmitters. (Wilson *et al.* 1984)

Radio-Québec, the Quebec educational television network, has recently entered a satellite distribution agreement for its broadcast services and the Télé-université du Québec employs ANIK C to deliver credit courses to remote communities. Mount St Vincent University's Distance University Educational Television (DUET) service has also used satellite distribution, and the Atlantic Association of Universities is co-operating in the distribution of university courses on time provided on a commercial satellite channel.

In January 1985, ACCESS NETWORK introduced a new satellite-based educational television service for the province of Alberta. With 84 hours per week of formal and informal educational programming, this service is available primarily via satellite-to-cable and satellite-to-TVRO distribution systems. A grant programme assists schools and other non-profit organisations in communities without cable to install TVRO equipment in community learning centres. Programming on the ACCESS NETWORK includes daytime broadcasts that are directly relevant to school-based curriculum. In the evenings, credit telecourses from various postsecondary institutions in the province are available to adult learners. Non-credit 'how-to' series, cultural programmes and programmes for pre-schoolers fill out the broadcast schedule.

Telecourses

First introduced in Canada by Laurentian University in 1972, formal credit telecourses are worthy of special attention as they represent an important and rapidly growing addition to the list of distance education services provided over wide areas by satellite-based educational broadcast systems. Some institutions, such as Wilfrid Laurier University, Seneca College, Carleton University and Mount St Vincent University, also work closely with cable system operators to provide telecourses locally or regionally (Burge 1984), while other institutions circulate videocassettes to their distance education students. Telecourse offerings number from less than 10 to more than 40 courses per semester on the various systems, and in subject matter vary from second language instruction to business and computer studies and continuing professional education in nursing, medicine and dentistry.

The television component is usually only one of several instructional elements in a distance education telecourse. For example, the introductory French 101 telecourse from Athabasca University (Ensemble) has been offered with at least seven significant media components. These include broadcast television, broadcast radio, audiocassettes, printed materials, individual telephone tutor, group audio teleconferencing and residential week-end study/practice sessions. All of these media have been used, individually or in combination, in other telecourses along with at least trial use of telephone-based oral testing, computer-managed learning and computer assisted-instruction.

Telecourses are especially important since they add to the distance education experience the visual dimension that is so critical in conventional education. With telecourses, a full range of material can be provided to address the instructional imperatives of the course and the subject matter, and accommodate the diverse learning styles of students. Well designed telecourses also attract and inform the general viewer, with two significant outcomes: first, informal learning occurs, resulting in a generally increased level of public awareness about various subjects; and second, a number of individuals are enticed to re-enter the education system in order to systematically strengthen and expand their formal educational backgrounds. These significant and desirable spin-offs from telecourses may ultimately be as important as or more important than the direct instructional impact on registered telecourse students.

Audio teleconferencing

Audio teleconferencing is the least expensive, most flexible, most readily implemented telecommunication technology for distance education. (Ellis 1981; Jeffrey 1983; Shobe 1983b) In its simplest form it can use standard telephone equipment and existing telephone conferencing facilities to link an instructor with a few widely-scattered students. As the number of locations, the number of participants and the frequency of teleconferences increase, specially designed station and bridging equipment must be employed, but the telephone system remains as the basic communication channel.

The primary purpose of audio teleconferencing is to accommodate interaction among isolated students and their instructors. Printed materials, videotapes, slides, textbooks, films and other materials are usually circulated to students for use between and during class sessions. Media that can be transmitted via telephone lines can also be employed to complement the auditory interaction. Electronic blackboards, slow-scan video, graphics tablets, videotex or teletext and computer-supported instruction are among the media that can be used in this way. (Graham 1984) Audio teleconferencing is also used by the University of Victoria, Simon Fraser University, the Open Learning Institute and several other postsecondary institutions in British Columbia to complement telecourses delivered over the Knowledge Network. Reports from Memorial University suggest that teleconferencing is overshadowing the telecourse initiatives for which that university is renowned and that students are unanimously enthusiastic about combined teleconference/telecourse offerings.

Memorial University has used a dedicated audio teleconference system (a private telephone circuit) to provide interactive audio communication in conjunction with satellite broadcast television and circulated videocassettes. (House *et al.* 1981, 1982; Jeffery 1983; McNamara 1978) At the University of Calgary (Ellis 1981, 1982; Zukiwski 1982) and Athabasca University (Jacobsen 1982; Shobe 1982, 1983b), audio teleconferencing and videotex (Telidon) technology have been combined effectively. Teleconference students at both institutions invariably applaud the added visual focus that the colour graphics provide. (Ellis 1982; Jacobsen 1982)

Athabasca University has used teleconferencing primarily to complement its home-study courses. (Shobe 1982, 1983b) Bi-weekly teleconference seminars enhance the individual telephone tutoring that is standard for Athabasca University courses. Students work through their home-study materials before attending teleconference sessions which accommodate the discussion and debate absent from most home-study courses. Results suggest that teleconferencing could be employed as an inexpensive alternative to the residential schools that many distance education programmes have incorporated.

The University of Ottawa has employed audio teleconferencing in combination with an electronic blackboard to deliver a wide range of courses including engineering, liberal studies and education courses, many of which were offered in French. (McDonell 1984) With assistance from the secretary of state, this audiographic teleconferencing technology was used during 1984-5 to deliver courses for teachers of French Immersion programmes nationwide. This combination of media is very comfortable from a conventional instructor's point of view as it can originate from a classroom and the electronic blackboard can be used by the instructor much like a conventional blackboard. Aside from the capital costs of installing the equipment, operational costs can be high because the system requires two telephone lines - one for the verbal interaction and one for the electronic blackboard - thereby doubling long-distance toll costs.

In Alberta, four teleconference systems are now in operation, several more institutions are contemplating acquisition of teleconference bridges and at least twelve postsecondary institutions have continuing teleconference programmes, are experimenting with individual courses or are collaborating with other providers to broker teleconference courses into their regions.

The independent teleconference systems in Alberta were established by each programming agency in a pattern which accommodates its individual requirements, but within a framework of strong interinstitutional communication and co-operation. In each new community served, the initial programming institution would establish a new teleconference facility and make necessary personnel arrangements. Other agencies would ordinarily share the use of that facility, but when scheduling conflicts arose, the institution would establish an additional temporary facility. As general learner demand for programming increases and scheduling conflicts or overlapping multiply, the temporary facilities become permanent. This evolving, co-operative approach has optimised the use of equipment, space and personnel, and it has led inevitably towards voluntary province-wide co-ordination of programming, scheduling, and facility and personnel utilisation.

While co-operating in facility and personnel development, Alberta's teleconferencing institutions, in co-operation with community-based educational consortia, have also joined together in a very strong lobby to elicit greater government support in offsetting long-distance charges. As a consequence, government grants that enable leasing of FX (foreign exchange) lines to interconnect regional teleconference bridges have been approved. As well, the recently approved after-hours access to the provincial government's RITE Telephone Network accommodates toll-free connections in the evenings to virtually every community in the province where a government office has been established.

The use of the FX Network and the RITE Network for instructional teleconferencing means that the programming institution, wherever it is located in the province, can establish a toll-free network that connects numerous centres in virtually every other region of the province. There may or may not be additional (less expensive) toll calls from those regional centres to smaller rural communities to complete the teleconference network for a particular course.

At this time, efforts are under way by the programming institutions and related agencies to establish an Alberta Teleconferencing Council. The council would seek to co-ordinate equitable access by all users to the inexpensive FX and RITE teleconferencing networks; to encourage communication and co-ordination in respect to programming in order to avoid course and programme duplication; to co-ordinate access to teleconferencing facilities and support personnel in various communities; and to encourage transferability of credit among programming institutions. The continuing success of this province-wide co-operative approach to the development of a distance education delivery system, including co-ordination of both programming and facilities, may be instructive to institutions in other jurisdictions.

Computer-based Distance Education

'All information in all places at all times. The impossible ideal. But the marriage of computers with existing telecommunications links will take us far closer to that goal than we have ever been'. (Godfrey and Parkhill 1980) The focus of educators in the 'information society' will be to help people learn to learn. People will be taught how to seek information through available technological resources and how to analyse, evaluate, interpret and apply what they discover. Rote knowledge will be taught by multi-media computer-based instructional systems (frequently in the home) in a more patient, entertaining, efficient and effective manner - and at a much earlier age - than human teachers could manage. Conceptual learning will include both mediated and interpersonal dimensions and children will go to 'school' not so much to acquire their basic education, as to develop their social, cultural and recreational skills.

At this time, however, our best computer-assisted instruction (CAI) often appears artificial and simplistic, and most computer-managed instruction (CMI) and computer-based course authoring systems follow objective instructional design strategies that many instructors reject. Few of the existing computer-based education (CBE) projects address programme development in contrast to module or course development; fewer still consider the operational exigencies of large-scale computer-based education-at-a-distance; and virtually none consider how to address the fundamental social and cultural issues that would be associated with the introduction of a computer-based education system. These gaps between 'promises' and 'products' must be closed if the potential of CBE is ever to be realised.

One of the more interesting Canadian initiatives in computer-managed learning (CML) has already been applied effectively for course-specific distance education. Developed initially by the Southern Alberta Institute of Technology (SAIT), this CML system includes course authoring, student assessment and feedback, and student records capabilities. (Ruggles et al. 1982) Students taking CML-based courses receive a variety of home study materials - texts, workbooks, audio and videotapes, kits, etc. - and proceed through their course independently or with some telephone tutorial assistance. Tutorial assistance via computer conferencing is also possible though not widely used as yet. Assignment and examination answers are entered on remote terminals with marking, feedback and record updating managed by the software. The SAIT/CML software and similar, but somewhat enhanced, software available from a private Alberta software company have been successfully marketed around the world.

A provincial software licensing agreement recently negotiated by Access Network provides the most recent, enhanced version of this CML software free to more than twenty of Alberta's postsecondary educational institutions. Access Network has also undertaken to support the activities of a provincial users' group that will work collectively with the software developer on software enhancements. The group will also attempt to co-ordinate development, sharing and marketing of courseware and item banks compatible with this CML system. The short-term savings to the provincial education system arising out of this licensing agreement will approach $400,000. Longer term savings arising out of courseware sharing among participating institutions and avoidance of duplication in courseware development activities will undoubtedly run into the millions of dollars.

At the present, time this CML software system is used primarily for on-campus CML activity. However, for several years, SAIT has used this software to support province-wide delivery of an ambulance attendant (paramedic) training programme. Grant MacEwan Community College is also using the CML software to support province-wide and, indeed, interprovincial delivery of a post-basic nursing and nursing refresher programme. (Nakonechny 1982) Other Alberta institutions are now moving rapidly in the direction of computer-supported off-campus instruction as well.

The Open Learning Institute of British Columbia has developed an extremely useful software package called the Distance Education and Training Resource Management System. Although this software relates to institutional management rather than direct instruction, it must be regarded as significant to distance education since it facilitates many of the support systems-registration, student records, assignment grading and course materials management - that are vital to excellence in distance education services. The Open Learning Institute is also developing computer assisted learning packages for several of its course. (Mugridge 1985)

Another major learning-related computer application developed in Canada is CHOICES, a computer-assisted career counselling programme available from the Government of Canada through its Department of Employment and Immigration. At the present time, over 225 terminals located across Canada enable career exploration (in conjunction with counsellor assistance) in an interactive, on-line mode.

Most CBE systems are developed for on-site, on-line use. While modern communication technologies enable them to be used off campus as well, communications costs have tended to limit those applications. This is true for the SAIT system, the Grant MacEwan Community College applications (Nakonechny 1982), the TVOntario Academy system (Waniewicz 1982), and the PLATO system developed by Control Data Corporation in the United States and now used by a number of Canadian institutions. (Szabo 1983)

The University of Quebec, the University of Alberta and the Alberta Vocational Centre in Edmonton, among others, have used PLATO extensively for both on-campus and off-campus instruction. PLATO offers an extensive range of ready-to-use educational software, an excellent course authoring system, course evaluation and student record facilities and an impressive range of teaching methods (with accompanying audio and video display devices). Until recently, however, remote PLATO locations faced excessive communications costs that have deterred widespread adoption of the system. Control Data Corporation has now introduced a microcomputer-based PLATO system which avoids these costs. CHOICES, the Canadian computer-based career counselling service, is also moving towards the use of microcomputers.

Most new applications in computer-based distance education attempt to minimise the problem of communications costs by taking advantage of the computing power now available in new microcomputer systems. 'Stand-alone' instructional activities are designed which require only brief and infrequent connections with host computers for assignments and examination purposes. Properly integrated into computer-based education systems, communications networks, publicly-accessible data bases and information services, bulletin boards and computer conferencing systems have the potential to alter radically the nature and meaning of the word education.

While the information society has the potential to permit a whole new concept of schools and schooling, there is a difficulty that may be foreshadowed by our previous experience with the adoption of telephone technology for distance education. Unlike many other new technologies, the telephone system was not used for formal instruction for nearly 100 years after its development, largely because the communications costs were very high. Even more important, those costs depended on distance, time and the number of locations involved and they increased more or less in direct proportion to those factors. Economies of scale could not be achieved except by collecting more and more people into groups, and this led to fewer opportunities for true interaction, one of the key reasons for considering the use of telephone. Widespread use of instructional audio teleconferencing was not encouraged in Canada or elsewhere until significant government support was made available to offset these volume-sensitive costs. Thereafter, user demand has increased and the development of the required switching and signal processing equipment has followed as a natural consequence of this demand.

At this stage in the development and application of computer-based instructional and information systems to distance education, many costs related to remote computer applications are very volume sensitive. Every connection, every minute of on-line interaction, even the rate (therefore the volume) of communication increases these costs. Even the use of relatively inexpensive Datapac services for Telidon graphics transmission has been found by the Alberta Correspondence Branch to be too expensive for routine support of distance education services. As each connection to a system ordinarily represents a single person, the achievement of economies of scale through grouping of individuals, as was possible to a degree with teleconferencing, becomes very problematic. One might predict, therefore, that significant, creative, wide-spread applications of computer-based education strategies to conventional and distance education will be delayed until these volume-sensitive cost factors are addressed. The Edulink system in Alberta, whereby Alberta Government Telephone offers special rates for connection to the PLATO system at the University of Alberta is, one hopes, only the first of many examples of government support for computer-based educational communication. Co-ordination and co-operation among distance education institutions will also be essential if the very high costs of instructional software development is not to delay further the introduction of computer-aided distance education services.

Optical Disc Technology

Optical disc (videodisc) technology will take a deserved place in the forefront of educational technology in the very near future for several reasons:

it accommodates virtually every instructional medium including audio, full-motion video, graphics, print, still photographs, and computer programmes;

information stored on a disc in any format is rapidly accessible and access can be controlled by computer programmes;

the discs are not subject to wear and thus are long-lived;

once a master disc is prepared, copies can be produced inexpensively in large volumes; and

earlier technical difficulties with preparing and using optical discs are being overcome. (D'Antoni 1982)

Optical discs can be used in combination with other interactive technologies such as microcomputers and teleconference networks to provide multi-media education independent of time and place. In the short term, this multi-dimensional technology will be available on campus or in local learning centres, since few people have the necessary play-back equipment. In time, however, this limitation will disappear as the equipment involved also accommodates home entertainment and is available in most households.

Two types of videodisc are available - those where there is contact between a stylus and the surface of the disc and those which involve the use of reflected scanning laser beams which read the disc without contact. For a variety of reasons the reflective optical disc - or laserdisc - technology seems likely to emerge as the winner in this battle of alternate technologies, and it is already a clear favourite in the compact disc technology for audio disc and microcomputer application in the home.

Both public sector and private sector organisations are convinced of the dramatic potential of optical disc technology for education and many are actively developing laserdiscs for educational use. Most of these applications are intended for in-school use, but the nature of the technology dictates that distance education applications are limited only by the availability of appropriate equipment to the off-campus learner. There are two generic applications of laserdiscs for education: first, as an audio, video, graphic-print or software *database*; and second, as a pre-planned *instructional package*. In the former case an enormous amount of software, print, graphic, audio and video pictures - up to 108,000 still frames on a single 12" disc-can be stored and accessed very rapidly under external control. In the latter case, a carefully designed multi-media instructional programme is encoded on the disc, often with multiple pathways, feedback loops, planned simulations, sources of additional information and both formative and summative assessment exercise built into the process.

The encyclopedic or database approach to laserdisc development is being considered by a number of Canadian publishers on a subject area basis. One noted publisher of texts for the health sciences is exploring the development of a 'Medical Terminology' videodisc. Using an external computer to control such a disc, one could quickly call up still photos of equipment, instruments, typical histological specimens and lesions and other practical illustrations related to health care. Sequences illustrating proper procedures with accompanying graphics, print or 'voice-over', could also be recalled repeatedly and conveniently as required, taking advantage of the branching and random-access capability of the laserdisc which is one of its major advantages over sequential videotape. Other Canadian publishers are considering laserdisc database for Canadian flora and fauna, biology, engineering and the visual arts.

Much of the current development of pre-designed instructional videodiscs has been undertaken by the private sector for industry-based training. This is a hidden and often overlooked area of distance education since it usually occurs outside the sphere of interest of distance education practitioners. The number of examples of such training materials is increasing rapidly with the majority of development work being done in eastern Canada by private entrepreneurs on contract to major corporations. Noteworthy examples include the laserdisc-based training programme developed by Interactive Image Technologies of Toronto to train Bell Canada employees to use that company's new electronic messaging system, and those developed by Michael J. Petro Ltd. for training salesmen and mechanics for General Motors and American Motors.

Nevertheless, interactive instructional laserdisc programmes are also being developed by public education agencies. In co-operation with various educational institutions in Alberta, especially the Alberta Vocational Centres in Calgary and Edmonton, Access Network has been involved in the development of interactive instructional laserdiscs that teach urinary catheterisation, sign language for the deaf, cell search techniques for correctional officers, and English as a second language for new Canadians. The Ontario Institute for Studies in Education is also heavily involved in videodisc applications with several other agencies, and Simon Fraser University has developed videodiscs for school-based instruction. The University of Alberta has developed a laserdisc-based simulation on classroom teaching for student teachers and many other public education institutions elsewhere in Canada are beginning to explore the use of this powerful though somewhat expensive multi-media resource for both conventional and distance education. (Tobin 1984)

Optical Fibre Communications

Three factors inhibit the use of existing technologies to give most households access to a variety of available databases;

poor organisation and maintenance of the databases;

high cost of extended, long distance communication; and

inadequate capacity and transmission speed of existing telecommunications systems.

Fibre optics systems, which transmit light pulses rather than electrical currents, could help to overcome the last two difficulties. As light transmission is unaffected by electromagnetic and radio frequency interference, the speed and the capacity of fibre optics systems are potentially 10,000 times greater than copper cable systems. (Ruggles *et al.* 1982) As a result, fibre optics transmission systems could minimise or eliminate problems of capacity and transmission speed, thus truly opening the door to the information society for the vast majority of the population.

Recent Canadian experiments in this area have been described as unqualified successes. In Manitoba, thousands of kilometres of fibre optics cable have been installed in the test communities of Elie and St Eustache to handle telephone calls, video transmissions, FM service and computer communications. Although these tests do not involve instructional applications directly, they have clearly demonstrated the enhanced communication possibility with these systems and suggest that this technology will help to resolve the coming transmission capacity bottleneck.

In Saskatchewan the SCAN (Saskatchewan Communications Advanced Network) optical fibre network now connects a significant number of communities in the major population corridors between Saskatoon in the north and Regina and Moose Jaw in the south. Conceived as an alternative to conventional microwave and copper wire communication networks that will accommodate future and vastly increased telecommunication requirements, it exhibits the major advantages of both systems. Like the terrestrial microwave system, it accommodates both narrowband (audio) and broadband (video) communication channels. Like the copper wire network that it will eventually replace, it can go everywhere in the province that wire now goes, and provide enhanced, *interactive* communications opportunities equivalent to those provided by the most sophisticated metropolitan coaxial cable systems. In addition, like the copper wire system for telephone communications, optical fibre systems can be configured as switched networks, meaning that fully interactive two-way video communication between individuals or indeed, among a number of independent sites as in audio teleconferencing, will be possible.

Optical fibre systems will also encourage the development and use of centralised visual databases analogous to existing computer-based information services and databases. Current technology does not allow general public (or student) dial-up access to visual database, as the broadband capability for downloading the information, especially moving images, is not in place. Optical fibre networks will eliminate this restriction and open an entirely new kind of resource for general information services and public education systems. Unfortunately, most provincial governments are taking what seems to be a short-sighted view and are avoiding the issue of switching from copper wire to optical fibre technology. A reversal of this situation would be very desirable.

At present, the SCAN system in Saskatchewan is being used to extend a limited range of classroom-based instruction carried out at the University of Regina to community college centres and into homes that are connected to the system. Lectures on campus are televised and broadcast live over the SCAN system to viewers, with registered students receiving additional support in the way of print materials and tutorial support. Although the use of the SCAN system for distance education is only in its preliminary stages, the potential for providing a diverse array of distance education services is obvious.

Videotex and Teletext Systems

Videotex and teletext systems such as Canada's Telidon protocol will not be examined in this chapter, as they basically represent textual and graphics display software systems. They can be used in the context of satellite or cable broadcast services and to provide enhanced displays for CAI, videodisc and audio teleconferencing systems. In basic terms they represent communications or software/graphics protocols that can be employed by several other technologies rather than being technologies in and of themselves. This does not, however, negate their importance or the fact that some of the very best protocols have been developed in Canada.

Evaluation of Distance Education Technologies

It is obvious from this overview that Canada's experience in applying a very broad range of new media and communication technologies to distance education is extensive and impressive. Both in experimental projects and in an increasing number of continuing, government-funded distance education services many technologies have been evaluated from scientific/technical, instructional and human points of view. The available data are extensive, and seven key factors, identified by that research as determining the success or failure of these technological innovations for distance education, can be summarised:

1. *Responsiveness to Learner Needs:* The formal and informal educational needs of geographically-isolated students must be addressed directly by distance education agencies. Many of these learning needs parallel in kind, if not in number, the educational needs of the general population. Most distance learners demand that the distance education curricula be transferable to and qualitatively equivalent to on-campus programmes.

2. *Programme Quality:* Effective media use requires co-operation among media, content and process specialists. This is costly but essential, and costs can ultimately be spread over large aggregates of learners through interinstitutional co-operation. Excellence in programme design, media selection and media production must accompany excellence of the technical delivery system.

3. *Interactive Components:* Telecommunications technologies can be used to broadcast instructional material, but they also facilitate interaction in a variety of forms between remote learners and instructors. The interactive capability of an instructional system is at least as important as the multi-media capability of the distribution/broadcast technologies used.

4. *Reliability of the System:* Communications technologies must be 'transparent' to their users. That is, simple instructions and simple activities should allow learners and instructors to use the system effectively. Equipment should be thoroughly tested for reliability of operation and back-up channels must be available in case of failure of the main communication system. Where complex technical activities cannot be avoided, trained aides must be available to assist users.

5. *Cost and Accessibility:* Telecommunications costs are a major limiting factor in interactive technology-based distance education. Subsidy of educational telecommunications costs must be addressed as a political issue as it is becoming increasingly easy, in technological terms, to offer interactive instruction directly to the home.

6. *Student Support Systems:* The administrative support systems of educational institutions rarely reflect the time-lines and lifestyles of off-campus learners. Many administrative and student support activities could be handled by electronic mail (admissions and registration forms, transcripts, assignment and examination processing) or audio/video conferencing (academic tutorials and student counselling). Reduced response time and increased

operational flexibility must be a major consideration in the design of such systems.

7. *Institutional Commitment:* As instructional technologies evolve, governments and institutions will be confronted with fundamental questions about the nature of the education system. Institutions which would use the new technologies to serve both on-campus and off-campus learners must make an early and continuing commitment to a long-range transition programme if they are to be successful. Unless learners, educators and the public clearly see that institutions and government are confident in and committed to these changes, they will be reluctant participants in the exercise.

It is worth remembering that the technological capabilities of a medium, especially in the current era of microelectronic evolution and innovation, are usually far in advance of the actual techniques that have been adopted. In large part this relates to an unfortunate tendency to use new technologies to do the same old things in more or less the same old way. New technologies usually accommodate new strategies, but the necessary creative insight into those new options is frequently obscured or constrained by conventional wisdom.

It is also worth noting that, while Canada has a rich background in the use of new technologies for distance education, much of that experience has been gained under 'soft money' research grants. Several of the more interesting applications mentioned earlier in this chapter no longer exist as the term of the research grants (and therefore the funding for the projects) has run out. Among very few others, the significant examples in British Columbia and Alberta of continuing provincial government funding for major distance education initiatives can be pointed to and used by educators in other jurisdictions to lobby their governments for a longer term approach to the development and delivery of improved distance education services.

As a final observation, it must be stressed that the hardware or technological component of new instructional delivery systems is nearly always the least expensive element. While the front-end costs of installing a super computer, satellite transmission system or fibre-optics network can appear to be very significant, they are usually single, capital expenditures which can be amortised over a relatively long period and a relatively large audience. In contrast, the operational costs associated with courseware development and maintenance are recurrent and substantially larger over the longer term than are the hardware costs.

It is these courseware related costs - needs assessment, design, production, delivery, evaluation and revision costs - that impose an unavoidable requirement for communication, co-operation and co-ordination among distance education resources. Only when a high degree of collaboration exists will conventional and distance education be able to take full and effective advantage of the educational potential inherent in today's emerging media and communications technologies. It is apparent that, on a number of fronts, the necessary collaboration is beginning to occur either by way of mutual agreement among interested institutions, or by government intervention. It is equally clear that, if the former approach is not adopted, the latter response can be expected. To provide equitable, universal access to the resources of the public education system is the ultimate goal of distance education. Canadian experiments in the use of telecommunication technologies for education serve this goal and provide information, advice and leadership to others with similar goals.

REFERENCES

Portions of this chapter have been excerpted, with permission of the publisher, from an article previously published by the author in *Open Campus*, Occasional Papers, Victoria, Australia: Deakin University.

Bottomley, J. (1981) 'The satellite tele-education project (STEP): A western Canadian experiment in interactive television teaching', in J.E. Gough, B.J. Garner, and R.K. Day (eds.), *Education for the Eighties: The Impact of New Communications Technology*, Deakin University Press, Victoria, Australia

Burge, E.J. (1984) 'Information and Communications Technologies and Distance Education in Canada', in Ignacy Waniewicz (ed.), *New Technologies in Education: Working Paper No. 5*, Ontario Educational Communications Corporation, Toronto

Daniel, J.S. (1981) 'Satellites in education: experimenting forever?', in J.E. Gough *et al.*, *Education for the Eighties*, Deakin University Press, Victoria

Daniel, J.S., A.D.D. Miller, R.G. Lyons, and D.A. George, (1977) *The use of Satellite Delivery Systems in Canada: The Costing of Two Networks and a Preliminary Needs Survey*, Department of Communications, Ottawa

Daniel, J.S., M.L. Cote, and J.M. Richmond, (1978) 'Project report: Education experiments in Canada with the communications technology satellite (CTS)', in L.A. Parker and B. Riccomini (eds.), *The Telephone in Education*, Book II, University of Wisconsin - Extension, Madison

Daniel, J.S., C. Keating, and R. Marchand, (1978) 'Guide de l'animation téléphonique', *Télé-université du Québec*, November

D'Antoni, S.G. (1982) 'Videodisc and videotex: new media for distance education', in J.S. Daniel, M.A. Stroud, and J.R. Thompson (eds.), *Learning at a Distance: A World Perspective*, Athabasca University

Ellis, B. (1981) 'University of Calgary's new educational teleconferencing system', *Journal of the Alberta Association for Continuing Education*, 9, no. 1

Ellis, G.B. and R.S. Champman (1982) 'Academic equivalency of credit courses by teleconference', in J.S. Daniel *et al.* (eds.), *Learning at a Distance*, Athabasca University, International Council for Distance Education

Fitzpatrick, J. (1982) 'The Australian schools of the air: the conundrum of who teaches', *Distance Education*, 3, no. 2

Forsythe, K. (1982) 'Knowledge network - a new hybrid for learning systems', *Distance Education*, 3, no. 2

Godfrey, D. and D. Parkhill, (eds.) (1980) 'Gutenberg two', in *Press Porcepic Ltd.*, Toronto

Graham, M. (1984) 'Educational Teleconferencing in Canada', in I. Waniewicz (ed.), *New Technologies in Canadian Education: Paper No. 14*, Ontario Educational Communications Authority, Toronto

Gray, J. and B. Watson (1985) *School Broadcasting in Canada*, University of Toronto Press, Toronto

Guild, P.D., D.A. George and D.C. Coll (1976) 'The Carleton University educational communications project', in L.A. Parker and B. Roccomini (eds.), *A Report on University Applications of Satellite/Cable Technology*, University of Wisconsin - Extension, Madison

House, A.M., J. Roberts and E. Canning (1981) 'Telemedicine provides new dimensions in Newfoundland and Labrador', *Canadian Medical Association Journal*, March

House, A.M. (1982) 'Teleconferencing at Memorial University', in M.L. Mandville (ed.), *A Man's Reach Should Exceed His Grasp: Distance Education and Teleconferencing at Memorial University*, Memorial University of Newfoundland, St John's

Jacobsen, E. (1982) 'Use of Telidon to Teaching Macroeconomics', Internal Report, Athabasca University

Jeffery, G.H. (1983) 'Multi-point teleconference and regular classroom teaching', *Canadian Journal of University Continuing Education*, 9, no. 1

Jenkins, J. and H. Perraton (1978) 'Distance learning in Africa', in J.W. Brown and S.N. Brown (eds.), *Educational Media Yearbook 1978*, R.R. Bowker, New York

Lambert, R.S. (1963) *School Broadcasting in Canada*, University of Toronto Press, Toronto

McDonell, P.J. (1984) *Tracking Psychology by Telephone*, Bulletin of the Social Science Federation of Canada, Ottawa

McNamara, W.C. (1978) 'Educational television in Newfoundland - from studio to satellite: 10 years toward interaction' in L.A. Parker *et al.* (eds.), *The Telephone in Education*, Book II, University of Wisconsin - Extension, Madison

Mugridge, I. (1985) 'Application of Computer Technology in Distance Education: The Case of The Open Learning Institute', *Canadian Journal of Educational Communications*, 14

Nakonechny, G. (1982) *Computer-managed Learning: A Nursing Refresher Programme*, Internal Report, Grant MacEwan Community College

Polcyn, K.A. (1976) 'Some potential learning community competitors for the use of the allocated broadcast satellite frequency spectrum', in L.A. Parker *et al.* (eds.), *A Report on University Applications of Satellite/Cable Technology*, University of Wisconsin - Extension, Madison

Queen's University (1979) 'History of the University', in *Queen's University Arts and Science Calendar, 1979-80*, Queen's University, Kingston

Ruggles, R.H., J. Anderson, D.E. Blackmore, C. Lafleur, J.P. Rothe and T. Taerum (1982) *Learning at a Distance and the New Technology*, Educational Research Institute of British Columbia, Vancouver

Ryan, M.G. (1975) *Canadian-American communication Symposium: The Influence of Teleconferencing Medium and Status on Participants' Perception of the Aestheticism, Evaluation, Privacy, Potency, and Activity of the Medium*, Buffalo, New York

Shobe, C.R. (1982) *Proposal for Long Term Teleconference Programming at Athabasca University*, Internal Report, Athabasca University, Edmonton

Shobe, C.R. (1983a) *Telecommunications Technologies and Distance Education: A Report in Recent Canadian Initiatives*, Open Campus, Deakin University. Victoria, Australia

Shobe, C.R. (1983b) 'Audio teleconferencing', in *Proceedings of the 5th Biennial Forum of the Australia and South Pacific External Studies Association*, Toowoomba, Queensland (in press)

Smith, R.W. (1982) 'The misfortune of college courses on television, or why "big bird" can't teach thermodynamics', *The Chronical of Higher Education*, November

Stephen, A. (1981) *Computer Managed Learning in A Technical Institute*, Internal Report, Southern Alberta Institute of Technology

Szabo, M. (1983) *Recent Developments in Computer-based learning using PLATO at the University of Alberta*, Internal Report, University of Alberta, Edmonton

Waniewicz, I. (1982) 'The TVOntario Academy', in J.S. Daniel, *et al.* (eds.) *Learning at a Distance*, Athabasca University

Wilson, J., B. Bell and W. Powell (1984) 'The Provincial Educational Communications Organisations in Canada: Paper #7', in *New Technologies in Canadian Education*, Ontario Educational Communications Authority

Zukiwski, J. (1982) 'Use of the black box in teleconferencing', *Telematics*, *1*, no. 1, Alberta Educational Communications Authority

Use of Audiocassettes

James D. Leslie

CHOICE OF DELIVERY MEDIUM IN DISTANCE EDUCATION

Education can be delivered at a distance by a variety of means like print material, audiocassettes, videocassettes, videodiscs, broadcast radio, broadcast television, computer assisted instruction, either separately or in combination. The choice of delivery medium is often a crucial factor in the success of the resulting programme, but what determines the optimum choice?

The choice of delivery medium should be based on the following factors:

1. the characteristics of the subject matter;
2. the purpose of the distance education programme;
3. the anticipated size of the group to be educated;
4. the anticipated cost of the delivery system; and
5. the suitability of the delivery medium to the needs of the groups involved.

These factors will not be discussed in detail until after a presentation of the characteristics of the use of audiocassettes as a medium in distance education. At this point, however, some general comments on all media will be made.

First, in any discussion of factor (5), it must be remembered that there are three groups involved in any distance education delivery system: the institution offering the education, the instructors who produce and deliver the material, and the students who participate in the education programme.

It is usually the institution which chooses the delivery medium, and the choice is sometimes based on its needs, rather than on a reasoned consideration of the factors mentioned. However, the institution must clearly realise that the needs of the other two groups are equally important. If the instructors do not feel comfortable with the delivery medium, then they will not be able to produce good material. Also, the students participating in the education programme are the ultimate decision makers of the success or failure of the programme. If certain characteristics of the delivery medium do not suit their needs, they will not register in the programme.

Economic considerations, mentioned in factor (4), are very important, because if the delivery system is too expensive for the market contemplated, even if it could be the best in the world, it will still fail because no one will be able to afford it. However, in any discussion of costs, one has to be very careful about cost definitions. One has to differentiate clearly between preparation cost, per unit distribution cost and per student delivery cost.

These cost definitions can be easily explained as fixed and variable costs. The preparation cost is a fixed cost and is the total cost for zero involvement. It includes the cost of preparing the masters of the course material, and the capital cost associated with that portion of the delivery system needed to deliver this course. The per student delivery cost depends on the enrolment.

In our experience at Waterloo, most costs increase linearly with enrolment. However, additions to personnel or equipment to handle extra students produce jumps in cost at particular enrolments. This does not change the definition of preparation cost or of per student cost, and per unit distribution cost can be thought of as the slope of the straight line from the cost of zero enrolment to the cost for current enrolment.

It is the per student delivery cost, rather than the preparation cost or distribution cost separately, that determines the cost effectiveness of the distance education delivery system. This will be discussed again, when the costs of audio tapes as a distance education medium are compared with other possibilities.

AUDIOCASSETTES AS A DISTANCE EDUCATION MEDIUM

Origin of the Use of Audiocassettes in Distance Education in Canada

The use of audiocassettes in distance education in Canada started in 1968 when the University of Waterloo Correspondence Programme was established. The growth in enrolment and the growth in the number of courses in the University of Waterloo Correspondence Programme from its inception in 1968 until the present day has been outstanding. From four courses in Physics in 1968-9 with a total enrolment of 252 student-term courses, the programme has grown until there are now 303 courses in 25 departments in 1984-5 with a total enrolment of 19,722 student-term courses. (A student-term course is one student taking a course for one term.) The University of Waterloo Correspondence Programme has been a great success, showing remarkable growth in both courses and student enrolment. It has the largest offering of distance education courses in Canada. What are the reasons for the success of this distance education programme?

The main reason for its success is that it tried to make the distance education experience as close as possible to the on-campus experience of a regular student. Lectures can be thought of as having three channels of communication. First, there is the **formal visual** channel, i.e. textbooks, printed notes, maps, slides, the various formally prepared material the professor may assign or supply to the students. Second, there is the **informal visual** channel, what the professor writes on the blackboard. Finally, there is the **audio** channel, what the professor says in the lecture. In a regular lecture, the latter is the glue which holds the formal and informal visual material together. The approach to distance education in the University of Waterloo Correspondence Programme provided an AUDIO channel which allowed the professors to comment on the formal and informal visual material just as they would in a regular lecture.

During the remainder of this discussion of the University of Waterloo Correspondence Programme, a description will be given of the way things were done during my tenure as director from 1968 until 1980. For this reason, the situation will be described in the past tense.

A professor prepared a University of Waterloo correspondence course in the following way. The professor sat at his own desk with a tape recorder, the formal visual material and a pad of paper. Each professor was told to imagine that a student was looking over his shoulder. By talking into the tape recorder, a professor could direct a student's attention to material in the textbook, discuss the information on a slide, present some notes or work an example. The pad of paper played the same role as the blackboard in a classroom, in that a professor could write notes or draw diagrams. Thus the lectures tended to be more informal, more in the style of a tutorial. Each distance education student received copies of the lecture tapes, lecture notes and the formal visual material and could reconstruct the lecture in his own home.

Format and Operation of a University of Waterloo Correspondence Course

A term course consisted typically of 20 forty-minute lectures recorded on C-90 monaural audiocassettes. It was found that most professors could cover more material in 20 forty-minute taped lectures than they could cover in 36 fifty-minute live lectures. Thus there was a packing factor of approximately two-to-one. The reason for this was that in many live presentations one has to spend the first part of a lecture reviewing material from the previous lecture or in setting up some problem that one was doing at the end of the previous lecture. In a taped lecture this is not necessary: the student can always look back at the previous lecture notes to see the set up of the problem or listen to the previous lecture if he wants to review something. Eventually, however, there were a few courses where the professors could not present their course material in 20 forty-minute lectures. The simplest solution was to allow them to use more tapes.

Most of the lectures were taped in professors' offices or homes. The lectures were taped in final form by the professors. Typically, a professor would prepare his course notes and then, using his notes as a prompt, lecture into the tape recorder much as he would deliver a lecture based on these notes to a live class. Most professors would tape each lecture in 5 to 10 minute portions. At the end of taping each portion, they would listen to what they had prepared. If they were happy with it, they would go on and prepare the next portion. Otherwise they would go back and retape it if they felt that they could do it better. Professors were taught how to set the volume on the tape recorder and where to clip the microphone to get best signal-to-noise ratio on the finished tape. While this approach appears to put the whole responsibility on the professor of getting a good tape master, it meant that there was no sound engineer or tape technician between the professor and the preparation of his lecture. Beside the obvious fact that this was a low cost approach, it also was good pedagogically in that it allowed the professor to prepare things at his own rate, in his own way, and in a certain sense forget that the tape recorder was there and concentrate on effective communication with the student. Most professors were able to produce reasonably good master tapes by this approach. Normally, professors were encouraged to submit tapes as they were prepared, so that they could be screened to ensure that the audio quality was acceptable and to detect errors professors were making at a stage where this error could be corrected.

More recently, the rooms in the correspondence programme facility used for listening to tapes have also been used for taping lectures by some professors who have found it difficult to prepare good lectures in their offices or homes.

Professors also taped their own lectures. Many audio-visual people have commented that better tapes could have been produced if the professor had only prepared a script and had a trained announcer read the final version of the lecture. While it might have been a better sounding tape, it would have been an inferior lecture. The reason is that the professor really understands his material and this comes through in his presentation. An announcer, who usually does not understand the material, can only read the script as he is told to read it, so that subtle differences in emphasis are often missed. It is also important for the tape to be informal, because the student should feel that the professor is a real person rather than just a disembodied voice. Therefore, the professor was encouraged to be informal. My favourite was a mathematics professor who, while taping at home, said, 'Well that's enough mathematics for now ... anyone join me for a beer?'. One could then hear the sound of someone walking across a room, opening a refrigerator door, taking the top off a bottle and pouring the contents in a glass! After many requests from students, a picture of the professor with a short biography was supplied as part of the course package. This personal contact is important for communication; an announcer reading scripts would get in the way.

The course notes were photocopied or offset-printed copies were made of the set of course notes prepared by the professor. Initially, these course notes were almost always handwritten by the professors. As time passed, some of them were typed by secretaries in the professor's department. Because the correspondence programme did not have the resources to type the course notes being supplied, it relied on the course notes being provided in final form by the professors. It has to be remembered that the University of Waterloo Correspondence Programme started with only a small capital investment ($2,000 to buy a tape duplicator) and, although it has now grown to be a large operation, it has always been under pressure to justify any growth in staff and resources. Consequently, the whole approach to production of course material was a low cost one, and the course materials were generally received quite well by the students. However, one of the problems of this successful low cost approach is that later, when trying to improve the approach by more costly procedures, the administration was reluctant to increase costs.

Course packages consisting of all lecture notes, lecture tapes, assignments, textbooks and other resource material were supplied to students before the start of the course. This was a different approach to many correspondence programmes that divide a course into separate lesson packages and only send one out at a time to a student. The approach used at Waterloo had a number of benefits to the student. First, he could get a more realistic assessment of what was involved in the course because he saw all the course material including the required assignments. Sometimes students who had been admitted to a course without having the prerequisite would switch into the prerequisite course once they saw what was really involved in the course. Students could also work ahead since they had the whole course package right from the start.

Almost all courses in the University of Waterloo Correspondence Programme operate on a term basis. There are three terms per year, although all courses are not available each term. Thus courses start and end on fixed dates. During a course there is a fixed schedule of assignments, and an examination at the end of the course. The decision to operate this distance education programme on a term basis was initially made because that was the way the courses operated on campus in the regular programme, and the correspondence programme was meant to be as close as possible to the experience of a regular student. The students were treated as members of a class, although that class was geographically distributed.

Treating students as members of a class led to the concept of treating the feedback on a class basis. Students sent their assignments in according to a set schedule. The assignments were graded and the students were sent back their assignment, a model set of solutions showing how the assignment should have been done, and a tutorial tape addressed to the class as a whole. When the feedback performance is handled on a class basis, the professor can emphasise common difficulties with the material and share questions that individual students have raised. Students perform better when they know that others are having the same problems. They can profit from the individual questions raised, in that it might have been a question that they were puzzled about but had been afraid to ask.

Although most courses operated on a term basis, there were three courses that evolved into a different mode of operation. Since our experience with these courses affected the later approach to audio-taped courses for technical training, a rather detailed description of their evolution will be given here. These were the three pre-university courses, Chemistry 001, Mathematics 001 and Physics 001. These courses were created at the request of the faculty of engineering a few years ago, at the time when students in the high schools of Ontario were being allowed great freedom of choice in selecting courses. Some good students in the last year of high school were finding that they were missing one of these critical courses when they finally decided that they really wanted to enter the engineering programme at Waterloo. The faculty of engineering wanted in a correspondence course version three remedial courses that would cover all the chemistry, mathematics and physics a first-year university student would need.

These three courses were created in the usual format of taped lectures with accompanying lecture notes, and they were initially offered on the regular correspondence programme term schedule. However, it soon became apparent that this was not meeting the need. Each course could only be offered if there was enough demand for it, but usually a student wanted to start the course right away and did not want to wait for the start of a term. It was finally decided that these three courses should be available as soon as a student wanted to start.

However, there still remained the question of how to provide the students with a feedback component. Since students would start the courses at various times and progress through the course material at different rates, it was not possible to provide 'real' feedback. However, the following 'instant feedback' scheme was proposed. The course professors selected a set of questions as exercises. Then they prepared an instant feedback package consisting of model solutions plus audio tapes, leading the students through the assignments. Students were told that they should try the assignments on their own and then check their solutions with the instant feedback material. The reasoning was as follows: if a student tries a problem, there are three possible outcomes. The first is that he will not be able to do the problem because he cannot get started, or makes a mistake along the way. The second is that he will do the problem in the same manner as the solution given in the instant feedback. The third is that the student will get the correct answer but do it by such a remarkably different method from the solution given, that he would not be sure whether his method was correct. It seemed obvious that the instant feedback package would handle the first two cases, and the third case would be so rare that the best way to deal with it was to tell the student to send such unique solutions to us for a response. The instant feedback approach worked very well for several years. The final examination was available every two months and a student could sign up at any time and tell us later when he wanted to write one of the six examinations available each year.

Why Instructors Like Audiocassette Courses

The first reason why instructors like an audiocassette course is that it is very similar to live classroom instruction. As they are very familiar with the latter, they feel very comfortable with the former. They do not have to learn new skills for they can carry over most of what they have found works in a live classroom situation.

Various disciplines have different mixes of formal visual material, informal visual material and audio presentation. If you studied lecture presentations by instructors in different disciplines, in one case you might find that 80 per cent of the information content is in the audio presentation and the visual material consists of just a few key dates and names, as in a lecture on history. But another lecture, say on mathematics or physics, might have 80 per cent of the information content in the written material and the audio presentation is only contributing the remaining 20 per cent while reinforcing the written material. The strength of the audiocassette course approach is that it can handle this wide mix as has been demonstrated by the success of the University of Waterloo Correspondence Programme in such an extensive range of disciplines and subjects. It could be argued that, if 80 per cent of the information content is in the written material, it would be easy to dispense with the taped portion for those courses. But one can use audiocassettes to provide the other 20 per cent of the information in teaching the material, stressing certain things, commenting on others and to add some personality to the material. The problem with doing everything in written form is that the course material can quickly become very heavy and boring. A completely written presentation is a book, and it takes a lot of talent to write a good textbook.

The second reason why instructors like audiocassette courses is that a reasonably good instructor can produce very effective distance education course material using this approach. Third, instructors like audiocassette courses because it is easy to incorporate a wide range of resource material into any course. The instructor can comment on rock samples, microscope slides, pictures, maps, etc., along with any other visual material.

Why Students Like Audiocassette Courses

First, students like audiocassette courses because they find that audio tapes and course notes give a more complete presentation than written material alone. If instructors give written presentations, they tend to start abbreviating their presentation, because they find it too painful to write it all down. They also start thinking about style and a written presentation can then become too formal to be really effective teaching.

Second, students feel that this approach is more personal and eliminates some of the remoteness from distance education. At the University of Waterloo Correspondence Programme, a party was held once a year to which all students in the programme were invited to meet their professors. It happened many times that a student was talking to me when a professor walked by talking to someone else, and the student would suddenly become very animated and say 'That's my professor! Excuse me, I must meet the person I have been listening to for the past 3 months!' Early in the programme before every tape was screened, one of the French professors taping a course in his office finished his lecture with time remaining on the tape. He took his microphone off, but accidentally he left the tape recorder on and proceeded to go about his business making telephone calls, talking to students in French. This tape was sent out to students as part of the lecture package. The students were enthralled by this private peek into the life of a French professor and, when they discovered that it was a mistake, they urged us not to cut it off the taped lecture.

Third, the discipline of an audiocassette course produces a very structured course. In a live lecture, after the sound waves die away and the blackboards are erased, mistakes have vanished. Even if a student comes up the next day and shows you a mistake in the notes, you can probably convince him that he copied it down incorrectly from the blackboard! But in an audiocassette course, the instructor commits himself in print and on tape. Many professors at the University of Waterloo have stated that preparing an audiocassette course has been the best pedagogic experience that they have ever had.

Finally, students like the fact that they have their own set of course materials and can fit their studying around other commitments. Unlike broadcast television courses, they do not have to block out specific times in the week to participate in the course. Women with young children like the fact that they can wait until the children are asleep and then study their course materials. The course materials (tape recorder, cassette, course notes) are so portable that students can take a lecture with them and study it on the way to work in public transit.

Why Institutions Like Audio Cassette Courses

Audiocassette courses have much lower preparation costs than other distance education media. Thus an institution without the financial resources to invest in television production can easily consider preparing an audiocassette course. It is much easier to get a good course out of a typical instructor than with other distance education media. Print distance education courses need good writers, and this is much more difficult to find than you might think. An official at the Open University in Britain said that they had to teach their people how to write course material. In fact, he referred to it as almost the same as teaching someone a new language. Television-based distance education courses, whether broadcast or videocassette, need very good production values and performers. This is because people compare video courses to commercial broadcast television, and if the production looks amateurish, then it is rejected. Audiocassette courses do not need good production values. The sound does not have to be high fidelity. It may be claimed that this is because people compare an audiocassette course to radio, and commercial radio on the whole has been taken over by the mindless patter of disc jockeys, so a reasonable production standard is quite acceptable. Finally, since the audiocassette approach has been shown to work in a variety of disciplines, an institution can be reasonably sure that it will be successful in their field.

DEVELOPMENTS IN THE USE OF AUDIO CASSETTES IN DISTANCE EDUCATION

Distance Education Programme of the Canadian Society of Laboratory Technologists (CSLT)

In 1979, the Canadian Society of Laboratory Technologists approached Waterloo Distance Education Inc. for a collaborative effort to produce a programme of technical training using audiocassettes. CSLT is the professional association of the technologists who do laboratory tests in Canadian hospitals. CSLT has been operating a series of upgrading courses for their members using print-only materials for several years. However, the CSLT administration felt that their programme needed to be updated and that the audiocassette approach pioneered at the University of Waterloo Correspondence Programme was the method to use. Waterloo Distance Education Inc. (WDE) had just been formed by J.D. Leslie and A.E. Dixon to apply the audiocassette approach to distance education to the field of technical training. So collaboration between CSLT and WDE was a natural development.

In the past six years, nine courses (Antimicrobial Susceptibility Testing, Hemostasis, Laboratory Management, Modern Blood Group Serology, Modern Immunology, Normal Histology I and II, Red Cell Disorders, and Toxicology) have been developed and two more courses are presently being prepared. The collaborative effort has worked in the following way:

CSLT provides the instructors, who are technologists in the field with an expert knowledge of the course content but have no experience in preparing a distance education course in an audiocassette format. CSLT also administers the final operation of the programme and handles the grading of assignments and examinations. WDE supervises the development of the audio taped courses and the production of course material. WDE starts by training each new instructor to prepare course material in an audio taped format. Instructors submit rough course notes along with the masters of the audio taped lectures. WDE personnel prepare the course notes on a word processor so that they can be easily updated and illustrations are professionally prepared. Each lecture is carefully examined by WDE distance education experts to ensure that the audio taped presentation is effective and a critique of each lecture is prepared so that any flaws can be corrected in collaboration with the instructor. WDE handles all details of packaging the course material and supplies finished course packages to CSLT on demand as well as duplicating any tutorial tapes used in class feedback.

These CSLT courses operate on a term basis with the class sending in assignments on a fixed schedule. The students receive back their own graded assignment, a model set of solutions and, at the choice of the instructor, a tutorial tape addressed to the class as a whole. Each course has a final examination which is written on the same day across the country. So, the CSLT programme operates closely on the model of the University of Waterloo Correspondence Programme.

These CSLT courses represent two significant developments in audiocassette courses. First, they demonstrate that good distance education courses can be produced by content experts who are not experienced teachers. While some of the instructors had taught their material before in classroom sessions, others had very little teaching experience. Second, the collaboration between CSLT and WDE has meant that a professional association with no experience in distance education can mount a first-class programme without the problems of learning how to do it on their own. These CSLT courses have been very successful, have received good reviews and are starting to be marketed in the United States and Canada. They represent a good model of what could be done in other areas of training by other professional associations.

High Technology Training Courses by Waterloo Distance Education Inc.

In addition to contract work such as that with CSLT, Waterloo Distance Education Inc. has also been developing distance education audiocassette courses to teach high technology subjects to practicing professionals. Course 801, Microprocessing Essentials, was the first of these courses to be developed, in 1979, and it is now available in a third edition released in 1985. It teaches programming microprocessors in machine language and how a microprocessor can control things in the real world. Microprocessors, when combined with memory devices and input/output devices, produce microcomputers. Microprocessors can be incorporated into products to give them intelligence. Knowing that many practicing engineers, scientists, technologists, and technicians had graduated before such training was available, it was decided that a course on microprocessors should be available in a distance education format.

Following the approach used earlier with the pre-university courses in the University of Waterloo Correspondence Programme, it was decided that this course should be available as a self-study package, because, in industry, it is often imperative that training commence as soon as a need is identified. Because such training needs hands-on experience, a single-board computer is included as part of the self-study package. A student listens to the instructor on audiocassettes while studying the course notes, and then tries exercises on the single board computer with 4 plug-in boards. If the student has any difficulties, he can study the solutions in the software library.

Course 901, Structured Programming in BASIC, is a new distance education course which teaches programming of computers in BASIC. Again it is a self-study audiocassette course, where students can work through a theory package and then try examples which are taken up in the 'instant feedback' practical package. Students do their practical exercises on an IBM PC microcomputer.

With courses 801 and 901, the technical level of such audiocassette courses has been pushed to a new high. In addition to course notes typed on a word processor so that they can be rapidly updated and professionally illustrated, the method of handling the taping of the lectures has been changed. The instructor tapes the original lecture, which is then transcribed and edited to provide a script. The original instructor then retapes the final version of the lecture using the script as a guide. In this way, the spontaneity of the original is preserved while eliminating all pauses and inaccurate references. The original instructor is still used in the final version of the lecture, because as mentioned earlier, it is better that the person doing the taping of the lectures really understand the course material.

Use of Audio Cassettes in Distance Education by other Institutions in Canada

Apart from the University of Waterloo, there are not any other extensive university distance education programmes based on audiocassette courses. Many universities have occasional courses which use audiocassettes as part of the multi-media mix; however, most university distance education programmes have tended to be either print-only based or television courses supplemented by print-based materials.

This is not surprising for several reasons. First, until the development of the University of Waterloo Correspondence Programme, most large distance education programmes were primarily print-based. The British Open University, the Fernuniversitat in Germany and various distance education programmes in Norway and Sweden all use print materials as their basis of instruction; and new programmes have tended to emulate these international examples. Second, certain media people have pushed television as an educational medium. At one point, there were attempts to teach on campus by television, but these failed almost universally and have been abandoned. However, television is still being pushed as a medium for distance education. Some people mistakenly think that the Open University uses television instruction, whereas OU people admit that they use television primarily to attract people to take courses. Finally, since print-based distance education has been used for a number of years and most academic institutions are so conservative in their approach, it appears to be difficult for them to change.

Most community colleges appear to have been limiting their distance education efforts to 1 to 3 day intensive courses in high tech training. However, Fanshawe College in London, Ontario has started a distance education programme for converting technicians into technologists. However, because of lack of funds, they have used primarily print-based material.

Audiocassette distance instruction appears to be catching on in the private market. In addition to the WDE and CSLT courses cited earlier, there are a number of other examples. Audiocassette courses are a natural for language instruction and one can walk into bookstores and see audiocassette based language courses for sale. Some firms are offering audiocassette based training courses, for example, a Canadian manufacturer of a word processor has its training course in the form of an audiocassette self-study package. Recently, a large manufacturer of personal computers has offered a brief audiocassette course introducing people to the use of their computer.

STRENGTHS AND WEAKNESSES OF AUDIO CASSETTE COURSES

Subject and Purpose

The University of Waterloo Correspondence Programme has demonstrated that a variety of subjects can be taught effectively by audiocassette courses.

The audiocassette course is best, however, when the purpose is to give detailed serious instruction. Thus it is well suited to technical training or advanced instruction at the community college or university level. On the other hand, if the purpose of a course is to entertain or give general impressions about some subject, television is much better. However, this does not mean that television can necessarily handle detailed technical training better than an audiocassette course. The director of technical training for a large Canadian high technology company said that his company had purchased a supposedly good technical training programme on videocassettes for employee training. Tests indicated that information transfer was very poor. He finally realised that the problem was that the employees were so used to regarding television as a medium for entertainment that it was difficult for them to really concentrate. In contrast, this same company bought a number of Course 801 packages and found them to be a most effective industrial training package. The combination of the informal approach of audio-taped instruction and hands-on experience with the single board computer and plug-in boards drew the student into the training and made for a very effective learning experience.

Cost

Audiocassette courses have a much lower preparation cost than television courses. The preparation costs of print-only courses are not always lower than audiocassette courses. A typeset print-only course can be more expensive than a audiocassette course with word-processed course notes. Also, the preparation costs of some print-only distance education courses can be quite high. Officials of the British Open University indicate that it cost approximately $250,000 to develop a new print-only course. This was because to produce effective print-only material they felt that they needed to have teams writing the material and other teams testing and rewriting it until they obtained effective course material.

The per unit distribution cost is higher for audiocassette courses than for print-only or broadcast television courses, because the package of materials in the case of an audiocassette course is more expensive per student. However, in the case of a videocassette course, the cost of the videocassette per hour of play is probably at least three times that of audiocassettes. The audiocassettes used for distribution to the students do not have to be of ultra-high quality; in fact, the most important feature of the cassette is that it should have a good transport mechanism so that it will duplicate well in a high speed duplicator without jamming.

While an audiocassette course has a higher per unit distribution cost than either a print-only course or a television course, the per student delivery cost can be much lower than either if the total course enrolment is low. In a comparison of two distance education delivery systems, one with a low preparation cost and a medium distribution cost (the situation for an audiocassette course) and a second with a very high preparation cost and a very low distribution cost (typical of a broadcast television course), the first system always has a lower per student delivery cost until the enrolment reaches a much higher level in the second type of course. Since many high technology courses have rather small total enrolments, the high preparation cost of television courses makes it almost impossible to recover costs.

Inherent Limitations

The greatest limitation of the audiocassette is connected with the fact that it is a linear-access medium rather than a random-access one. This means that one cannot get access rapidly to some portion of the tape. Thus the audiocassette is best in a situation where a student is to be given a good presentation of a subject once, but is not going to have to make extensive returns to a particular portion for restudy. Course notes with section numbers allow fairly quick access to a portion of the instruction material, but it is not possible to browse through material as in a book. Of course a person can fairly quickly locate the part of the tape associated with a particular section, but not rapidly enough for this medium to be used as a reference source.

Another limitation is that audiocassette courses assume the existence of another delivery system (mail or courier service) to deliver course packages and return assignments. Related to this is the limitation associated with the delay in getting feedback on assignments to the student. Of course, this is an intrinsic limitation of any distance education course that requires students from afar to submit assignments for grading. The choice between real feedback with delays and instant 'feedback' with self-study packages has already been outlined.

POSSIBLE FUTURE USE OF AUDIO CASSETTES IN DISTANCE EDUCATION

High Technology Training Programmes

With the speed with which technology is changing, it is commonly recognised that workers will have to be retrained frequently during their careers. It would be best if such retraining courses were available in a distance education format, so that workers could do this retraining while at their place of employment. In this way, the required retraining would occur if the employee had to be sent to some central location for retraining.

Audiocassette courses would be a natural for such programmes of high technology retraining. First, the potential enrolment in some of these highly specialised technical training courses would be small, and as has already been indicated, audiocassette courses are more cost effective than others when total enrolments are small. Second, courses could be prepared quickly and readily updated. This is a necessity when dealing with high technology courses but, while it is easy to make a change on a master of a set of course notes on a word processor and retape a portion of an audio tape, it is much more difficult to reshoot some portion of a television programme. Third, such technical courses will require the incorporation of a wide range of resource material and again this shows one of the strengths of audiocassette courses. Finally, instructors may have to be drawn from industry who have little teaching experience and experience with CSLT courses shows that such inexperienced teachers can still produce good distance education material when audiocassette courses are used.

Use of Audio Cassettes in Computer Assisted Instruction (CAI)

Computer assisted instruction implemented on microcomputers has great

245

potential for distance education. With the advent of powerful personal computers such as the IBM PC or AT, it is now possible to do computer assisted instruction without the need to have a connection to a powerful central mainframe computer. The greatest strength of CAI is its ability to do simulations. For example, if one wants to show a student how some electrical circuit works, one can have the computer simulate the circuit and then let the student see how things change as particular quantities are verified. CAI can also be used to test a student's responses to questions. However, the greatest weakness of CAI is in the area of direct instruction on some subject. The problem is that all instruction has to be in the form of written words on the screen. Thus at present CAI is like silent screen movies and what is needed is some speech to go along with the simulations and key words on the monitor screen.

Computer generated speech is possible but it is difficult to give tone and emphasis to words. Also, it takes a lot of memory to produce even a little speech. While some attempts have been made to give computer control over delivery of speech by random access of recorded messages, the equipment is probably too expensive for a distance education format. Instead, the use of cheap stereo audiocassette recorders will be interfaced with personal computers to improve distance education CAI. One track of the audiocassette would contain cues to tell the computer what information to display or programmes to run and the other would contain the audio information to be delivered during the instruction phase. In this way, the instructional abilities of CAI could be strengthened by providing audio instruction to go with the visual material being presented on the computer monitor. Since the audio track would be on the same tape as the track controlling the computer, it would not be possible for the audio presentation to lose synchronisation with the monitor display. If the student wanted to repeat a portion of the instruction, the student would just rewind the tape to the start of that portion and the computer control track would reload the appropriate programmes from floppy disc so that the simulation and visual display is repeated. When the instruction phase is finished, the control track would switch the programme back to keyboard control and the student would be told to turn off the tape recorder. Then the student would be able to continue with the non-tape controlled portion of the CAI programme and either explore some aspects of the simulations or undergo testing and evaluation.

ACKNOWLEDGEMENTS

I would like to thank the University of Waterloo Correspondence Programme and in particular Mr C.N. Sochasky.

Educational Radio

Margaret Norquay

Educational radio in Canada began in the 1930s and was directed exclusively towards the concerns of the rural and farm population. The Antigonish movement at St Francis Xavier University, headed by Dr M.M. Coby, pioneered the use of the small community group for study, discussion and action around issues of common concern. The result was the organisation of many co-operatives, credit unions and other self-help services that had substantially improved the economic position of the rural Nova Scotian community. These efforts fired the imagination of adult educators throughout Canada and the United States. A natural extension of Coby's methods took shape, using radio to reach people who could not be reached by the kind of direct personal contact used in the initial stages of the Antigonish movement.

An early experiment was tried in 1935 by the Workers Educational Association in co-operation with the Canadian Broadcasting Corporation (CBC). A series of half-hour broadcasts was aired on Saturdays from 6:30 to 7:00 p.m. offering panel discussions on rural economic issues. Study bulletins were prepared and sent on request to local groups called Agricola Study Clubs. These efforts were apparently well received but did not have the benefit of field workers to organise the groups or receive feedback from them. Participation was scattered and there was no way of measuring the impact of the programme. In 1937, the United Farmers of Ontario used the local radio station at Wingham for another series of programmes directed to the farming community in Grey and Bruce Counties. The educational secretary of the Bruce County United Farmers organised about thirty local groups who studied a booklet on co-operation, written by H.H. Hannam, secretary of the United Farmers provincial organisation, called *The Plan for Tomorrow which Works for Today*.

The first attempt to use the national network of the CBC for rural education began in November 1937 with a series offered on the national network called 'Enquiry into Co-operation'. It ran for nine weeks from November 1937 to April 1940 with a lengthy break in February and March because the policy regarding federal elections prohibited 'any controversial programming'. The radio series was jointly sponsored by the Canadian Association for Adult Education and the CBC. Neil Morrison, later to become the CBC director of public affairs, was employed to organise study groups across the country. Study material for the series was prepared by Dr W.H. Brittain, the dean of MacDonald College, the agricultural extension service of McGill University. Some 350 study groups participated.

The Agricultural Extension Service at MacDonald College was primarily directed at the English-speaking farmers in the eastern townships of

Quebec. In 1939, Dr Brittain employed R. Alex Sim as director of a new extension programme called The Rural Adult Education Service. Sim was a farmer's son from Holstein, Ontario and a recent graduate in sociology from the University of Toronto.

In April 1939, the CBC had established a farm and fisheries department and hired as director Orville Shrugg, a farmer and a former organiser of the United Farmers of Ontario. Sim and Morrison proposed to Shrugg an intensive demonstration project to be tried in Quebec that would test the potential of radio study discussion groups. The rural Adult Education Service would organise the groups and prepare discussion outlines and scripts for the programmes. The CBC agreed and Radio Station CJLT at Sherbrooke presented a new series in February-March 1940 called 'School of the Air'. It was a weekly programme about farm and community concerns with a mail-in open line called 'Community Clinic Questionbox'. The programme was designed for isolated communities which could only be reached by radio and from which response could only come via mail, which, in those days, could be sent after a specific broadcast and arrive well within the week in time for the next programme.

'Community Clinic' featured Alex Sim and Neil Morrison in dialogue about farm issues. These included topics such as the fixing of farm prices; the revision of rural taxation; the need for a rural health programme; and weekly half-holidays for farmers. The series was also carried by CBM Montreal and local stations in Hull, New Caledonia and Chicoutimi. The success of these efforts led to the establishment of 'National Farm Radio Forum' with the first official broadcast held on 10 November 1941.

Neil Morrison was employed jointly by the CBC and the Canadian Association for Adult Education as an organiser of discussion groups and was asked to work through trade unions, existing study groups, co-operatives, women's institutes and so on. The group programme was. to provide full information to farmers about CBC programming, collect requests for further material and to discover regional needs which might need special treatment.

The project was launched in every province in that first year. Two thousand copies of the *Farm Forum Guide* and over 7,000 copies of the *Farm Forum Handbook* were distributed. The programmes were produced by the CBC with advice and support from the Canadian Association of Adult Education, who co-ordinated the efforts of their constituent groups, including the Canadian Federation of Agriculture and the extension department of several participating Canadian universities.

Roger Schwass, who served as a 'Farm Forum' secretary, estimates that, at its height, 'National Farm Radio Forum' involved about five per cent of the farm families in Canada. 'If one assumes that forums were useful as learning centres for a period of five years, perhaps as many as fifteen to twenty per cent of the farm families in Canada participated for a period of time lengthy enough to be worthwhile.' One of the goals of 'Farm Forum' was to mobilise Canadian farmers for food production during the Second World War. Food production did double between 1940 and 1944 but it is rather difficult to estimate the extent to which the programme effected this increase.

A typical 'Farm Forum' consisted of a group of neighbours which varied in number from four or five to twenty. They would meet weekly in one another's homes half an hour in advance of the broadcast. The discussion guide for each programme was distributed a week in advance and members were expected to have read it. The group would discuss the topic and debate their answers to the questions asked in the guide. Their secretary would report their answers, opinions and further questions on the form provided and mail it to the provincial office.

The writer worked in the Quebec 'Farm Forum' office during the 1943-4 season and recalls that the mail services of the day were such that the reports from over eighty groups always arrived within the week, in time for the provincial 'Farm Forum' secretary to summarise the findings and present them over the air during the programme. 'Farm Forum' had such immediate success that the Canadian Association for Adult Education recommended to the CBC that a weekly national public affairs broadcast should be offered, based on the 'Farm Forum' model but designed for people living in urban areas. This led to the launching of 'Citizens' Forum' in the fall of 1943. By this time, Neil Morrison had been appointed supervisor of the CBC's department of 'Talks and Public Affairs'. He and his staff were already experienced and committed to small group discussion around radio broadcasts.

The 'Citizens' Forum' was a three-way project of the CBC, the Canadian Association for Adult Education (CAAE) and the Institute of International Affairs. The institute provided research facilities and the study guide; the CBC organised the programmes; and the CAAE organised the listening groups. There were over 1,000 'Citizens' Forums' at the conclusion of the first season on air. By the next year, this was down to 800 and levelled off in the early 1950s to about 400. Although programmes originated in different parts of the country, it proved very difficult to have a national programme which dealt with issues which were of equal importance to all regions of the country. 'Farm Forum' also had problems meeting the needs of all the regions and by the middle 1950s participation was in serious decline. Finally, the mechanisation of agriculture, the decline of the family farm, the urbanisation of rural areas and the coming of television, so weakened 'Farm Forum' participation that the programme closed in 1964.

'Citizens' Forum' met a similar fate. Some attempts were made to accommodate to television but CBC scheduling relegated the programmes to 10:00 at night, too late to be used as a stimulus for discussion. Since the forum programmes folded in the 1960s, few, if any, attempts seem to have been made to use radio as a deliberate educational tool in any kind of structured learning.

Ryerson Open College began broadcasting its first course in January 1971. It was initiated by the dean of arts of Ryerson Polytechnical Institute who had been inspired by reports about the launching of the Open University in Britain and was possibly spurred on by the publication of *The Learning Society*, a report of the Commission on Postsecondary Education which recommended the use of radio and television to increase access for education. Like the early farm programme on CHLT in Sherbrooke, Open College was designed as an experiment. The aim was to find ways in which radio, with some assistance from television, could be used effectively to deliver a university-level course and to assess the potential market for such education.

Ryerson had its own radio station, CJRT-FM, with an educational non-profit licence. The station had originally been used as a facility for training students enrolled in the Department of Radio and Television Arts. In 1965, the station began to employ professional staff and, by 1970, offered a programme schedule which consisted mainly of classical music interspersed with short news breaks and BBC talk shows. It also featured late-night jazz programmes six days a week, and the occasional series of talks presented by professors from the University of Toronto and Ryerson. The dean, supported by the vice-president academic, doubling as acting president, was able to announce, without any prior consultation that is anywhere recorded, that Ryerson was establishing an Open College.

They decided to offer 'Introductory Sociology' as a first course. There was a tenured teacher in the sociology department who had written and broadcast several well-received documentaries for the popular television programme 'Take 30'. In the late 1960s early 1970s, sociology was a popular subject. The teacher and office staff were borrowed from other Ryerson departments and housed at CJRT-FM. The teacher was merely asked to find out how to run a credit course on radio. It was to be an experiment that could fail. Approval of the course for credit presented no difficulties because a tenured teacher was presenting the same course in the classroom: it was only the delivery system that was different. The subtle antagonisms that academe would later direct towards any form of education via the media did not immediately surface, probably because very few faculty were aware that the experiment was taking place. Later, the comment would be made that some of the problems which arose at Open College stemmed from the fact that it had been conceived without benefit of clergy; that is, without the consultation and approval of academic council, the body that was later charged with accrediting the course. One could speculate that, if the approval of that body had been sought, Open College might never have been launched.

The first course attracted 83 students. Considering the limited range of the station's signal, this number was quite remarkable. The station antenna at that time was on the top of a three-storey Ryerson building and the listening range was not only limited but the FM signal somewhat unpredictable. Wind, weather and any new highrise could suddenly block the signal. CJRT staff were constantly asked to give advice about how to get the signal: they regularly told people to carry a portable radio around the house and stop when they caught it. One student reported he could only get the signal if he attached his antenna to the kitchen sink; another reported getting in her car and driving to the lakefront where she would park, hear the programme and take notes. Eighty-five per cent of the students were women and one-third defined themselves as housewives. This was no doubt related to the fact that, in 1971, there were no opportunities in Toronto to study for a degree part-time, no university education available at a distance, and no such education allowing for open registration. Open College required no entrance qualification.

From the beginning, Open College took the position that, if people thought they could do the work, they could take the course. Toronto had not yet felt the full force of the Women's Liberation Movement, but many women were beginning to think about possible opportunities for their own growth and development. Their delight at being able to take a course without fear of exposing what they perceived as their ignorance, was palpable.

The hour-long radio programmes consisted of a talk, an interview, feedback on weekly assignments, and a phone-in for registered students. Sociology is a discipline that can be made immediately relevant to every-day life and efforts were made to relate theoretical concepts to what was happening in the news and what was being viewed on TV commercials and sitcoms. In addition to the response from students, numerous letters and phone calls were received from regular listeners who wanted to argue about something said in the programme or to provide their own comment on an assignment that had been read over the air. Coffee klatches of young mothers sent in their own questions which, if relevant, were discussed on the programme in the feedback section. Public response to the first course was sufficiently positive that the minister of education urged Ryerson to continue the experiment.

From the beginning, it was a stated objective of Open College to offer courses in response to community needs. Over the years, continuous contact and consultation have been maintained with a wide variety of community groups, social agencies and educational institutions to ensure that courses selected for development reflect some evidence of demand.

Open College has offered two kinds of programming: university credit courses, supported in part by government funding; and non-credit programming which includes short courses to fit the needs of specific target groups and a variety of general interest programmes directed towards the broader community. Open College/CJRT-FM, the only radio station offering degree-level credit courses, provides a model for the delivery of postsecondary education by radio. It is located on Ryerson campus in downtown Toronto in the offices of CJRT-FM Inc. CJRT-FM is a private, non-commercial, educational radio station funded in part by the Ontario ministry of citizenship and culture.

HOW OPEN COLLEGE WORKS

An outline for a proposal credit course is carefully scrutinised by the relevant Ryerson faculty. It is assessed as academically equivalent to a degree course listed in the Ryerson day-school calendar and approved by academic council, a body that corresponds to the senate in a university. Since 1973, Open College courses have been accredited by Atkinson College, York University. Proposed outlines, together with the qualifications of the teachers, are now also sent to Atkinson. The course, when approved, is assigned an equivalent number from their calendar.

Today, a typical credit course from Open College will have the following components: an orientation at which students meet their tutor and broadcast instructors; broadcasts of two one-hour radio programmes per week for about six months; written assignments marked by a tutor; two study week-ends; a mid-term and a final examination. A typical programme will have a talk by the instructor interspersed with two or possibly three interviews. There will sometimes be feedback on assignments. The student phone-in was dropped, as it became impractical and students said it was not very useful. Student enquiries are handled individually by tutors who can be contacted by phone or mail.

Open College has offered sixteen credit courses in its fifteen years of operation. These include courses in psychology, politics, sociology, biology, history, literature, economics and management studies. Open College offered the first courses in gerontology available at a distance.

NON-CREDIT COURSES

These are shorter courses designed to fit the needs of a specific group wishing to upgrade its skills. Such courses have often been offered in response to requests from community groups or agencies, and are often designed in consultation with potential students. A course for volunteers working with emotionally-disturbed children was requested by the Metro Volunteer Centre and put together after lengthy consultations with volunteers and staff from some forty agencies serving such children. Similarly, a course for family daycare providers, requested by a branch of the ministry of community and social services, was designed only after lengthy consultation with daycare providers and parents. Detailed notes were taken of all these consultations, a committee of potential students struck and a curriculum outlined. Open College then employed qualified professionals to develop and present the course. The consultations provided a built-in commitment for people to enrol because they were assured the course would deal with information they had requested. These shorter, non-credit courses are less intensive and less costly than courses at a university level. However, they do not merit government funding and have only nominal student fees, as they are almost totally developed with general station funds.

The non-credit courses are useful for upgrading when an entire degree or diploma is not required. They have also served as a vehicle for getting people back into the educational stream who are initially afraid to register in a credit course. These students often go on to register in full-time degree programmes at university, having tested themselves and learned that they can cope with the work.

A typical non-credit course would include an orientation with tutors, twelve to twenty one-hour programmes over as many weeks, a mandatory study week-end, no examination but careful evaluation by a tutor of assignments based on the programmes. Students who complete all assignments and attend the study week-end are given a certificate outlining the extent of their participation.

Credit courses are aired three different times each week to provide maximum listening opportunity for people with irregular work hours or heavy family responsibilities. The programmes are also available on cassette in the Ryerson Library and Open College office for students who miss a broadcast. Once a course has been presented on air, it is revised and released on cassette to students outside the CJRT listening range. Unlike Britain's Open University, Open College uses radio for direct teaching and not only to build student morale or to add enrichment to what, at Open University, is essentially a correspondence course. At Open College, the radio programme *is* the course.

In the early years, radio was supplemented by weekly half-hour telecasts presented by the Ontario Educational Communications Authority. These were not specially produced programmes but were films selected for their relevance to the subject matter. Television was abandoned for two reasons: less than one-third of the students watched the programmes, and negotiating for suitable broadcast times became too difficult. Furthermore, TVOntario could not guarantee that broadcast times, once established, would not be changed. Since the substantive material in the course was on radio, no student ever complained about the loss of the television programmes.

All students are provided with a tutor who meets them at orientation sessions at the beginning of the course and during study week-ends. The tutor marks assignments and the mid-term and final examinations, and is available by telephone or mail for consultation. Tutors are expected to make detailed written comments on all assignments so that the reason for grading and the possibilities for improvement are made clear. This tutorial function is carefully monitored. All tutors must have a graduate degree in the discipline and are selected for their nurturing and supportive qualities.

WHO BENEFITS FROM OPEN COLLEGE COURSES?

Open College students come from a variety of backgrounds. Age distribution and educational level vary somewhat according to the particular course. Generally speaking, the educational level ranges from students with Grade 8 to those with graduate degrees who have not studied the discipline being offered. Until about 1980, twenty per cent of the student body would not have gone beyond Grade 12. In the non-credit courses described above, 20% had not gone further than Grade 11 and some 10% only had Grade 8. To date, the student age range is from 16 to 84. However, roughly one-third are divided nearly evenly in the 21-30 and 41-50 age groups. About 2 to 3% are under 21 and over 60.

Open College now offers a complete certificate in Gerontology consisting of six university credit courses. The programme has been extraordinarily popular and individual gerontology courses have attracted more students than anything Open College has ever produced. However, the majority of these students, unlike those in other courses, are professionals: nurses, teachers, social workers, occupational therapists and administrators in retirement homes and health care facilities. This has raised the average educational level considerably. Seventy-five to 85% of Open College registrations are still women but there is a wide occupational range. Almost one-third are professionals or managers; the remaining students have included clerical and sales staff, draughtsmen, nursing and teaching assistants, child care workers, blue collar workers, actors, journalists, security guards and letter carriers.

Many Open College students are people who have dropped out of the educational system. Working with Open College students in the early years provided ample evidence that the vast majority of Canadian women over the age of 35 were brought up to believe that they did not have the intellectual capacity to aspire to postsecondary education. Many qualified women were too intimidated to enrol in a conventional educational institution, and many women reported that their husbands were thoroughly opposed to their taking courses.

A course on radio can be taken at home and no one need know about it. Handicapped persons, people working on irregular shifts, or homebound housewives with small children can usually manage to catch the programmes at one of the listening hours. A major finding from the Open College experience has been that there is a large number of people who feel inferior because they have not earned a degree. And an equally large number is held back by low self-esteem which instils a fear of the classroom. Open College students can test their abilities in private. By the time they go to a study week-end to mingle with other students, they have had feedback from their tutors and their confidence has begun to build.

Open College students are exciting to teach. They work very hard; they do all the required readings and most of the optional; and during the breaks at study week-ends, they talk about the books they have read. Teachers and tutors working with Open College students sometimes feel postsecondary education is wasted on the unmotivated young.

AFTER OPEN COLLEGE

When Open College students get a credit for a course, they have a new sense of capability and is ready to move on to something else, and they do. For example, a 51-year-old man who worked as a security guard took the course for volunteers working with disturbed children. He did very well in his assignments and became a volunteer for an agency serving children. Six months later, he enrolled in a two-year diploma course in child care at a community college: yet he had begun to think that educational doors were closed to him. Another student, a 24-year-old woman, who had left school at Grade 10, was considered an unrepentant drop-out by her father and husband, both of whom were teachers. She secretly registered in an Open College credit course. Terrified of failure but supported by her tutor, she achieved an A grade, astonishing both herself and her family. She then went on to earn a Bachelor of Arts degree.

Some 3,000 students have taken one or more credit courses from Open College. However, since education at Ryerson Polytechnical Institute is primarily oriented towards a specific career, few Open College students complete their degree at Ryerson. They take their liberal arts credit and go off to Atkinson College at York or a number of other Ontario universities. A conservative estimate indicates that perhaps as many as 1,500 students have gone on to degree programmes in other institutions.

Open College students are officially registered at Ryerson. They are included in the Ryerson student count and receive transcripts from the Ryerson registrar. Technically, Atkinson credits Open College courses as transfers from Ryerson degree programmes. Atkinson attracts most of the Open College students because it is specifically organised for part-time, mature adults and is directed towards people who are working in full-time jobs. Not all successful Open College students continue their formal education, but many report increased achievement in their jobs and greater satisfaction in their personal lives.

RECRUITMENT AND TRAINING OF TEACHERS

When a course has been chosen and a tentative outline approved by the relevant academic department, applications for the teaching team are invited. The relevant faculties at Ryerson and Atkinson are informed and advertisements placed in two Toronto daily newspapers requesting applications and resumés. The resumés are checked for academic suitability and preliminary interviews are held to select a number of people to go through the initial trial process of learning to write for the ear and to broadcast. Applicants write a ten-minute script on some aspect of the subject to be taught, interview another academic on a related matter, and are interviewed by someone on Open College staff about some area of his or her expertise.

An Open College producer works with the applicant and edits the script to make it suitable for broadcast. It must be written to create the illusion being spoken spontaneously. It is a process Open College staff dub 'wiring the script for sound'. The applicant is given some elementary voice training and the work they do is taped. This process may take the better part of a week or ten days. When it is completed, Open College producers listen to the tapes and select two teachers who will comprise the teaching team for the course. The purpose of this process is to give the prospective teachers some hint of the time and effort required to prepare the course. It also gives Open College staff some indication of the applicant's willingness to be edited and to be taught the necessary skills. Applicants are told that, if they are employed, they may need to rewrite their first script six or eight times while they learn to write for the ear in a way that allows the material to be appropriated by the students. The object of this selection process is not to find an academic who can immediately function like a professional broadcaster, but to find people who are teachable and willing to put in the necessary time and effort. They will normally be employed for an eighteen-month period, expecting to spend a full year in course preparation before the actual broadcasts. Students in class may put up with whatever the teacher imposes, but when an educational institution takes to the public airwaves, the teaching must be well done. Credit courses, like justice, must not only be demanding but be seen to be so. They must be prepared with great care.

There is nothing difficult about learning to write and speak for broadcast but the skills do have to be learned. Academics accustomed to being the supreme authorities in their classrooms are not often ready to have their work criticised or being asked to rewrite it. Learning to write as if one is speaking, and speaking the script as if it has not been written, is not easy to do. So teachers find the first three or four months rather painful; however, the process of training is just as arduous for Open College producers who are responsible for the training and the production.

Some educational broadcast systems employ academics to supply content and hire professional writers and broadcasters to prepare the material for air. Open College, however, has opted to train the teacher to write and broadcast his or her own material. This provides a more personal approach to students and the broadcasting experience is often of great value to the teacher, all of whom report benefits to their teaching when they return to the classroom. Some who have learned to broadcast through Open College have become respected educational broadcasters elsewhere. The most notable example is Jay Ingram, the host of CBC's 'Quirks and Quarks'. He was serving as a sessional instructor at Ryerson when he was recruited for the teaching team to prepare and broadcast a course called 'Biology and Twentieth Century Man'. For two or three years following the presentation of that course, Jay did a weekly half-hour science journal on CJRT-FM and subsequently was employed by the CBC.

ACCREDITATION OF OPEN COLLEGE COURSES

From the beginning, Open College aimed to present courses of such quality as to merit accreditation by other academic institutions. As indicated, this goal has largely been realised but it has not come easily. When government funding became tied to student registration, university administrators and their faculties have been nervous lest there be a decline in enrolment. Despite the fact that Open College draws on a completely different clientele from the Ryerson day school and has only been able to produce one new credit course a year, some faculty have viewed it as a possible competitor for students. Consequently, the path to accreditation, even at Ryerson, has been rocky. Courses have never been rejected on academic grounds but there have been serious bureaucratic delays. Atkinson College has been receptive to crediting Open College courses because they recognise that Open College serves as a recruiting ground for their students. When they arrive at Atkinson, their credit in hand, they have already been screened. Several Open College students who have gone on to Atkinson have won scholarships and prizes.

The selection of courses to be produced by Open College is somewhat limited by the need to select a course that is found in the regular Ryerson calendar. Some flexibility is possible if the department concerned does not demand an exact equivalence of content, only equivalence of discipline and academic level.

Faculty fears of displacement are unfounded but are very real and still exist. Consequently, a great deal of energy, if not ingenuity, is expended in seeking departmental approval for course accreditation.

RELATIONS WITH THE COMMUNITY

From its inception, Open College and CJRT-FM have had very warm and continuing relationships with the listeners and the broader community. There has never been any lack of academic expertise available for interviews. Scientists, scholars and artists have always been willing to contribute some time to a non-profit station who takes its listeners seriously and offers something for the mind that is not offered through other media.

In addition to the faculty at Ryerson Polytechnic Institute, there are two universities and four community colleges in Metro Toronto. Open College is within an hour and a half drive from four other Ontario universities and has facilities for doing interviews over the telephone from anywhere in the world. Recently, for example, Richard Sheldrake was interviewed from Wales for a new series called 'Mysteries of the Mind'. Open College also tries to keep abreast of conferences, seminars and workshops in the Metro Toronto area and so is often able to tape talks or interviews with visiting experts who have a contribution to make to a course currently under production, or to an informal lecture series which runs from May to October.

Open College courses may feature interviews with twenty to forty specially qualified people. A course in introductory economics called 'Money, Power and Politics' had interviews with Kenneth Boulding, John Kenneth Galbraith, the Governor of the Bank of Canada, and some thirty other economists from around the world. Most scholars are pleased to be interviewed by Open College and freely offer their services to what they perceive to be a genuine educational process. They will be interviewed by another academic who is knowledgeable about their subject, not by a host needing a three-minute quick fix for a talkshow. They can also count on being given the time to make a substantive contribution that will not be distorted through editing by someone who may not understand the importance of what is being said.

The strength of the relationship between CJRT-FM and its listeners was most vividly illustrated in 1974, when a shortfall in Ryerson student enrolment led to an announcement by the Ryerson president that both Open College and the station would close. As mentioned previously, CJRT-FM and Open College were financed from Ryerson's general budget. The president's announcement of possible closure led to dozens of letters of protest which were sent to the editors of the *Toronto Star* and the *Globe and Mail*.

Toronto record stores organised petitions that were eagerly signed by their patrons who enjoyed the diet of classical music and jazz provided by the station. It was reported that a petition organised by a University of Toronto professor was signed by some 2,000 names and sent to the provincial government. Open College students prepared a brief which they delivered to all MPPs in Ontario. Not wanting Open College staff to be accused of financing their own survival, the students mimeographed the brief themselves and took up a collection to finance the mailing. The brief was well-documented and requested the government to guarantee funding for Open College for a three-year developmental period.

Margaret Scrivener, a Conservative MPP, attracted by the astonishing public outcry, met with the students and offered her services to organise a panel of prominent citizens to discuss the issue at a public forum in the Town Hall, St Lawrence Centre. The students co-operated by coming out in large numbers and bringing enough friends and supporters to all but fill the hall. Scrivener assembled another group of citizens from business and education who prepared a detailed brief for the Davis government. Their proposal is summarised as follows:

> It is proposed that the Open College/CJRT be established, with its own Board of Trustees as a non-profit, community-based, educational, informational and cultural foundation, under the laws of the Province of Ontario; that the Government of Ontario request the several members of the Board of Governors of Ryerson Polytechnic Institute to transfer their interest in and responsibility for radio station, CJRT-FM, and Ryerson Open College to the Board of Trustees of Open College/CJRT; that the Government of Ontario provide financial support for the operations of the Open College/CJRT on a descending percentage scale during the period 1973-78, with a balance of funds required coming from various private and public sources.

Open College was closed during the 1973-4 academic year but hardly a week went by when the director did not receive a letter, a phone call or a visit from a listener protesting its closure. A letter arrived from a group of young mothers in a bedroom community well out of the city saying that Open College must not close because it was the only thing that kept them alive during the long winter. In the meantime, letters continued to flow to the newspapers and, in December 1973, Premier Davis announced to the legislature that an independent corporation would take over both Open College and CJRT-FM and that funding would be provided for a three-year period, after which it was expected that the newly appointed board would be able to raise its own funds. Open College came back on the air the next fall offering a revised edition of a course that had previously been offered.

It took time to effect a transfer of staff and equipment from Ryerson and to negotiate with Ryerson a continuing academic participation in Open College. Since a radio station cannot offer university credits, this participation was essential if the courses were to continue to have any academic credibility in the community or if the students were to receive credits that would be useful to them.

In November 1974, CJRT-FM was incorporated, retaining the noncommercial educational status of the station. The board, under the energetic leadership of its chairman, set to work immediately to increase the station's listening range and, in June 1975, increased the power from 27,000 watts to 50,000 and moved the antenna to the CBC tower. The signal could then be heard within a 45-mile radius. The transmitter has subsequently been installed on Toronto's CN Tower, giving a transmission range of 100 miles.

FUNDING

It was not until the third year of the guaranteed funding period that the board was able to embark on fundraising. Their first efforts carried out over the radio raised $107,000. Fundraising efforts have continued until the station now raises over forty per cent of its budget from its listeners, small businesses and corporations. Continuing community support is evidenced by the fact that last year some 11,000 listeners donated $510,000 to the station.

The production and first broadcast of a two-semester university course costs approximately $150,000 in direct salaries for instructors, producer, transcript typists, tutors and supplies. This figure does not include studio or broadcast costs. Some contribution to station finances is made through government funding for credit courses. However, since Open College students are deemed to be additional to Ryerson's base student population, full-time equivalent funding (FTE) is heavily discounted. The amount available from this source, together with student fees, does not begin to cover the cost of course production and administration, even if amortised over several years. No university could afford to spend the money on course development that is expended by CJRT-FM on Open College. This expenditure is justified, however, because CJRT-FM is required by licence to offer structured learning and the courses double as radio programming. It has been estimated that the cost of non-credit programming of comparable quality would cost as much or possibly more. In order to provide such quality, the station would need to hire outside professional broadcasters, researchers and writers as the station staff, as it now stands, could not accommodate such programming.

Open College attracts a large listening audience. According to the last survey of the Bureau of Broadcast Measurement, some 59,000 people listened to Open College weekly and each course attracted an average of some 20,000 listeners. Many listeners undoubtedly become donors. The move to the CN Tower in January 1981 has put the station within the reach of some six million listeners, seventy per cent of the Ontario population.

ADVANTAGES OF EDUCATIONAL RADIO

Perhaps the greatest advantage of educational radio is that students need no academic entrance qualifications. A student who is unable to keep up cannot hold back the class. Portions of assignments can be read over the air and commented upon in a way that no teacher could ever do in class. The student who prepared the assignment recognises it as his but no one else does. And s/he is saved the embarrassment of public praise or criticism. Students many times over express appreciation of this feature.

When programmes have had open-line phone-ins meant for the students, the listening public often contributed as well. In 'Developmental Psychology', for example, a student telephoned on air and asked a teaching psychologist a question in genetics which the teacher was unable to answer. A leading geneticist from the University of Toronto heard the exchange, phoned the Open College office the next day and offered to come to a study week-end and conduct a seminar. That scientist so enjoyed the experience, she returned every year the course was offered.

Properly presented, a radio talk can create the illusion of one-to-one communication. The teacher can convey and inspire enthusiasm and, if appropriate, reasonable doubt. S/he can clarify meaning which may be obscure in the textbook and give clues about what kind of attention should be paid to what. Education via radio requires concentrated listening but leaves the eyes free to take notes. The mind is not distracted by visual stimuli which have little relevance to the material being studied.

Another advantage of educational radio is its great flexibility. The number of interviews included in a typical Open College course would never be possible if television were the medium. With radio, one can do an interview on a portable tape recorder in a hotel room if necessary, or even over the telephone.

Radio also does a great job of public education. Courses have often served as an encouragement to listeners who want to return to the educational stream but are initially afraid to register. They listen to a course one year, gain some courage and register the next time the course is offered.

REFERENCES

Bates, A.W. (1985) *The Growth of Technology in Distance Education*, St Martin's Press, New York

MacKenzie, Norman *et al.* (1975) *Open Learning: Systems and Problems in Post-Secondary Education*, Unesco Press, New York

O'Houle, Cyril (1976) *The Design of Education*, Jossey-Bass Publishers, San Francisco

Perry, Walter (1977) *The Open University - History and Evaluation of a Dynamic Innovation in Higher Education*, Jossey-Bass Publishers, San Francisco

Schwass, Rodger (1972) *National Farm Radio Forum: The History of and Educational Institution in Rural Canada*, Unpublished Ph.D. thesis (Toronto)

Wilson, Isobel (1980) *Citizens' Forum*, Ontario Institute for Studies in Education, Toronto

Use of Television

Barry Brown and Danielle Fortosky

Over the past decade a short-order diet of fast-maturing microchips has served Canadian educators a smorgasbord of technological choices which have nurtured advances in educational communications and information systems. The occurrence has re-ordered and in some cases re-defined the functions of established media, particularly television. While the television evolution has offered instructors exciting new options, the resulting diversity has also challenged educational planners by widening the horizon of the untested potential for this medium. Furthermore, the history and development of television in Canada is a sober reminder to educators that the pedagogical potential of this medium has traditionally been refined or restrained more according to the dictates of the boardroom than the classroom. Seasoned educators who responded enthusiastically to the Age of Television now enter the Information Age more experienced with the parameters of promise, while today's initiates enter from a broader spectrum of technological taste and expectation. Within this climate, the changing face of television continues to beckon and draw Canadian educators to re-examine its potential and to explore its new meaning for learners at a distance.

THE MEANING OF TELEVISION AND DISTANCE EDUCATION IN CANADA

The debut of television in Canada took place 'on-the-air' so that its original meaning was wrapped up in broadcasting characteristics. As videotape evolved, followed by cable transmission, satellite communications, fibre optics and videodisc, the meaning of television became more encompassing, to a point where its distinctive properties were becoming obscured by the branching and merging of electronic systems. The basic definition of television has always denoted a process whereby images are transmitted by converting light rays into radio waves. However, transmission has two related connotations: to convey or communicate to others as well as to transport across an intervening space. In the same sense, television can be interpreted in two stages. First, by encoding light rays as radio waves, the process employs a unique symbol system for thought transfer in order to communicate ideas to others. Second, the transportation over distance of thought and image encoded as electronic signals, connotes the distribution features of television which, today, take many forms. Therefore, television means not only the process by which pictures are transported to your television set, but also implies a unique technology for encoding ideas in the same way that a pen and paper is a particular system for encoding written or drawn symbols as a representation of thought. These symbol-producing features of television have been multiplying through such developments as computerised editing, character generation and graphic systems. Also, a new kind of symbol system in the form of the interactive programme has been introduced via computer-controlled videotape or videodisc. To a similar extent, the transportation of the image has also been affected by technological progress. Signal transmission has been revolutionised by the efficiency of fibre optics technology, where radio waves are converted by laser into digital pulses travelling at the speed of light, through hair-thin strands of glass. Because laser technology can completely regenerate a digital signal every ten kilometres, a fibre optics system is not subject to the same signal degradation as a cable system, which must amplify the original signal every few kilometres. Cable thus cannot stretch its coverage much further than a 15 kilometre radius. While fibre optics improves on the distance limitations of coaxial cable, communications satellites make distance irrelevant. Like super high microwave towers or transmitters in space, they transmit or relay television signals to and from any point on the globe, via their position in a geostationary orbit at 35,887 kilometres above the equator. The implications of this expanding facility to bridge space and time, combined with an ever evolving system to communicate thoughts and ideas through symbols, will help to determine the impact of television on the nature of distance education.

Just as the definition of television has unfolded through various technological developments, the meaning of distance education has evolved through a variety of connotations, since the time when the most common name for remote learning was 'correspondence'. A recent definition which has gained acceptance among researchers describes distance education as 'learning situations where teachers and learners carry out their essential tasks apart from one another, although they communicate in a variety of ways. This definition does not include provision of courses in off-campus centres by travelling instructors'. (Daniel and Stroud 1980:1)

At the British Open University, the 'variety of ways of communicating', has traditionally implied the interaction of tutors and students with a combination of print, telephone, radio, and television. Printed texts have provided the core and largest segment of the instructional process. More recently, videocassettes, audiocassettes, and microcomputers have also been introduced into the distribution format, and researchers continue to explore the merits of teletext, viewdata, and videodisc for Open University courses.

It is difficult to compare Canadian initiatives in using television for distance education with the experience of the British Open University. First, in the sphere of education, the British Open University was created as a national commitment to distance education and has consequently secured a separate funding agreement with the government. Among the 48 conventional British universities, grants are allocated through the University Grants Committee (UGC), a body set up in the interests of these universities, to disburse funding on behalf of the Department of Education and Science (DES). In the case of the Open University, grants are issued directly from the DES. Although the British Open University has always retained the capacity to foster regional differences as in such programmes as the *History of Wales*, customarily the national interest overrides regional activity. In Canada the situation is reversed. Historically, education has been a provincial jurisdiction. This political reality reinforces regional diversity, especially in a country where a small population is scattered over a vast distance.

In that context, distance education institutions such as Télé-université, Athabasca University and the Open Learning Institute developed in response to regional needs. Although recently these institutions have begun to direct their attention across provincial borders, regionalism continues to take precedence over a national focus. As a result, the concept of funding a national distance education agency for Canada has never realised support.

Second, while education is a provincial jurisdiction in Canada, broadcasting is a federal responsibility, partly because airwaves do not respect provincial borders. In order to accommodate provincial broadcasting licenses for education, a compromise was established in the form of a provincial educational communications authority. Organisations such as TVOntario, ACCESS Alberta, and the Knowledge Network in British Columbia broadcast both credit and non-credit educational programmes within the mandate of their respective provincial authorities. In theory, the number of educational broadcasting networks could equal the number of provinces. In fact, many provinces, such as those participating in the Atlantic Satellite Network, are attempting to co-operate in the sphere of educational broadcasting. Nevertheless, the provincial independence of educational broadcasting authorities promotes fragmentation of a national audience, a determining factor in achieving economies of scale. Comparatively, a critical factor in the creation of the British Open University was its partnership with the BBC. The alliance of the national public broadcasting system with a nationally-recognised university produced opportunities to develop the use of television for distance education which are unparalleled in Canada.

Therefore the concept of television for distance education in Canada is related to certain underlying factors:

1. Television implies the symbolic characteristics of encoding the image as well as sending it;

2. The progress of television technology has developed various means whereby educators create and distribute their message. In the context of distance education, these developments increase the variety of ways that learners and teachers communicate at a distance. These options create a challenge of choice whereby educators must become more responsible for assessing the most appropriate and cost-effective method to serve the need;

3. Broadcast television for distance education in Canada implicates federal-provincial agreements in the area of education and communications. Although educational broadcasters have been negotiating their way through these conventions, the geographical and political realities of Canada have impeded a singular or concentrated approach to distance education;

4. Other forms of television distribution including satellite, cable, videocassettes, and videodisc have either circumvented broadcast conventions or rendered them obsolete; but they have also introduced other complications for distance education. For example, videocassettes, which are as portable as printed learning packages, allow a distance education institution to transport its 'signal' across provincial borders without contravening the broadcasting act. This facility encourages distance educators to become more venturesome about marketing their media beyond provincial borders. Such activity could sponsor a competitive skirmish for scarce resources.

The meaning of television for distance education in Canada therefore establishes that there is no single formula or recipe for development. Choices are being fashioned according to the regional context or individual situations. Although these decisions are presently being buffeted by rapid technological change, they should ultimately be guided by the needs of the learner.

WHY USE TELEVISION? THE QUESTION OF NEED

An observation of Schramm (1974) sets the stage for considering the most appropriate medium for distance education programmes: 'given a reasonably favourable situation, a pupil will learn from any medium - television, radio, programmed instruction, films, filmstrips or others.' (p. 22) Schramm points out that hundreds of experiments confirm this conclusion and that factors controlling learning in face-to-face contact also figure heavily in learning from educational media. He lists the controlling factors, among others as: 'the relevance and clarity of the content, individual abilities, motivation to learn, attention, interest in the subject, respect and affection for the teacher, emphasis and replication of the central points to be learnt, and rehearsal by the learner.' (p. 22)

Bates (1982), a full decade later, in a paper presented to the International Council for Correspondence Education's 12th World Conference, discussed trends in the use of audio-visual media in educational systems on a world basis. His conclusions were: (1) there is a clear movement *away* from using broadcasting by distance learning systems; (2) the range of audio-visual media suitable for distance education is rapidly increasing; and (3) the educational potential of audio-visual media still tends to be under-exploited by distance learning systems. (p. 1)

Bates cited 'academic distrust' as the main reason distance learning institutions did not make greater use of broadcasting. He indicated that few individuals responsible for distance education courses had received training in the use of audio-visual media and that:

There is a lack of an educational theory which can provide clear guidelines as to the unique educational advantages of television or radio over print or face-to-face teaching ... most teachers and educators are unable or unwilling to see the *educational* (as distinct from the *distributional*) advantages of television and radio over print and face-to-face teaching. (p. 4)

Pichette (1985) in a collection of papers titled *Learning in Society: Toward a New Paradigm*, delivered at the Symposium on Learning in Society in 1983 in Ottawa, listed a series of ten 'musts' in 'Creating a New Educational Environment and Helping it Grow'. He points out that:

We must bridge the false gap between what is 'Educational' and what is not ... We 'must' make educators, social interveners and researchers aware of the qualitative effect of the media and the new technologies on learning methods and cognitive structures. What are the positive and truly educational effects of television, computers, the print media, electronic games, omnipresent audio-visual and communications displays and the like on continuing learning? (p. 113)

Paper 5 (Burge *et al.* 1984) of TVOntario's series titles, *New Technologies in Canadian Education*, describes the many issues and problems facing the application of information and communications technologies to distance education in Canada:

> If technology is to be used effectively, a conceptual framework is needed. Such a framework can offer theoretical guidance in the design and use of different media so that learners can use a fully integrated set of learning materials appropriate to their learning styles and interests. A related issue is that of matching types of technology, both hardware and software, to types of learners ... Resistance to the use of new technologies for distance education is common among educators who are unfamiliar with technological applications. (p. 48)

The capacity of television to teach in any of its many formats is scarcely an issue in the current literature. The concerns expressed by the foregoing comment are prevalent in current literature. Posing the question, 'Why Use Television in Distant Education?' elicits the response that 'individual needs require individual solutions.' Television is a unique medium offering great potential for delivery of distance education. Television as the 'universal' or 'integrating' medium perhaps inspired the introductory comment to TVOntario's Paper 5:

> The evaluation of information and communications technologies has increased the potential for providing education to those who would otherwise not have access to educational resources ... only with the recent integration of technologies into education have the possibilities for learning at a distance become so comprehensive, credible, and popular. (p. 1)

The uniqueness of television as a delivery medium is well-known and well-documented. The effectiveness of television to promote learning is determined by directing it to fulfil a clearly defined learning need of a specific learner in an appropriate setting. This can best be accomplished by the needs analysis approach. This approach should involve a carefully developed conceptual framework supported by formative and summative evaluation. It is important that evaluation be systematic and continuous as it is in the effective face-to-face instructional process.

THE UNIQUE CONTRIBUTION OF TELEVISION TO DISTANCE EDUCATION

In 1968, Roderick MacLean, a man who organised one of the earliest and most comprehensive university television services at the University of Glasgow, assessed television's contribution to learning in his book, *Television In Education*. Almost twenty years later, his following remark is still relevant: 'If a man *wants* to learn - and this is true, whether he is a small farmer learning to keep his books, or a teacher catching up on statistics, or a doctor keeping abreast of the latest techniques - he neither needs nor wants to be cosseted along with every adventitious trick that television offers.' (p. 53)

The 'tricks' of television have multiplied considerably since this observation was published, but they have evolved out of four qualities, basic to television, which MacLean describes as a measurement of capacity: the capacity to magnify, to distribute instantaneously or relay, to store and ultimately to assemble, that peculiar characteristic which allows television to fuse a variety of symbolic permutations and technological capabilites. Intrinsic to these four capacities are the same symbolic and distributional features that were earlier described as characteristic to the meaning of television. However, in spite of whatever capacity or meaning television purveys, MacLean's point emphasises that the unique contribution of television to education, regardless of its technical sophistication or uniqueness, is only as remarkable as its effects on the learner. In many cases, the simplest offering is the most significant contribution. The following examples illustrate various ways that television is being incorporated with distance education in Canada and meeting learners' needs according to these basic capacities.

Some institutions such as Mount St Vincent University in Nova Scotia and the University of Regina in Saskatchewan are using studio-equipped classrooms to televise live lectures and transmit them via cable, satellite, or microwave to students scattered within their transmission range. This relay capacity of television literally allows the instructor to be in two places at once. Such applications of the 'narrowcast au naturel' justify a lack of production sophistication by the commitment of a specific student body requiring specialised information. This form of television also provides for interaction via telephone and promotes a sense of immediacy and community which is not as spontaneous with videotapes distribution. Although when given a choice students prefer live instruction, this system can sometimes be less expensive than sending out a fleet of itinerant faculty, because they are frequently travelling long distances, in separate directions, on the same evening to teach the same course, to a small number of students.

Many organisations involved in distance education use television 'clips' of medical operations, interviews, demonstrations, or dramatic scenes to provide short sequences of illustrative evidence for points being made by a lecturer, who could also be televised. Often the lecturers use these clips strictly for their visual attributes, and talk to the video just as they would talk to a slide. In fact television is increasingly replacing film and slides for this purpose because it is becoming more user-friendly, a phenomenon which is partly related to the growth in the home video entertainment industry. Furthermore, television offers the facility to portray movement as well as changing relationships.

Another contribution of television to distance education which stretches its full capacity to relay, store and assemble, is the documentary. The documentary assembles a sequence of visual testimony to support a pre-scribed format which not only creates a reality for the learner, but can also interpret its meaning or provide a perspective, within the limits of television's capacity to manipulate images. A subtle attribute of the documentary is that even where it has not been designed for an educational purpose, it can have an educative effect. That is why certain educational broadcasters such as TVOntario have been successful in designing learning support materials or experiences to wrap around an existing and successful documentary series. By altering the support materials, the course can be adjusted to various levels of distance studies.

The advantages of information storage which are so useful to the documentary are also valuable for archival and record-keeping purposes in education. The one-time-only event can be taped and stored for raw replay at any future date. It can also be edited according to various purposes to be used on later occasions.

Like the documentary, the drama comes close to tapping the full potential of television with all its capacity to communicate. The drama creates illusion in a paradoxical fashion. On the one hand it magnifies reality by focusing, expanding and dramatising a human situation. On the other hand, it minimises or simplifies the reality because those conflicts and complications which are so basic to the human condition must be resolved within a tightly controlled time schedule. This paradox has contributed to the fall of television into superficiality. The challenge of producing a thought-provoking and meaningful dramatic presentation within a regulated time frame is often superseded by a less expensive, yet highly saleable product. This tendency is manifested by a fast-paced, plastic taste for situation comedies or those cops-and-robbers shows that have recently introduced centerfold detectives, to play out unsubtle games of Eye Spy and Twenty Questions. Yet, apart from any commercial use or abuse of television drama, educators can still take advantage of the power of this medium to relay time and space by recreating real or imagined scenes from any point in history. Then the capacity of television to store and assemble allows these scenes to be organised, mixed and enhanced both aurally and visually, by the symbol-producing properties of this technology.

An example of the variety of ways these elements of dramatic television can be treated in distance education is occurring at the University of Saskatchewan. A few years ago, the College of Education in co-operation with local school divisions produced a drama entitled 'Learning The Game', which dealt with a number of issues relating to Saskatchewan education such as school closure, lifelong learning and educational accountability. The issues were couched in a 'soap opera' centred on the life of a Saskatoon family. The style of the series was not unlike the format of 'The Archers', a long-running radio show in Britain designed to provide information to farmers via a continued story of the day-to-day life of the fictional Archer family. Initially, 'Learning The Game' was a video-based package and the series was broadcast on a local CTV station. A panel discussion followed with viewers phoning in questions and comments. A short discussion guide also accompanied the series, which was subsequently distributed on videotape to educational administration classes and discussion groups.

More recently, two separate applications have evolved from the series. In one instance, a local technical institute is using sections of the series to motivate discussion on a city-wide cable programme about lifelong learning. In a second application, the College of Education has selected five short scenes from the series to support themes in another learning package that has recently been developed for school administrators. The administrative package is print-based and will incorporate these scenes to reinforce written material as well as to motivate interpretation and inspire discussion. This facility to stimulate feeling, to cause people to identify or react, to inspire a sense of relationship, importance or even an overview of the situational context, is one of the strongest attributes of dramatic television. This capacity to communicate at one of the highest levels of human sensibility must be protected, especially in educational spheres, from the kind of electronic wizardry which is distracting producers from exalting an idea to worshipping technique. Electronic techniques such as computer graphics or squeeze zooms may be effective for selling soap, but when used for their own sake may also represent another form of those 'adventitious tricks' which contribute little to the learning process. In the final analysis, the challenge for educators is to remain vigilant in securing a balance, because even though the pitfalls for oversubscribing to technical wizardry are very real, there are also opportunities to be gained from these technological developments.

The facility of television to assemble, integrate and network other media has multiplied significantly since MacLean wrote about this concept in 1968. Computerised graphics and animation systems offer a whole new dimension to teaching abstract relationships. However, one of the most exciting of these developments for distance education is interactive television. This facility is a progression of television's capacity to integrate computer technology, producing such results as the interactive videodisc and computer-controlled, interactive videotapes. The potential of this medium for self-instruction is only as limited as the programme design. But therein lies the rub.

Ultimately a fifth capacity of television transcends the other four: the capacity to mystify and confound. When television mesmerises its masters through digital dexterity, its contribution to distance education is as insubstantial as the substance of the image. On the other hand, if educators explore and direct the technology, they can surpass its mystification by pushing it to the outer limits of learning effectiveness. Therefore, television's contribution to distance education, or any form of education, is proportional to the extent that its cold technology can be animated by human design and expression.

TELEVISION PRODUCTION FOR DISTANCE EDUCATION

The television production system involves more of a team effort than most other programming systems. In order for it to be successful for distance education, planners and production personnel must be able to communicate effectively, remaining sympathetic to each other's needs. Schimeck notes that 'it takes a number of years for an educational agency to develop the skilled manpower necessary for striking a balance between the requirements of TV production and the objectives of the educators.' (1982:272) Stevenson remarks cryptically that 'myths like you can't teach mathematics by television' should be firmly ignored. He points rather to the responsibility of the media team saying that this statement really means, 'the producer of a particular mathematics programme in collaboration with his academic colleague is unable to teach mathematics.' (1979:10) Together with Scupham (1975) he emphasises that the academic should have knowledge of the media while production personnel should be understanding of the needs of instruction. This alliance is one of the least understood but most essential factors in the successful production of educational software. Furthermore, this alliance has recently been strained by technological advances which have de-mystified production to a point where fewer specialists and technicians are required to create an acceptable product and where educators can become more closely aligned to the production system. Bates (1984) indicates that current developments in media allow for different alternatives to the mass media models that were so fashionable in the 1960s and 1970s and which produced the Open University. He points out that smaller and less central-ised models are now possible:

> This could mean a move away from large national systems of audio-visual production and distribution for education, to more diversity of provision and more local initiatives. There will be much greater opportunities for 'do-it-yourself' production of audio-visual materials by teachers, or for buying audio-visual materials from sources other than broadcasting organisations. New media allow local schools and colleges to develop their own on-campus, and more significantly, off-campus multi-media courses at reasonable cost. (p. 236)

Because a number of educational institutions in Canada such as community colleges and universities are now equipped with either 1-inch C-Format or 3/4-inch videotape editing facilities, a certain amount of basic production can occur in-house. This kind of production access can sometimes lend itself to an improved alliance between educators and audio-visual personnel. Because the production organisation is uncomplicated, generally the teachers and producers are working as part of the same 'family', namely their loyalties and career paths are focused within the same institutions. In cases where professional production houses align with educational institutions, the disparity in career direction and modes of operation can sometimes become a source of disharmony.

On the other hand, the production of sophisticated telecourses, which sometimes need to feature global geographical phenomena or interviews with world experts, requires the skill and facility of a dedicated, well-funded production house. In these instances it is more prudent to purchase an existing telecourse, and package it with in-house educational components, than to try to reproduce it locally.

Despite the exceptional needs for elaborate production and in spite of the cold Canadian winters, educational studies have moved outside. The need for expensive and elaborate production studios is being replaced by a requirement for light, portable single camera units which offer the world as a studio at much less cost. Therefore local initiatives in production are becoming more viable as the technology becomes more refined. It could conceivably be argued that, in the future, producing television in any of its forms could be as accessible to the educator as publishing a textbook. In that context, the evolution of television production for distance education may have reached the same turning point that Gutenberg inspired when he advanced the quills of the monks. His technological leap not only revolu-tionised ideas, but produced them in tangible printed form, placing the power of the word in any hand that could reach out to a printing press.

CARRIER TECHNOLOGY AND DISTANCE EDUCATION

Initially, established telecommunications systems could be conveniently classed as telephony, telegraphy, and broadcasting, but the recent advent of satellite, fibre optics and a plethora of playback devices, has caused an exponential increase in the possibilities for delivering the television signal. Although these latest technologies have expanded the potential for using television in distance education, they have also complicated the decision making process.

Any brief description of carrier technology must be categorised as cursory and can only set the stage for the consideration of options in programme delivery. Transmission of electronic communication is characterised by two major modes of signal distribution; airwaves and cable. In order to send a signal any distance through the air it must be mixed with a carrier wave of a certain radio frequency, a process known as modulation. Frequency is usually expressed in hertz and indicates the number of alternating cycles per second. Signals can be transmitted using amplitude modulation (AM), frequency modulation (FM) or pulse code modulation (PCM).

Bands of radio frequencies are allocated by international agreement and extend from 10 KHz to 300 GHz on the electronic spectrum (see Figure 1). Bandwidth refers to the range of frequencies required to convey the visual and/or aural signals transmitted. For example, the bandwidth required for a standard colour television signal is 6 MHz, while a standard voice channel requires only 4 KHz. The higher the frequency of a channel, the more information it can convey and at a higher information rate because there are a greater number of cycles per second available to carry the information.

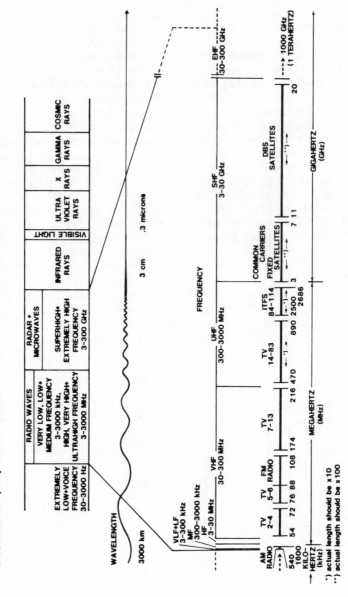

Figure 1: The electromagnetic spectrum and broadcast bands. In D.M. Fortosky, *Distance Education and Communications Technology at the University of Saskatchewan: Options For The Future* (Unpublished master's thesis, University of Saskatchewan, 1983), p. 173

Signals travelling via airwaves can interfere with one another. Therefore, the radio frequency spectrum is strictly controlled by international agreement and in Canada is regulated by the Federal Department of Communications (DOC). Since there has been limited spectrum space, allocations have been a scarce and prized commodity. Therefore only common carriers are assigned frequency bands by the DOC to carry telephone signals, data or network transmission of television and radio signals intra- and interprovincially. Broadcast undertakings receive a network signal from a common carrier which usually brings the signal from a distant location by microwave. The undertaking then broadcasts that signal, combined with the signals of its locally produced programmes, through its local transmitter which is assigned a broadcast frequency by the DOC for its own area.

Regions of the spectrum have come to be known for the kind of information they carry. The region between 3 and 30 KHz is known as very low frequency and is used for telephone, telegraph, voice, and low speed data. The region between 30 and 300 MHz is designated as very high frequency (VHF) and is used for radio channels and the television channels 2-13. Ultra high frequency (UHF) is between 300 and 3,000 MHz and can carry television channels 14-83 as well as instructional television fixed service (ITFS) for channels 84-114. Super high frequency signals, from 3 to 30 GHz make available large bandwidths for microwave and satellite transmission of voice, data, and television signals.

Microwaves carry television signals, radio or voice channels by multiplexing their carrier frequencies to occupy a bandwidth measured in gigahertz (GHz). Frequency division multiplexing is the process of taking the original frequencies of a number of signals, transposing them to higher frequencies and arranging them to constitute one wide-band signal. For example, 1,200 phone calls (4 KHz voice channels) or one colour television channel (6 MHz video channel) occupy about the same amount of channel bandwidth. Time division multiplexing, where the signals are sampled repetitively and the decimal equivalents of their amplitudes are transmitted sequentially is another form of multiplexing.

Microwaves travel in a focused, line-of-sight beam that must be relayed approximately every 60 kilometres across the earth's curvature. Microwaves can provide multiple, high bandwidth highways for the delivery of telephone conversations as well as television and business data over intercontinental routes. This form of signal distribution supports long haul, city-to-city transportation of distance education messages.

Cable distribution is another main classification of signal delivery giving distance educators a vast array of means by which to deliver their messages. Cable technology spans a period of rapid development from early Morse code signals carried on a single strand of conductive cable to the present-day, high-capacity, broad-band fibre optics cable which seems to have unlimited message capacity.

Today, pairs of twisted wires have become the standard channel for transmitting telephone calls and low speed data, whereas coaxial cable is capable of carrying signals with frequencies of up to 300 MHz. Coaxial cable consists of a central copper wire conductor surrounded by a metallic shield. The entire cable is covered with a protective coating. The signal is contained within the wire and not being free to propagate in space does not interfere with neighbouring signals. Therefore cable signals, if not derived from through-the-air broadcast, are considered self-contained or closed circuit and are not subject to the same regulatory controls as radio communications.

Cable companies are also capable of distributing data or voice, a service which traditionally comes under the purview of telecommunications carriers. Because of this flexibility, cablehas a great deal of potential for distance education. However, its status in remaining so undefined has also sparked much federal-provincial controversy in the area of communications. The situation has been further complicated by new developments in distribution technology.

One of these developments, fibre optics, which in operating principle is not that different from coaxial cable, has greatly extended the capacity of cable. Fibre optics, which employs a thin strand of pure glass to transmit a digitally modulated beam of laser light, opens up an entire new frequency and bandwidth range: light frequencies which exceed 1,000 GHz in the upper regions of the electromagnetic spectrum. Therefore, because the information capacity of a channel for a given bandwidth is directly proportional to the frequency, the principle of light communications through fibre optics cable opens up information highways well beyond the radio spectrum.

The province of Saskatchewan has implemented one of the earliest and most ambitious fibre optics networks in the world. This system has been designed to network 56 communities and is capable of serving 190,000 households. SaskTel is laying 3/4-inch fibre cable that is composed of 12 fibres, each capable of transmitting at least 672 phone calls, 2 television channels, and 90 million bits of data per second. By multiplexing different colours of light, each strand could be capable of many times this capacity. Therefore, SaskTel's 'light highway' could conceivably transform Saskatchewan into the 'wired wonder of the West', especially if fibre optics technology can be effectively integrated with communications satellite technology (see Figure 2).

Figure 2: Satellite-fibre communications. In G.C. Bradley and E.L. Florence, *Long Haul fibre optics in the Western Canadian Plan* (SaskTel, 1981), p. 2.

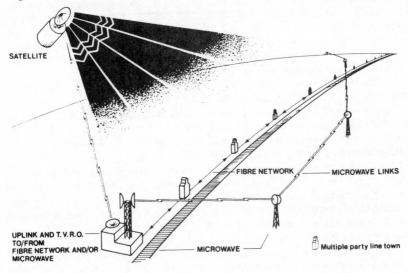

Communications satellites are positioned in geostationary orbits 35,867 kilometres above the equator so that their position remains constant in relation to the earth. They receive microwaves transmitted from an uplink on earth, amplify them and retransmit them to an earth receiving station. The device on the satellite which performs this task is called a transponder. Canadian communications satellites began with the launch in 1972 of Anik-A. Since then, many have been launched providing more than adequate space for present communications needs in Canada. The current Canadian satellites have up to 24 transponders, each capable of accommodating at least 36 MHz of bandwidth (see Table 1).

Table 1: Comparison of Canadian Satellites

	ANIK-A	HERMES (experimental)	ANIK-B	ANIK-C	ANIK-D
Frequency Band (GHz)	6/4	14/12	6/4 + 14/12	14/12	6/4
Number of RF Channels	12	2	12 + 6	16	24
Channel Bandwidth (MHz)	36	85	36 + 72	54	36
Number of Transponders (4 Spares)	12	1	12 + 4	20	24
Antenna Coverage	All Canada	2 Spot Beams (965 Km wide)	All Canada 4 Spot Beams	4 Spot Beams + Switching	All Canada
Power Output (watch)	5				
Design Life (yrs.)	7	200	10 + 20	15	11
Mission Life (minimum)	---	2	7	10	10
		4		8	8
Launch Dates (Series) (1)	Nov. 72	Jan. 76	Dec. 78	Apr. 84	Aug. 82
(2)	Apr. 73	---	---	Apr. 83	Oct. 85
(3)	May 75	---	---	Nov. 82	---
Orbit Location (1)	194° N	116° N	109° N	109° N	104° N
(2)	106.5°N			116° N	114° N
(3)	114° N				

Two types of transponders are in use in Canada, a low frequency (6/4 GHz) which has a foot-print or beam covering the entire country and a high frequency (14/12 GHz) which provides spot beams focused on four geographical areas of the country: west, west central, east central, and east. Low frequency transponders are very much like regular microwaves and are used in very much the same manner. High frequency transponders have opened satellite communications to individual users with their own small diameter receiving dish antennas. This form of message transfer is termed direct broadcasting satellite (DBS). DBS is of great interest to distance education because it is a direct electronic thoroughfare which cuts through the limitations of distance.

As a receiver-transmitter system for distance education and other message traffic, satellite transmission is not that different from microwave relay, but in terms of its position in space, satellite technology has certain advantages over microwave. First, from its vantage point in space, a satellite can retransmit signals to forty per cent of the earth's surface. Three satellites could cover the entire globe. Second, signals being transmitted to and from satellites are less subject to degradation in that the greatest portion of their journey is through a vacuum. Third, satellite communication does not require a number of relay stations to direct and amplify the signal, as in microwave relay.

A great deal of experimentation has occurred across Canada throughout the past decade in developing strategies for delivery of distance education programmes by satellite. Among these, the Knowledge Network of British Columbia, ACCESS Alberta, and TVOntario, have established major programmes delivering learning materials to all levels of education in each province and beyond.

THE UTILISATION OF TELEVISION IN DISTANCE EDUCATION

The scope and nature of strategies employed by distance educators is limited only by their imagination and available resources. The spectrum of use spans the gamut, from VHS videocassette to fully interactive satellite broadcasts; from local cable educational channels to computer based videodisc learning systems.

Carrier technology gets the message from location to location but often the time of reception is not convenient or conducive to learning. In this case other technologies employing storage-distribution systems are used to store or extend the television material. Each carrier-distribution-storage system has specific advantages and disadvantages in respect to its application to the learner or group of learners. Any account describing the parameters involved in selection and deployment of television in distance learning systems would require chapters of considerable length. A capsule account can be little else than a menu or listing.

In distance education learning systems, television is used to deliver instantaneous messages to the learner via commercial or educational broadcast stations, cable television companies, or direct broadcast satellite. The programme material may be delayed by storage on a videotape, videodisc or a digital storage device such as a computer disc. Videotape, videodisc and computer disc may also be employed as a method of direct physical distribution of learning material to the learner.

Specialised techniques of television utilisation may employ interactive strategies whereby the learner provides feedback to the teacher, either directly by telephone return or indirectly, by computer-based techniques. Specialised message creation systems combined with computer technology such as videotext, teletext and viewdata greatly extend the utilisation of television or television-like images in distance education. The Canadian version of interactive teletext and graphic communications is called Telidon.

Videotext uses a computer as a data base, telecommunications to carry the data and a modified television receiver to display it. The teletext form of videotext is broadcast as a part of a television signal. Pages of information which are stored on a computer are digitally integrated into the television scanning system in the vertical banking interval. The teletext material is conveyed simultaneously with a television picture and broadcast into a home receiver. A keypad and decoder enable the viewer to call up pages on the screen or superimposed over the regular television image. In the Viewdata version of videotext, users can connect directly to a computer and interact with it in the form of question, answer and search. Telidon has many advantages for distance education. It allows interaction to students and instructors with a database and it posses high quality colour graphics, as well as simulation functions. Furthermore, the creation or editing of Telidon pages is relatively simple.

Daniel *et al.* (1982) caps this brief discussion of television utilisation in distance education with the following comment describing 'telematics' as the amalgam of all these systems: 'As we move into the mid-1980s, it will be increasingly difficult to discuss an individual medium in isolation. Television, telephone, and computer are merging into a single technology called either *communications* or *telematics* depending on where one lives.' (p. 264)

CANADIAN APPLICATIONS OF TELEVISION FOR DISTANCE EDUCATION

The application of television to distance education in Canada has been affected by five distinct factors. First, geography has played a considerable role in defining signal patterns. A look at a map of Canada helps to explain why British Columbia's Knowledge Network and ACCESS Alberta are using direct broadcasting via the Anik-C satellite to beam educational programming to remote populations scattered throughout a terrain that discourages terrestrial systems. By the same token, it is understandable why the Atlantic Satellite Network evolved to serve the four Maritime provinces, whereas the flat plains of Saskatchewan offered an opportunity to install the longest fibre optics network in the world.

Second, the population patterns, to some extent, complement these geographical influences. For example, Ontario and Quebec hold the majority of Canada's population and the consequent economies of scale fostered earlier development as well as a greater diversity of systems than in other parts of Canada. That is partly why TVOntario is able to network a number of distance education interests in the province and broadcast their tele-courses using satellite or terrestrial systems, depending on the situation. The same is true for the level of educational programming in Quebec. A consortium consisting of thirteen educational institutions has quite recently evolved to form Télévision Educative du Québec (TVEQ). However, Télé-université has been developing distance education programmes and delivery systems in Quebec since 1974.

A third factor affecting the development of television for distance education is the availability of production and distribution facilities. As mentioned earlier, the recent progress of technology has allowed educators to get closer to the medium. Past practices of equipping large production houses to serve mass requirements have dissolved into lighter systems which permit local initiatives. Although these may not be as sophisticated in production technique, they can be just as effective in serving the learner's needs. In Canada, a country which has produced some of the most outstanding telecommunications research and applications in the world, the distribution system often leads the other elements of a distance education programme. Therein lies the greatest danger for distance education in Canada: the temptation is to allow technology to upstage the learner in directing the delivery and components of the programme.

Related to this factor is a fourth factor affecting Canadian applications of television for distance education: the role of telecommunications experiments for distance education in Canada. Since 1972, the federal department of communications has been active in sponsoring trials across Canada using various telecommunications systems for education. One specific thrust grew out of the space industry and the department supported a number of projects in direct broadcasting via satellite. During the peak of this experimental period many questions were asked about 'experimenting forever' and the future implications of these highly subsidised experiments for educational programmes which necessarily required a longer-term financial commitment. Today, some of the results of those experiments are manifested by such examples as Knowledge Network, ACCESS Alberta, and TVOntario's Northern Service, which have all moved from experimental, subsidised status to the role of paying customer. To what extent these organisations are subsidised by other provincial or federal government departments is dependent on the particular organisation.

The fifth factor affecting the use of television for distance education in Canada is the most elusive because it pertains to the present and historical roles of Canadian politics in all of its complexity. The growth of television in education occurred simultaneously with federal-provincial negotiations regarding the constitution and its repatriation. Agents who sought to engage broadcasting to education acted against a backdrop of federal-provincial bickering, a situation which from a certain perspective could be compared to attempting a betrothal between Romeo and Juliet. The results of this political situation had varying effects. In the opinion of certain educational planners, political wrangling retarded the progress of television in Canadian education. Also, certain telecommunications systems can be obliquely connected to policy issues of the mid-1970s. Technological progress is not the sole reason that Saskatchewan's broadband fibre optics network is a closed-circuit communications system for the province and does not impinge on any federal broadcasting regulations. It is also noteworthy that Knowledge Network and TVOntario received at least a year of subsidised experimental space segment time, while Manitoba shared TVOntario's signal and Saskatchewan only applied for and received sixty hours of satellite time. Certainly the previously identified factors of geography and population played a role in these circumstances, not to mention the viability and organisational support of these projects. However, it would also be incomplete to overlook the role that politics has played in these initiatives.

Paper 5 (Burge *et al*. 1984) of TVOntario's series entitled *New Technologies in Canadian Education* identifies a large number of educational institutions in Canada that are presently using television for distance education and the various ways it is being applied. This research helps to illustrate the following summary of applications.

On the east coast, Mount St Vincent Distance University Education via Television (DUET) is beaming credit and non-credit courses to the four Atlantic provinces, via satellite, microwave and cable. The University of New Brunswick is also providing credit and non-degree telecourses to distant learners via cable television. Memorial University in Newfoundland is one of the longest-running examples of using television for distance education. In 1961 it began broadcasting credit courses via television and in 1969, it also began to distribute them on videotape. Since 1974, the Extension Service of

Memorial University has been using television in community development. Remote communities make videotape programmes about local issues and bring them to the attention of government as well as the rest of the province. The resulting videotapes are also used to stimulate meetings, seminars and conferences.

In Quebec, TVEQ provides interactive television for all members of the Université du Québec network as well as three other universities, a CEGEP and two business schools. It offers both credit and non-credit programming on cable television networks throughout the province. In Montreal and Quebec City an entire channel is devoted to these programmes whereas in other communities, a channel is designated four to five hours a day for this purpose.

In Ontario, TVOntario networks a consortium of universities who co-operate in the production and development of telecourses, as well as help to share the costs. In addition, institutions such as Wilfrid Laurier and Carleton Universities are highly committed to using television as a primary mode of delivery for distance education. Carleton notes however that it does not consider courses such as graduate seminars can be effectively conveyed via television.

In Manitoba, Assiniboine College at Brandon has been offering a credit course in business management via cable television in 17 towns in Manitoba. In Saskatchewan, the University of Regina is offering four credit courses to five locations via televised lectures which are distributed from Regina on the fibre optics network. The University of Saskatchewan in Saskatoon is planning its third satellite project entitled Uplink '86. This initiative is a continuation of two previous trials, Uplink '83 and Uplink '84, in which credit and non-credit programmes were beamed via the Anik-B and C satellites to the four western provinces. Because the University of Saskatchewan is the home of the Western College of Veterinary Medicine, it has a mandate to provide continuing professional education to veterinarians across western Canada.

In Alberta, ACCESS has been broadcasting 84 hours of educational programming per week on Anik-C(3) since January 1985. Athabasca University is making use of some of this air time to broadcast television programmes which support a certain number of its credit courses, and the Universities of Calgary and Alberta are also co-operating with ACCESS to provide a few telecourses for distance education in outlying regions.

The Knowledge Network in British Columbia has been broadcasting television for distance education via satellite since its inauguration in January 1981. During its developmental period, it has been successful in attracting the participation of the major provincial educational institutions. The University of Victoria has broadcast a number of courses such as public affairs, educational administration and professional development for registered nurses. The Open Learning Institute uses the network to beam telecourses to support its distance learning packages. The University of British Columbia and Simon Fraser University, as well as community colleges and the technical institutes, are also linked into the network and have used its television facility for various distance educational needs.

The TVOntario Series (Burge *et al.* 1984) acknowledges that the diversity offered by broadcast television and videotape for programme presentation and delivery has transformed this medium into an accepted vehicle for distance education in Canada. However, the study is also realistic about the associated drawbacks of this technology: 'The major problems with the use of television and videotapes and their delivery technologies (such as cable and satellites) are the cost and access to production and distribution resources. And, as with other technologies, there is a recognition that television and videotapes are suitable only for some types of teaching and learning styles.' (Paper 5, p. 29) This statement thus reiterates the earlier observation that there is no simple solution or recipe for the successful distribution of distance education. Each situation must be evaluated in its own context, beginning with the educational need.

TELEVISION AND THE NEED FOR INTERACTION

Combining the unique characteristics of the television programme with the organisational and management capabilites of the computer has produced an exciting new learning system. Videodisc development appears to be one enabling technology in this new media mix which holds great future promise. Because it provides a rapid, random access to any sequence or still frame in the television programme, this technology appears to reduce or remove the adoption barrier which has held back the widespread development of this type of instructional strategy.

Schwier (1985) in the introductory statements to a textbook nearing publication, deals with interactive video succinctly:

Interactive video is a recent development in instructional technology, merging the popular extant technologies of computers and television. Instructional television has suffered pedagogic criticism because programming most often lacks strategies for involving learners actively in the content, but has long been recognised as a powerful tool for 'bringing the real world into the classroom.' Like so many of the promising young students it is designed to instruct, it has never quite lived up to its potential. Computer assisted instruction, usually based upon modular branching paradigms familiar in print-based programmed learning materials, successfully involves the students actively in the instruction, but due to inherent limitations, lacks realistic illustrative capacity and the immediacy of television. By marrying these technologies, an instructional developer has the capability of exploiting the strengths of each, resulting in a hybrid technology which can provide the structure and involvement of computer assisted instruction and the realism of television. (p. 1)

Training for industry and the military has exploited interactive video throughout the past decade. High front-end cost and more than a little distrust of yet another new learning medium has prevented the transfer of this large-scale research and development activity to the educational sector. Low-cost microcomputers which interface with equally low cost videotape and videodisc players have rejuvenated interest in interactive video by the academic community. Systems available today exhibit various instructional and economic strengths and weaknesses, but each configuration depends upon well-designed and produced video and computer components for the success of the instructional product.

In the past, hardware was a formidable obstacle to early development of interactive video, but costs have rapidly fallen due to technological developments, competition and mass production. Software and production costs have not enjoyed a similar reduction because of the labour-intensive planning, production, and post-production phases involved in the development of high quality programmes.

Describing interactive video Schwier (1985) comments:

Interactive video production is characterized by a series of modules, or segments, constructed in such a way as to promote efficient access to other segments based upon the branching architecture of computer assisted instruction. Successful modular television design is contingent upon the quality of post-production; that is, constructing, organising and enhancing the television material following its production. In traditional television production, this is primarily the function of editing. In interactive video, editing is nestled among a larger array of post production activities. Post-production for interactive video includes making decisions about learner involvement, ordering and reordering instructional components, constructing remedial strategies, and building a solid, yet flexible instructional context. (p. 2)

In Canada educators have not invested to any significant degree in videotape-based interactive video. Videodisc technology with its markedly faster random access of still or motion sequences seem to have caught the imagination of Canadian educators. Videodiscs have been produced and are in various stages of production from coast-to-coast. Early adopters of interactive video technology based upon videodiscs include in a non-exhaustive listing: Simon Fraser University, ACCESS Alberta, University of Alberta, University of Saskatchewan, Ontario Institute for Studies in Education, Sheridan College, National Library of Canada, and consortia such as the Goldcoin group in Kitchener, Ontario.

Real excitement exists among users of interactive videodisc concerning possibilities for instructional application at all levels of education. Several presentations at AMTEC 85, the annual conference of the Association of Media and Technology in Education in Canada held in Calgary, underlined the optimistic feeling educators hold for this advancing technology. Distance education among other applications stands to derive major benefits from interactive video. A production workshop presented by the Faculty of Education Instruction Technology Center, at the University of Alberta during the summer of 1985 dealt with 'The Design and Production of Interactive Videodiscs'. This workshop highlighted the facility of videodisc to merge high quality video with computer control so that the user can decide which material will be viewed, in what order, and at what speed. The following comment is an excerpt from a descriptive brochure on the workshop and capsulises the bright future for this medium:

Interactive laserdisc technology is making major inroads into many areas of education and training. Its rapid search, freeze frame potential, and high video quality lend themselves to a variety of situations involving teaching and learning. Since it is readily interfaced with existing microcomputers, the potential exists for startling new and effective approaches to learning and information retrieval. For sophisticated analysis in research, or for training and instructional use, this new technology is being applied in medicine, sociology, education, space sciences, biology, physics ... every field of human endeavour. (p. 1)

Interactive communication across a distance between three or more individuals or groups in two or more locations utilising one or more forms of education telecommunications media is generically termed 'teleconference'. Generally teleconferencing encompasses audio conferencing, video conferencing and computer conferencing. Either separately or in combination, these comprise the best known formats to conduct electronic meetings.

Audio conferencing is a logical extension of a telephone conversation between two individuals. Addition of a video image in real-time or slow-scan where the television image is built up over a period of time enhances the simulation of face-to-face communication. Computer conferencing or networking is text based linking individuals computer terminal to computer terminal. The link is commonly the regular telephone line and interactivity is not usually in real-time. Each type of conferencing has definite strengths and weaknesses and the process becomes more effective in combination of each type.

Cost is one major factor which often determines the type of network and form in which the teleconference is held. Two varieties of transmission network links are used for teleconferencing in Canada. The regular telephone network, utilising an electronic bridge to convene or join three or more telephone lines is the least expensive type. Dedicated networks such as telephone lines, cable systems, or satellite channels are considerably more expensive to utilise and maintain over time.

Incorporation of the television image either by linking two or more video screens or by sending regular television programming ahead of time by videotape is generally felt to be a more effective mode of communication than by audio conference alone. Teleteaching is the term coined to represent teleconferencing strategies in education. Teleteaching is the transfer of educational information via one or more forms of telecommunications media to students located at several remote sites. Television figures prominently in the 'distance education' form of teleteaching. The television image in video conferencing is very effective when a visual component is called for by the educational task. Television in its common forms, such as direct transmission, videotapes, or videodisc, are important adjuncts to teleconferencing in delivering an educational programme over distance. In many cases economy is achieved by inserting pre-packaged programme material into the teleconference. In that way, the cost of high quality production for these events can be amortised over a number of sessions.

Television combined with teleconferencing produces a powerful vehicle for the delivery of distance education and Canada has been exploring a rich variety of strategies to capitalise on its potential. Specific examples can be found in every geographic area in Canada and educational literature is available regarding the numerous applications of teleconferencing in distance education situations.

THE IMPLICATIONS OF COST

Cost associated with television used in conjunction with distance education is a kaleidoscope of contrast. The cost of delivery varies from a few cents postage for mailing a videocassette to a considerably higher expenditure for channels on a satellite, which can be measured in terms of hundreds of thousands of dollars per year. Similar contrasts are evident in personnel expertise and cost of production. The low end may find a content specialist preparing video material with a self-contained camera/video recorder combination costing $1,500. At the high end, twenty production specialists may be required to develop video messages using a production facility costing millions of dollars. The line of demarcation between profession-al/novice and adequate/inadequate production practices and their associated costs is definitely blurred.

In Canada it appears that the cost of television for distance education is a widely fluctuating variable and that cost is not always proportional to programme effectiveness. Canada's geographical expanse and the singular characteristics of its regions, not to mention the uniqueness of the federal-provincial political framework which supports both education and communica-tions, prescribes that future developments in these areas must necessarily occur in response to special problems and opportunities of the individual regions. No single formula will satisfy the entire nation, but leaders in these fields must work to co-ordinate and promote their regional activities in order to benefit from each other's diverse endeavours and experience.

REFERENCES

Bates, Tony (1982) 'Trends in the Use of A/V Media in Distance Education Systems Around the World', Paper presented for the International Council for Correspondence Education's 12th World Conference, Vancouver, Canada. Published in *Learning at a Distance: A World Perspective*, J.S. Daniel, M.A. Stroud, and J.R. Thompson (eds.)

Bates, Tony (1984) *Broadcasting in Education: An Evaluation*, London: Constable

Bradley, G.C. and E.L. Florence (1981) *Long haul fibre optics in the western Canadian plain*, Regina: SaskTel

Burge, Elizabeth J., Joy Wilson, and Audrey Mehler (1984) 'Communications and Information technologies and distance Education in Canada', Paper 5 in the series *New Technologies in Canadian Education*, published by TVOntario Office of Development Research, Toronto, August

Daniel, J.S. and M.A. Stroud (1980) *Distance education: The lessons of a decade*, Paper presented at the annual meeting of the American Society for Engineering Education, (Pacific Northwest Section), 'Teaching and the new technologies.'

Daniel, J.S., M.A. Stroud, and J.R. Thompson (eds.), *Learning at a distance: A world perspective*, Edmonton: Athabasca University/International Council for Correspondence Education

Faculty of Education (1985) 'The Design and Production of Interactive Laser Videodiscs', Brochure describing Summer Workshop 3-7 June 1985 at the University of Alberta

Fortosky, Danielle M. (1983) 'Distance Education and Communications Technology at the University of Saskatchewan: Options for the Future', Unpublished Master's thesis, University of Saskatchewan, Saskatoon, Canada

MacLean, R. (1968) *Television in Education*, London: Methuen Educational Ltd.

Pichette, Michel (1985) 'New Directions in Continuing Education: What are the Stakes in Today's "New Technological Revolution"?', Paper delivered at the Symposium of Learning in Society, Ottawa, Canada, May 1983. Published in Occasional Paper 51 *Learning in Society: Toward a New Paradigm*, Canadian Commission for UNESCO, Mariette Hogue and Carmelia Quinn (eds.), Ottawa, May

Schimeck, Wolfgang (1982) 'Television in distance education', J.S. Daniel *et al.* (eds.), *Learning at a distance: a world perspective*, Edmonton: Athabasca University

Schramm, W. (1974) *Men, Messages, and Media: A Look at Human Communication*, New York, Harper and Row

Schwier, Richard A. (1985) *Demystifying Interactive Video*, Unpublished manuscript, College of Education, University of Saskatchewan, Saskatoon, Canada

Scupham, John (1975) 'The Open University of the United Kingdom', in *Open Learning*, the UNESCO Press

Stevenson, Jim (1979) *General applicability of the principles of Open University broadcasting to other university level distance - teaching systems*, Paper 56 presented at 'The Open University Conference on Education of Adults at a Distance', Birmingham, England, 18-24 November

Use of Audio Teleconferencing

William Robertson

Telephone technology is rapidly becoming an indispensable tool for distance education programmers. During the 1980s, audio teleconferencing using the regular telephone networks grew from an occasional experimental delivery method in distance education to a routine part of the delivery strategies of institutions throughout Canada and many other parts of the world. Programmers found that they could reduce communication costs and improve the quality of service to external learners without compromising the academic integrity of their programmes. The flexibility and low capital and operating costs of audio teleconferencing make it of special interest to institutions serving students who live in small, widely separated communities.

Recent surveys (Knowles 1984) suggest that the trend is accelerating. The interest in using audio and related visual data that can be transmitted over regular telephone lines appears to be related to the growth of distance education as a legitimate institutional activity. Another significant factor stems from the deliberate attempts of the Canadian Department of Communications to stimulate interest in communications technology in general. Between 1975 and 1982, the department sponsored a series of educational telecommunications experiments on the Canadian domestic satellites, Hermes and Anik-B, and developed and actively promoted their Telidon videotex system. Following the experimental period and the withdrawal of temporary equipment, distance education programmers experimented with audio teleconferencing and found it to be a very acceptable and affordable substitute for the high profile satellite-delivered television.

Over the past four years, users in colleges, institutes, and universities have moved from one or two experiments per year to regularly scheduled courses being delivered through private or public teleconferencing networks. During the 1984 International Symposium on Teleconferencing, evidence for strong educational support of audio teleconferencing became apparent through the papers presented. Key points were:

1. Most of the potential students are widely scattered among communities that are commonly several hundred miles apart and each centre may have less than ten students in a given course or programme;
2. The costs for starting and operating an audio teleconferencing system are relatively low in comparison with other available methods of serving remote students;
3. The technology is readily available and is familiar to instructors and students;
4. The systems used can be adjusted quickly to serve large or small groups;

5. The mode of instruction is similar to that of a seminar with the instructor being in charge of the discussion and able to stimulate multi-location interaction;

6. Scheduling adjustments can be made almost as readily as for on-campus classrooms;

7. Access to the instruction or programmes can be controlled through a limited number of off-campus centres;

8. The quality of the instructional materials is often improved because of a need for careful and early preparation;

9. Immediate cost benefits can be shown;

10. Properly organised, it has the potential for generating operating profits; and

11. Very useful working relationships can be developed with community groups having dispersed memberships.

TECHNICAL DESCRIPTION

Teleconferencing is the bringing together by electronic means of three or more people in two or more locations to share discussion or information. In common use, the term is limited to audio teleconferencing alone or in combination with other communications sources ('audio plus'). Typical supplemental or specialised teleconferencing techniques include the use of two-way and one-way video, both full motion and slow scan, electronic blackboards, facsimile, computer graphics, radio, satellites, and videotex. However, the most essential part of all the forms of teleconferencing is good quality audio. Without good audio, teleconferencing loses its main strength which is the immediate interaction of the participants for information exchange. Except for special applications, the visual portions of teleconferencing, such as in multi-point video conferences, have been judged by established users to contribute relatively little additional essential information over what would have been provided by a carefully prepared audio teleconference, and the very large costs of the video component cannot be justified. Audio teleconferencing alone or supplemented with appropriate telephone line-carried graphics is the current choice of most users because it is effective and cost efficient.

Audio teleconferencing requires a multi-telephone line electronic switch or interconnection device called a bridge to which the user can attach a wide variety of telephone and data transmission devices. The normal limitation is one device per line connected into the bridge. Typical types of audio equipment used with the bridge are regular telephone handsets, speakerphones, headsets, radiotelephones, and microphone-speaker units often called convenors. While it is possible to connect computers and other types of non-audio information transmission devices into the same bridging system as the audio equipment, there are usually operating problems. Until recently, audio and data had to be carried on separate telephone lines, doubling the cost of all telephone line charges and bridge rentals. The University of Calgary passed data and audio sequentially on the same telephone lines during a series of course delivery experiments in 1983 and 1984. The switching between audio and data and back again was done by hand at each centre on a visual and audio cue. The results were mixed, with some people missing the cue and having to request a second data transmission. They have since developed a relatively low cost switch that automatically detects and routes any data signal to the appropriate output device. Recently, a corporation in the United States developed a simple device for carrying both audio and data signals on a single telephone line. Tests of the equipment are being carried out in 1985 and 1986 in Southern Australia. Preliminary results indicate little difficulty in multiplexing audio and data signals.

Audio teleconferencing uses regular telephone lines provided by local public telephone companies. The general experience in Canada is that the quality of standard business or household telephone lines is good enough that virtually any available line can be used. Most sources of noise have been found to be in exchanges and the most noisy connections have been those in large metropolitan areas where a call is often routed through a series of exchanges. Normal operating procedure is for the bridge operator or the callers to listen for line noise when the connection is first made and to reconnect before the teleconference begins if the background noise is judged to be unacceptable. During teleconferences lasting several hours, line noise can often appear spontaneously on one or more lines. The only effective solution is to reconnect the problem line, hoping to obtain a cleaner path through the public network system. Some organisations with large teleconfrencing schedules and relatively short distances to cover, such as Memorial University, Acadia University, the University of Wisconsin and the University of Washington, have purchased or leased dedicated lines hoping to improve the line quality or to reduce their annual long distance charges.

Teleconferencing can originate from almost any reasonably quiet environment, although long-term users normally acoustically treat dedicated rooms to reduce overall noise in the system and to draw attention to the service availability. Occasional users normally purchase their services from the local telephone company, teleconferencing consultants, or a major user that is willing to sell available time on its system. Vendors normally sell time on their equipment by the minute along with some form of per line surcharge. Any specialised terminal equipment is usually rented by the week or month. Training in the use of equipment and in making efficient use of the teleconference is not normally supplied. Consultants, however, commonly provide a range of services including all necessary equipment, long distance toll charges, and user training. Heavy users of teleconferencing normally buy their own bridges which can be connected into private telephone exchanges or directly onto additional business lines that by-pass the exchange. Serious users will select dedicated rooms that have a height to width to length ratio of approximately 1 to 1.5 to 2.5. In addition, the walls may be adjusted so that they are no longer parallel or at right angles. The walls should be covered with sound absorbing materials but the ceiling and floor left somewhat hard. (Botros 1984) New microphone and telephone terminal designs can provide for generally hands-free operation with excellent sound quality.

An excellent summary of teleconferencing equipment types and uses is provided in the Ontario Educational Communications Authority 1984 Paper on Educational Teleconferencing in Canada. In brief, some of the key elements regarding various components of teleconferencing systems:

1. *Bridges:* The heart of any teleconferencing system is the electronic switch or connection point that allows many information circuits to be connected so that each circuit or line has equal access to the inform-

ation in the system. In common terminology, a large party line is set up so that everyone on the line can hear and be heard or see if visual data are included. Typical bridges can be controlled by operators or one of the callers who has been given the necessary passwords and operating codes. Bridges usually have ten to twenty 'ports' or connection points to which the owner has connected an equal number of telephone lines. It is usual to have the lines set up with one or two numbers with an 'over lining' function so that callers will automatically be shifted to the next open line on the bridge without having to call through a series of numbers looking for an open line.

Two important functions of bridges are to control the level of audio coming in from each line, reducing high levels and raising faint signals, and to control the flow of information so that only one message is in the system at one time. Typical bridges can range from complex pieces of equipment about the size of a four-drawer filing cabinet to simpler designs about the size of a small microwave oven.

2. *Audio Input Devices:* The most common device that is connected to bridges during educational audio teleconferences is some form of portable microphone and speaker-amplifier system. The Darome Corporation produces the unit that is widely available and their trade name, Convenor, has become the most common name of most similar units. These units vary in appearance but usually consist of a small box containing an amplifier, a speaker, and a small amount of related electronics, and a series of microphones connected to the amplifier box. The microphones normally have some type of press-to-talk switch to help control the audio traffic. For large groups, the microphones can often be extended with extra audio cables or additional microphones can be added to form a long chain. Since only one microphone can be used at a given time, the additional units do not affect the quality of the signal. Convenor-type units are normally used for groups up to twenty or thirty. For larger groups it is necessary to connect into a local public address system.

Other common telephone devices are the common handset and speaker telephones. Handsets are the most common choice for short, small group teleconferences. Depending on the characteristics of the bridge used and the size and familiarity of the group, handsets can be used to give a very easy, freeflowing feeling to the discussion that is not always possible with press-to-talk microphones. The largest disadvantage is that the number of people who can participate is limited to the number of lines on the bridge. Speakerphones are often selected when the group at a given location will be less than about eight to ten. Unless the unit has a switch that can turn off the microphone, there is a tendency for extraneous noise to be picked up by the unit's microphone and transmitted into the system.

3. *Electronic Blackboards:* An electronic blackboard looks like a regular blackboard except that its surface is somewhat flexible. When a user writes on the surface with chalk or some other erasable material, the pressure of the chalk is sensed by a grid behind the flexible surface and an electrical signal is sent to any television sets connected to the blackboard. Because the grid is quite fine and virtually every place on

the blackboard surface is represented by a point on the grid, anything drawn on the surface can be reproduced on the television screens. Each television unit has a device for storing the signals from the blackboard so that a complete image rather than a moving dot is presented on the screen. If the blackboard is connected into a bridge, any television unit with the memory function can receive the signal simultaneously. Until data and voice could be handled on the same line, it was necessary to have two lines through the bridge to each centre. Even now, the dual line system is commonplace and is a restricting factor in adding visuals to audio systems. Two-way communication is possible if both locations are equipped with blackboards and suitable monitors.

4. *Slow Scan Television:* Slow scan television is the transmission of a series of still video images at a rate varying from about one per ten or thirty seconds. The system uses a standard television camera, usually black and white, to produce a picture that is captured and electronically dissected. A string of signals representing each point on the screen is sent to each of the receiving units which is also capable of storing the image. As the image is received, it appears on the monitor screen line by line until a complete picture is sent. While slow scan does permit the sending of spontaneously generated graphics to each classroom, the lack of motion and high cost of the equipment has limited its use. Like the electronic blackboard, the data are normally sent over a second telephone line.

5. *Compressed Video:* A relatively new technique that has potential for educational teleconferencing if the price of the equipment drops significantly is video compression. Each image produced by a video camera is quickly analysed and compared with the previous image to identify those parts of the image that have changed. Only the changes are sent to the monitor which has a storage device that uses the new information to update the image held in storage. In this way, as long as the amount of motion in the image is small it is possible to send all the required data over regular phone lines. If too much change is generated by motion in the image, the system cannot handle all the data and the received picture tears and breaks up until the amount of motion is reduced.

6. *Facsimile:* Facsimile transmission of graphics has been used by the business community for many years as a simple and relatively inexpensive method for sending almost any type of document to another location by telephone. The document is scanned electronically at the sending location to detect where dark spots appear on the page. At the receiving location, those dark spots are reproduced and the graphic is regenerated. When the scanning is slow enough and the scan line is narrow enough, high resolution is possible. The problem with earlier experiments with teleconferencing and facsimile, is that the receiving machine had to receive a 'ready to transmit' signal and then return a 'ready to receive' signal to the sending unit. With many units in the system, conflicting signals were sent. Although the problem has been solved, the cost of machines has generally been outside the budgets of educational institutions. For point-to-point teleconferencing, facsimile is

an excellent extra feature.

7. *Computer Graphics:* All forms of computer graphics including those produced by the Telidon videotex system can be transmitted over telephone lines and through teleconferencing bridges. The only limitation will be compatibility of the equipment in the system. With the wide availability of computers and the new voice and data multiplexing equipment, computer graphics should start appearing with greater frequency in teleconferencing.

8. *Other Devices:* There is no theoretical limitation to the type of equipment that is used along with the audio signal in a teleconference as long as the equipment produces signals that can be sent over a telephone wire, there is some form of receiving equipment that can produce an understandable product or signal, and the original signal can be sent to many locations at the same time (broadcast). Practical concerns of cost or transmission time may eliminate some possibilities.

CURRENT CANADIAN USE

In a national survey conducted in 1983 (Knowles 1984), forty Canadian tertiary education institutions indicated they were using or planning to use audio teleconferencing in their programming, primarily for continuing professional education. The most common reasons given for their interest were to cut travel costs and to improve services to small groups in remote areas. In particular, the problems of travelling during winter were seen as being decreased by an increased use of telecommunications. Resistance of faculty to using telephones for instruction was not considered to be a likely deterrent for those who were planning new use, and those who had experience had found that faculty and students quickly became comfortable with audio teleconferencing systems. During the 1983-4 academic year, an informal consortium of the British Columbia Institute of Technology (BCIT), the Open Learning Institute (OLI), Simon Fraser University (SFU), the University of Victoria (UVIC), and the University of British Columbia (UBC) used audio teleconferencing to provide 467 hours of instruction to aproximately 3,800 students. (Robertson *et al.* 1984) The Ontario government used teleconferencing to reduce travel costs and managerial time in an experiment conducted between 1979 and 1982. Over an 18-month period in 1979-80, the Ontario ministry of transportation and communications saved $49,000 in travel and 2,078 hours of managerial time. (Cukier 1984) In a further 26 months, the ministry of the environment saved an average of $2,000 per month in travel and time. The level of satisfaction of the government users with audio teleconferencing was generally very high. In 1983, the Bank of Montreal began using audio teleconferencing for a wide range of administrative business and quickly demonstrated travel and time savings. More important, they discovered they were able to improve communications and produce more informed decisions. (McGibbon 1984)

Other major users of audio teleconferencing in credit and non-credit programmes have been the University of Calgary which added Telidon graphics in teaching four education courses in grammar education and classroom management. Thirty centres are reached with a wide variety of programmes. Memorial University began experiments in teleconferencing in 1977 and has developed its own dedicated system. Their use of teleconferencing is the most extensive in Canada and includes selected videotapes in courses such as Shakespearean Literature. The University of Ottawa is the only centre using electronic blackboards to supplement audio teleconferencing. There service is of special interest because it involves partnerships with business and industry in supplying specialised courses to industrial students if the firms provide the necessary equipment.

An extensive summary of the educational activity in Canada is provided in the Ontario Educational Communications Authority Paper on educational teleconferencing. They report four institutions using teleconferencing in British Columbia, nine in Alberta, three in Saskatchewan, two in Manitoba, three in Ontario, one in Quebec, one in Prince Edward Island, three in New Brunswick, four in Nova Scotia, and one in Newfoundland.

Of special interest is the interprovincial system centred on Mount St Vincent University in Halifax. Their Distant University Education via Television (DUET) uses one-way video to supplement audio teleconferencing that links centres in Nova Scotia, Prince Edward Island, Newfoundland, and New Brunswick. Benefits usually identified by users are: travel cost savings; time savings; reduced staff stress; quicker and more informed decisions; increased programming to remote sites; new services provided to small class groups; reduced costs per student hour for external students; improved planning and preparation of course materials; improved communication skills in presenters; improved relations with professional societies and community groups; and increased revenues from course tuition.

OPERATING MODELS

Potential users of audio teleconferencing should not consider it simply as a money-saving replacement for some of their current activities. It is true that audio teleconferencing is a technique that organisations with a dispersed membership or operating centres can quickly employ to reduce their overall operating costs. To gain the maximum benefits from audio teleconferencing most users have had to modify to varying degrees how they prepare and handle the activity that is conducted over the telephone. In particular, educational users should think of audio teleconferencing only as a portion of an integrated learning system. The key elements of that system are: the instructor; the students' printed instructional materials; visuals, including photographic slides, overhead transparencies, film and video; site co-ordinators and/or teaching assistants; and audio teleconferencing equipment.

It is a mistake to assume that if a good audio teleconferencing system is provided all the other elements of the learning system can be transferred directly from the conventional classroom or external studies systems. Some short but specialised instruction is required for most instructors and students, and class handouts and print packages will have to be prepared more carefully and earlier than is normal for on-campus classroom instruction.

Some of the successful operating models are:

The Authoritative Presenter Model

The Continuing Legal Education Society of British Columbia provides professional development seminars several times a month for lawyers and legal profession workers. Approximately one-third of the presentations are by audio teleconference. A typical seminar lasts for one day and may involve a panel of four to eight people with a moderator. They are all selected because they are considered to be experts in the topic to be discussed. The group will have worked on a specific topic for several months and their papers are printed for distribution at the start of the seminar. The panel meets in a large hall capable of seating from 200 to 600 people. External students in up to eighteen remote sites are connected to the large group by a teleconferencing bridge and the public address system in the hall. The usual number of external students is between eight and fifty per site. Although it is possible for any of the people present to ask a question through a floor microphone and take part in the seminar, the size of the group and the nature of the topics tends to make the presentations very much one way. The major benefit is that the large group can generate many questions that grow directly out of the reference papers and the presentations and expansions of the panel. The society has generated over $30,000 in revenue in a single day on some of their seminars. Estimated costs for them on such a seminar are less than $10,000.

All their evaluations point to very high acceptance of teleconferencing as a method of bringing the seminar into communities that are a day or more away from the seminar origination point. Many respondents prefer the teleconference seminars to the in-person type because they can have a side discussion on the topic, formulate a group question, and then review the answer without disturbing the larger group. Some have made a social event of their seminar by bringing a special lunch and beer and wine to their meeting place which could be a private home, office or board room. In that way, they can take part in only that section of the seminar that interests them and conduct some local business during the remaining time.

The University of Calgary Model

The University of Calgary Teleconferencing Centre under Dr Barry Ellis has done extensive experimentation into modes of delivery by audio teleconferencing. They discovered that the students in remote locations felt disadvantaged in comparison with the on-campus students because the campus students could talk with the instructor before and after the class and they could use their presence in the classroom with the instructor to dominate the discussion. As a result of those findings, most of the university teleconference classes are now held with the on-campus class being placed in a separate room away from the instructor so that all students are reached through the teleconferencing system and the instructor cannot see any of them. This has placed all sites on an equal status and has required the instructor to depend on audio signals and questioning rather than visual signals for feedback from the students. The initial reactions from on-campus students were somewhat negative because they thought they were receiving poorer treatment than they would have had if they had been in a regular class. Later in the year, their evaluations ranged from little difference to preference when compared to regular class instruction. It has been suggested that the teleconference instructors' increased preparation and careful listening more than compensate for the lack of their presence in the classroom.

The University of Wisconsin Model

The relatively short distances among all the centres connected in the University of Wisconsin's private teleconferencing system allow instructors to visit each class in rotation. Since all points in an audio teleconferencing system are equivalent as far as being capable of initiating a teleconference, the instructor is able to be with each group in the class at some time during the course of the term. All students can then benefit to the same extent from the private and extended discussions with their instructor that is normally reserved only for the on-campus students. This is a good instructional model but heavily dependent on reasonable travelling distances.

The British Columbia Instructional Model

The usual audio teleconferencing instructional model used by British Columbia tertiary education institutions is to have a small number of students in a teleconference room along with the instructor. Up to eighteen external sites are connected into the electronic classroom network with an operator controlled bridge, usually at BCIT. Each external site has some type of co-ordinator or teaching assistant who is responsible for all the on-site administrative details such as room equipment, materials distribution and collection, message passing, and, in some cases, local advertising and course promotion.

Courses that are put on by or directed to professional groups such as dentists, accountants, nurses, or community associations such as the YWCA or Outdoor Recreation Council, are planned and delivered in co-operation with the local members of those groups. As soon as an interest is expressed or a potential course is planned, contact is made with the representative central body to involve them from the outset in deciding which are the appropriate external sites, what emphasis or topics should be in the course, who can assist in building up local interest, and when the programme should be presented. It is common for some type of cost and revenue sharing to be agreed. In the programmes organised by the BCIT Distance Education department, one objective was to show such organisations that the teleconferencing system was a multi-point communication system that could be used by anyone who had a telephone, to reach a limited number of other people anywhere within reach of the telephone system. We found that users quickly thought of other uses for the system, and some started planning for events that originated in sites that most thought of as being very remote and having some of the 'external students' located in major urban centres. Others brought special guest lecturers to the class for an hour or so by using the international long distance telephone system.

COSTS

The costs for starting a university or college-based private audio teleconferencing system are not large if the local telephone system has relatively quiet lines, is readily accessible, and has acceptable local and long distance rates. There may be some legal or regulatory prohibitions that will prevent organisations from owning or connecting private equipment into the phone system. For those who can own and connect, the initial capital costs in Canadian dollars will be approximately:

Teleconference bridge, 20 line	$35,000 to $80,000
Portable microphone speaker set	$800 to $1,500
Speakerphones	$150 to $400
Miscellaneous cable and equipment	$800 to $2,000

In addition, some form of permanent location is needed for the bridge and, if possible, a mini-classroom immediately beside the bridge area. If acoustic treatment is considered, costs can be as low as several hundred dollars or as high as tens of thousands. An effective centre was created at BCIT in a portable building of about 500 square feet with an approximately $2,500 expenditure. That provided for a combination office and bridge operating centre and a ten-person seminar room equipped as the teleconference origination site.

A typical system consists of a ten or twenty line bridge, eight to twelve portable microphone speaker sets, ten or more speakerphones with a 'mute' switch for their microphones, and a box of cable, in-line amplifiers and connectors for setting up in local halls or hotel conference rooms.

Operating costs are dependent on local telephone rates and salaries and the following figures may not have much relevance for many jurisdictions. However, for guidance, the following is a typical planning budget an evening professional continuing education programme handled by BCIT:

COMMUNITY	REGISTRANTS
Vancouver - BCIT Site	16
Kamloops	12
Prince George	10
Fort Nelson	6
Kitimat	9
Fernie	8
Tofino	5
Merritt	7
Hope	6
Castlegar	13
	--
Total registrations	92

Programme duration	2 hours/session for 6 sessions
Course fee	$60
Long distance charges ($3.36/min total)	$2,520
Production of print packages	$85
Bridge time	$840
Instructional costs	$600
Terminal equipment transportation costs	$320
Projected costs	$4,365
Number of registrations to cost recovery	73
Projected cost per student contact hour	$3.95

In comparison, to deliver the same type of seminar to the same centres with a travelling instructor, the estimated cost for a twelve-hour seminar over one and a half days is $8,475 and the staff travelling time is a conservative 65 hours.

OBSERVATIONS

1. The most effective use of audio teleconferencing has been in professional continuing education and some of the least effective has been with introductory courses. The considered opinion is information that is additional to a solid theoretical or practical base among a group known to have similar experiences is much easier to communicate by teleconference than new materials to a mixed group. While this is probably also true in a regular classroom, the absence of visual cues can reduce the instructor's ability to recognise communication problems particularly when dealing with a mixed group that is not familiar to the instructor.

2. Initial instructor and student resistance to audio teleconferencing is very common but becomes insignificant after three to four exposures providing there are minimal technical problems.

3. Audio teleconferencing equipment can be very reliable. Most problems can be attributed to human error or poorly maintained phone lines. In three years of operating a bridge at BCIT there was only one major failure and that was caused by a local power outage.

4. All the institutional, government, and corporate surveys of the past few years related to the use of audio teleconferencing in Canada confirm that it is an effective, cost-efficient communication technique.

5. Many experienced teachers and other professional people who are used to dealing with the public do not believe that some form of practice or training is needed before they will be effective users of the technology.

6. There are very few topics that, with some imagination, cannot be taught by audio teleconferencing.

7. More than 86 per cent of users of audio teleconferencing systems who have experienced more than four or five sessions, rate their experience as good to excellent.

SUMMARY

1. Audio teleconferencing is a very cost efficient and educationally effective technique for providing or supplementing programmes for external students.

2. Audio teleconferencing is within the reach of almost any tertiary education institution. The technology is relatively simple and easy to maintain, and the costs are modest in comparison with other communication systems.

3. There are operating techniques unique to audio teleconferencing that must be mastered by both the instructor and the students before effective use can be made of the system capabilities.

4. Institutions that are considering a variety of communications technologies for reaching external students should examine audio teleconferencing before investing large amounts of time and funding in more expensive and less proven technologies.

REFERENCES

Bell, Bonnie and Wendy Cukier (1984) *Human and Organizational Factors in Implementing Teleconferencing*, Transportation and Energy Management Programme (TEMP), Government of Ontario

Botros, Radamis (1984) *Audio Teleconferencing: Room Acoustics*, Darome Teleconferencing Division, Canada Branch, Ottawa

Botros, Radamis (1984) *Audio Teleconferencing Terminals: Some Recent Developments*, Darome Inc., Ottawa

Bransford, Louis A. (1984) *Audio conferencing: An Affordable Option For the Information Poor*, ConferTech International

Collins, John (1984) *The Human Factor in Teleconference Techniques*, Council of Adult Education, Melbourne, Australia

Cukier, Wendy (1984) *Teleconferencing in Ontario: Survey Results to Date*, TEMP, Government of Ontario

Flavell, Elsa (1984) *The Peacesat Project, Wellington Polytechnic*, New Zealand

Graham, Lee G.A. (1984) *Cost Benefit Analysis for Teleconferencing: Definition and Design*, Optel Communications, New York

Knowles, Arther F. (1984) *Teaching and Learning Through Teleconferencing: A Survey of Activities and Plans in Canadian Universities and College*, Humber College, Toronto

McGibbon, C. Ian. (1984) *Initial Experience in Teleconferencing*, Bank of Montreal, Toronto

Ostendorf, Virgina A. and Harry Z.A. Orenstein (1984) *Acceptance of Audio Teleconferencing: Views from the United States and the United Kingdom*, Colorado and London

Parker, Lorne (1984) *Teleconferencing Application and Markets*, University of Wisconsin

Roberts, J.M. *et al.* (1984) *Telemedicine for Ontario*, Toronto

Robertson, W.D. *et al.* (1984) *A Consortium for Educational Audio Teleconferencing in British Columbia*, Toronto

Vezina-Shamlian, J. (1984) *Audio Teleconferencing in the Business World: The Use and the User*, Université de Montréal

Note: All of the above papers are published in the Proceedings of the International Teleconference Symposium, 3-5 April 1984 in either the International or Toronto sections.

Ellis, Barry (1984) 'Educational Teleconferencing', Paper presented at ICEM, Banff

Graham, Mary (1984) 'Educational Teleconferencing in Canada', *New Technologies in Canadian Education*, Paper 14, Ontario Educational Communications Authority

Parker, Lorne and Mavis Monson (1980) 'Teletechniques, An Instructional Model For Interactive Teleconferencing', *Educational Technology Publications*, Englewood Cliffs

Robertson, W.D. (1984) *Audio Teleconferencing - Using Old Technology to Reduce Course Delivery Costs and Improve Services to Rural Students*, Vancouver

Computers in Distance Education

David Kaufman

In this paper, the strengths and weaknesses of distance education are discussed and suggestions are given for using computers to overcome its limitations. A description is presented of some uses of computers in two major areas of distance teaching: development of course materials and delivery of these materials to students. Applications in computer-aided learning, computer-managed learning, computer conferencing and student support are discussed. Finally, three brief case studies are given: the Open Learning Institute, Athabasca University and Simon Fraser University. The paper ends by examining trends and looking to the future.

THE ROLE OF THE COMPUTER

Holmberg (1981:11) describes distance study as: 'Learning supported by those teaching methods in which because of the physical separateness of learners and teachers, the inter-active, as well as the pre-active, phase of teaching, is conducted through print, mechanical or electronic devices.' He points out that the main general characteristic of distance study is that the learner is at a distance from the teacher for much, most, or even all of the time during the teaching-learning process.

As a result, distance education systems have important strengths besides providing flexibility to learners as to the timing and location of their study activities. These may be described as providing an opening of educational opportunities to new target populations previously deprived either through geographical isolation, lack of formal academic requirements or employment conditions. (Kaufman 1984a; Kaufman and Sweet 1983) Flexibility in curriculum and content can be provided by the use of modules, and learning can be improved through careful instructional design of student material. Finally, a planned use of a wide range of media and other resources can be used to enhance both the efficiency and effectiveness of learning. Examples include the use of television, teleconferencing, computer-aided learning and even local support groups. Distance education has its roots in the tradition of print-based correspondence study, using the postal service for two-way communication between teacher and learner. This model is still the predominant one throughout the world, although many distance education systems also use the telephone as a communication device. As a consequence of this model, most distance education systems suffer from several limitations. Among these are the isolation of the distance learner, lengthy waiting periods for feedback on assignments, inability to cater to the extremely wide variability in learner backgrounds and abilities, limited access to library resources and difficulty in providing instruction for psycho-motor objectives.

The major question being addressed here is the following: how can the computer help to overcome the limitation of distance education systems and increase their effectiveness, efficiency and flexibility? For example, can the computer assist in developing better courses at lower cost? Can it decrease the isolation of the distance learner during course delivery? Can it be used to better instruct certain types of material?

Computers have been used extensively in education for more than twenty years, yet they have had little impact on distance education. Ehin (1973) wrote about this more than ten years ago and remarked on the absence of literature dealing specifically with computer applications in correspondence education. However, recent advances have led to increased capabilities at substantially lower costs. Two developments can be identified as most important. The first is the development and mass distribution of microcomputers; the second is the marriage of computers with communications technology, making direct and inexpensive computer communication both possible and relatively inexpensive. Computers can be used in distance education systems in two modes, referred to as local mode and transmitted mode. Local mode is synonymous with 'off line' since the computer stands alone as an independent system. Peripheral devices such as disc drives or printers are often used to enhance the system. In transmitted mode, a computer or terminal is connected to another computer ('on line') and the operation depends upon communication between these devices. By the interconnection of computers, it is relatively simple to create a complex learning network which could theoretically link all distance learners with their teachers and with a central institution. An electronic university could be created as described by Turoff (1982) and recently established by a private enterprise firm in San Francisco. (*HED* 1983) Other examples include word processing to aid course development, and data processing to aid administration and student registration.

APPLICATIONS IN DISTANCE EDUCATION

Instructional Uses

The instructional process in distance education is divided clearly into two stages. The first stage involves the design, development, physical production and storage of instructional materials. Cooper and Thompson (1982) have discussed text processing as a powerful tool for authors and editors. Its use in creating and editing documents facilitates the development of manuscripts before the production stage. Editorial changes, additions and deletions no longer delay development or add major costs. By also providing a course writer and a course designer each with microcomputer, communications software, and a modem to connect to the telephone lines, the development process can be even more significantly enhanced. (Kaufman 1984a) With this addition, all of the text processing options are still available, but electronic mail can be used to communicate changes and exchange materials. If a course team approach is used with multiple writers and other professionals, this approach can be extended by using computer conferencing (described below in more detail). By adding computerised page-composing, computer graphics, and computerised photo-typesetting, the production process could also be automated, where the manuscripts (with inserted graphics) could simply be left on a data base for electronic access by learners. At the present time, text processing is used by most institutions dedicated to distance teaching or having major distance education departments. Some institutions such as the Open Learning Institute and Athabasca University also use computerised photo-typesetting systems. The course material is then stored in a warehouse using a computerised inventory control system to maintain and route material.

The second stage of the instructional process involves delivery of the material to learners. Significant contributions to this area will begin to occur when distance learners have their own personal computers (or computer terminals), although limited benefits are possible if access to centres is provided.

Although text processing is a useful tool for student use in their assignments, the real breakthroughs here will occur through the use of computers to provide direct instruction. Computer-aided learning (CAL) has already been used at the Open University in Britain to provide diagnostic feedback, remedial help and revision aids. (Jones and O'Shea 1982) A learning centre approach was used which met with limited success. This was attributed by the authors first to problems associated with the practical difficulties of accessing a terminal, and second, to the problems of accessing programmes, which for novices include their fear and embarrassment, the problems of logging-in, and the possibilities of the machine malfunctioning. The future of computer-aided learning in distance education appears to be tied to development in two areas: high-quality courseware developed for use on home-based microcomputers, and access from home to courseware at reasonable rates through the telephone lines or cable networks. For example, the Control Data Corporation has made its PLATO courseware available in this mode on the information utility called the SOURCE. (Larsen 1983) Another possibility in this country is the videotex system called TELIDON. Love (1982) experimented with this system in a computer-aided learning format. She prepared lessons in three different subjects (Math, French, Business) and evaluated these with adult learners. Although the experiment was considered a success, it was found that TELIDON did not have powerful enough software at the time to support effective computer-aided learning. Also, microcomputer systems have recently proven to be more useful and less expensive than TELIDON.

White (1983) reviewed the research on computer-aided learning (CAL). She discovered that there has been very little research on its defects and that most of what we know is based on anecdotal reports. She focused on the effects on children, and some of her more important conclusions included:

1. Computers can improve learning and can motivate;
2. More learning in the future will be electronically based; less will be in print or lecture form;
3. Electronic learning is attractive to students partly because it is interactive and partly because of the allure of technology;
4. Computers increase rather than decrease socialisation;
5. 'Good' software depends on who judges it. Some 'bad' software is rated good by users;
6. Future electronic learning will benefit from technological advance-

ment;

7. A large part of electronic learning will be in imagery;

8. As a result of the electronic learning revolution, education will never be the same.

Kaufman (1985a) in a proposal presented to the Open Learning Institute argued for the development of computer-aided learning courseware. In this paper, he presented several reasons why the institute should involve itself in software development. These include:

1. An increase in microcomputers available in all sectors of society and particularly in the home;

2. A shortage of high-quality courseware, particularly for adult learners;

3. High courseware standards expected by the marketplace, requiring the use of a course team approach. (This approach is already in use at the institute);

4. High levels of interest at both the provincial and federal levels in creating and supporting a significant software industry;

5. Current interest of publishers and hardware manufacturers in creating and marketing educational software;

6. The excellent reputation worldwide already gained by the institute for the quality of its courses;

7. Current development by the author and the OLI Data Processing Department of an authoring language (OLIAS) which would be available for courseware development at the institute. This language would permit the development of quality courseware for three microcomputers (Apple II, IBM-PC, Rainbow 100).

Kaufman (1985a) argued that the institute should consider establishing a development process, similar in principle to its print and audio processes, which would permit the efficient development of CAL modules to serve learners as well as to generate additional revenue. He argued that the main limitation to the effective delivery of computer-aided learning software to learners is the lack of access to a microcomputer. However, several factors support the limited delivery of CAL materials to learners at the present time. These include:

1. Use of college centres and institute advising centres, as well as other sites such as business and industrial settings, libraries, public schools and community centres;

2. Programme and courses delivered by the institute which will require microcomputer support lend themselves to the use of CAL as well. Areas include computing courses, some business administration courses and some mathematics courses;

3. A large number of microcomputer owners already exists and would be a prime target audience for non-credit offering in a print-CAL format. Some credit courses could also be offered to this audience.

It appears that many courses would benefit from the use of CAL modules. The ability of a computer to simulate real-life situations which are not available to learners due to high cost, danger or other factors, is a resource which should be brought to the distance learner. Examples are courses requiring laboratory work (such as chemistry), practical work (such as process control), decision making (such as business or economics). Baath (1982) and Phillips and Young (1982) both presented evidence to show that the use of CAL increased completion rates in distance education courses. Many learners have or can be provided with access to suitable microcomputers for at least limited periods. This would permit the inclusion of shorter CAL modules (perhaps four to six hours) where appropriate.

Another area which promises to increase the efficiency and effectiveness of distance education is computer-managed learning. TVOntario has already begun to make use of this method to a limited extent in its Parents and Computer Academies. (Waniewicz 1982) In these continuing education courses, learners throughout Ontario return their assignments on computer-marked sheets. The computer-managed learning software marks the assignments and automatically generates personalised letters with results and appropriate feedback. These letters are then mailed to the students using the mailing labels also generated by the computer. Software to enable distance learning institutions' departments to carry out this function is available from Miami-Dade Community College, where the RRSP system was developed. Recently, the National Extension College in Great Britain has also developed a computer-managed learning programme which runs on microcomputers. One can anticipate that many distance learning institutions or departments will soon be making use of this type of software. Most recently, a new software package called the Computer Based Training System (CBTS) has been adapted by several Canadian institutions using independent learning on their campuses. This comprehensive computer-managed instruction software also allows for the integration of computer-aided learning. The British Columbia Institute of Technology is one institution which is using this package to support learners. This package has significant potential to aid distance learners and will likely be used when it is 'discovered' by distance education institutions. Details of this software are available from Stephen (1985).

The most recent and major innovation in this whole area is computerised communications. This includes electronic mail and computerised conferencing, which permit one-to-one and one-to-many communications among many people using computers and communication lines. An additional powerful feature is the ability to search and retrieve information from large-scale computerised data bases, opening up the possibility of remote libraries such as already available with the abstracts on the ERIC system. Computer conferencing as understood here is the use of computers to link people together across time and space. Cross (1983) has observed that 'computer teleconferencing is a system which enables two or more individuals at two or more locations to communicate.' Without having to interrupt their work schedules and to pay for costly travel, these individuals can exchange information and learning aids. Through keyboards, terminals, printers and telephone lines, participants access a common computer for extremely efficient direct communication.

Harasim and Johnson (1985) have outlined several general features of computer conferencing systems. These include text editing, sophisticated searching capabilities for conference items, access to external data bases, and electronic messaging. In addition, computer conferencing systems usually maintain a permanent record of proceedings during the course of a conference, thus serving as a type of electronic filing cabinet. Kaufman (1985b) listed several other features of these systems, including:

1. Directory - for identifying participants on the system and finding adresses where messages are to be sent;
2. Electronic mail - for one-to-one and one-to-many communications;
3. Conferences - for group discussions, with a permanent transcript of the proceedings;
4. Private work spaces - for collecting ideas and personal files;
5. Word processing - for composition and modification of messages or documents;
6. Bulletin board - for access to announcements of general or particular interests;
7. Newsletter or journal - for access to articles or papers of general and particular interest;
8. Data bases - for access to data or information on a variety of topics.

One useful feature of these systems is that it is a relatively simple matter to produce a printed copy of the information stored electronically. This permits the user to avoid reading on the screen and to read material at a more convenient time or place.

Several proposals recently have been advanced across the country for use of these electronic communication networks. Montgomery (1984) prepared a draft proposal for the establishment of the Alberta Digital Education Network. In Ontario, Harasim and Johnson (1985) suggested a strategy for professional development of teachers and trainers in Ontario, using computer networks and conferencing systems. They listed many potential benefits of such a system, including:

1. Encouraging teacher networking;
2. Encouraging the use of technology and professional development;
3. Encouraging the use of technology to facilitate communication among educators and to encourage information sharing at various levels;
4. Introducing distance education and providing quality learning opportunities to small communities and to learners who are physically and demographically isolated;
5. Applying electronic linkages between the home, the work place, professional associations and educational institutions.

They argued that certain characteristics of computerised conferencing systems make them well suited to professional development activities and the adult learner. For example:

1. Access to experts and respected peers;
2. One-to-one or one-to-many communication;
3. Active learner participation;
4. Linking of new learning to concrete on-the-job problems;
5. Follow-up, feedback and implementation support from peers or experts;
6. Self-direction - control over stop or start, time, pace, and place of the learning or communication activity.

In British Columbia, Kaufman (1984) presented a report to the Learning Systems Working Groups, representing the universities, institutes and colleges across the province, in which he recommended that the University of British Columbia computer and associated software be used to establish a provincial educational electronic communications network. The report also recommended that the provincial network established above should be linked to other appropriate educational networks and should also be used as a gateway to information utilities such as The Source, EIES, and the Knowledge Index. He suggested that a further report should be prepared as soon as possible, to outline the design and implementation of network. Kaufman (1985a) also prepared a proposal for the Open Learning Institute in which he suggested that this area be explored in more detail. He suggested that the institute consider the delivery of some of its courses using computerised conferencing. He also suggested that the institute establish its own computer conferencing system. This system would naturally serve as a resource for sister institutions choosing to purchase time on this service, as the British Columbia Institute of Technology and the University of Victoria have already done with their audio teleconferencing bridges. The report argued that the advantage of such a system would be its ability to virtually eliminate the major constraints of distance learning: isolation, slow feedback, lack of individualised instruction, and lack of library resources. Athabasca University in Alberta is planning to use electronic mail and conferencing for co-ordinators and tutors in their courses. The US-based privately financed electronic university provides an initial model for how this form of remote education (*HED* 1983). This system has generated tremendous interest and has received endorsements from high officials including the vice-president and the education secretaries. Proponents of this medium agree that even today it is a cost-effective solution to delivery of remote instruction. There is little doubt that this will be the case in the very near future if it is not already true. The same problem exists here as in the delivery of CAL courseware; namely, the lack of universal access to microcomputers. Simon Fraser University has recently offered a course in reading education which utilised electronic mail between the tutor and students. This is described in more detail in a later section of this paper.

The final area where the computer has been extremely useful and will continue to be so, may be termed 'instructional support'. For example, the Open Learning Institute has been using computers in most of its internal operations. Examples include a computerised student registration system, tutor records, course development, an inventory system in the warehouse, library research data base, and internal communications. The area of instructional support has been described in an earlier paper (Kaufman and McInnis-Rankin 1983) and includes several operational systems. In the area of career counselling, the CHOICES system is Canada's most widely used computerised career information system. This is an interactive, computerised, career information service which allows users to explore a comprehensive, current and provincially relevant data file of occupations. In the area of academic advising relevant to a particular institution, Simon Fraser University is developing a two-way computerised information system called the 'Automated Academic Advisor'. Information available will include programme and course prerequisites, registration information, class availability and schedule, and the new system will be 'user friendly' in that it will use natural language. In the area of the registry, the Open Learning Institute and Athabasca University have developed highly sophisticated student services record systems which are used by internal staff as well as by tutors and advisers. By providing on-line computer terminals in the regional centres, information is available at all sites to enable students to be better served. Another important feature of the terminal is the provision of electronic mail and conferencing capability. Instead of waiting one to two weeks for a reply to a memo by mail, a message and response can be sent the same day at much lower cost than standard voice telephone calls. This feature helps to alleviate some of the staff frustrations of operating at a distance. The computer also permits reports to be prepared very quickly and circulated instantly. Even an electronic institutional newsletter can be prepared for staff and students. Finally, the computer is an invaluable tool in helping to control operations in the warehouse. This area of distance education systems is extremely critical and depends on accuracy and speed to serve learners, qualities which are best provided by computers.

Administrative Support

This area traditionally has been the most highly developed with respect to computer use and has included the student services areas described above as well as financial systems such as payroll, accounting, general ledger and budget preparation, control, and reporting. Other areas include personnel records, library resources, scheduling of courses, decision support such as enrolment projections, inventory control, and report preparation. Montgomery (1983), Friedman (1983) and Lampikoski (1983) have discussed this in more detail. As distance education is being examined closely as a cost-effective option, the computer has important contributions to make in the administration of distance education systems and in developing appropriate methodologies for cost-benefit analyses such as those being developed by Rumble (1983). At the Open Learning Institute, computerised course and tutor-evaluation systems have been developed and are currently being used to assist in decision making. (Love 1983)

CASE STUDIES

Athabasca University

Athabasca University has been using computers in its course development process for some time now. (Cooper and Thompson 1982) However, several innovative uses of computers in course delivery are beginning (Holt 1985): a Digital Equipment Corporation VAX 785 computer will be used for a student monitoring system. The system will eventually allow all tutors to enter student data on-line and to use the electronic mail and the Cosy conferencing system. A prototype system has been running on a Sperry personal computer. The conferencing system will be used by course co-ordination and tutors starting in January 1986. Thirty-five Sperry personal computers are being used for computing science courses and a microcomputer in a business course. Twenty-eight are permanently placed in four sites; the others are moved around for a course which uses audio teleconferencing.

In the area of computer-aided learning, two pilot projects will be implemented in 1986 on the Sperry microcomputers. These both will be in the area of Remedial English. It is also planned in 1986-7 to use computer laboratory work in a number of other courses requiring simulations and other computer adjunct use. A five-year plan for using microcomputers for home delivery of courses is currently under review.

Simon Fraser University

During the past year, the distance education programme (DISC) and the faculty of education collaborated on a project using computer conferencing. (Bell 1985) An education course entitled 'Designs for Learning: Reading' was offered twice using conferencing as an option. In order to participate, students had to have access to a microcomputer. Two or three students in each course took advantage of this option and used the system to communicate with their professor, using microcomputers and modems connected to the university computer. However, the second session eventually became a dialogue between the professor and one student.

Several lessons were learned from those projects, and the university plans to continue using this medium. Improvements will include better documentation, better access to microcomputers for students, and placing a computer into an area where several students are clustered. It has been suggested that a course should be chosen having minimum print materials (other than the textbook), and that those materials be made available on-line.

The Open Learning Institute

Several applications and plans regarding the use of computers at the Open Learning Institute have been discussed above. Specifically, several activities have already occurred in the past few years. These include:

1. Preparing and evaluating CAL materials for use on the TELIDON systems;
2. Preparing a ten-module course in a computer-aided learning format in the area of Introductory Accounting. This project was funded by McGraw Hill Ryerson in Canada and will be marketed in 1986;
3. Implementing an international computerised conference to discuss the use of technology in education. Computer accounts were given to several dozen experts in the field across Canada, the United States and Europe. An on-line discussion then took place over a period of approximately six months;
4. Developing a science module in a computer-aided learning format in the area of food and nutrition. This module includes a print and audio component and will be available for use by OLI students. This package will also be marketed widely by the institute.

The most recent initiative in this area has been the preparation of a report which investigated information utilities. (Kaufman 1985b) It described several well-known systems such as the SOURCE, Compuserve, EIES, MATRIX, the University of British Columbia system called *FORUM, and local bulletin board systems.

An interesting and unique approach to computer literacy was developed at the Open Learning Institute. (Kaufman and Meakin 1982) A computer literacy course entitled 'Introduction to Personal Computing' was developed. In this course, students received a set of course units dealing with a variety of topics which included: What is a Microcomputer?, Technical Terms, What the Computer Can do for Me, and How to Choose a Personal Computer. The unique feature of this course was that students were actually provided (on a rental basis) with their own microcomputer. The computer chosen was the Radio Shack TRS-80 Colour Computer. The computer and all printed materials were provided to learners in a typical course package, prepared in an Open Learning Institute cardboard box. Students were able to pick up the course package at the institute regional offices. This course was found to be effective in meeting learners' needs as well as in generating revenue to pay for itself. Learners who decided to keep their computers after the course ended were able to purchase these at a discount rate. This allowed the institute to replenish its stock with new computers.

The most recent efforts at the institute have involved the development of its own authoring language for the development of computer-aided learning materials. This language called OLIAS (Open Learning Institute Authoring System) was developed by the author and the institute's data processing department. The system will be marketed in 1986 and is available for the RAINBOW 100, IBM Personal Computer, and Apple II Microcomputers. It is planned to use this language at the institute for the development of other computer-aided learning materials. An important strength of this language is that material authored on any of these three machines also will be capable of running on any of them.

Finally, some important work in the area of course development has been carried out in recent years. This work involves using a microcomputer and text processing system to automate the course development process. A course designer, working with the course writer and consultant, are able to define a 'Template' for course units. Headings and sub-headings for the course unit are defined in advance, and all formats are pre-set. Material is then slotted into the template using a text processing system. This process, although not widely used yet, is extremely efficient and makes use of good instructional design techniques for forcing the team to define clearly the material ahead of time.

DISCUSSION

It is clear from the above discussion that the computer is already playing a significant role in distance education systems across Canada, and that this will grow rapidly. As institutions gain more experience with this medium, the materials and approaches used will improve. For example, current experience with computerised conferencing already indicates that there are several reasons why computer conferences fail. Hiltz and Turoff (1978) list the most important ones, which include:

1. Lack of convenient access to a terminal;
2. Lack of a need or desire to communicate with other people on the system. This is related to a condition in which the group itself lacks a shared goal to which all members are willing to contribute several hours a week of their time;

3. Lack of adequate training material in an acceptable form. Many users' manuals are too long and badly written. Alternative training, such as in-person sessions, videotapes, or on-line lessons, is necessary in order to motivate learners;

4. Lack of strong or adequate leadership. It is necessary for a moderator to take hold and set an agenda as well as to keep the group working towards its goal;

5. Lack of a 'critical mass' within a conference or group. This has to do with both a minimum number of active participants and a minimum number of geographic locations. The minimum number seems to lie somewhere between eight and twelve active participants in three or more geographic locations. Below this critical mass there are not likely to be enough new messages or conference comments entered so there would not always be new items to receive and respond to when a member signed on. Above these minimum numbers, enough activity and controversy is generated to motivate members to sign on frequently and to participate actively in these changes.

In the area of computer-aided learning, two major areas will lead to the widespread use of this medium. The first is the interactive nature of this medium, as opposed to traditional print materials. As developers become more skilled in the use of computer-aided learning, and as more high quality material becomes available, distance education institutions will begin to incorporate these into their courses. Also, in this age of fiscal restraint in education, institutions that can develop effective computer software will have found an important source of external funds from the marketplace. These funds can, of course, assist the institution in better fulfilling its mandate.

In the area of computer-managed learning, it is clear that the computer can perform an important function, which has been well received by learners who have used the system. As appropriate software becomes available and Canadian educators become aware of this approach, increased use will be made of this medium.

Finally, in the area of instructional support, it is expected that the computer will continue to play an important role in areas such as computerised course development, computerised counselling, computerised storage and distribution.

The three case studies provided indicate that both dedicated distance education institutions as well as distance education departments are beginning to make use of the computer to better serve learners.

THE FUTURE

Kaufman (1984) has listed six outcomes which could be expected in this area. These are:

1. A personal computer will be available for every distance learner;

2. The Electronic University will become the predominant model of distance education;

3. Private enterprise will enter the distance education field in significant ways;

4. Intelligent (or 'expert') computer-aided learning systems will become

available for use in distance education;

5. Computer and communications technology will be used to make available multi-media learning systems using print, audio and video messages for delivery;

6. Developments in distance education systems will have profound effects on traditional education systems.

Several important questions have yet to be properly addressed and other social factors will surely limit or reshape some of the above predictions. Some of these questions are:

1. What are the appropriate designs for these computer-person systems?
2. What is the role of personal contact, i.e., face-to-face interaction?
3. What is the place of the effective dimension in learning and how will it be addressed?
4. What are the emotional and social effects of computer automation on people?
5. What is the effect of 'computer anxiety' exhibited by many people? How can it be reduced?
6. What are the social, educational and political impacts of the computer on society as used in these ways?

Our experience in predicting the future would lead to the conclusion that these and other questions will likely reshape the vision presented here in surprising ways. However, an exciting start has been made in this country and there is reason to believe that this beginning will continue to develop in several important directions.

REFERENCES

Baath J.A. (1982) 'Experimental research on computer-assisted distance education', *Learning at a Distance: A World Perspective*, J.S. Daniel *et al.* (eds.), pp. 303-5, Athabasca University/ICDE, Edmonton

Bell, D. (1985) Simon Fraser University Course Using Computer Conferencing, Personal Communication

Cooper D.W. and J.R. Thompson (1982) 'Text processing; the revolution in word manipulation', *Learning at a Distance: A World Perspective*, pp. 301-2

Cross T.B. (1983) 'Computer tele-conferencing and education', *Educational Technology*, 29-31

Ehin C. (1973) 'Suggested computer applications in correspondence education', *Educational Technology*, 60-3

Friedman H.Z. (1983) 'The contribution of data processing to student administration at the Open University', *Learning at a Distance: A World Perspective*, pp. 292-5

Harasim, L. and E.M. Johnson, (1985) 'Educational applications of computer conferencing for teachers in Ontario', Workshops on Computer Conferencing and Electronic Mail, University of Guelph, Guelph, Canada, 22-3 January

Higher Education Daily (HED) 'Corporation launches "electronic university"', Capitol Publications, 13 September

Hiltz, S.R. and M. Turoff (1978) *The Network Nation: Human Communication via Computer*, Addison-Wesley Publishing Company, Inc., Advanced Book Program, Reading, Massachusetts

Holmberg B. (1981) *Status and Trends of Distance Education*, Kogan Page, London

Holt, P. (1985) Brief Description of Athabasca University Use of Computers in Educational Delivery, Personal Communication

Jones A. and T. O'Shea (1982) 'Barriers to the use of computer assisted learning', *British Journal of Educational Technology*, 207-17

Kaufman D. and D. Meakin (1982) 'Delivery of a home-based course in personal computing', Paper presented at Microcomputers in Education Conference, University of Victoria

Kaufman D. and E. McInnis-Rankin (1983) 'The humanistic application of technology to student services in distance education', Paper presented at the Joint Annual Conference of CACUSS/NASPA, Toronto

Kaufman, D. and R. Sweet (1983) 'Increasing Educational Opportunity for Adults: A Canadian Example', *Higher Education in Europe 8*, (3)

Kaufman, D. (1984a) 'A computer-based instructional system for distance education', *Computers and Education*, 8, 479-84

Kaufman, D. (1984b) 'Practice and theory of distance education: course blueprint', *Distance Education*, 5, 239-52

Kaufman, D. (1984c) 'Electronic Mail and Computer Conferencing for the Learning Systems Working Groups', Report prepared for the Knowledge Network, Vancouver, Canada, September

Kaufman, D. (1985a) 'Computer-aided learning at the Open Learning Institute: The next step', Proposal prepared for the Open Learning Institute, June

Kaufman, D. (1985b) 'Computer networks: exploratory study', Internal report, Open Learning Institute, April

Lampikoski K. (1983) 'Towards the integrated use of the computer in distance education', *Learning at a Distance: A World Perspective*, pp. 296-8

Larsen D. (1983) Personal Communication to Author, Control Data Corporation

Love L. (1982) 'Use of TELIDON for computer-aided learning in distance education', Internal Report, Open Learning Institute

Love L. (1983) 'A course and tutor evaluation system at the Open Learning Institute', Internal Report

Montgomerie D. (1983) 'Administrative uses of computers in education, Alberta Printout 50-1

Montgomerie, T.C. (1984) 'The Alberta Digital Education Network', *Alberta Printout*, 5, (1), May

Phillips C.A. and R.G. Young (1982) 'Increasing completion rates with computer-assisted lessons', *Learning at a Distance: A World Perspective*, pp. 298-9

Rumble G. 'Responding to economic austerity: can economic models of distance teaching help us?', *Learning at a Distance, A World Perspective*, pp. 199-201

Stephen, A. (1985) Computer-Based Training System. CBTS Computer-Based Training Systems, Ltd., Calgary, Alberta

Turoff M. (1982) 'On the design of an electronic university', Briefs of a conference on Telecommunications and Higher Education sponsored by New Jersey Institute of Technology and New Jersey Department of Higher Education

Waniewicz I. 'The TV Ontario Academy', *Learning at a Distance: A World Perspective*, pp. 285-6

White, M.A. (1983) 'Synthesis of Research on Distance Learning', *Educational Leadership*, May

Contributors

ABOUT THE EDITORS

David Kaufman, Training Supervisor, Computer Technology, City of Vancouver, Vancouver, British Columbia. Formerly Director of Course Design and Educational Technology, Open Learning Institute.

Ian Mugridge, Dean of Academic Affairs, Open Learning Institute, Richmond, British Columbia.

ABOUT THE CONTRIBUTORS

Roger Bédard, Director, Undergraduate Studies, Télé-université, University of Quebec, Quebec City, Quebec.

John Bottomley, Director, Programme Support, Open Learning Institute, Richmond, British Columbia.

Jane Brindley, Senior Counsellor, Athabasca University, Athabasca, Alberta.

Barry Brown, Head, Department of Communications, Continuing and Vocational Education, University of Saskatchewan, Saskatoon, Saskatchewan.

Jocelyn Calvert, Co-ordinator, University Programme, Open Learning Institute, Richmond, British Columbia.

Dan O. Coldeway, Instructional Developer, Athabasca University, Athabasca, Alberta.

John Daniel, President, Laurentian University, Sudbury, Ontario; Chair, Canadian Higher Education Research Network; and Past-president, International Council for Distance Education.

John Dennison, Professor, Department of Educational Administration and Higher Education, University of British Columbia, Vancouver, British Columbia.

John F. Ellis, Professor, Faculty of Education, Simon Fraser University, Burnaby, British Columbia. Founding Principal, Open Learning Institute.

Glen M. Farrell, President, Knowledge Network of the West Communications Authority, Vancouver, British Columbia.

Danielle Fortosky, Head, Instructional Television, Division of Audio-Visual Services, University of Saskatchewan, Saskatoon, Saskatchewan.

Patrick Guillemet, Media Designer, Télé-université, University of Quebec, Quebec City, Quebec.

Margaret Haughey, Programme Co-ordinator, Distance Education, Division of University Extension, University of Victoria, Victoria, British Columbia.

Christopher Hope, President, Granton Institute of Technology, Toronto, Ontario.

Abram Konrad, Professor, Department of Educational Administration, University of Alberta, Edmonton, Alberta.

Francine Landry, Research Agent, Télé-université, University of Quebec, Quebec City, Quebec.

James D. Leslie, President, Waterloo Distance Education, Inc., Waterloo, Ontario. Formerly Director, Correspondence Programme, University of Waterloo.

Ethelyn McInnis-Rankin, Adviser, Open Learning Institute, Richmond, British Columbia.

Norman McKinnon, Chairman, Research and Development, Independent Learning Centre, Ministry of Education, Toronto, Ontario.

Margaret Norquay, Director, Open College, CJRT-FM, Toronto, Ontario.

Ross Paul, Vice-President, Learning Services, Athabasca University, Athabasca, Alberta.

William Robertson, Graduate Student, Faculty of Education, University of British Columbia, Vancouver, British Columbia. Formerly Head, Distance Education Unit, British Columbia Institute of Technology.

J. Peter Rothe, Manager of Research and Evaluation, Insurance Corporation of British Columbia, North Vancouver, British Columbia Formerly Visiting Professor at Fernuniversitat, West Germany.

Kate Seaborne, Programme Co-ordinator, Science and Technology, Division of University Extension, University of Victoria, Victoria, British Columbia.

Charles R. Shobe, Director, Formal Learning, Alberta Educational Communications Corporation, Edmonton, Alberta. Currently President, Canadian Association for Distance Education.

James M. Small, Professor, Department of Educational Administration, University of Alberta, Edmonton, Alberta.

Robert Sweet, Teacher, Pitt Meadows Senior Secondary School, British Columbia. Formerly Research and Evaluation Officer, Open Learning Institute.

John Tayless, Director, Academic Programmes, North Island College, Comox, British Columbia.

Arlene Zuckernick, Co-ordinator, Distance Education, Division of University Extension, University of Victoria, Victoria, British Columbia.

Index